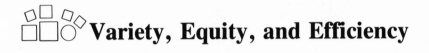 **Variety, Equity, and Efficiency**

**Columbia Studies in Economics 10**

# Variety, Equity, and Efficiency

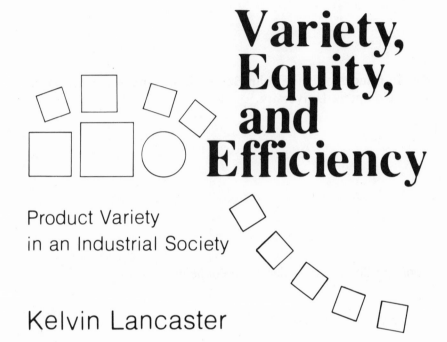

Product Variety
in an Industrial Society

Kelvin Lancaster

Columbia University Press/New York/1979

Kelvin Lancaster is the John Bates Clark Professor of Economics at Columbia University.

Library of Congress Cataloging in Publication Data

Lancaster, Kelvin.
  Variety, equity, and efficiency.

  Bibliography: p.
  Includes index.
  1.  Diversification in industry.   I.   Title.
II.   Product variety in an industrial society.
HC79.D6L36      338.5      78-24616
ISBN 0-231-04616-2


Columbia University Press
New York and Guildford, Surrey

To Clif and Gil

# Preface

THE ECONOMY WHICH has traditionally formed the subject of analysis by economists is one in which there are a finite number of goods, the exact number and properties of which are assumed to be part of the given data. One of the more obvious features of modern industrial economies, however, is that products can be designed to any set of specifications within some range, which is wide for some classes of products and relatively narrow for others. The present work is devoted to the analysis of such economies, in which the number and specifications of the goods to be produced form part of the solution instead of part of the data.

The analysis given is, I believe, the simplest possible which is still capable of generalization without error. My earlier paper on the same subject (Lancaster, 1975) was too simple, and many of its results do not hold up in more general cases. If the analysis seems lengthy, it is because the framework must be built up from scratch, and even such basics as demand theory must be reworked from the beginning. Techniques have been kept as simple as possible, and the analysis uses only the kind of basic calculus that is now part of every economist's toolkit.

Although there is no existing formal analysis of economies with variable product numbers and specifications, there are long-standing presumptions as to what such an analysis would reveal. Some of these presumptions are found to be totally incorrect, and some are found to be correct—the latter often for the wrong reasons.

The author wishes to acknowledge the assistance of the National Science Foundation, which has supported the research on which this book is based from its very beginning, and of the Institute for Advanced Studies of the Hebrew University of Jerusalem.

Columbia University                                             K.J.L.
April 1978

 **Contents**

# Variety, Equity, and Efficiency

Chapter 1

# Introduction

## 1.1 The Problem

SUPPOSE THERE IS a city administration that can reduce the costs
of its fire department by closing every second firehouse and replacing
the existing equipment and communication system by a new one that
doubles the speed with which fire-fighters can respond to an alarm
at any given distance from the nearest firehouse. Since the average
distance from a potential fire to the nearest firehouse is doubled and
the speed of response is also doubled, the average response time is
unchanged. With total cost lessened without any change in average
response time, the change would clearly satisfy one acceptable criterion of efficiency. Yet a proposal to make the change would not
receive a unanimous vote, for a good reason.

Suppose for simplicity, that the city is a linear one, spread along
a main street with firehouses every mile, in the initial situation. The
average distance from a firehouse is then a quarter of a mile, with
the maximum distance a half-mile. If the response time is 60 minutes
per mile, the average response time is 15 minutes, and the maximum
30 minutes. Under the modernized system, the firehouses are 2 miles
apart, the average and maximum distances a half-mile and a mile,
and the response times 15 minutes (average) and 30 minutes (maximum), the same average and maximum as before. But consider a
fire at a distance of two-thirds of a mile from one of the new firehouses,

for which the response time is 20 minutes. Under the old system, this would have been only one-third of a mile from the nearest firehouse, with a response time of 20 minutes, even with the original equipment. Any fires more than two-thirds of a mile from the nearest firehouse on the new system will have response time of between 20 and 30 minutes, and these would have had response times of less than 20 minutes under the original system. Residents of these zones are worse off under the new system than under the old, whereas other residents are better off under the new system. Assuming a uniform distribution of population, one-third are worse off and two-thirds are better off; however, it can be shown that those who are worse off have their response times increased, on the average, by 15 minutes, whereas those who are better off have their response times reduced, on the average, by only 7.5 minutes.

Thus the change, which brings *efficiency* (lower cost for the same average response) by reducing *variety* (fewer firehouse locations), introduces problems of *equity* by making some better off while making other worse off.

One way of solving the equity problem would be to have those who lose from the change compensated by those who gain. In this example, real-estate taxes might be adjusted appropriately since there is no problem in identifying each individual's gain or loss. If, after *compensation* has been duly arranged, no one is worse off under the new system and net cost is less than that for the old system, it would be possible to say that the new system is better than the old. The new system could be unambiguously referred to as *optimal*.[1] But if there is some institutional bar to differentiated real-estate taxes or other methods of compensation, it might still be appropriate to consider the new system an improvement because it reduces cost but leaves the population as well off, on the average. The new system without compensation could be regarded as a *second-best optimum*[2] on these grounds.

1. A simplified economic analysis of the variety–efficiency problem is given in Meade (1974). The author's more general analysis was developed independently (see Lancaster, 1975). Both of these analyses were limited in scope.

2. There is one tradition in welfare economics (to which the author does not subscribe) in which a move is considered fully optimal if compensation *could be paid*, even though it is not. This idea is essential for such techniques as consumer surplus and most methods of cost–benefit analysis, techniques which are avoided here.

This locational example is simple and clear-cut, but it sets the stage for a large and important class of problems for which analysis is neither simple nor obvious, the class of problems with which this work is concerned.

Consider the Ministry of Automobile Production in a planned economy, which must decide how many different types of automobile are to be produced. It knows that different consumers prefer different kinds—some want black four-door sedans, some gray station wagons, some red two-door sedans, for example—but that there are considerable economies of scale in the production of any one kind. The greater the variety that is produced, the less the production of any one type and the higher the average cost per car. Is it better to produce one type at lower cost? If only one kind is produced, the industry is more efficient as measured by average cost per car, and the consumers who happen to prefer the type chosen are very happy; those consumers who prefer other types are less happy, unless the cost saving is so great that they can buy the somewhat less-desirable model for much less than they would have had to pay for their most-preferred kind. Even in the latter case, there is an equity problem; i.e., whatever model is chosen, the choice is more desirable for some and less desirable for others.

In the automobile example, as contrasted with that of the firehouses, the consumers who would prefer one model rather than another cannot be identified by an objective external parameter such as the location of their home relative to the firehouse. Although those whose most-preferred model is not produced could, in principle, be compensated (by being charged a lower price for the available model or by a cash rebate), it would be very difficult to identify them or assess compensation. Furthermore, if a decision is made to produce only the gray station wagon, for example, those for whom a gray station wagon is the ideal kind of automobile will find it difficult to accept that others should be given a rebate for accepting precisely this type. This is the problem of *manifest equity* that arises when individual preferences for one kind over another are not directly related to objective external parameters.

If automobile production is left to a private sector, the same type of questions can be asked. How much variety will the industry produce, given its competitive structure? Is this the optimal variety, given some desired balance between equity and efficiency? If it is not optimal, does the market produce too little variety or too much?

Take a different example. Suppose a town has two newspapers, one more "liberal" and the other more "conservative," with newspaper readers evenly divided between the two. Economies of scale are such that there would be a great saving in resources if only a single newspaper were produced for everyone. In this case, the preferences of any individual for one paper would be quite strong, with a marked loss in welfare if this paper were eliminated in favor of the other. Assuming that a "middle-of-the-road" solution is not possible, there would be a good case for keeping both papers, by subsidy if necessary, even though this may be inefficient on a purely cost basis. The difficulty of compensation in this case is very clear—imagine conservative readers being asked to pay more for the conservative paper, if this is the only one in town, so that liberal readers could be charged less for it!.

It is obvious from these examples that the variety, equity, and efficiency problem arises when three elements are present in a situation:

*1. When there is variety in individual preferences.* If everyone lived at the same location (in the firehouse example), wanted precisely the same kind of automobile, or liked the same newspaper, there would be no conflict between variety and efficiency. It is also obvious from the newspaper example that the problem is most acute if individuals have strong preferences for one variant over another. If each individual prefers one variant to others but is nearly indifferent between them, the overall welfare loss incurred by producing a single type is relatively small, and efficiency considerations can easily outweigh all others.

*2. When there is potential variety in the product.* If it is technically possible to make only one kind of automobile in only one color, there is no variety possible in the first place. Technological change which introduces the possibility of variety brings a potential gain in welfare along with the problems associated with choice within that potential variety.

*3. When there are economies of scale in production.* If there are no economies of scale, then there is no reason why every product should not be custom made to suit every individual's preferences.

Production is not restricted to the narrow sense of manufacturing, and scale economies may occur at any point between the raw materials and delivery to the final consumer, including, in particular, economies in distribution and inventory holding due to standardized products. There can be other reasons for the existence of predesigned, as opposed to custom-made products, such as the impatience of consumers who need a suit today and not next month, but the emphasis here will be on scale economies of some kind.

These three elements—variety among individual preferences, potential variety among products, and economies of scale—are all present in the consumer-products sectors of advanced industrial societies. This book, therefore, can be considered as an exploration of the problems associated with technologically advanced economies. Although the emphasis is on the consumer-products sector, similar problems arise in other sectors, as shown in Chapter 10. Note that the problems apply as much to planned or socialist economies as to market economies and are, in fact, more acute in planned economies, in which the Ministry of Production must face the equity–efficiency choice directly.[3]

In Chapter 2 will be set out the specific way in which preference variety, potential product variety, and economies of scale are modeled into an analysis that can then be carried through to examine variety, equity, and efficiency in both a pure welfare setting and a number of different market settings. The remainder of this chapter will be devoted to some broad general considerations that come prior to such specifics.

## 1.2 Variety in Tastes

It will be assumed throughout this work that individual variations in tastes or preferences are real and substantial in the sense that individuals consider themselves to be better off (or have a higher welfare) when they have a product which exactly fits their view of the ideal

3. In a market economy, the choice does not appear in any direct form to any individual economic agent. It arises, as here, only in examining the overall performance of the market or in deciding whether the government should intervene or not.

design for that class of products than when they do not. It may seem strange to make a point of this, but there is a school of thought, represented by the work of Galbraith,[4] which suggests that the average consumer (the authors of these views presumably always exempt themselves) is little more than an empty shell into which cunning advertisers can implant whatever tastes happen to generate the highest profits. Some practitioners in advertising and marketing may even believe this, despite the legendary evidence of the Edsel.[5]

Were it true that tastes could be created or manipulated in this way, the problems with which this book is concerned would simply not exist. If all these advertising and other manipulative skills were employed to induce all consumers to have the *same* tastes, everyone would be happy with one kind of each product, which could then be produced with the maximum use of economies of scale. Efficiency would be fully served with no problem of equity arising from the lack of variety.

A planned economy would be very much easier to organize if everyone had the same tastes, not only because there would be economies of scale but also because the planning process itself would be greatly simplified when there was minimal variety. For this reason, it is safe to assume that a planned socialist society would not go out of its way to generate variety in tastes where none already existed, and there is certainly no evidence that any such society has done so. Yet product variety is clearly an important policy issue even in the Soviet Union—with a whole generation and more of consumers who have been isolated from the blandishments of capitalist selling techniques. Premier Kosygin spoke of "expanding and modernizing the range of manufactured goods"[6] as a high-priority economic goal.

Marx himself, in his famous brief glimpse of the final utopian state of true communism—"from each according to abilities, to each

4. See Galbraith (1967).

5. For the younger readers it might be pointed out that the Edsel was a new automobile model introduced by Ford in the 1950s. It was a sales disaster, in spite of one of the most carefully designed advertising and marketing campaigns ever put together.

6. A. N. Kosygin, "On Improving Industrial Management." Excerpt from a report to the Central Committee of the Communist Party of the Soviet Union, September 1965 (reprinted in Nove and Nuti, 1972).

according to his need"[7]—clearly visualized individual differences, existing even after a presumably long period of the intermediate state of socialism.

The point does not need to be labored. Even the socialist theorists, who would have the most to gain by supposing that individuality was invented by capitalists in order to increase profits, do not suppose that consumers are a uniform and undifferentiated mass.

To take tastes to be real and substantial is not necessarily to assume that they are innate and not influenced by environmental and social pressures, only that, however they have been developed, they have some inherent stability and do not change in response to relatively trivial stimuli. To the economist, individuals are represented in the system by their preferences, which determine both behavior in situations in which individuals are able to exercise choice on their own behalf and also their own rating of themselves as better or worse off in one situation as compared to another. These preferences are, in fact, the individual's economic *persona*.

The tastes which are accepted as given for each individual are not preferences over collections of specific goods but deeper preferences over objectives which are to be achieved by the consumption of goods. It is the attributes or characteristics of different goods which provide the means for conveying embodied characteristics which contribute to consumption objectives. It is not food as such but the taste, hunger-abating, nutritional, and other characteristics of food that directly impinge on the consumer's preferences.[8]

By viewing goods as intermediaries in the consumption process, and only by so doing, it is possible to maintain an orderly view of the relationship between a consumer with stable tastes and a world of changing goods, as is essential to the study of product variety. Although the goods in some identifiable class or group (like automobiles or shoes) change, the characteristics they possess do not change in kind, only in relative quantity. Automobile models vary in seating room, power, or other characteristics, shoes in color, heel

7. Marx (1891).

8. This is the foundation for the approach to consumer theory developed by the author and which is used throughout this work (see Lancaster, 1966, 1971). The analysis is set out more fully in Chapter 2.

height, or size, and each model can be related to the assumed stable preferences of the individual over the relevant characteristics. A completely new model can be immediately fitted into the system by comparing its characteristics content with that of existing or previous models, so that consumers do not have to start their preferences from scratch every season. Every so often a good may appear (like a radio or movies or pocket calculators) that either has characteristics that would be regarded as different in kind from those of all previous goods or has existing characteristics in proportions so different from those of previous goods[9] that a genuine new product group is formed, within which variety then develops. This work is concerned with product variety within a group, not with the expansion of the number of product groups.

Those who argue that tastes are easily changed often mean only that the particular mix of goods used to achieve an underlying consumption objective may change rapidly in response to the appearance of a new product variety or to new information as to the true characteristics of an existing product. A very high proportion of cigarette smokers who formerly smoked unfiltered cigarettes switched to filtered cigarettes within a relatively short time after the smoking and lung cancer link became widely known. There is no reason to consider that the preferences of these individuals between the sensory pleasure of cigarette smoking and the objective of long life changed in any way. All that happened was that a hitherto unknown characteristic of cigarettes became known, which led to a change in the collection of goods, with no change in the underlying preference structure.

There are classes of goods in which the characteristics which vary over the class may be less important in achieving major consumption objectives than characteristics which are essentially possessed to the same degree; few thirsty Pepsi drinkers, for example, would refuse a Coke if that were all that was available and feel a

---

9. In some sense airplane and taxicab transportation share the same basic characteristics, but the proportions differ so much that a situation in which a choice needs to be made between the two is so unlikely to occur that they should be regarded as in two different groups—long-distance transportation and short-distance transportation.

significant welfare loss in so doing. The products in such a class are very good substitutes for each other, and a consumer may change from one variety to another with little loss of welfare. An individual's "tastes," in the sense of the particular product variety he or she chooses, may appear unstable, but this merely reflects the existence of several almost equal ways of achieving the same consumption objective. Because of market properties, it is in just such product classes that the greatest resources have been devoted to advertising and marketing techniques, and it is from these that much of the folklore of marketing has sprung, which has led to an undue emphasis on the ease with which consumers might be persuaded to switch brands. Such apparent instability on the part of the consumers does not affect the analysis, since it merely implies that such goods are almost perfect substitutes for achieving consumption goals and thus that the level or distribution of welfare is almost the same whether there is one variety or many.

In whatever way preferences come to be developed, it can be accepted that the process is some type of interaction between post-natal environment and genetic, or prenatally determined, predispositions and thus that the degree of preference variation over the population may vary from one society to another. This degree of variation is itself an important economic parameter, as shown in the economic simplifications that would result from total lack of variation. It might be expected that societies with a large degree of ethnic and cultural homogeneity (Scandinavian countries, for example) would have less variation than societies with more diverse populations (like the United States or the Soviet Union), but this is merely an informal guess.

A deeper problem is that tightly knit societies or subsocieties may reveal less diversity of preferences than truly exists, because of social pressures to conform. Individuals may fail to reveal their underlying personal preferences in such cases, although they have certainly revealed that their preference for remaining within the subsociety dominates their personal difference in taste with respect to other matters, which thus poses the problem of what is "true" preference. In other societies, there may even be social pressures to emphasize individual differences, which would lead to another kind of distortion.[10] It will be assumed here, as in traditional in welfare economics, that the "true" preferences are those that are, or would be, revealed by actual choice.

Since preferences are taken to be based on the characteristics of goods in relation to the fulfillment of specific consumption objectives, it is not unreasonable to assume the existence of some hierarchical properties in the relationship between the objectives and thus in the relationship between characteristics.[11] It is not necessary to go as far as the Austrian school and assume a strictly hierarchical consumption theory,[12] but the existence of some hierarchy generates the presumption that the degree of preference variety across a population will be an increasing function of real income. The argument is that product varieties in a class will typically perform some basic function (giving shelter, satisfying hunger, providing transportation) to much the same degree but will vary greatly in attributes ranking lower in the hierarchy (esthetic properties, flavor, comfort). Consumers at minimum real income levels will strive to satisfy the basic functions first and will only consider other characteristics when they have some surplus over minimum basic needs. The set of relevant characteristics in a situation will be greater at high income levels than at low income levels, which gives more scope for diversity as incomes rise. The analysis given here concentrates on situations in which all consumers are at approximately the same level of real income, but this kind of income effect on diversity would appear in comparing the optimal or market structures of different economies with different income levels.

The concept of "manifest equity," introduced in the opening section of this chapter, implies some relation between the preceived welfare of others and the welfare of the individual. In general, however, it is assumed throughout this work that there are no consumption

10. It is sometimes argued that capitalist society, by emphasizing competition and individual achievement, fosters variations in revealed preferences that are, in some sense, false, whereas socialist society, by emphasizing cooperation, enables the inherent similarities to emerge. Even if the facts and the argument were accepted, preferences so thoroughly conditioned would be considered "true" preferences.

11. See Lancaster (1971, pp. 145–147).

12. See Menger (1950). Ironmonger (1972) also uses a strictly hierarchical system.

externalities, unless they are specifically introduced into a case, and that an individual's welfare depends only on his or her own consumption.

## 1.3 The Technology of Production

The variety-equity-efficiency problem arises from the interaction of varied preferences with a production technology which permits variations in the specifications of products to be produced but gives economies of scale in the production of large quantities of a product to any single specification.[13] That much of modern technology possesses both these properties is obvious enough and calls for no particular argument.

There are some points worth noting, however. One is that the development of modern technology has expanded the potential variety of products while simultaneously creating the opportunity for economy through standardization.[14] The two aspects of the technology with which this book is concerned have largely grown up together. Before the development of machine-based manufacturing, the handcraftsman had few scale economies on which to draw, and it might be expected that he could produce in infinite variety. In fact, the craftsman was severely limited by his materials, his tools, and his own skills, and potential variety was quite small even though there were no apparent economies from standardization.

Under conditions of handcraftsmanship there were, in effect, economies of scale, but in a different form from those associated with modern technology. These were economies arising from investment in "human capital"[15] rather than physical capital. A craftsman would spend several years learning how to do things in a certain way and,

13. By a "specification" is meant an exact combination of characteristics in specified proportions such as would appear in a supply contract between a manufacturer and a distributor—a man's two-piece suit of a certain size, color, style, and fabric, with certain specific details of finish, for example.

14. Note that expansion in potential variety through technology is not confined to manufactured products but has also occurred in agriculture.

15. See Schultz (1961).

having done so, could produce a limited range of products with the skills acquired. To produce something different would require the craftsman to devote time to thinking through how it should be done, and thus the custom article would be produced at higher cost than the standard product. In the preindustrial era, only princes could afford the unstandardized product, and the products available to the ordinary consumer were of remarkable uniformity, as they are in contemporary peasant societies.[16]

In the main analysis which follows, it will be assumed that the economies of scale are specific to a particular product variant. This is obviously a simplification, since joint economies of scale between different products of the same group are clearly important in practice. Automobile manufacturers might use the same engine in several automobile models, for example, and obtain economies of scale in engine production much greater than could be obtained from production of a single model. Although "interproduct" economies, which include joint economies in production, are discussed in Chapter 9, they will be ignored elsewhere. In deriving conditions for optimal product differentiation, it is implicitly assumed that all possible joint economies of this kind are utilized. This is covered by the usual efficiency assumption in welfare analysis, that everything is produced with the least possible use of resources for the quantity given. The effect of such joint economies on market structures is confined to the discussion in Chapter 9.

Another assumption that is also an obvious simplification is that goods can be produced to any specification within some feasible range. Characteristics of products cannot always be varied continuously, and there are some characteristics that are inherently discontinuous. The specifications of many products may be defined partly by the presence or absence of "features," such as the various controls, input options, extra speaker terminals, and so on, in high-fidelity audio equipment, and only partly by continuously variable characteristics like power, distortion, or other measurable parameters of the same equipment.

16. Peasant craftsmen have an inordinate pride, shocking to the urban traveler with romantic notions about preindustrial societies, in being able to produce pots or baskets which are almost as uniform as if produced by a machine. From their point of view, they are succeeding in producing to an exact specification and minimizing random error.

All these simplifications are reasonable in a general analysis of product variety which is designed to establish broad patterns, not to produce specific solutions for individual cases.

## 1.4 The Scope of the Study

This is a theoretical study of the problem of the optimal degree of product variety in an economy in which the technology exhibits economies of scale and the population has varied tastes, both characteristics of advanced industrial societies.

The study commences with the establishment of a framework for analysis, formalizing the approach which has already been sketched out into an economic model with well-defined properties on which all the succeeding analysis is based. This formalization is set out in Chapter 2, and the result is a model in the true sense of a simplified representation of reality with acceptable basic properties. The most heroic simplification is the *uniformity assumption* on the nature and distribution of preferences, which can be compared to the assumption of a flat featureless plain in location theory. Although real populations are unlikely to exhibit such regularities, the uniform case provides the workable basis for analysis, to which the effect of nonuniformities can later be added.

Using the basic model, Chapters 3 and 4 examine the conditions for optimal product differentiation in a pure welfare economics setting, that is, without reference to any specific institutional arrangements such as markets.

Chapter 3 examines optimal differentiation in a highly simplified setting in which the only goods in the economy are those in a single product class. Although this is a model which is stripped to its bare essentials, it is referred to as the "paradigm case" because it illustrates both the optimum problem and its solution in the least complex manner possible.[17] Chapter 4 expands the analysis by considering the problem of optimal product variety within a group when that group

---

17. This is the case analyzed in Lancaster (1975). At that stage it was not realized by the author that there are no viable market structures in the paradigm case, and thus there are some important errors in the paper.

is embedded in a larger economy producing "outside goods" which are not within the product class being investigated.

The optimum analysis produces one conclusion of particular interest, since it appears to contradict much traditional thinking:

1. It is not optimal to produce any good at minimum average cost.

What this implies is that, if any good is being produced at minimum average cost (that is, all the economies of scale have been drawn upon), it is always better to increase product variety and produce more goods, each at an output below the minimum average cost level.

Following the solution of the problem of optimal product differentiation is a series of chapters which examine the market structures that are possible within the kind of economy with which the book is concerned and compare these structures with the optimum. The series commences with the analysis of market demand under conditions of continuously variable product differentiation (Chapter 5), an analysis that necessarily breaks new ground. Chapters 6, 7, and 8 are devoted to the study of market structures which consist only of single-product firms, structures which are analogous to, but not identical with, traditional monopolistic competition. The crucial difference between the firms in this model and those in traditional analysis is that here the firms must choose both the price and *specification* of the goods they produce. The following are among the important conclusions which emerge from these studies:

1. There are viable market structures only over a restricted range of economic parameters.

2. The "most-competitive" possible equilibrium is one in which every firm produces a unique product, receives zero monopoly profit, and produces at an output less than that which gives minimum average cost. This is the equilibrium associated with perfect information on the part of firms and consumers, costless and continuously variable potential product-specification changes, and free and willing entry into the group, for which reasons it is called "perfect monopolistic competition."

3. The traditional perfect-competition structure is not possible in this economy under conditions of full flexibility. This traditional structure can only be generated by imposing restrictions on the freedom of

firms to decide on the specifications of their products, and is then suboptimal.

4. The market may provide more or less than the optimal degree of product variety, depending on the parameters of the system.

5. In those cases in which the market produces more than optimal variety, the loss in efficiency is balanced, in part, by the greater degree of equity due to greater variety.

The analysis is not confined to the "perfect" monopolistic case; Chapter 8 considers the effect of such imperfections as incomplete information, costs of specification change, and costs of entry. In general, such imperfections tend to reduce the degree of product variety.

Chapter 9 is concerned with market structures based on multi-product firms, including true monopoly, and the possibility of quasi-monopoly power being created by virtue of a single firm's control over several products. It is shown that a monopolist will, in general, produce a variety of products in his group, but fewer products than would be optimal or would be produced under a monopolistic-competition structure. The possibilities for quasi-monopoly are shown to depend on how the products under single control are related to each other in the spectrum of all products within the group and not on the number of products as such which are produced by a single firm. The effect of interproduct economies on market structure is also examined in this chapter.

In examining market structures, the emphasis is on how the degree of product variety is affected by the structure. More conventional considerations, such as the effect of market structure on prices and price distortions, are discussed to some extent, but the effects are generally the same as in the traditional analysis with goods of fixed specification and thus do not require extensive treatment.

The study concludes with a series of brief sketches in which the principles established in the previous chapters are applied to a series of special problems, such as trade in differentiated products, development strategy, optimal variety in public programs, variety and the measurement of GNP, and product differentiation in capital goods. These topics constitute the substance of Chapter 10 and are designed to provide suggestions for further research rather than to be complete studies in themselves.

Chapter 2

# A Framework for Analysis

## 2.1 Introduction

THE PROBLEM IN analyzing economic systems in which the goods
(or many of them) can be infinitely varied in design and specification
has always been that of finding a workable framework of analysis.
Chamberlin, who perceived the importance of variable product design, thought it impossible to carry through a full formal analysis of
its effects:

. . . "product" variations are in their essence qualitative; they cannot,
therefore, be measured along an axis and displayed in a single diagram." [1]

Some years prior to the appearance of Chamberlin's work, however,
Hotelling had provided a hint as to a possible solution of the product-
variation problem by extending his model of pure spatial competition:

The number of dimensions of our picture is increased to three or more
when we represent geometrically such characters as sweetness of
cider, and instead of transport costs consider more generally the de-
crement of utility resulting from the actual commodity being in a
different place and condition than the buyer would prefer. [2]

1. Chamberlin (1933, p. 79).

2. Hotelling (1929).

Hotelling himself did not develop this idea further, Chamberlin ignored it, and no one else took it up.

The Hotelling quotation gives the essence of the idea on which a framework for analyzing the economic consequences of infinitely variable product specification can be constructed, namely, that differences between products can be decomposed into differences in measurable characteristics of those products (like the degree of sweetness of the cider) and that consumers will react to those differences in characteristics. Many steps are involved in building up from the basic idea to the full framework, however, and the purpose of this chapter is to describe those steps.

## 2.2 The Characteristics Approach

The fundamental approach on which the analysis in this book is based is that developed earlier by the author[3] in which goods are considered not as entities in a gestalt sense but as bundles of properties or characteristics. These characteristics are objective, and the relationship between a good and the characteristics it possesses is a technical one, determined by the design of the good or by "nature"[4] if the good is not synthesized. Individuals are interested in goods not for their own sake but because of the characteristics they possess, so that the demand for goods is derived and indirect and depends on preferences with respect to characteristics and on the technical properties that determine how characteristics are embodied in different goods. Differences in individual reactions to the same good are seen as expressing different preferences with respect to the collection of characteristics possessed by that good and not different perceptions as to properties of the good. This is strictly true, of course, only if it can be assumed that full information as to the

3. Lancaster (1966, 1971). A somewhat similar analysis, which had been developed independently, appears in Ironmonger (1972). Note that the term "attributes" is often used instead of "characteristics," especially in the marketing and psychology literature.

4. But "nature" can be changed a great deal, and most agricultural products in a modern economy, from wheat and tomatoes to beef and chicken, have been subject to man-made redesign.

characteristics of the good is available to all; in the absence of full information, one consumer may be aware of certain characteristics, another consumer of different characteristics.

The characteristics which appear in the analysis are assumed to be objectively quantifiable as well as objectively identifiable, even though there are important characteristics (color, for example) that do not fit this specification. Although color can be objectively *defined* by primary color composition and degree of saturation, color differences cannot be put on a simple scale like size or horsepower or vitamin C content so that everyone agrees that good A has twice as much per pound as good B. The analysis, as given, does not apply to goods in which the only variations are in nonquantifiable characteristics; however, it is possible to handle some nonquantifiable characteristics in a context in which quantifiable characteristics dominate, as, for example, when an individual prefers large cars to small cars and red cars to blue but will always prefer a slightly larger blue car to a slightly smaller red car, which implies a lexicographic ordering of characteristics, with color as decisive only between cars of the same size.

The essential feature of the characteristics approach is that individual preferences are preferences with respect to collections of *characteristics* in the first instance, and preferences with respect to collections of goods are derived from preferences over characteristics only when the technical relationships between the goods and the characteristics they contain is given. The usual assumption that preferences are stable (meaning that they do not change in the short run or in an arbitrary way) is taken to mean that preferences over characteristics are stable but that preferences over goods may change if the characteristics composition of the goods changes. This is the key to the analysis of product differentiation: Variation in product implies a change in its characteristics composition, the effect of which can be read off against assumed stable preferences over characteristics.

Preferences over characteristics are taken to have the properties usually assumed for preferences over goods in traditional consumer theory. That is, if a diagram is drawn with quantities of different characteristics along the axes, instead of quantities of different goods, the indifference curves will have the properties of being convex toward the origin, of being nonintersecting, and of representing more-preferred collections when further from the origin, assuming all characteristics to be desirable ones. ("Bad" characteristics require appropriate modifications.) Similarly, the utility function will have the form $U(z)$, where $z$ is a vector of characteristics rather than of goods, but will possess the usually assumed properties.

The basic characteristics analysis is illustrated in Figure 2.1 for the two-dimensional case. The axes represent quantities of the two characteristics A and B, and IC is an indifference curve showing the conventional properties. Points $X$ and $Y$ represent the collections of characteristics possessed by unit quantities of goods X and Y, respectively. It is obvious that the individual represented will prefer one unit of good X to one unit of good Y. Good Y is now varied in such a way as to possess slightly more of characteristic B and slightly less of characteristic A, the collection of characteristics possessed by the varied product being represented by point $Y'$. The individual now prefers one unit of good Y, as varied, to a unit of good X. The preference ordering with respect to the two goods has been changed by a relatively small change in the specification of one product, although the basic preferences (in terms of characteristics) remain unchanged.

Figure 2.2 represents another individual, with different preferences. The same product variation as in the previous case results in

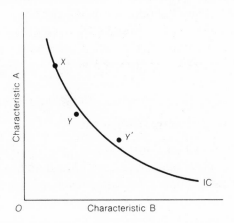

**Figure 2.1.** Preference diagram for goods with two characteristics.

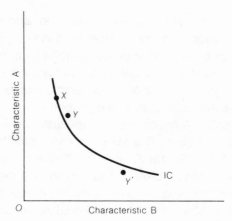

**Figure 2.2.** Diagram as in Figure 2.1, but for an individual with different preferences.

a change in the preference ordering with respect to goods in the opposite direction; the individual initially prefers one unit of good Y to a unit of good X, but after the product variation prefers a unit of the varied Y (Y'). Thus the characteristics approach can handle the analysis of opposite changes in preference ordering with respect to goods between two consumers when preferences are stable and product changes are the same for both individuals.

Most importantly, the characteristics approach accords with common sense. When a new model of a product appears, we decide whether or not we prefer it to the old model by taking note of how its properties have been changed and whether improvements in some characteristics have been outweighed by reductions in other desirable features. The ultimate judgment depends on individual preferences, unless all properties are improved and none is made worse.

## 2.3 Goods as a Transfer Mechanism

As pointed out elsewhere,[5] the combination of variable product design and individual preferences based on characteristics implies that goods are simply a transfer mechanism whereby characteristics are

5. Lancaster (1975).

bundled up into packages at the manufacturing end, pass through the distribution and marketing processes as packages, and are then, so to speak, opened up to yield their characteristics again at the point of consumption. The packaging occurs either for technical reasons, because it is impossible to provide the characteristics that make up an automobile separately (although the proportions of the various characteristics can be varied over some range), or for economic reasons, because it requires less resources to provide the characteristics as a fixed bundle than to provide the same characteristics separately.

Consumers do not, of course, merely open their "packages" at home and consume the characteristics separately, except in rare instances. The technology of consumption determines whether consumption of the good is combinable with that of other goods (breakfast cereals with sugar and milk, for example) to give a combination having characteristics derived from all components or whether it is noncombinable and the collection of characteristics contained in the good must be consumed as a fixed bundle.

The view of goods as a transfer mechanism, and thus as intermediaries rather than primary resources or objects of final consumption, leads to an important overview of the working of the economic system. Consumer welfare is determined by the characteristics available for consumption, and the ultimate constraints are those on resources, these two factors being linked by transfer through goods. The efficiency of the system cannot be measured simply by the output of goods from given resources but depends on how well the goods have been chosen to transfer characteristics to consumers. Thus the optimum problem involves the *design* of goods as well as their quantities. In fact, the level of welfare that can be attained from a given set of resources depends on:

1. the preferences of the individuals, which determine the welfare levels associated with different collections of characteristics;

2. the consumption technology, which determines the collection of characteristics that can be obtained by consumers from a given collection of goods of specified design;

3. the production technology, which determines both the potential

variations in the characteristics contents of the various goods and the resources required to produce a given collection of goods of specified design;

4. the choice of the number and types of the various goods to be used as the transfer mechanism between production and final consumption.

The structure of the problem differs from that of traditional general equilibrium analysis in the existence of potentially infinite variations in the properties of some goods in the system. It is essential in traditional analysis that the number of goods be finite and of fixed specification, although some flexibility is obtained by allowing for a very large number of goods, only some of which are produced in nonzero quantities.

## 2.4   The Consumption Technology

In the author's original paper on the characteristics approach,[6] it was assumed that the relationship between goods and characteristics was *linear* in the sense that quantity $x$ of a good contained exactly $x$ times as much of every characteristic as a unit quantity of the same good. It was also assumed that characteristics were *additive* in the sense that the characteristics obtained from joint consumption of specified quantities of two or more goods could be determined by adding up the quantities of each characteristic contained in the specified quantities of the two goods.

Both these assumptions, and especially additivity, are specialized. It will be appropriate to assume linearity whenever goods are *divisible* and can be consumed in any quantities (like sugar or soap), but it is both unnecessary and inappropriate to assume linearity when goods are *indivisible* (like automobiles and most consumer durables) and must be used in a fixed package size.

The assumption of additivity will be discarded for most of the analysis given here, and the property will be viewed somewhat different. A distinction will be made between *combinable* goods and

6. Lancaster (1966).

*noncombinable* goods, goods being combinable when different variants can be consumed together to give characteristics which are a combination of the characteristics of the two components (like different types of coffee) and noncombinable when two variants cannot be consumed simultaneously (like different automobile models). If goods are combinable, they may or may not be strictly additive in characteristics, although additivity will be assumed in the few cases of combinability that appear in the subsequent analysis.

It is the author's view that, although the original characteristics analysis was based on the combinable and additive model and a considerable literature has grown up around this model,[7] the true power of the characteristics approach is most evident in the analysis of goods, like consumer durables, in which noncombinability is the rule. The problems of optimal transfer through goods are most acute in the noncombinable case, since consumers cannot obtain a desired characteristics mix simply by consuming several goods simultaneously; for example, a large car plus a small car is not equivalent to two medium-sized cars. Noncombinable goods may be divisible (cigarettes or beer) or indivisible (automobiles), the distinction between divisibility and indivisibility being less important and less clear than that between combinability and noncombinability.

The existence of indivisibility may be as much a property of the production technology as of the consumption technology, since production of a good in one very large unit rather than many small units, even though it can be consumed in small units, may be determined by technology or economic advantage. The only variable characteristic of a refrigerator may be its size, for example, so that a model with 10 percent more capacity may be viewed by the consumer as equivalent to 10 percent more refrigerator. Such a good might be viewed as divisible as far as the consumption technology is con-

---

7. See, for example, Alcaly and Klevorick (1970); Archibald and Rosenbluth (1975); Auld (1972, 1974); Barker (1974); Barten (1977); Bernardo and Blin (1977); Brumat and Tomasini (1977); Colantoni, Davis, and Swaminuthan (1976); Geistfeld (1977); Graft, Lea, and Whitworth (1977); Hendler (1975); Hogarty, and MacKay (1975); Hori (1975); Klevmarken (1977); Ladd and Zober (1977); Leland (1977); Lipsey and Rosenbluth (1971); Muellbauer (1974); Nicosia (1974); Ratchford (1975); Roberts (1975); Rosen (1974); Sandmo (1973); and Stewart (1977).

cerned, but for production reasons may be made in only one size and thus appears as an indivisible good in the system.

The primary focus of the analysis will be on goods which are noncombinable and divisible, with analysis of the effects of indivisibility. There will be little emphasis on combinable goods, since it will be shown that these do not lead to the major problems associated with noncombinability. Noncombinability is strongly associated with high-technology manufactured goods, combinability with agricultural products or low-technology manufactures, so the analysis is especially applicable to advanced Western economies. There are, however, important implications for all economic systems and particularly for those economies on the brink of developing high-technology manufacturing.


## 2.5  The Group

Long before the introduction of the characteristics approach, when goods were simply goods as far as the theory of consumer behavior was concerned, it was found both convenient and in accord with common sense to consider goods in groups (in the crudest form, simple groupings like "food" or "clothing") for applied and empirical work. Such groupings are based on the implicit assumption that different items of food have more in common with each other, either on the production side or the consumption side, or both, than do a kind of food and a kind of clothing.

The idea of a group can easily be formalized in terms of characteristics, and indeed some implicit notion of characteristics has always lain behind the group concept. First it should be noted that the groups are groups of *goods*, not characteristics, so that the group property must involve the consumption technology and its structure. Then it should be noted that the group is only of interest if individuals react to the universe of goods through the groups into which it has been subdivided, which implies that the structure of preferences is also involved. Finally, it is usual, although not essential, to suppose that goods in the same group possess some similarity in production.

Formally, a subset of the universe of goods forms a *fully separable group* if the following conditions are met:

1. All goods in the subset possess characteristics in common.
2. None of the characteristics possessed by any of the goods in the subset (which can be referred to as the *group characteristics*) is possessed by any goods outside the group.
3. The welfare or utility functions of all consumers are separable between the group characteristics and nongroup characteristics; that is, the typical utility function has the structure $U(v_G, v_{NG})$, where $v_G$ is a subutility derived from the available collection of group characteristics only and $v_{NG}$ is a subutility derived from nongroup characteristics only.[8]

Full separability is a strong property and thus requires strong conditions. For most purposes, it is sufficient to have approximate full separability, where there are characteristics in common between group and nongroup goods but the proportion of the total nongroup characteristics obtained from the group goods and the proportion of group characteristics obtained from the nongroup goods are both so small as to be unimportant in decision making. That is, if the consumption technology is depicted as a matrix with each entry showing the quantity of characteristic (rows) obtained from given quantities of goods (columns), full separability requires that the matrix can be organized to show blocks of zeros, and approximate separability that the matrix shows blocks of very small numbers instead of zeros. Similarly, the utility function can be approximately separable, with the subutility $v_G$ derived from all characteristics, but with very small weights to nongroup characteristics, and the subutility $v_{NG}$ with very small weights to group characteristics.

It is assumed throughout this analysis that there exist groups which are at least approximately fully separable in the above sense— groups such as automobiles, college programs, radios, soft drinks,

8. Separability implies sequential budget decisions and guarantees that the choice between products in any group is independent of the choice between products in any other group. The effect of purchases in any group on those in any other group appear as income effects only. See Strotz (1957), Gorman (1959), Goldman and Uzawa (1964), Blackorby, Lady, Nissen, and Russell (1970), and Pollack (1972), also Lancaster (1971, Chapter 8).

housing, typewriters. In general, the analysis will concentrate on one group at a time, so that the relevant distinction is between *group goods*, meaning goods in the particular group being considered, and *outside goods*, meaning all other goods, whether or not these can be subdivided into their own groups.

It is also assumed that the groups being considered are such that there are strong production similarities between goods within the group, so that the producers of the group goods consider themselves to be in the same industry or subindustry and producing a different good in the same group is a realistic option for every producer. Although consumption grouping does not of itself imply production grouping, the two are commonly associated in fact, and it is reasonable to expect that technical similarities between goods sufficient to make them appear within the same frame at the consumption end will tend to result in their being produced in much the same way.


## 2.6   Product Differentiation

The distinction between differentiated products and different products can become somewhat shadowy. The term "product differentiation" is used here to mean variations in the characteristics contents of goods within the same closely defined group. In common terminology, product differentiates correspond to different "models" of automobiles or radios, whereas an automobile and a radio are products from different groups. The term "brand," used widely in marketing literature, is not properly synonymous with product differentiate, since there may be several models (and thus product differentiates) under a given brand name or identical products under different brand names.[9]

The basic model of the group on which the analysis is built is one in which the goods and potential goods within the group possess the same characteristics, all of which are taken to be quantifiable. Thus differences among the products within the group can be iden-

9. In marketing, it is normally assumed that different brands are different products in the eyes of the consumer, even if identical in all respects but name and packaging. The question is left open here, although there is some relevant discussion in Chapter 8.

tified by quantitative differences in characteristics content. The definition of product variations then depends on whether the goods in the group are divisible or indivisible. If they are divisible and there are, say, $m$ characteristics defining the group, a good can be identified by the $m - 1$ ratios of the quantities of the various characteristics to any one characteristic chosen as numeraire for one unit of the good. Since the characteristics content of $x$ units of the good is simply $x$ times the content of each characteristic in a unit of the good, because of the assumed linearity, goods with identical characteristics ratios can be considered identical goods since the same characteristics collections can be obtained by consuming appropriate quantities of either.

Goods which are indivisible, on the other hand, need to be identified by the $m$ quantities of each characteristic contained in a unit quantity, since goods having the same characteristics ratios but packaged in units of different sizes need to be identified as differentiated goods. Indivisible goods have identical absolute quantities of characteristics per unit will be considered as identical goods.

The information necessary to identify the good in the given context will be called its *specification.* The specification will depend on the characteristics ratios, in the case of divisible goods, or the characteristics per unit quantity, in the case of indivisible goods. Not all characteristics need be listed in the specification if membership in the group implies possessing certain characteristics in certain quantities—automobiles having four round wheels, for example. Specifications are assumed to be restricted to those characteristics which vary over goods within the group, and this gives the justification for analyzing models with small numbers of variable characteristics.

Product differentiation is then defined as varying the specifications of goods within a group, and a product-differentiated group is a group containing goods of different specifications.

An important distinction needs to be made between *vertical* and *horizontal* product differentiation. A further quotation from Chamberlin is relevant on this point: "The 'product' may be improved, deteriorated, or merely changed."[10] Chamberlin's "improvement" and "de-

---

10. Chamberlin (1933, p. 172).

terioration" correspond to *vertical* product differentiation, in which the absolute quantities of all characteristics per unit of the good are increased or decreased. It corresponds to what has come to be called quality change, a topic on which there is a considerable literature.[11] Vertical product differentiation, or quality change, is of importance only in the case of indivisible goods. If goods are divisible and there are two goods with the same characteristics ratios, one having more characteristics per unit quantity (higher quality), then either the prices or unit resource costs are proportional to the qualities (quality being unambiguously defined and measurable in this case), and the goods differ only in the definition of their units, or they are not proportional, in which case one or other of the goods can provide exactly the same characteristics collection as the other, but for less expenditure or resource use, and the other good drops out of the system.

This book is concerned with the analysis of *horizontal,* rather than vertical, product differentiation, in which the various product differentiates vary in specification rather than in quality—the goods are "merely changed," in Chamberlin's phrase. For the reasons given above, product differentiation is essentially horizontal when goods are divisible, and few problems arise in making the distinction between the two kinds of differentiation. With indivisible goods, which are also introduced into the analysis, such problems arise, however. Two goods, one of which has 20 percent more of every characteristic per unit quantity than the other, are obviously vertically differentiated. When one good has 20 percent more of some characteristics and no more of others, there is obviously a mixture of vertical differentiation and horizontal differentiation (the latter occurs because the characteristics ratios between the goods differ). When one good has 20 percent more of some characteristics and 20 percent less of others, there is obviously horizontal differentiation. Is there also vertical differentiation? This is a difficult question, which cannot be answered uniquely, and the problem has been investigated in the literature on quality change.[12] This literature is mainly concerned with the problem

11. But "quality" is sometimes used in the literature in a sense that does not necessarily imply vertical ranking. In this sense it corresponds to what has been called "specification" here. See, for example, Leland (1977) or Rosen (1974).

12. See Lancaster (1977) and contributions by Cagan, Dhrymes, Griliches, and Hall in Griliches (1971).

in its most troublesome form, having its origins in studies designed to assist in introducing quality change factors into cost-of-living indexes and other official indicators.

The common sense of the distinction between horizontal and vertical product differentiation is clear enough: Different models of basic compact cars represent horizontal differentiation, whereas the distinction between a Volkswagon and a Mercedes is one of vertical differentiation. Since the analysis here is developed primarily for divisible goods, and since indivisible goods are introduced in a context in which any important degree of vertical differentiation is ruled out by the structure of the situation, no great difficulties will arise from the distinction between the two directions of differentiation.

## 2.7   Differentiation Possibilities

It will be assumed, as in the author's earlier work on the subject,[13] that product differentiation is potentially continuous over the group, within some limits set by the potential differentiation range. For a group of divisible goods in which only two characteristics are variable over the group, and thus in which specification is given by a single parameter (provisionally taken to be the characteristics ratio), it is assumed that there is a maximum and minimum value for the specification parameter but that it is potentially possible to produce a good having any specification between those extremes. In the $n$-characteristics case, in which specification is determined by a point in $(n - 1)$-dimensional space corresponding to the $n - 1$ characteristics ratios, it is assumed that goods can be produced having specifications corresponding to all points in the convex set determined by the extreme points which delimit the potential differentiation range.

The production technology determines not only what specifications of goods can be produced but also what resources are required to produce goods of different specifications once the different goods have been normalized in some way to give comparable units. This aspect of the production technology will be approached by inverting the input–output relationship and considering what collections of characteristics can be derived from a fixed bundle of resources when

13. Lancaster (1975).

all those resources are used to produce a single good of given specification.

Consider a given bundle of resources, of arbitrary size, that will be considered to be the unit bundle. This bundle may consist of a single resource (labor, for example) or several resources (labor and capital), but it will be assumed that the resources are either used in fixed proportions or, in a market model, have fixed relative prices, so that the resources can be treated as a single aggregate resource. Henceforth the singular word "resource" will be used, implying either a truly single resource or an aggregate that can be treated as a single resource.

Take an arbitrary specification within the potential differentiation range and consider the production of a good having this specification, using the whole of the unit resource for the purpose. There will be some maximum amount of the good that can be produced (in whatever units it may be measured), and, since the ratios of the characteristics are given by the specification, this maximum amount of the good will correspond to a maximal collection of characteristics in the proportions determined by the specification. Figure 2.3 illustrates the two-characteristics case, in which the quantities of the two characteristics (not goods) are measured along the axes. The slope of the line $OX$ gives the characteristics ratio and thus the specification, and the point $X$ represents the largest collection of character-

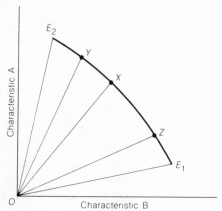

**Figure 2.3.** Product differentiation possibilities with given resources.

istics having that ratio that can be achieved for a single good produced with a unit of resource.

For every specification there will be some point representing the maximal collection of characteristics producible from a unit of resource by embodiment in a single good. Points $Y$ and $Z$ correspond to such collections in the diagram, for specifications given by the slopes of $OY$ and $OZ$, respectively. It is reasonable to suppose that if product differentiation is continuous over the potential differentiation range (determined in the figure by the extreme ratios corresponding to the slopes of $OE_1$ and $OE_2$), maximal collections will also vary continuously and thus the locus of all such collections will be a continuous curve. This curve will be defined as the *unit product-differentiation curve*, or *unit PDC*.

What shape can such a curve (or surface, in the many-characteristics case) be expected to have? In general, it can be expected to slope downward to the right, the amount of one characteristic being increased only by reducing the amount of the other. One possibility is that the curve is a straight line, in which case the implicit resource cost per unit of each characteristic is a constant. It seems more likely (and there is no guidance from theory or empirical study to help here) that the resource cost of embodying more of characteristic A relative to characteristic B will rise, relative to the resource cost of characteristic B, as the ratio of A to B increases, which gives a PDC having the same property of concavity toward the origin as in the traditional production possibility curve. This is the shape that will normally be assumed.

Because of the way in which the shape of the PDC is compounded with the shapes of indifference curves in formulating the compensating function at a later stage in the argument, the exact shape of the PDC will not appear directly in later analysis and is not critical.

The PDC corresponding to, say, $V$ units of resource can be derived in the same way as the unit PDC and can be expected to have the same general properties. The relationship between the unit PDC and the PDC for $V$ resource units is, however, assumed to be much stronger than that of having the same general shape: It is assumed that the two PDCs will be *geometrically similar*, the $V$-unit

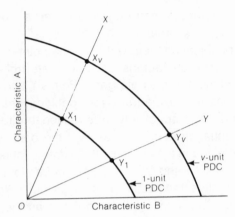

**Figure 2.4.** Product differentiation curves for different resource levels.

PDC being a pure homothetic expansion of the 1-unit PDC. By a homothetic expansion is meant that if $V$ is greater than 1, the $V$-unit PDC is larger (further from the origin) than the 1-unit PDC and geometrically similar to it, so that the ratios $OX_V/OX_1$ and $OY_V/OY_1$ in Figure 2.4 are equal to each other for all rays $OX$ and $OY$, but the ratio is *not necessarily equal to V*. That is, the quantity of any characteristic obtained by producing a good of given specification with different quantities of resources always increases if the quantity of resource increases, but not necessarily in proportion to the increase in the resource. The point is emphasized here because the analysis in this book is primarily concerned with production in which there are economies of scale of some kind. The assumption of homotheticity (geometrical similarity of the PDCs) ensures that all products within the group can be produced with the same economies-of-scale properties.

## 2.8   Measurement and Comparability

One of the major obstacles in the path of formal analysis of product differentiation is that of making quantitative comparisons between goods which are not identical. Monetary measures cannot be used, since prices are endogenous in the market models and do not appear in pure welfare analysis. Goods of different specification, therefore, can only be compared in terms of initial resource content or final utility value. Since it is the essence of the analysis here that there are many individuals with varied preferences, a single utility measure is out of the question, and thus resource input measures must be used.

Goods within a single group are defined and measured in the following way:

1. A good is defined by its specification, goods of different specifications being different goods.

2. Different goods are brought to the same measure by defining the unit quantity of any good to be the quantity that can be produced with unit resources.

3. Quantities of the same good are scaled in proportion to the content of any characteristic (characteristics proportions being fixed), relative to the content of that characteristic in a unit of the good, as defined above.

4. Quantities of different goods will receive the same measure if and only if the embodied characteristics collections lie on the same PDC and the quantities thus require the same resources. This follows directly from properties 1 through 3, the definition of the PDC, and the assumed property of homotheticity.

The definition implies that $Q$ units of any good contains $Q$ times as much of every characteristic as a single unit (giving linearity in the goods–characteristics relationship) and that $Q$ units of good X requires the same resources as $Q$ units of good Y, but *not* that $Q$ units of good X requires $Q$ times as much resource input as a single unit. Resource input requirements are only used to relate quantities of *different* goods, relative quantities of the *same* good being scaled directly from characteristics content. Equivalent quantities of different goods may or may not correspond to equivalent numbers of "natural" units of each, but different quantities of the same good will be measured proportionally to the number of natural units.

A more formal version of the above analysis, involving the introduction of a quantity function which has contours identical with those of the PDC, but in which the numbers attached to the contours are proportional to the distance from the origin, is set out in Appendix A.

## 2.9   Optimal Transfer for an Individual

As already pointed out, goods provide a transfer mechanism whereby characteristics are embodied in those goods at the production end and the final consumer's reaction to the goods is determined by the embodied characteristics. The possibilities for embodiment are determined by the PDC, and the consumers reaction is determined by his or her preferences.

For a single individual, the optimal transfer is by a good with its specification chosen to provide the characteristics collection most preferred by that individual among all the possible characteristics collections that can be derived from a given resource level by embodiment in a single good. Consider a one-person economy, with fixed resources available for the group under consideration. The PDC defines the characteristics collections that can be attained by using those resources to produce a single good (goods are assumed to be noncombinable), and the individual's indifference map defines his preferences over the potential characteristics collections. The optimal specification is given by the characteristics collection on the PDC which is most preferred by that individual, and this will obviously be

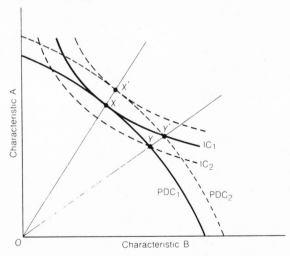

**Figure 2.5.** Diagram illustrating an individual's most-preferred good and also the idea of compensation.

at a point at which an indifference curve is tangent to the PDC, such as the point $X$ in Figure 2.5. The specification corresponding to this point (the slope of $OX$ in the diagram) is then the specification of the good which provides optimal transfer between resources and final utility or welfare for that lone individual.

To avoid later confusion from using the term "optimal" to refer to the best choice at different levels of multistage maximizing or minimizing processes, the good which represents optimal transfer for a given individual will be referred to as that individual's *most-preferred good*.[14] It is immediately obvious that (1) the specification of the most-preferred good for an individual is jointly determined by both the properties of the PDC and the preferences of the individual and (2) individuals having different preferences can be expected, in general, to have different most-preferred goods.

It is important to note that the most-preferred-good concept is derived by assuming the individual to be allocated a bundle of resources which are to be devoted *exclusively* to producing a good for his or her sole consumption. There may be economies of scale in the production of the good for the individual (these do not affect the analysis), but the individual is not allowed to obtain *additional* scale economies by forming a coalition with another individual in which both agree to accept the same good and obtain these additional economies. Such coalitions are treated at a later stage in the study.

Although the PDC is assumed to be homothetic, the most-preferred good for a given individual will not necessarily have the same specification at different resource levels, unless the individual's preferences are also homothetic, that is, unless the slope of the indifference curve at a point depends only on the characteristics ratio at that point and not on the absolute levels of the characteristics. It will be convenient, and is not unreasonable, to assume that preferences can be treated as homothetic over the relatively restricted range of variations in absolute characteristics levels that will appear in the analysis, so that the specification of the individual's most-preferred good can be taken as fixed over the range of variation which occurs.

14. This was called the consumer's "optimal good" in Lancaster (1975), hence the explanation for the new term.

## 2.10   Availability and Compensation

Consider Figure 2.5, which depicts events for a two-characteristic group and a single consumer. Given the resources corresponding to $PDC_1$, the most-preferred good for the individual depicted has specification given by the slope of $OX$, since there is tangency between one of the individual's indifference curves and the PDC at the point $X$.

Now suppose that, for whatever reason, the individual in question is supplied with a good having specification given by the slope of $OY$ instead of being supplied with his or her most-preferred good. This good will be referred to as the *available good*, and it gives suboptimal transfer, in the sense that the individual will be worse off (shown by $IC_2$ in Figure 2.5) if the resources are used to make this good rather than the most-preferred good. The individual can, however, be made just as well off as he or she would have been with the quantity of most-preferred good corresponding to the point $X$ by being given more of the available good than will be produced by the resources defining $PDC_1$. Given that the specification of the available good is given by the direction of $OY$, the required quantity of available good is that amount corresponding to the PDC passing through $Y'$, the point at which the ray through $OY$ intersects $IC_1$. This PDC has been labeled $PDC_2$.

Now, since the diagram is drawn with characteristics measured along the axes and relative quantities of the same good have been defined to be proportional to the characteristics content, the ratio of $OY'$ to $OY$ gives the ratio of the quantity of the available good needed to bring the consumer to the welfare level he or she would attain from the quantity of *most-preferred good* given by $PDC_1$ to the amount of *available* good given by $PDC_2$. But the definition of relative quantities of *different* goods implies that the quantities of the available good and the most-preferred good given by $PDC_1$ are the same. Thus the ratio $OY'/OY$ gives the ratio of the quantity of available good to the quantity of most-preferred good, when both quantities give the same welfare level for the consumer. This ratio, which is central to all the analysis that follows, will be termed the *compensating ratio.*

The compensating ratio, which is necessarily greater than or equal to unity, gives the relationship between a given quantity of an individual's most-preferred good and the quantity of any other good of given specification which provides the same level of welfare for that person. It is obvious that the compensating ratio depends on:

1. the properties of the PDC;
2. the individual concerned and the properties of his preferences; and
3. the specification of the available good (the specification of the most-preferred good is given by 1 and 2).

If preferences are homothetic over the range of variation being considered, the compensating ratio will be independent of the quantity of most-preferred good with which the comparison is being made.

A glance at the diagram (Figure 2.5) is sufficient to reveal that the compensating ratio will be larger the greater the curvature of the indifference curve, the greater the curvature of the PDC, and the greater the difference in specification between the available good and the most-preferred good.

Although it is convenient to introduce the compensating ratio through a simple two-characteristic diagram, the concept is, of course, quite general. Let $Q^*$ be some quantity of most-preferred good and $Q$ be the quantity of available good such that the individual is indifferent between $Q^*$ and $Q$. The compensating ratio is then the ratio $Q/Q^*$. Because of the previous steps that have been taken to ensure comparability between the measures of different goods, $Q$ and $Q^*$ are in the same units (resource units), and the ratio is a well-defined concept with the dimensions of a pure number.

## 2.11   The Compensating Function

Given the PDC, the preferences of the individual concerned, and the specification of the available good, the compensating ratio for that individual is determined, since the preferences and the PDC between them determine the specification of the most-preferred good. If the specification of the available good is changed, then the compensating ratio will change, and, if both the PDC and the indifferences curves are smooth, the compensating ratio can be expected to vary continuously with the specification of the available good. The variation of the compensating ratio with the change in specification of the available good, given the specification of the most-preferred good, is the *compensating function,* a key concept in the succeeding analysis.

In order to define the compensating function, the measurement of specification must be carefully considered. Until this stage, it has sufficed to take the ratio of characteristics (in the two-characteristics case) as defining the specification, since it was needed only to identify and order goods of different specification. For a variety of reasons, including infinite range, if goods with zero amount of one of the characteristics are feasible with the given PDC, the simple ratio is not a suitable measure for further analysis; instead, the specification will be defined by the distance *along* the PDC from one extreme of the potential differentiation range, as a proportion of the total length of the PDC from one permissible extreme to the other. That is, specification is measured in terms of *arc* distances along the PDC.

As a result of the homotheticity of the PDCs for different resource quantities, and because the distances along the PDC are normalized for the length of the PDC, goods having the same characteristics ratios will have the same specification on the new measure at all levels of output. Thus the arc measure is an order-preserving transformation of the ratio measure. In a sense, the arc measure is a "natural" measure since it gives equal changes in specification for equal distances along the PDC, the basic determinant of the possibilities for varying the product. In the case of $n$ characteristics, the simple arc measure is replaced by distances in $n - 1$ suitably chosen directions along the product-differentiation surface, normalized for the total length of the surface in that direction.

The chosen specification measure is equivalent to "straightening out" the PDC and then using a linear measure along it. A glance back at Figure 2.3, 2.4, or 2.5 makes it immediately obvious that, if the PDC is straightened in this way, the indifference curves and other constructions in the diagrams will then be distorted in a more or less complex fashion which depends on the shape of the PDC in ordinary characteristics space. The general effects of the distortions can be appreciated by considering two special cases.

Take first the case of a PDC in the shape of a quarter-circle, as

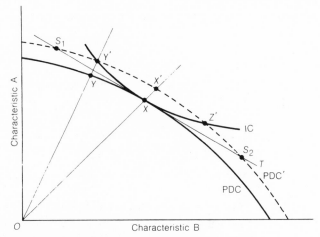

**Figure 2.6.** Product differentiation in characteristics space.

depicted in Figure 2.6 in its untransformed shape, along with the indifference curve which determines the most-preferred good and the common tangent ($T$) to the IC and the PDC. (Note that an elliptical PDC can always be transformed into a circular one by a simple change in the units of measurement of either characteristic.) Now by straightening out the PDC into a unit line segment, Figure 2.6 is transformed into a diagram in which specification is measured horizontally and quantity of good is measured vertically, as in Figure 2.7. Because of homotheticity and the circular properties, the radials $OXX'$ and $OYY'$ in Figure 2.6 become verticals in Figure 2.7. The origin, it should be noted, behaves strangely, and thus is not depicted; because of the normalization process, a PDC close to the origin, and

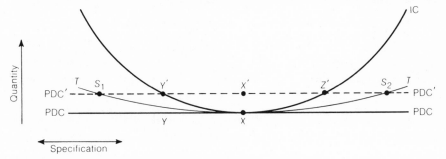

**Figure 2.7.** Product differentiation in specification-quantity space.

thus of infinitesimal length, is expanded into the unit segment by this process, and thus the origin is "stretched" from a point into the same unit segment. The mapping transforms the original diagram from *characteristics* space into *specification–quantity* space.

The circular PDC of Figure 2.6 becomes the unit line segment of Figure 2.7, and equal heights above PDC in the new diagram represent equal increases in the quantities of the goods represented by their specifications, as compared with the quantities corresponding to PDC. A second PDC, like PDC' in Figure 2.6, will appear in Figure 2.7 as parallel to PDC, the distance between the two curves corresponding to the quantity increase, which is the same for all goods by the properties of the PDCs and the quantity definitions. It is obvious that as the PDC of Figure 2.6 is straightened out into the line segment of Figure 2.7 and the radial distances are converted into vertical distances, the tangent line is transformed into a curve which is convex downward and the indifference curve becomes even more convex than before. The PDC, the IC, and the curved image of the former tangent line will all touch at point $X$ in Figure 2.7, since the transformation preserves the ordering of all points, although it does not preserve linearity. The identical labeling of points, lines, and curves in Figures 2.6 and 2.7 makes it easy to follow the effects of the transformation.

Consider now the case of a linear PDC, as depicted in Figure 2.8. No straightening out is required in this case, but normalization is still necessary. Figure 2.9 shows the already-linear PDC placed in a horizontal position, but with no other change (a simple rotation of Figure 2.8). The radials are not vertical except for $PP'$, lying on the normal to the PDC in Figure 2.8, and since PDC' is further from the origin than PDC, A'B' is greater than AB. The distances along $AA'$, $YY'$, $XX'$, and $BB'$, however, are all proportional to quantity changes. Normalization consists of a uniform shrinking of the length of PDC' to the same length as PDC, with the point at which the normal from the origin intersects the line in Figure 2.8 ($P'$) held fixed. This shrinking in from the ends (shown by the arrows in Figure 2.9) gives the final transformation of Figure 2.10, in which the convexity of the indifference curve is somewhat increased.

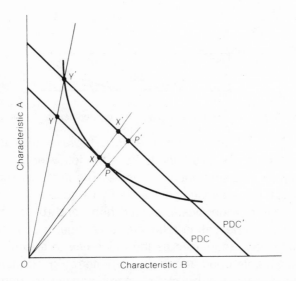

**Figure 2.8.** A linear product differentiation curve in characteristics space.

The properties of the compensating function can be visualized in either Figure 2.7 or Figure 2.10. A horizontal movement along the linearized PDC measures changes in specification, and the vertical distance from the PDC to the transformed indifference curve corresponding to the most-preferred good (the only indifference curve depicted in the diagrams) measures the *extra* quantity of available good necessary to give the individual the same welfare as attained from the most-preferred good. If $Q$ and $Q^*$ are the quantities of available and most-preferred goods, respectively, which yield the same utility for the individual, then the compensating ratio, which will henceforth be denoted by $h$, is given by $Q/Q^*$. The vertical distances $YY'$ in the diagrams do not measure $h$ directly but $Q - Q^*$, or

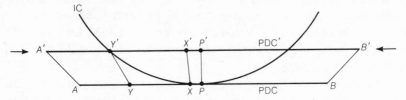

**Figure 2.9.** Partial transformation of Figure 2.8. See text for details.

**Framework for Analysis**

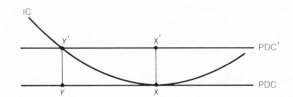

**Figure 2.10.** Final transformation of Figure 2.9 into specification-quantity space.

$(h - 1)Q^*$. Since $Q^*$ is fixed for a given PDC, however, the variation of $h$ with specification is easily seen to have the following properties, at least for the circular and linear cases: (a) The compensating ratio $h$ increases as the specification of the available good differs more from the specification of the most-preferred good and (b) the rate of increase of the compensation ratio with a change in specification of the available good increases as the difference in specification between the available good and the most-preferred good increases.

The properties can be stated more formally by denoting the specification of the available good by $x$, so that $h = h(x)$ for a given individual. If $x^*$ denotes the specification of the most-preferred good, then the properties of $h(x)$ are taken to be:

1. $h(x^*) = 1$.
2. $h'(x^*) = 0$.
3. $h''(x^*) > 0$.
4. $h(x) > 1$ for $x \neq x^*$.
5. $h'(x) > 0$ for $x > x^*$ and $h'(x) < 0$ for $x < x^*$.
6. $h''(x) > 0$ for all $x$.

Property 1 follows directly from the definition of the compensating ratio, properties 2 and 3 from the tangency at the most-preferred-goods specification and the condition that this is indeed the optimal specification, and property 4 from the implicitly assumed uniqueness of the most-preferred-good specification. Property 5 follows from the relationship between the assumed shapes of the PDC and the indifference curves, and property 6 is apparent from Figures 2.7 and 2.10 in the cases illustrated.

Of the six basic properties which $h(x)$ is seen to possess in the cases given, all are invariant with respect to the transformation from characteristics space to specification–quantity space except possibly property 6. Properties 1, 2, 4, and 5 are clearly invariant for any ordinal (positive monotonic) transformation, but signs of second derivatives are not necessarily preserved by such a transformation. Property 3 is preserved, however, as is property 6, for $x$ in some sufficiently small region defined by $x^* \pm \epsilon$, since any PDC can be well represented by either a straight line or a circular arc close to the point of tangency between it and the indifference curve.

It will be assumed henceforth that the property $h'' > 0$, which certainly holds for $x$ sufficiently close to $x^*$ if the most-preferred good represents a proper optimum as a transfer good, also holds for $x$ as far distant from $x^*$ as is necessary in the analysis. It seems better to make this assumption directly than to place restrictions on the shapes of the indifference curves relative to the shape of the PDC in order to guarantee the property.

Note that the properties of the compensating function depend on the properties of both the PDC and the indifference curve of the individual. In fact, the compensating function compounds the properties together (the relationship between $h''(x^*)$ and the convexity properties of the two curves is derived in Appendix A), which is why the exact shape of the PDC is not important, only its shape relative to the shape of the indifference curves. It is even possible for the PDC to be convex toward the origin (although this seems unlikely on a priori grounds), provided the indifference curves are even more convex.

Finally, the compensating function as derived is that for a single individual and a single base-quantity level. It will be assumed that individual preferences can be treated as homothetic (all indifference curves are geometrically similar) over the range of variation in base quantities which occur in any one analysis. The assumed relationship between compensating functions for different individuals will be taken up in the discussion of uniformity in Section 2.13.


## 2.12   The Preference Spectrum

The analysis up to this point has been entirely devoted to the study of a single individual. For a given PDC, the conditions determining this person's most-preferred good have been set out, a measure of specification has been established, and the compensating function for this individual has been derived.

If a second individual is introduced into the system, he or she will also have a most-preferred good and a compensating function showing how the quantities of other available goods must vary with their specifications if that person is to remain at the same level of welfare as could be attained with the most-preferred good. The PDC will be the same for both individuals, and so will the measure of specification since this is based only on the properties of the PDC. The specifications of most-preferred goods and the properties of the compensating function will differ between the individuals only to the extent that the structure of preferences differs between them.

In principle, individuals could have different preferences but the same most-preferred good, a situation that would occur if indifference curves of the two individuals happened to be tangent to each other at the point where both are tangent to the PDC. In such a case, the most-preferred good would be the same for both, but if the indifference curves were coincident only at the tangency point, the compensating functions would differ. As a first step toward setting up a model having certain properties of regularity that will be referred to as uniformity, such cases will be ruled out by the following:

If there are two or more consumers whose most-preferred goods are identical, those consumers will be assumed to have preferences which are identical in all other respects, at least over the characteristics of the group under consideration.

This assumption implies a one-to-one relationship between preference patterns and most-preferred goods, so that a particular preference pattern can be indexed by the specification of the most-preferred good associated with it.

From this point on, the analysis will be entirely concerned with economic systems having large numbers of individuals, with diverse preferences, the diversity of these preferences being manifest in the range of specifications of most-preferred goods. It will be assumed that the specifications of most-preferred goods, measured in the manner described in the previous sections, form a compact line segment in the two-characteristic case or a compact convex set in $n - 1$

dimensions in the more general case. This set will be referred to as the *preference spectrum* and will be treated as a continuum for analytical purposes. To avoid certain problems it is best regarded as a set of a very large but finite number of distinct points (suitably spaced) which is being approximated by a continuum to simplify the argument.

The difference in specification between the two extreme most-preferred goods in the spectrum will be referred to as the *range* of preferences. It will be assumed to be less than the potential differentiation range, so that there are no preferences without a feasible most-preferred good.

Associated with any point in the preference spectrum will be a population density, and the variation in this density over the spectrum describes the distribution of individuals with diverse preferences over the total population.

## 2.13 Uniformity

In this section will be introduced the most crucial simplifying assumption of the whole analysis, that of the uniformity of the compensating function over the spectrum of preferences.

As a first step toward establishing the concept of uniformity, it will be assumed that every individual's indifference curve, after transformation into specification–quantity space in the manner set out in Section 2.11, is *symmetric* about the point of tangency with the PDC. As shown in Figure 2.11, this property implies that the additional quantities of goods with specifications represented by $X_1$ and $X_2$ which are required to bring the consumer to the same welfare level as he or she would attain with the most-preferred good ($X^*$) will be the same if the specification differences from the most-preferred

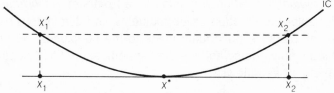

**Figure 2.11.** An indifference curve in specification-quantity space.

good, $X^* - X$ and $X_2 - X^*$ are the same. In terms of the compensating function, it implies that $h(x_1) = h(x_2)$ if $x_1 - x^* = x_2 - x^*$, and thus that the compensating function for the individual can be written in the form $h(u)$, where $u = |x - x^*|$.

Note that the required symmetry property is that of the image of the indifference curve after transformation from characteristics space into specification-quantity space. Since the transformation is made by straightening out the PDC into a line segment and measuring specification along the arc of the PDC, the symmetry property depends on the relationship between the properties of the untransformed indifference curve and the untransformed PDC. In particular, symmetry of both the original indifference curve and the original PDC about the radial corresponding to the specification of the most-preferred good is sufficient but not necessary for symmetry after transformation. If either curve is asymmetric in characteristics space, however, symmetry after transformation requires a counterbalancing asymmetry in the untransformed shape of the other curve.

The second step toward uniformity is to assume what might be termed *mutuality*—a relationship between two individuals with different preferences. Consider any two such individuals, whose most-preferred goods will necessarily differ given the uniqueness assumption of the previous section. Let the most-preferred goods of individuals 1 and 2 have specifications denoted by $x_1^*$ and $x_2^*$, respectively, let the compensating ratio for individual 1 with respect to the most-preferred good of individual 2 be $h^1(x_2^*)$, and let the compensating ratio for individual 2 with respect to $x_1^*$ as the available good be denoted by $h^2(x_1^*)$. Then the mutuality assumption is that $h^1(x_2^*) = h^2(x_1^*)$; that is, *the compensating ratios of two individuals with respect to each other's most-preferred goods as available goods will be identical*. In conjunction with the previous assumption of symmetry, this implies that $h^1(u) = h^2(u)$ for $u = |x_1^* - x_2^*|$. It will be assumed that *the mutuality relationship holds for all pairs of individuals*.

Repeated application of the mutuality and symmetry properties over many pairs of individuals leads to the conclusion that $h^i(u) = h^j(u)$ for all individuals $i$ and $j$ and all specification differences $u$. This can be stated as follows:

The compensating functions of all individuals can be represented by the single function $h(u)$, where $u$ measures the difference in specification between the available good and the most-preferred good for the individual in question. Individual differences in preference are represented wholly by the specifications of most-preferred goods and do not appear in the compensating function when this is expressed in terms of differences in specification between available and most-preferred goods.

This is the *uniformity property*. In geometric terms it implies that the transformed indifference curves in specification–quantity space are all of identical shape and are tangent to the PDC at the specification corresponding to the most-preferred good, as depicted in Figure 2.12.

Uniformity is a property involving both the relationships between the preferences of different individuals and the relationships of these preferences with the properties of the PDC. The assumption of uniformity is a heroic, and yet reasonable, simplification. It might be considered analogous to the assumption of a featureless plain in basic location theory—an assumption designed to provide a background of regularity against which variations in parameters of more immediate interest and importance can be investigated.

A clear distinction should be made between the above assumption of *uniformity of the spectrum* (meaning the existence of a single form for the compensating function) and *uniform density along the spectrum,* an assumption which is sometimes made and sometimes relaxed. The former refers only to a certain type of similarity in the structure of preferences over the population; the latter refers to the proportions of the total population having different preferences (that is, different most-preferred goods).

## 2.14   Measurability of the Spectrum Properties

The analysis in this book depends crucially on the existence of a well-defined spectrum of goods within the group and on the implicit

**Figure 2.12.** A uniform spectrum of preferences. See text for explanation.

measurability of distance along the spectrum. The method of constructing the spectrum from measures of characteristics and of goods by a transformation from characteristics space to specification–quantity space may have left the reader unconvinced as to the operational validity of the final product, the goods spectrum itself. It will be shown here, that *provided the uniformity property can be assumed to hold,* it is possible to devise hypothetical experiments that can (1) correctly order the goods along the spectrum and (2) correctly measure distances along the spectrum relative to any spectrum distance chosen as the unit distance.

The first thing to note is that the *compensating ratio* for any available good with respect to a consumer's most-preferred good can be, like indifference relationships in ordinary consumer-choice situations, determined by an outside observer, at least in principle. The consumer can be asked to state what quantity of the available good is equivalent to a specified quantity of most-preferred good. Suppose that a variety of such data on compensating ratios for two or more consumers, with respect to the same goods, were available, then it will be shown that the data can be used to determine the spectrum properties.

Assume it to be known that there are two effective characteristics in the group being examined, so that there is a line spectrum. Data are available for the compensating ratios for two individuals A and B with respect to six goods which are known to be in the group but for which the relative and absolute positions on the spectrum are unknown.

Let the data be as follows:

| Identification number of good | Compensating ratio | |
| :---: | :---: | :---: |
| | For A | For B |
| 3 | 1.12 | n.a. |
| 11 | 1.0 | 1.12 |
| 12 | n.a. | 1.12 |
| 19 | 1.12 | 1.0 |
| 23 | 1.04 | 1.04 |
| 47 | 1.04 | n.a. |

It is immediately obvious that A's most-preferred good is number 11 and B's is number 19. The compensating ratio for A with respect to good $i$ is denoted by $h_i^A$, and that for B by $h_i^B$.

To deduce the ordering of the goods along the spectrum, the procedure is as follows. Since 11 is A's most-preferred good and $h_{19}^A = 1.12$, whereas $h_{23}^A$ and $h_{47}^A$ are both 1.04, then either 23 or 47 must lie between 11 and 19 in the spectrum. Also, since 19 is B's most-preferred good and $h_{11}^B = 1.12$, whereas $h_{23}^B = 1.04$, it is 23 that must lie between 11 and 19. Thus the ordering of three of the goods, namely, 11, 23, and 19 is established. From the data for B, it is clear that 12 must be the closest good to 19 on the side away from 23; and from the data for A, that 47 must be the good next to 11 on the side away from 23 and that 3 must be the next good in that direction. Thus the full ordering is: 3, 47, 11, 23, 19, 12. To deduce relative distances along the spectrum, use is made of the uniformity property that equal compensating ratios represent equal distances both for a given individual and between individuals. From this, and the data, it follows that the distance between 11 and 47 is the same as the distance between 11 and 23 (using data for A) and that both are the same as the distance between 23 and 19 (from B). Denote this distance by $\bar{u}$, so that the distance between 11 and 19 is $2\bar{u}$. But this must be the same as the distance between 3 and 11 (from A), so that the distance between 3 and 47 must be $\bar{u}$ since the distance between 47 and 11 is $\bar{u}$. Finally, from the data for B, the distance between 19 and 12 must be $2\bar{u}$. Thus the goods 3, 47, 11, 23, and 19 are equally spaced at distances $\bar{u}$, and good 12 is at a distance $2\bar{u}$ away from 19. Not only has the ordering of the goods been established, but their spacing as well.

The assumption of uniformity is, of course, critical, but can itself be tested with further data. For the example give, since the distance between 19 and 3 is $4\bar{u}$ and the distance between 12 and 11 is also $4\bar{u}$, uniformity would require that $h_{12}^A = h_3^B$. Observations for these two compensating ratios would then give a test of the hypothesis of uniformity.

The example given has been chosen to give the maximum information from the least observations, but it is sufficient to establish the operational validity of the spectrum.

## 2.15    Properties of the Uniform Compensating Function

The basic properties of the uniform compensating function will be the same as those of the typical compensating function for the single individual, set out in Section 2.11. After making the substitution $u = |x - x^*|$, the six basic properties become:

1. $h(0) = 1.$
2. $h'(0) = 0.$
3. $h''(0) > 0.$
4. $h(u) > 1$ for all $u > 0.$
5. $h'(u) > 0$ for $u > 0.$
6. $h''(u) > 0$ for all $u.$

These properties can be summarized by the statement that the compensating function is a positive, increasing, strictly convex function of $u$ with special values at the origin $h(0) = 1$ and $h'(0) = 0$.

Extensive use will be made of the compensating function throughout the analysis, since it summarizes the essential substitution properties between different goods within the same group. The degree of convexity of $h(u)$, which is related to the magnitude of the second derivative $h''(u)$, expresses the degree of substitution in an inverse way. That is, if $h''(u)$ is very small, so that the transformed indifference curve is almost flat, then individuals require little compensation for receiving an available good which is not their most-preferred good, which implies that the goods are very close substitutes even when their specifications differ considerably. If $h(u)$ is strongly convex, however, the requisite compensation is large, even when the available good does not differ greatly from the preferred good in specification, because the goods are relatively poor substitutes.

Associated with the compensating function are three other functions derived from it, which are also used extensively throughout the analysis. These are:

1. The *elasticity of compensation* $e_h(u)$, which is the elasticity of the compensating function and is defined by

$$e_h(u) = u h'(u)/h(u).$$

2. The *cumulative compensating function* $H(u)$, defined by the

relationships

$$H'(u) = h(u) \quad [H(u) = \int_0^u h(v)\, dv] \quad \text{and} \quad H(0) = 0.$$

Under conditions of uniformity, this gives the total compensation required for all individuals up to a distance $u$ from the available good when the density of individuals is constant and equals unity.

    3. The *elasticity of cumulative compensation* $e_H(u)$, which is the elasticity of the cumulative compensating function $H(u)$ and is defined by

$$e_H(u) = uH'(u)/H(u) = uh(u)/H(u).$$

The properties of $H(u)$, $e_h(u)$, and $e_H(u)$ are derived in Appendix A, in which a more formal analysis of the compensating function is given. All are positive increasing functions of $u$ with the following properties at the origin:

$$H(0) = 0, \quad H'(0)\, [= h(0)] = 1;$$

$$e_h(0) = 0, \quad e_h'(0) = 0;$$

$$e_H(0) = 1, \quad e_H'(0) = 0.$$

Both $H(u)$ and $e_H(u)$ are strictly convex functions of $u$, but $e_h(u)$ may be convex or concave since the third-order derivative of the compensating function $h'''(u)$ is unrestricted as to sign.

    Occasional use will be made of the logarithm of $h(u)$, written $\underline{h}(u)$. The function $\underline{h}(u)$ is convex near the origin [$h(u)$ is then said to be *logarithmically convex* near the origin], with $\underline{h}(0) = 0$ and $\underline{h}'(0) = 0$.

    If there are $n$ characteristics and not merely two, as assumed in the last two sections, then the PDC is transformed into a hyperplane of $n - 1$ dimensions when mapped into specification–quantity space. The variable $u$ is then some appropriate measure of distance between two points representing different specifications on this hyperplane, a measure such as (but not confined to) the Euclidean distance. The preference spectrum is considered to possess the property of uniformity if the compensation for any individual with respect to any available good is given by the single function $h(u)$, where $u$ is the distance in specification between the available and most-preferred goods in accordance with the measure chosen. Obviously, the uniformity property in the $n$-dimensional case depends on the choice of distance measure, as well as the properties of preferences and the product-differentiation surface. Once uniformity is assumed, the properties of $h(u)$ are then similar to those for the two-characteristic case, since $u$ is a scalar and not a vector. The cumulative compensating function and compensation elasticities are analogous to those in the two-characteristics case.

## 2.16   Production and Economies of Scale

The discussion up to this point has been primarily with variations along, or in the vicinity of, a single PDC. This section is concerned with variations in the other direction—changes in resource input as different amounts of a single good of fixed specification are produced.

Since it is assumed that there is a single resource or a bundle of resources that can be treated as a single aggregate resource, it is convenient to work with the *input function*, giving input as a function of output, rather than with the conventional production function giving output as a function of input. Because of the single-resource property, the input and production functions are uniquely related as mutually inverse functions.

The input function will be written in the form $V = F^x(Q)$, where $V$ is the resource input needed to produce amount $Q$ of some good of fixed specification $x$. From the definitions of measure and the properties of the PDC, as discussed in Sections 2.7 and 2.8, quantities of different goods receiving the same quantity measure will require the same levels of resource input, and, because of the assumed homotheticity of production, this will be true for all levels of output of both goods. From this follows the fundamental property of the input function:

The input functions of all goods and potential goods in a single group are identical, provided the quantities of the goods are measured in accordance with the system laid out in Section 2.8.[15]

15. But the input functions may differ between groups in any way.

That is, if $Q^1$ and $Q^2$ represent quantities of goods of different spec-ifications, then $F^1(Q^1) = F^2(Q^2)$ if $Q^1 = Q^2$, so that the function $F$ need not be indexed for any particular good and all analysis can be carried out in terms of a single input function of the form $V = F(Q)$. Although the specification of the good does not need to be given, it is essential to note that the input function gives the input requirement for producing amount $Q$ of a good of a *single fixed specification*. The input required to produce quantity $Q^1$ of a good of specification $x_1$ and quantity $Q^2$ of a good of specification $X_2$ is given by the sum of the two input functions

$$V_T = V_1 + V_2 = F(Q^1) + F(Q^2)$$

and not by the input function for the sum of the quantities, $F(Q^1 + Q^2)$, unless $F(Q^1) + F(Q^2) = F(Q^1 + Q^2)$, which would imply constant returns to scale. In other words, any economies or diseconomies of scale are confined to the production of a single good and do not spill over into the production of other goods within the group. Some special assumptions are also needed to avoid large changes in input require-ments from trivial variations in specification.[16]

As a consequence of the above, the scale properties of produc-tion are the same for all goods within the group and are given by the properties of $F(Q)$. The analysis of this book is primarily concerned with production in which there exist *economies of scale* of some kind.

Before introducing the formal definition and measure of scale economies, the fundamental properties of $F(Q)$ need to be listed. These are:

1. $F(Q) > 0$ for all $Q > 0$ (no output without input).
2. $F'(Q) > 0$ (no additional output without additional input).

Neither of these properties calls for discussion, since both are re-garded as essential properties in all economic analysis. It might be noted, however, that $F(0) = 0$ is not assumed (input without output is permitted), nor is any restriction placed on the sign of $F''(Q)$, so that marginal input requirements may rise or fall with the scale of output.

In a market economy, the input function is identical with the *cost*

16. The author wishes to thank Menachem Yaari for bringing out this point. It will be assumed that there is some threshold effect in production such that specification can be varied over some very small range without incurring a new fixed cost or destroying the existing scale economies.

*function* (except possibly for a constant of proportion representing the input price level), provided inputs are available at fixed prices.

Economies of scale will be measured by a *degree-of-economies-of-scale parameter* $\theta(Q)$, which is simply the inverse of the elasticity of the input function, or the ratio of the average to the marginal input requirement (ratio of average to marginal cost in a market setting), and is given by

$$\theta(Q) = F(Q)/QF'(Q).$$

The parameter is written $\theta(Q)$ because it will, in general, vary with output. If $\theta$ is a constant, it is easily seen that $F(Q)$ then has the form

$$V = V_o Q^{1/\theta},$$

with inverse (the production function)

$$Q = aV^\theta.$$

The production function is immediately recognizable as that of homogeneous function of degree $\theta$ (degree of returns to scale). There are constant returns to scale if $\theta = 1$, and increasing returns to scale if $\theta > 1$. Thus values of $\theta$ greater than unity will represent *economies of scale* if $\theta$ varies with $Q$ and increasing *returns to scale* if $\theta$ is a constant. The analysis which follows is not confined to constant $\theta$, and thus covers more general economies of scale than is implied by the restricted concept of increasing returns to scale.

In terms of traditional cost curves, $\theta > 1$ implies that marginal cost is less than average cost and that average cost is falling. Thus economies of scale, as used here, implies falling average cost (in a market context) or a falling input–output ratio (in a price-free context). If $\theta$ varies with output, then there may be economies of scale at some output ranges and different economies of scale (or even diseconomies of scale) at others. The following restrictions will be assumed to be satisfied by the economies-of-scale parameter in all subsequent analysis:

$$\theta(0) \geqq 1,$$

$$\theta'(Q) \leqq 0 \quad \text{for all } Q.$$

The first condition confines the analysis to production in which there are no initial diseconomies of scale and average cost (or input–output ratio) is either constant or falling for outputs near zero. The second restriction rules out production in which the degree of economies of scale increases with output or, equivalently, production in which the average cost (input–output ratio) falls at a more rapid rate as output increases and is thus concave downward. It is obvious that $\theta'(Q) > 0$ would lead to an explosive situation—not only are there economies of scale (potentially explosive in themselves), but these economies actually increase with output.

Together the two restrictions imply that $\theta(Q) = 1$ for all $Q$ if $\theta(0) = 1$, so that constant returns to scale near the origin imply constant returns to scale throughout. It will normally be assumed that $\theta(0) > 1$.

A wide variety of cost or input curves is consistent with the restrictions assumed.[17] Average cost (input) may fall over all outputs, or may be U-shaped with a minimum (at which $\theta = 1$) for some finite output. Marginal cost (or marginal input requirement) must be positive but may be constant, falling, rising, or falling to a minimum and then rising. The economies of scale may be due to true increasing returns to scale (constant $\theta$), to fixed costs, or to a combination of subfunctions, each showing different returns-to-scale properties. Some cost functions which are consistent with the restrictions are depicted in Figure 2.13.

Two representative types of cost or input function are of particular interest and are widely used in both traditional analysis and here. The first is the pure increasing returns-to-scale type, characterized by homogeneous production, $\theta$ constant and greater than unity, and falling marginal cost or marginal input–output ratio ($F'' < 0$). The second is the U-shaped curve (typically associated with a fixed cost or input), characterized by a value of $\theta$ commencing above unity and falling through unity (at the minimum of the curve) to be less than unity (diseconomies of scale) at large outputs. The marginal curve in this case may be falling initially, but must rise ($F'' > 0$) after some level of output.

17. See Hanoch (1975).

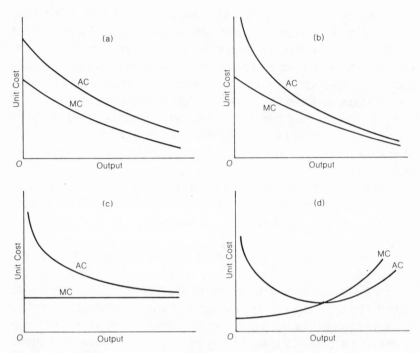

**Figure 2.13.** Average (AC) and marginal (MC) cost curves for four different technologies: (a) A homogeneous input function with increasing returns to scale; (b) A fixed cost combined with falling marginal cost; (c) A fixd cost combined with constant marginal cost; (d) A fixed cost combined with rising marginal cost.

## 2.17  A Note on Combinable Goods

If goods are combinable, so that two goods can be consumed simultaneously to give a characteristics collection that is a combination of the characteristics of the separate goods, the analysis of compensation given above for noncombinable goods cannot be used, and the problem must be approached anew.

The PDC and input functions depend only on the production conditions and can be expected to possess the same general properties (subject to some restrictions commented upon later) whatever the consumption technology. The measures of quantity and of specifications will be unchanged, although it will be more convenient to carry out the analysis in original characteristics space than after transformation into specification–quantity space.

A most-preferred good, derived in the same way as before, will exist for every individual, and if there is only a single individual and a single available good, there is a compensating ratio for that individual with respect to that good. But once the system produces two or more different goods in the group, the whole analysis changes.

Consider a two-characteristic group with a single consumer but with two available goods, neither being the consumer's most-preferred good but having specifications on opposite sides of the most-preferred specification. Figure 2.14 illustrates such a case, with the specification of the most-preferred good corresponding to the point $X$, the specifications of the two available goods to $Y$ and $Z$. If the goods were noncombinable, the individual could consume $Y$ or $Z$, but not both, with the amounts of respective goods needed to give the same welfare level as the most-preferred good being determined by the compensating ratios $OY'/OY$ and $OZ'/OZ$. It is obvious that, in an optimizing framework, the consumer would choose the good with the lower compensating ratio (less resource use or less expenditure), which would be called the *best-available good*, given that the choice is restricted to goods with specifications $Y$ and $Z$ only.

In the combinable case, however, the individual could attain exactly the most-preferred collection of characteristics (that is, the collection he or she would obtain from the most-preferred good, if it

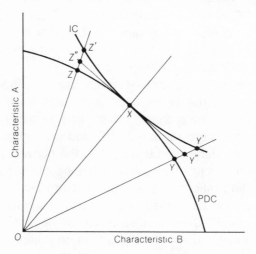

**Figure 2.14.** Compensation for combinable goods. See text for explanation.

were available) by consuming goods $Y$ and $Z$ together. Assuming that the goods are *linearly* combinable, the appropriate combination is found by extending the tangent at $X$ to cut the rays $OY'$ and $OZ'$ (at $Y''$ and $Z''$, respectively); the two goods will then be consumed in proportions corresponding to the ratio of $XY''$ to $XZ''$. The individual is able to construct the most-preferred good by combining the two available goods. The quantity of good $Y$ consumed is equal to the quantity represented by the distance $OY''$ times the proportion of $Y$ in the mix, the quantity of $Z$ by $OZ''$ times the proportion of $Z$ in the mix. Since all goods are in comparable units (a consequence of the system of measure chosen), the quantities of goods with specifications $Y$ and $Z$ can be added to give the combined quantity of both available goods which is equivalent to the quantity of most-preferred good represented by $OX$. The ratio of the combined quantities of the two goods to the quantity of most-preferred good is the compensating ratio for goods which are combinable.

This compensating ratio is a weighted average of the ratios $OY''/OY$ and $OZ''/OZ$, with weights corresponding to the proportions of the two goods in the combination. Clearly it is much less than either $OY'/OY$ or $OZ'/OZ$, the compensating ratios when the goods are noncombinable. The reason is obvious from the diagram: The curvature of the indifference curve does not contribute to the compensating ratio for combinable goods, which depends only on the curvature of the PDC. If the PDC is linear, the points $Y''$ and $Z''$ will coincide with $Y$ and $Z$, and the compensating ratio will be unity for all individuals whose most-preferred goods lie in the range between $Y$ and $Z$, with respect to $Y$ and $Z$ as available goods.

The property of the compensating function for combinable goods which will prove to be of importance in later analysis has been established above: The properties of the compensating function depend only on the curvature of the PDC and are independent of the shapes of the indifferences curves. Thus the convexity of the compensating function is much less than with noncombinable goods, and the compensating ratio may even be constant at unity if the PDC is linear. It could also be argued that this effect is heightened by the likelihood that the PDC will be less curved in the combinable cases, since if it is easy to combine the goods in consumption, it may well be easy to combine the characteristics into the goods at the production end. Perhaps the most realistic cases of combinability are when the goods are themselves blends or mixtures, which can easily be blended with each other at the consumption stage and presumably blended out of their basic components at the production stage, giving a linear or near-linear PDC.[18]

Note that the analysis of combinability holds only if there are available goods with specifications which span the specification of the individual's most-preferred good. In the $n$-characteristics case, this requires $n$ goods with linearly independent characteristics vectors, so that individuals' most-preferred goods can be expressed as convex combinations of available goods.

## 2.18   Comparison with Spatial Models

Because of the depiction of the goods spectrum in a spatial manner in this analysis and the fact that Hotelling-type models have provided hitherto the only analyses that could be considered to approach the problem of economies with variable goods specifications, it is important to compare the present model with the spatial model in order to make clear where the similarities and differences lie.

In the basic Hotelling spatial model, all events take place in a one-dimensional linear space embedded, usually, in two-dimensional space, like a road or a railroad surrounded by desert. Goods may be produced anywhere along the line and if they are to be consumed other than at the point of production, must be transported there at a fixed cost per mile. The line is obviously analogous to the potential goods spectrum in the analysis given here, the possibility of locating at any place is analogous to continuously variable goods specifications, and the dependence of transport cost solely on the distance from point of production to point of consumption is analogous to the uniformity property. It is usually assumed that consumers

18. This is a class of products such as household cake mixes, spice mixtures, and paints, in which essentially combinable goods are successfully sold as predetermined combinations. Presumably, this occurs because the labor or information required can be supplied at lower cost by the manufacturer than by the household.

are located evenly along the line, and this assumption is analogous to uniform density over the spectrum.

The location of a given individual along the line corresponds to the specification of his most-preferred good in the characteristics model, and the location of a point of production corresponds to the specification of an available good. When it comes to the concept of the compensating function, however, the exact analogy between the models no longer holds.

In the spatial model, the only difference to the consumer between an available good (a good at the point of production) and his most-preferred good (a good on his doorstep) is the cost of transport between the two points. It makes no sense to ask what quantity of available good is equivalent to a given quantity of most-preferred good (especially since it is usually assumed in the Hotelling model that the individual will consume a single unit only), only what payment for an available good would be equivalent to a given payment for a unit of most-preferred good. The compensating ratio cannot be expressed in price-free terms, because the transport cost, the crucial element in the model, is in price terms.

Denote the transport cost per unit of distance by $a$ and the distance between the location of the consumer and the location of the producer by $u$, where $u$ is directly analogous to the similarly denoted variable in the characteristics spectrum. If the price of the most-preferred good (the good at the consumer's location) is $P^*$ and the price at the factory (that is, the price of the available good) is $P$, then the analog of the compensating ratio will be that ratio of $P^*$ to $P$ at which the individual will be indifferent in a choice between a most-preferred good at price $P^*$ and an available good at price $P$. If this compensating ratio analog is written $\hat{h}$, then it is given by $\hat{h} = P^*/P$ when $P$ and $P^*$ are related by the equation

$$P^* = P + au.$$

The "compensating function" is a function of the price $P$, as well as the distance $u$, and has the form

$$\hat{h}(u, P) = 1 + \frac{au}{P}$$

Taking $P$ as fixed, consider $\hat{h}$ as a function of $u$ only, so that its properties can be compared with those of the compensating function proper as set out previously. These properties are:

1. $\hat{h}(0) = 1$.

2. $\hat{h}'(0) = a/P$.

3. $\hat{h}''(0) = 0$.

4. $\hat{h}(u) > 1$ for all $u > 0$.

5. $\hat{h}'(u) > 0$ for all $u$.

6. $\hat{h}''(u) = 0$ for all $u$.

Comparison of these with the list of properties given in Section 2.15 will show that only properties 1 and 4 are identical for $\hat{h}(u)$ and $h(u)$. The differences, which result in major differences in system properties as between the spatial model and the characteristics model, are that $\hat{h}(u)$ is linear in $u$ instead of strictly convex and $\hat{h}(u)$ has a cusp, or angle, at $u = 0$ instead of a tangency to the spectrum.

In addition to the differences between $h(u)$ and $\hat{h}(u, P)$, when variations in $u$ alone are considered, there is also the dependence of $h$ on the price level. This means that the price-free analysis of optimal product differentiation cannot be carried out for the spatial model in the manner given in Chapters 3 and 4. A comparison of the two models can, however, be made in a market context, and the spatial and characteristics versions of monopolistic competition are compared in Chapter 6. As might be expected, there are crucial differences between the models, showing that system properties derived from spatial models cannot be assumed to hold by analogy in characteristics models, in spite of the existence of common features between the two models.

 **Chapter 3**

# Optimum Differentiation I: The Paradigm Case

## 3.1 Introduction

THE CORNERSTONE OF traditional microeconomic theory is the analysis of the market under conditions of perfect competition. This has the multiple virtues of being the simplest model, being a situation that might sometimes be a reasonable approximation to reality, and, most of all, being a structure that can be shown to give an optimal solution to the problem of efficient attainment of many social welfare criteria. Having made the analysis of perfect competition, its properties can then be used as coordinates against which the performance of other market structures can be measured.

In the present context, there can be no perfectly competitive market structure, because such a structure would be inconsistent with the combination of economies of scale and essential heterogeneity of goods that characterize the situation to be analyzed.

It is necessary, therefore, to commence the analysis by setting up a simple situation that possesses the essential properties of a differentiated product world, to determine the properties of its optimal configuration, and then to use these properties as a basis of comparison with more complex structures and with market solutions of various kinds.

The situation chosen for initial analysis is simple indeed: an economy in which the only actual or potential goods are those belonging to a single group and which possess identical characteristics but in differing proportions. Furthermore, it is assumed initially that the consumption technology is characterized by noncombinability (goods cannot be combined to give characteristics in proportions intermediate between those of the goods themselves), so that each individual consumes but a single good.

In spite of its simplicity, the solution for the optimum in such a case is nontrivial. Furthermore, its designation as the *paradigm case* is well earned since the broad features of the optimal solution in this case provide a pattern which recurs in the more complex cases discussed at a later stage, and the understanding of the paradigm case provides the essential insights for all analysis of product differentiation.

It will be shown that there is a well-defined optimum at which resource use is a minimum for given target welfare levels for all consumers, which is attained with a finite number of goods by compensating individuals for whom the goods being supplied are not to their most-preferred specification. Under conditions of a uniform preference spectrum and a uniform distribution of welfare, the spectrum of consumers will be divided into segments of equal size, each supplied with a good of specification at the center of the segment. The optimum segment size is clearly defined by a certain relationship among elasticities of compensation and of production. This property, that the solution is a relationship among elasticities, will be found to recur in more complex optimal structures and also in market solutions. It implies that if the production function is homogeneous (of constant elasticity), the optimal degree of product differentiation is not affected by the size of the economy. Another important property of the optimum (which is also replicated in more complex cases) is that if production is such that there is a minimum cost level of output (a U-shaped cost curve), the optimum output is never at this minimum cost level. This implies, of course, that the traditional proof of the inefficiency of monopolistic competition—by showing that production is not at minimum cost—is not valid when specification is variable, and a much more complex proof of the proposition is required.

The full optimum requires compensation based on the relationship of every individual consumer's most-preferred good to the good actually provided. Difficulties in making such compensation are discussed, and this leads to the solution of a "second-best" optimum, in which such compensation is not made.

Also discussed in this chapter are the effects of variation in system parameters on the optimal degree of product differentiation and the effects of relaxing some of the initial assumptions. Among the modifications considered are nonuniform welfare densities, indivisible goods, combinable consumption, analysis in many dimensions, and consumers who like variety. These modifications can be studied with relative ease within the context of the paradigm model, and it can be assumed that the kind of effects which result will also hold in the more general model. Except for the case of indivisible goods, these modifications are not considered elsewhere.

## 3.2 The Optimum Problem

Given a continuous spectrum of consumer preferences over goods in the group, the problem is to place all consumers on predetermined target welfare levels with the minimum use of resources. There is no equity-versus-efficiency conflict in the problem as thus stated, since the distribution is predetermined and the solution gives the efficient means of attaining that target. There will be different solutions for different target distributions, but the paradigm case is restricted primarily to the problem of attaining a uniform welfare distribution with the least resources, although some relaxation of the uniform welfare distribution will be made at a later stage.

A uniform welfare distribution means that welfare density is independent of position in the spectrum. This can be interpreted as equal welfare levels for all (if individuals have identical welfare functions in terms of most-preferred goods) or as distributions of welfare over individuals at a point in the spectrum which are identical over all points in the spectrum.

A continuous spectrum of preferences implies a continuous spectrum of most-preferred goods—those goods which consumers would specify for themselves if they were given their share of resources to be used to produce a good exclusively for their own use. Under conditions of constant returns to scale, it is well known that the operation of the economy at competitive equilibrium is precisely the same as if all individuals were given their share of all resources and produced goods for themselves, provided the resources are optimally distributed. In the case of differentiated products, therefore, there are no gains from the pooling of resources under constant returns to scale, and thus every individual's most-preferred good would be produced—an infinite degree of product differentiation.[1]

If there are economies of scale, however, those consumers whose most-preferred goods are close in specification might gain by pooling resources, producing a single good (which cannot be the most-preferred good for all) at a lower resource cost per unit, and using part of the resource savings to compensate those members of the pool for whom the good is not their most preferred and still have spare resources to produce a bonus amount of the good for everyone.

The optimum problem is essentially that of finding the optimal pooling arrangement. The total population is to be divided among pools or sets such that all individuals in each set receive the same good, in such quantities as to bring each up to the preassigned target welfare level, with the pooling arrangement designed to achieve these targets with the least resource use. It is obvious that the division into sets will not be optimal unless the good made available to each consumer is his or her best available good, that is, unless there is no other good actually available such that the individual would prefer a unit of that good to a unit of the one he or she is provided with, where units of different goods are chosen to represent identical resource costs.

The assumption of uniformity of the preference spectrum implies that, if a certain good is the best available good for some individual, it is also the best available good for any other individual whose most-

1. In a preindustrial society with few economies of scale, a predominance of custom-produced goods would be expected. That such societies often exhibit a limited range of variety is due to reasons other than scale economies. These include limited technology and information, so that producers know how to produce only a limited range of products, and social pressures to conform that lead to a narrow spectrum of overtly revealed preferences.

preferred good is even closer in specification to it. Thus the optimal sets of consumers will necessarily be convex and will correspond to segments of the spectrum, and the division into pools will be a proper partitioning of the preference spectrum into these segments.

The variables of the problem are the number of segments into which the spectrum is to be partitioned (the degree of product differentiation), the size of each segment, and the specification of the good with which each segment is to be provided. The optimum problem can be decomposed into these three subproblems, which can be solved sequentially. First the optimal specification can be determined for an arbitrary segment, then the relative sizes of the segments can be determined for an arbitrary number of segments with optimal specification in each, and finally the optimal number of segments can be determined on the assumption that the two preceding conditions are fulfilled.

There are no restrictions as to the means of achieving the target welfare levels in the full optimum problem. It is obvious that, since the good made available in any segment is the most-preferred good at only one point in that segment, target welfare levels can be attained only if individuals not receiving their most-preferred good are compensated appropriately. In the paradigm case, the only goods in the system are the group goods themselves, so compensation necessarily consists in giving consumers more of the available good than would have been required to achieve the target welfare level if the good had been their most-preferred. All compensation is "inside" compensation—compensation in group goods themselves. In the next chapter, the optimum problem will be widened to an economy in which there are goods other than group goods and compensation is possible in "outside" goods.

It should be noted that achieving equal welfare levels, even with identical consumers (identical except as to their choice of most-preferred good), implies a nonuniform distribution of the good within each group, since those consumers whose most-preferred good is more distant from the available good than others will need to be given more in order to compensate for the "distance" of the good from the most-preferred specification. There are several major problems associated with such compensation, and these are discussed later in this chapter.

## 3.3 Optimal Specification

At this stage, the following problem is to be solved: Assuming the set of all individuals to be supplied with the same good has been determined, what will be the optimal specification for that good? Since the overall problem is that of minimizing resource use, it is obvious that the optimal specification is that which minimizes the total quantity of the good required to bring all individuals in the set up to their target welfare levels.

Individuals or groups of individuals with the same preferences will be identified by the specification of their most-preferred good, where the specification is represented by a parameter $x$ which places it on the spectrum of potential goods. To save some verbiage, an individual whose most-preferred good has specification represented by parameter value $x$ will be said to be an individual "at $x$" in the spectrum.

The highest and lowest values of the specification parameters for the most-preferred goods of any members of the set will be denoted by $\bar{x}$ and $\underline{x}$, respectively, and the specification of the good to be made available to members of the set by the parameter value $b$. Under the assumptions of continuity and uniformity of the preference spectrum, the set of consumers to be provided with the same good at the optimum will be compact and will be the segment of the preference spectrum defined by $\{x \mid \bar{x} \geq x \geq \underline{x}\}$ since if it is optimal to provide the good to consumers at $\bar{x}$ and $\underline{x}$, it must be the best available good for them and thus for all consumers at $x$ where $\bar{x} \geq x \geq b$ or $b \geq x \geq \underline{x}$.

The welfare density at $x$, denoted by $\bar{q}(x)$, is defined as follows. Consider the consumers at $x$, for whom the most-preferred good is one of specification $x$. Then there is a certain quantity of that most-preferred good that will bring the consumers up to the target welfare level. This quantity is $\bar{q}(x)$. (Since the spectrum is a continuum, $\bar{q}(x)$

is strictly speaking a density and is the limiting value of $\Sigma/\epsilon$ as $\epsilon \rightarrow$ 0, where $\Sigma$ is the total quantity of the good required to bring all individuals in the subsegment $(x, x + \epsilon)$ up to target welfare levels; however, the less accurate description is simpler and will be used throughout the analysis.)

The welfare density depends on the combination of target welfare levels and population density, and a given density may be derived from lower population density and higher welfare levels or lower welfare levels and higher population density. For the purposes of the analysis, it is only the level of $\bar{q}(x)$ that matters, not how it is derived.

It is assumed that the welfare density is uniform, at least over any single segment, so that $\bar{q}(x)$ is a constant that will be written $q_0$. The target welfare levels are now built into the analysis as $q_0$, as is the assumption of uniform welfare density.

Within the segment under examination, the good provided to all individuals in the segment is the most-preferred good only for those at $b$. For these individuals, quantity $q_0$ of the good achieves the required welfare density. For all other consumers in the segment, the good is only the best available, and these consumers need to be compensated by being given more than $q_0$ of the good. From the definition of the compensating function $h(u)$, the amount of the available good required to bring individuals at $x(> b)$ up to the target welfare levels will be given by $q_0 h(u)$, where $u = x - b$. For individuals at $x < b$, the quantity will be $q_0 h(u)$, where $u = b - x$. Under the assumed conditions of uniformity of compensation, the compensation function depends only on the distance measure between $x$ and $b$, and not otherwise on the location of $x$ or $b$ in the spectrum.

The total quantity of the good required to achieve the target welfare levels over the whole set of consumers is then given by

$$2Q = \int_0^{\bar{x}-b} q_0 h(u) \, du + \int_0^{b-x} q_0 h(u) \, du.$$

(It is convenient, for reasons that will soon be obvious, to use symbols to represent half-quantities over segments rather than full quantities.) Using the cumulative compensating function

$$H(u) = \int_0^u h(v) \, dv,$$

the above equation can be written:

$$2Q = q_0[H(\bar{x} - b) + H(b - \underline{x})].$$

Since the input function is independent of the specification (by the assumed homotheticity of production and the definition of unit quantities), the optimal value of $b$ is that which minimizes $2Q$. This is given by

$$\frac{\partial H(\bar{x} - b)}{\partial b} = -\frac{\partial H(b - \underline{x})}{\partial b}$$

or

$$h(\bar{x} - b) = h(b - \underline{x}). \tag{3.1}$$

Since $h(u)$ is single valued, this implies that

$$\bar{x} - b = b - \underline{x}$$

or

$$b = \tfrac{1}{2}(\bar{x} - \underline{x}). \tag{3.2}$$

That is, if the welfare density is uniform over the set, the optimal specification for the good to be provided to the set is the mean between the specifications of the most-preferred goods of the extreme consumers in the set, as would be expected in a context of such uniformity.

Henceforth it will be assumed that the good provided to any set under discussion is optimal in specification and will be centered in the set if the welfare density is uniform. With the width of the segment denoted by $2\Delta$ ($= \bar{x} - \underline{x}$), the quantity of a good of optimal specification required to give a uniform welfare density of $q_0$ over the segment is given by

$$2Q = 2q_0H(\Delta). \tag{3.3}$$

Finally, it should be noted that the second-order conditions for optimal specification depend only on the condition that $h'(u) > 0$, which is satisfied for all $u > 0$.

## 3.4 Relative Segment Size

Having determined the optimal specification for the good to be provided to any segment and before moving on to the main problem of determining the optimal number of segments, it is provisionally assumed that the number of segments is given and that the relative sizes of these segments is to be determined.

Suppose that there are $n$ segments, the width of the $i$th segment being $2\Delta_i$, and that each segment is supplied with a good of optimal specification. Then the quantity required of the $i$th good is given by $2Q_i = 2q_o{}^i H(\Delta_i)$, where $q_o{}^i$ is the welfare density over that segment. The total resources required to attain the target welfare densities over all segments is then given by

$$V = \sum_1^n F[2q_o{}^i H(\Delta_i)], \qquad (3.4)$$

where the variables of the problem are the $\Delta_i$ values. Since the segments must cover the whole spectrum, the variables are constrained by a relationship

$$\sum_1^n \Delta_i = R, \qquad (3.5)$$

where $R$ is a constant.

Minimizing $V$ with respect to each of the variables gives the following set of conditions, which must hold for all $i$ and $j$:

$$q_o{}^i h(\Delta_i) F'[2q_o{}^i H(\Delta_i)] = q_o{}^i h(\Delta_j) F'[2q_o{}^j H(\Delta_j)]. \qquad (3.6)$$

If the welfare density is uniform over the whole spectrum, so that $q_o{}^i = q_o{}^j = q_o$, it is obvious that these conditions are satisfied by $\Delta_i = \Delta_j = \Delta$ for all $i$ and $j$, since the input function $F$ is the same for all goods (homotheticity of production).

The second-order conditions for the above minimization of $V$ are not trivial, but they can be shown to be satisfied for equal segment sizes if $d(hF')/d\Delta > 0$. The sign of this derivative is not itself at all obvious, but it can be shown to be positive if both the first- and second-order conditions for the optimal number of goods (set out in the next section) are satisfied.

Thus it has been shown that to achieve a uniform welfare distribution over a uniform preference spectrum in an optimal way with $n$ goods:

1. the whole spectrum should be partitioned into $n$ segments of equal width.
2. each segment should be supplied with a good having its specification at the center of the segment.

The results have obvious intuitive appeal.

With uniform welfare density $q_o$, therefore, the output of all $n$ goods will be identical and given by $2Q = 2q_o H(\Delta)$, where $2\Delta$ is the uniform segment width and $2n\Delta$ is the width of the spectrum.

## 3.5 Optimal Product Differentiation

It has already been established that in an economy where the only goods are group goods, which is characterized by uniformity of the preference spectrum, and for which the target welfare distribution is uniform, the optimal way to achieve this target with some specific number of goods is to partition the spectrum into equal segments and supply each segment with a good having specification at its center. To complete the basic analysis of the optimum in the paradigm case, the optimal number of segments must be determined.

The analysis will be conducted in terms of the optimum segment width, rather than the number of goods per se. Given the range of the spectrum and the condition that the whole spectrum is to be covered, the segment width will be reciprocally related to the number of segments, and thus the number of different goods. There is one problem that should be noted: The segment width is a continuous variable, whereas the number of goods is necessarily an integer. In a real situation, the optimally determined segment width divided into the range of the spectrum may not yield an integral number of goods. Obviously there is then a choice between taking either the integer above or below, and the best choice depends on comparing resource use in the two cases and cannot be determined from inspection of the marginal conditions which will be determined here. In the generalized context of the analysis presented here, problems of this kind can be ignored.

Since the optimal segment size (the same for all segments) is to be chosen so as to minimize the use of resources over the whole spectrum, this objective will be achieved if the size is chosen so as to minimize the average resource use per unit of segment width. It is convenient to refer to this somewhat loosely as minimizing resource use per capita over the segment, on the presumption that the uniform welfare distribution is associated with a uniform population distribution—although this need not necessarily be the case.

Since the segments are identical in properties, it is sufficient to concentrate attention on one segment. If the segment width is $2\Delta$ and the target welfare density is $q_o$, the quantity of the good required to achieve the uniform target welfare level when the good is of optimal specification is $2Q = 2q_o H(\Delta)$. If $F(2Q)$ is the input function (or resource cost function), resource use per capita over the segment is given by

$$v(\Delta) = \frac{1}{2\Delta} F[2q_o H(\Delta)].$$
(3.7)

From this is obtained

$$\frac{dv}{d\Delta} = \frac{q_o h(\Delta) F'}{\Delta} - \frac{F}{2\Delta^2}$$

$$= \frac{q_o H(\Delta) F'}{\Delta^2} [e_H(\Delta) - \theta]$$
(3.8)

after making the substitutions for the elasticity of the cumulative compensating function $e_H(\Delta) = h(\Delta)\Delta/H(\Delta)$ and the elasticity of the input function (degree of economies of scale) $\theta = F/2QF'$. (Note that the argument of $F$ is $2Q$.)

Thus the optimal segment size in the paradigm case is given by the condition $dv/d\Delta = 0$, which implies

$$e_H(\Delta) = \theta,$$
(3.9)

that is, the optimal segment size is to be such that the elasticity of the compensating function is equal to the degree of economies of scale in production, or elasticity of the input function.

The interpretation of the condition in economic terms is quite simple. The elasticity of the compensating function $e_H$ shows the percentage increase in goods quantity required to maintain the target welfare levels if the segment size is increased by 1 percent. The economies of scale parameter $\theta$ gives the percentage increase in output obtained from a 1 percent increase in resources. If $\Delta$ were such that $e_H(\Delta)$ was larger than $\theta$, a 1 percent decrease in the segment size would require $e_H$ percent less of the good and use ($e_H/\theta$) percent (>1 percent) less resources, so that resource use per capita would be reduced by making the segment smaller. If $e_H(\Delta)$ were less than $\theta$, an increase in the size of the segment would reduce resource use per capita, and thus when $e_H(\Delta) = \theta$, the segment size is optimal.

The second-order conditions in the paradigm case are very simple, and will be satisfied if the expression

$$e_H{}'(\Delta) - 2q_oh(\Delta)\theta' \tag{3.10}$$

is positive. (Note that the prime on $\theta$ refers, as always for the production function, to its derivative with respect to its natural argument, quantity. The prime on $e_H$, as always for compensating functions, refers to its derivative with respect to distance along the spectrum, in this case $\Delta$.) Now $e_H'$ is certainly positive (see Appendix A), and $\theta'$ is either zero, if the degree of returns to scale is fixed (homogeneous production), or negative, since returns to scale which themselves increase with output have been ruled out (see Chapter 2). Thus the second-order conditions are satisfied.

Existence of a solution to the optimal-segment-size problem can be guaranteed for degrees of economies of scale which are not too great. It is shown elsewhere that the elasticity of the compensating function is unity when $\Delta = 0$ and is an increasing function of $\Delta$ for values of $\Delta$ at least out to some finite distance from the origin (see Appendix A). Thus the graph of $e_H(\Delta)$ against $\Delta$ commences at the point (0, 1) and rises at least out to some $\Delta_o$. Now $\theta$ is either a constant (homogeneous production) or declines with output and thus with $\Delta$, and so its graph is either a horizontal line or a downward-sloping curve commencing at (0, $\theta_o$), where $\theta_o \geqq 1$. Thus, provided $\theta$ is not too much greater than unity, the curves intersect and a solution exists.

There are extreme cases. If $\theta_o = 1$ (constant returns to scale at very small output levels), the solution will be at $\Delta = 0$; that is, there will be an infinite degree of product differentiation. The other case is if $\theta$ is too large to have $e_H(\Delta) = \theta$ for any $\Delta$, in which case $dv/d\Delta <$ 0 for all $\Delta$ and there will be a corner solution with $\Delta$ as large as possible, that is, with a single good and no product differentiation.

The solution in terms of optimal segment width gives what might be termed *product density*—the number of products per unit distance along the spectrum. The total number of goods depends on the product density and the range of the spectrum. This can sometimes create confusion as to what is meant by a greater or lesser degree of product differentiation. In most cases, it will be assumed that the range of the spectrum to be covered is always the same, so that a smaller optimal segment width will be unambiguously associated with a larger number of products and thus with a greater degree of product differentiation. In any circumstances in which the range is potentially variable, the description of product differentiation as being greater or less must be handled with due care for the distinction between an increase in product density (which might justifiably be regarded as increased product differentiation) and an increase in the number of goods.·

## 3.6 A Historical Error

The first attempt to analyze product differentiation in a context that permitted comparison of the market solution with what was presumed to be the optimum, and the only such analysis until recent years, was the Chamberlin model of monopolistic competition.[2] The essence of the analysis was the use of the traditional U-shaped cost curve, in which it was assumed that the optimal output was that corresponding to the point of minimum average cost—the bottom of the U—and the suboptimality of monopolistic competition was apparently proved by showing that this led to output at a point before the bottom of the U, where average cost was still falling.

The analysis presented here has made no explicit use of the U-

---

2. Although the earlier Hotelling model can also be given a welfare analysis by the use of consumer surplus procedures (see footnote 4).

shaped cost curve (here average input curve), but has been cast in terms of the degree-of-returns-to-scale parameter, which is the ratio of average to marginal input (cost). The only restriction placed on the input function was that this parameter $\theta$ should not be increasing with output. The input function used here is quite consistent with a U-shaped average input curve. In fact, if $F(X)$ has the form

$$F(X) = A + f(X),$$

where $f(0) = 0$ and the parameter $\beta(X)$, the degree of economies of scale of the variable input function $f(X)$, is nonincreasing with output $(X)$ and less than unity for some $X_o$ (and thus for all $X \geqq X_o$), then $\theta$, the economies-of-scale parameter of the total input function $F(X)$ can easily be shown to commence at an infinite level and converge asymptotically towards $\beta$ and thus necessarily pass through unity. The corresponding average input curve has the classic U shape.

Even when the average cost curve is U-shaped, however, any optimal solution over a continuous spectrum of consumers is necessarily at a point on the downward-sloping portion of the curve, where $\theta > 1$. This is because the elasticity of the compensating function $e_H(\Delta)$ is always greater than unity when $\Delta > 0$, and thus the optimum condition $e_H = \theta$ can only be satisfied at a value of $\theta$ greater than unity. The only case in which an optimum is possible at a value of $\theta$ equal to unity is at the origin (as occurs when there are constant returns to scale at all output levels), but this is impossible with the U-shaped curve because $\theta > 1$ at the origin.

The optimum condition implies that if the configuration were such that production was at the point of minimum average cost, efficiency would be increased by producing more goods so that production of each good was below the minimum average cost level. The higher resource cost per good is more than covered by the saving in compensation from the reduction in the segment size.

If monopolistic competition is inefficient, it cannot be proved to be so merely by showing that the monopolistic-competition equilibrium results in firms producing at an output less than that which gives minimum average cost, as in traditional analysis. It must be shown that the point on the cost curve at which there is monopolistic-competition equilibrium differs from the poin at which the optimum occurs, and in particular that the former is to the left of the latter, if the classic conclusion that monopolistic competition leads to greater-than-optimal product differentiation is to be demonstrated. It is obvious that it is much more difficult to produce a proof of this kind than to make the relatively simple demonstration that monopolistic competition gives rise to output below the minimum average cost level. This difficulty will become apparent in Chapter 7.

## 3.7 Influences on Product Differentiation

In order to determine the factors that influence the degree of product differentiation and the direction of that influence, it is necessary to make the distinction, introduced in the preceding section, between *product density* and the *number* of different products. It will be convenient to refer to increased product density (more products per unit distance along the spectrum, or smaller average segments per product) as *increased product differentiation*. When comparing different market structures, comparing market equilibria with the optimum, or comparing the effect of parameter changes, all within the context of a given economy, it is reasonable to suppose that the range of consumer preferences is a basic property of the population and is therefore stable. For comparisons of this kind, the number of goods (range divided by average segment size) will increase along with the product density, and there is no ambiguity in the idea of greater product differentiation. For long-run comparisons or comparisons between different economies, however, the range may vary, and thus the product density and the number of products may not move in the same direction.

Assume initially that the range is given and thus the product density (appearing in its reciprocal form, as the segment size) is an unambiguous indicator of the degree of product differentiation. Now the optimal segment size in the paradigm case is given by a condition in the very simple form $e_H(\Delta) = \theta$, from which it is immediately apparent that the degree of product differentiation is determined only by those factors which influence $e_H$ or $\theta$, or both. The elasticity $e_H$ is determined by the properties of the compensating function $h$, and thus these properties affect the degree of product differentiation. The economies-of-scale parameter $\theta$ is either an exogenous parameter (with homogeneous production) or a function of output, and thus of the compensating function and the welfare density.

Consider a general system parameter $\alpha$ which might, in principle, affect $e_H$ or $\theta$, or both. The effect of a variation in $\alpha$ on the optimal segment width is found by differentiating through the equilibrium conditions and can easily be shown to be given by

$$\frac{d\Delta}{d\alpha} = \frac{-(\partial e_H/\partial\alpha) + (\partial\theta/\partial\alpha)}{e_H' - 2q_0 h\theta'}, \tag{3.11}$$

where $e_H'$, as always, is $de_H/d\Delta$ and $\theta'$ is $d\theta/d(2Q)$. The denominator in the above expression is necessarily positive, so the sign of $d\Delta/d\alpha$ is the sign of the numerator; it will be unambiguous if $\partial e_H/\partial\alpha$ and $\partial\theta/\partial\alpha$ have opposite signs (or one is zero).

Consider first a variation in $\theta$ itself, if a constant, or a parametric variation that increases the value of $\theta(2Q)$ at all output levels. This will obviously increase $\Delta$. Thus an increase in the degree of economies of scale (if constant) or an upward shift in the economies-of-scale function $\theta(2Q)$ will always reduce the degree of product differentiation. This is an important result that will be shown to hold for all structures studied, including market equilibria and optimum configurations.

Now consider a variation in the welfare density $q_0$. Since $e_H$ is an elasticity, it is unaffected. But $2Q = 2q_0 H$, so a change in the density affects the level of output and thus the degree of returns to scale unless this is constant. Formally,

$$\frac{\partial\theta}{\partial q_0} = 2H\theta', \tag{3.12}$$

which is negative if $\theta'$ is negative. Thus an increase in the welfare density will increase the degree of product differentiation if the degree of economies of scale varies with output (negatively) but have no effect on the degree of product differentiation if the degree of economies of scale is constant. The latter implies that, with homogeneous production, the "size" of the economy (with range held constant, this is the welfare density) has no effect on the degree of product differentiation, in spite of the economies of scale. These economies will be apparent in the lower average resource use per unit of output in the large economy but do not affect the amount of product differentiation because this depends only on the *ratio* of the average to the marginal resource use and not on the absolute levels. If the degree of economies of scale declines with output, however, the larger economy (in this sense) will show a greater degree of product differentiation.

Finally, consider the effect of variations in the compensating function. This is potentially a complex matter, since the function might change in a variety of ways, but interest in the compensating function is really centered on how it is related to the degree of substitutability between goods in the group. As shown in an earlier chapter (Chapter 2), the degree of convexity of the compensating function (the size of the second derivative $h$ ") is inverse to the substitutability across the group: The greater is $h$ ", the less adequate as substitutes are two goods at a fixed spacing from each other in the spectrum. Take the parameter $\alpha$ to be such that it increases $h$ "$(u)$ at all values of $u$. Now $\alpha$ affects both $e_H$ (which is obvious) and $\theta$, since

$$\frac{\partial \theta}{\partial \alpha} = 2q_o \theta' \frac{\partial H}{\partial \alpha} . \tag{3.13}$$

If $\alpha$ increases $h$ " everywhere, it is shown in Appendix A that both $\partial e_H/\partial \alpha$ and $\partial H/\partial \alpha$ are positive, so that $\partial \theta/\partial \alpha$ is negative, and thus $d\Delta/d\alpha$ is negative. Thus an increase in the convexity of the compensating function will increase the degree of product differentiation.

Finally, if the range of diversity among preferences increases but the population remains the same, this must be accompanied by a reduction in the welfare density. If the economies-of-scale parameter is constant, the welfare density does not affect the product density, and thus the increase in diversity will increase the number of products but leave the optimal segment size the same. Since the output per good must then fall, the average resource use per capita will rise. If the degree of economies of scale falls with output, the lower welfare density will reduce the product density by increasing the optimal segment size. The number of products will still rise, but not in proportion to the increase in the range of diversity, as contrasted to the constant-$\theta$ case, in which the number of goods is proportional to the range.

Since the directions of the influences will be shown to hold in contexts other than that of the paradigm case, the following summary is useful:

1. The degree of product differentiation at the optimum will be greater if (1) the degree of economies of scale is less, (2) the degree of substitutability between goods in the group is less, or (3) the welfare density increases *and* the degree of economies of scale depends on output.

2. An increase in the population will (1) increase the degree of product differentiation if the range of diversity is unchanged *and* the degree of economies of scale varies with output, but have no effect if it is constant, (2) increase the number of goods (and the degree of product differentiation in that sense) if the range of diversity is increased, and (3) lower the per capita resources required for a given level of welfare per capita, whether or not the degree of economies of scale varies with output.

3. An increase in the range of diversity of preferences with a constant population will increase the number of goods in any case, but the increase will be less if the degree of returns to scale depends on output than if it is constant.

## 3.8 Nonuniform Welfare Density

It has been assumed up to this stage, at least in the formal analysis, that the welfare density was uniform across the spectrum in the sense that the target welfare distribution would be achieved by allocating the same quantity of most-preferred good at every point in the spectrum. The target is achieved in the optimum analysis by allocating the equivalent in available goods of the most-preferred good, but the welfare density parameter $q_0$ still remains a factor of proportionality throughout the analysis. In this section, the effect of a cautious modification of the uniform density assumption will be made, the first of several modifications to the basic simplifying assumptions in the paradigm analysis.

First it should be noted that the density parameter can be interpreted in a variety of ways, since it merely specifies the required total allocation of a hypothetical good over the total number of consumers for whom that good is most preferred (strictly speaking, the total density of consumers at the point, not the number), without reference to how the total is distributed. If all consumers are identical except as to their most-preferred good and the target welfare level is the same for everyone, the density parameter can be taken to reflect population density at each point in the spectrum. On the other hand, the population density might be uniform and the density parameter reflect goods per capita and thus welfare levels assigned at different points. Nor is it necessary to assume that all consumers at a point receive the same quantities of the good. There may be a specific distribution of goods over individuals at each point, so that density variations in $q_0$ can be interpreted in many ways—but it is most convenient to consider them as typically reflecting variations in population density over the spectrum while target welfare per capita remains uniform.

The analysis here is confined to the effect of small variations in density across the spectrum, variations sufficiently small for the following assumptions to be reasonable:

1. Variations in density over a single segment or between adjacent segments can be considered negligible.

2. Variations between segments at different points in the spectrum can be treated as small deviations from the standard optimum of the paradigm case.

The first assumption permits the use of the intrasegmental properties derived in the standard case—in particular, the centering of the good within the segment. The second assumption enables the analysis to be carried out by commencing from the standard paradigm optimum with uniform density $(e_H(\Delta) = \theta)$ and considering the effect of small deviations from uniform density.

The problem to be solved is essentially that of determining if the optimal segment size will differ from the mean segment size when the segment density differs from the mean density, and the direction of the deviation. It is assumed that the variations not only are small in the sense already given but occur in both directions in such a way that the average segment size, and thus the number of goods, is not changed. The effect of a change in the mean density will be essentially similar to that of a change in the level of a uniform density, which has already been studied.

Suppose that there are $n$ segments, the density and width of the $i$th segment being $q_o{}^i$ and $2\Delta_i$, respectively. Then the condition for optimal relative segment size is that given earlier in the chapter (Eq. 3.6):

$$q_o{}^i h(\Delta_i) F'[2q_o{}^i H(\Delta_i)]$$
$$= q_o{}^j h(\Delta_j) F'[2q_o{}^j H(\Delta_j)] \quad \text{for all } i \text{ and } j.$$

If $q_o$ is variable over segments, instead of constant as in the earlier analysis, this condition is equivalent to requiring that the expression $q_o h(\Delta) F'[2q_o H(\Delta)]$ be constant over all segments. By taking the arguments $\Delta$ to be understood and making the substitutions $e_H = h\Delta/H$ and $\theta = F/2q_o HF'$, it is easily seen that

$$q_o hF' = \frac{q_o e_H F}{\theta \Delta}. \tag{3.14}$$

By differentiating the condition that the above expression be constant and using the optimal condition $e_H = \theta$, it can be shown that

$$\frac{d\Delta}{dq_o} = -\frac{\Delta}{q_o} \frac{\theta}{e_H{}'\Delta - \theta'}. \tag{3.15}$$

Since $e_H{}' > 0$ and $\theta' \leq 0$, $d\Delta/dq_o$ is unambiguously negative for small variations away from uniformity.

Thus, for deviations from uniform density which are not too great, the degree of product differentiation will be greater in those portions of the spectrum with higher-than-average density and lower in those with lower-than-average density. Note that this effect will occur even when the degree of economies of scale is a fixed parameter ($\theta' = 0$), although a change in the *mean* density will not affect the *overall* degree of product differentiation in this case.

## 3.9 The Feasibility of Compensation

It is possible, in principle, to set any desired goal for the distribution of welfare over the population and then determine the most efficient means of attaining this objective. The general method of solving the problem is implicit in the preceding analysis, although it was confined to the particular objective of a uniform welfare distribution—an objective that is likely to be given serious consideration in a real situation and which happens to lead to the simplest solution. Later in this chapter, some modification of the uniform-welfare-density target will be discussed, but the purpose of the present section is to focus on problems concerning compensation that are best seen in the uniform-welfare context, although they apply to all distributional targets.

The special feature of efficiency under conditions of product differentiation is that the optimum is only achieved by the use of compensation. That is, since it is possible to save resources by limiting the number of distinct goods that are produced, consumers not receiving most-preferred goods are compensated so that they can be satisfied with some other good. In the case of a uniform target distribution of welfare, this is achieved optimally by a *nonuniform* distribution of goods. Individuals whose most-preferred good happens to be one of the goods chosen to be produced will receive less of that good than will other individuals whose most-preferred good is not made available. Therein lie the problems to be discussed.

In putting any theoretically devised scheme of economic policy into practice, there are, of course, a myriad of basic technical problems. Most of these are what might be termed "low-level" feasibility problems, e.g., clerks, data processing, physical handling, and so on, which always occur and which are not within the scope of policy discussion at the abstract level, even though they are often sufficient to render infeasible a theoretically desirable policy measure.

The concern here is with "high-level" feasibility problems that arise in the case of compensation, which leave the optimum desirable in principle but possibly impracticable. They are labeled "high level" because they cannot be solved merely by brilliant public administration. There are two, in particular, that stand out, the problem of *information* and the problem of *manifest equity*.

The information problem can be stated most simply. To calculate the optimal degree of product differentiation, it is sufficient to know the *distribution* of preferences over the population in some aggregate statistical sense. To achieve that optimum requires that the appropriate compensation be carried out, which requires information concerning where the preferences of every individual (identified as to name) lie in the aggregate spectrum. It is obvious that information as to where individuals fit into the spectrum is several orders of magnitude greater than information as to the statistical properties of the spectrum. Thus the degree of information required to make proper compensation may prevent such compensation from being made, unless the population has such a degree of honesty that each can be permitted to take what he or she needs in the way of compensation. It may still be possible to work out what goods ought to be produced and in what quantities, but whether the optime' quantities and specifications are still the best when compensation cannot actually be made is a problem in the analysis of *second best*, discussed in the next section.

The other problem, that of manifest equity, can be appreciated by considering individual A, whose most-preferred good happens to be one of those actually produced. Will A believe that individual B, who is being given more of that same good—the very one that A regards as ideal—is being treated equally and not preferentially? There is a real policy dilemma here, one that occurs very frequently in real situations and which cannot fully be resolved. What is true equity may be seen to be inequitable, and what is apparently equitable may truly be inequitable. The dilemma does not arise in the naïve classical welfare analysis, in which the welfare of individuals is determined only by what they themselves receive, but it does arise if there are externalities and individuals are not omniscient. (Omniscient individuals will, of course, know that individual B needs more of the good just to enable him to reach the same welfare level as A.)

Because of the above dilemma, it is appropriate to consider an alternative optimum solution in which manifest equity (equal quantities of goods for everyone) is required, rather than true equity. This leads to a second-best solution, as in the information case.

In spite of the feasibility problems, the full optimum will be used as the primary reference against which other configurations (including second-best solutions) are compared. The second-best solution will be used as a secondary reference, not only because of the above reasons but because realistic market solutions, in which individuals are not compensated, can be compared only with the second-best formulation.

## 3.10 Second-Best Formulations

If the accepted objective is to attain some target distribution of welfare with the minimum use of resource, compensation of those individuals who are not receiving their most-preferred goods will probably be required—and will certainly be required if the target is uniform welfare, as in the paradigm analysis. Should there be constraints on the use of compensation, either because of political unacceptability or because of unavailability of relevant information, then it will generally be inefficient to adopt the degree of product differentiation, in the absence of compensation, that would be optimal if compensation were made. This is a direct application of the theory of second best.[3] There will be new solutions to the problem, based on some kind of optimization that takes explicit account of the constraint that prevents compensation, and such solutions will be second-best solutions.

Reformulation of the problem into one from which a second-best solution can be obtained cannot necessarily be done in a unique way. If the original targets cannot be attained—as in the paradigm case, when compensation is not possible and a uniform welfare distribution thus cannot be attained with finite product differentiation—then new targets must be substituted or weights assigned for proximity to the original targets versus other considerations such as additional resources required.

Equity-versus-efficiency considerations arise in the second-best analysis which were absent in the optimum analysis, since the desired equity goals were fully achieved in the latter by means of compensation. The particular second-best solution that is arrived at will depend on the balance between equity and efficiency, when the additional constraint is imposed.

Consider a specific case, namely, that in which the optimum solution is that of the paradigm, which is characterized by a uniform

3. See Lipsey and Lancaster (1956).

spectrum of preferences and a uniform target level of welfare, achieved by full compensation when required. Suppose that the constraint imposed is that only a uniform distribution of the available goods is politically acceptable, so that every individual supplied with a particular good is supplied with the same amount of that good, whether it is close to or more distant from the specification of his most-preferred good. The distribution of welfare will necessarily be nonuniform if the number of goods is finite, those consumers for whom the available good is most preferred being better off than those for whom it is not.

Obviously, with a greater degree of product differentiation, the distribution of welfare will be more uniform (when the distribution of goods is uniform), but scale economies will be less, and thus the use of resources will be greater. This is the equity-versus-efficiency problem.

If the balance is entirely toward equity, then equity can be attained by producing every good that is anyone's most-preferred good. One possible second-best solution, therefore, is for an infinite degree of product differentiation with no gains from economies of scale at all. This attains the original welfare targets with the maximum use of resources, short of actual waste.

Another possible second-best approach is to emphasize efficiency rather than equity by adopting a utilitarian approach and minimizing the resources required to attain a target level of average "welfare" per capita without assigning any weight to equity. From the assumption of uniformity of preferences, it is a small step mathematically—but a large step philosophically—to add the welfare indexes of the individuals and average them.[4]

It is assumed that individuals have identical welfare functions in

4. Consumer surplus analysis, which can also be used to derive a version of the second best, merely hides the problem. The author has always possessed a strong distaste for the use of consumer surplus analysis because it is based on the difference between the actual situation and hypothetical situations which do not occur, rather than the actual welfare of the actual situation as in the analysis used. There are, in addition, a series of major objections to the use of consumer surplus in a general-equilibrium setting. For a welfare analysis of product differentiation in terms of consumer and producer surpluses, see Dixit and Stiglitz (1977), Salop (1976), Spence (1975, 1976a, b), and Willig (1973). Surplus analysis always gives a second-best solution in the sense used here, since no compensation is actually made.

the sense that all individuals receiving the same amounts of their most-preferred goods (which may be the same or different) would reach identical levels of welfare and, further, that individuals receiving amounts of any goods which are equivalent (through the compensating ratio) to equal amounts of most-preferred goods would also reach identical welfare levels. The utilitarian social welfare function, in its pure classic form, assumes that an increase in welfare to one individual is just as good as, but no better than, an equivalent increase in welfare to any other individual, and thus that welfare is simply added over all consumers. If $w(u)$ is the welfare derived by an individual at distance $u$ from the good being supplied, then the total welfare over the segment being supplied by that good is given by

$$W = \int_0^{\bar{\Delta}} w(u) \, du + \int_0^{\underline{\Delta}} w(u) \, du, \tag{3.16}$$

where $\bar{\Delta}$ and $\underline{\Delta}$ are the distances from the good specification point to the segment edges in both directions.

In the particular context of the present type of analysis, the straight utilitarian welfare function can be given a special justification as an acceptable social welfare function. This is because, *ex ante*, no individual can know exactly where the specifications of the goods to be produced will lie. Under conditions of uniformity and uniform population density, therefore, the average welfare level, computed as $W/(\bar{\Delta} + \underline{\Delta})$, with $W$ as above, is also the expected value of welfare for any individual, given that the specification of the good to be produced is yet unknown. Thus *ex ante* agreement on the utilitarian form could be obtained from all individuals under conditions of Rawlsian ignorance,[5] provided they were risk-neutral.

The straight utilitarian welfare function is, of course, neutral with respect to the distribution of welfare among individuals. It is possible to use instead a simple concave welfare function of the form

$$W = \int f[w(u)] \, du, \tag{3.17}$$

where $f$ has the properties $f > 0$, $f' > 0$, and $f'' < 0$. Such a welfare

5. See Rawls (1971, p. 136).

function gives, in effect, a weight to each individual, which declines as the welfare of that individual increases relative to that of others, and thus gives implicit bias towards equity. In the following section, in which second-best solutions are derived, it is found to add little in difficulty if a special form of such a concave function is used, so that solutions are derived for both the straight utilitarian function and the concave version.

## 3.11 A Second-Best Solution

As has already been pointed out, there is not necessarily a unique formulation for a second-best problem, even when the constraint (in this case, a uniform goods distribution) is unambiguous, since inability to attain a primary target may leave a variety of options as to secondary targets.

The solutions given here are for a class of social welfare functions which includes the straight utilitarian case and one form of concave function. The form of the social welfare function is

$$W = \int [w(u)]^\beta \, du, \tag{3.18}$$

where the limits of integration cover half-segments and $\beta$ is a fixed parameter not greater than unity. If $\beta = 1$, it gives the straight utilitarian case, if $\beta < 1$, a concave social welfare function. (A further interpretation of this form is given later.)

The second-best problem is now set up in the following form. All individuals are to be partitioned among sets, and all members of each set are to be supplied with the same quantity of the good made available to the set—this amount also being equal to the quantities of goods made available to other consumers in other sets. The sizes of the sets, the specifications of the goods, and the per capita quantity of goods are to be chosen to minimize the resources required to achieve a specified level of average welfare per capita, determined by means of the welfare function set out above.

It is obvious that, under conditions of uniformity and uniform population density across the spectrum, the sets will be segments of the spectrum of equal size and that each will be supplied with a good of specification at the center of the segment. Thus the analysis can be carried out in terms of a typical single segment, as in the previous analysis of the full optimum, thus minimizing resource use per capita across the segment.

Consider an individual whose most-preferred good has specification at distance $u$ from that of the good supplied to the individual's particular segment. If the quantity of the good supplied is $q$, its equivalent in terms of the most-preferred goods will be $q/h(u)$, where $h(u)$ is the usual compensating function. The individual's welfare level is some known function of $q/h(u)$, which is the same for all individuals. If the range of variation in $h(u)$ is relatively small, marginal welfare or utility can be taken to be constant, so that the welfare level is proportional to $q/h(u)$ plus some base-level value, with the same proportionality factor and base-level value for all individuals. (An interpretation of the welfare function being used in terms of diminishing marginal utility is given below.)

Thus the welfare per capita over a segment of width $2\Delta$ is given by

$$
\begin{aligned}
w &= \frac{k}{\Delta} \int_0^{\Delta} [w(u)]^{\beta} \, du + w_o \\
&= \frac{k}{\Delta} \int_0^{\Delta} [q/h(u)]^{\beta} \, du + w_o,
\end{aligned}
\tag{3.19}
$$

where $k$ is the proportionality factor and $w_o$ is the base-level value. Note that $q$ is constant, since equal distribution of goods is specified.

If $z(u) = h(u)^{-\beta}$ and $Z(u)$ is defined by

$$
Z(u) = \int_0^u z(v) \, dv \qquad Z(0) = 0,
\tag{3.20}
$$

then per capita welfare can be written as

$$
\begin{aligned}
w &= \frac{kq^{\beta}}{\Delta} \int_0^{\Delta} z(u) \, du + w_o \\
&= \frac{kq^{\beta} Z(\Delta)}{\Delta} + w_o.
\end{aligned}
\tag{3.21}
$$

If the target welfare level is $w_o + \bar{w}$, then

$$q^\beta Z(\Delta) = \frac{\bar{w}}{k} \Delta, \tag{3.22}$$

and the value of $q$ required to attain this target level is a function of $\Delta$. By differentiating, writing $e_Z$ as $\Delta z/Z$, and substituting for $\bar{w}/k$ (from Eq. 3.22) it is found that

$$\frac{dq}{d\Delta} = \frac{q}{\beta \Delta} (1 - e_Z). \tag{3.23}$$

Resource use per capita is given by

$$v = \frac{1}{2\Delta} F(2q\Delta),$$

so that

$$\frac{dv}{d\Delta} = 2\Delta \frac{dq}{d\Delta} + 2q \frac{F'}{2\Delta} - \frac{F}{2\Delta^2}. \tag{3.24}$$

After substituting for $dq/d\Delta$ from above and using the degree-of-scale-economies relationship $\theta = F/2q\Delta F'$, this becomes

$$\frac{dv}{d\Delta} = \frac{qF'}{\Delta} \left[ \frac{1}{\beta} (1 - e_Z) - (\theta - 1) \right]. \tag{3.25}$$

Thus the second-best condition, $dv/d\Delta = 0$, implies that

$$1 - e_Z = \beta(\theta - 1). \tag{3.26}$$

Note that, since $z = h^{-\beta}$ and $z' < 0$, $Z$ is concave and $e_Z < 1$, so that a solution will exist.

Does the second-best solution lead to more or less product differentiation than the full optimum? That question is the chief interest here, and the answer permits the relationship between the two solutions to be determined. No relationship between the solution above and the optimum solution, $e_H(\Delta^*) = \theta$, can be discerned from inspection, so further analysis is required.

Since $z = h^{-\beta}$, use can be made of Lemma 3a (Appendix B), which gives

$$e_Z - 1 > -\beta(e_H - 1)$$

or

$$1 - e_Z < \beta(e_H - 1). \tag{3.27}$$

The segment width at the optimum is denoted by $\Delta^*$ and that at the second best by $\Delta$. If $\theta$ is constant, the full optimum implies

$$e_H(\Delta^*) - 1 = \theta - 1.$$

Using the inequality above in conjunction with the condition for the second-best solution gives

$$\beta[e_H(\Delta) - 1] > 1 - e_Z(\Delta) = \beta(\theta - 1)$$

$$= \beta[e_H(\Delta^*) - 1]. \tag{3.28}$$

Thus $e_H(\Delta) > e_H(\Delta^*)$, which implies $\Delta > \Delta^*$ since $e_H$ is an increasing function, showing that the degree of product differentiation is less at the second best than at the full optimum. Note that this result is independent of the value of $\beta$, provided it is positive, and thus holds for both the straight utilitarian case ($\beta = 1$) and the concave social welfare function ($\beta < 1$). For the straight utilitarian case, the result is not surprising, since no weight is given to equity, and the rapidly rising cost of compensation at the segment fringes, which tends to reduce the advantages of scale economies from large segments in the optimum case, is partly offset here by increasing the welfare of those at the segment center relative to those at the edges as the segment size increases. Since individuals at the center gain more welfare from the same goods than those at the edges but count equally in the averaging, larger segments result. It is more surprising that the same relationship holds for values of $\beta$ much smaller than unity, in which implicit weight is being given to equity.

Small values of $\beta$, however, do give a higher degree of product differentiation than the straight utilitarian welfare function, which accords with the equity-weighting role of a small $\beta$. This is easily seen by differentiating the second-best condition (Eq. 3.26) with respect to $\beta$ to obtain

$$\frac{d\Delta}{d\beta} = -\frac{\theta - 1}{e_Z'}. \tag{3.29}$$

Since $Z$ is concave, $e_Z'$ ($= de_Z/d\Delta$) is negative, so that $d\Delta/d\beta$ is positive and a higher degree of product differentiation is associated with a lower value of $\Delta$. As $\beta$ declines, the degree of product differentiation increases, but never reaches the level of the full optimum. As $\beta \rightarrow 0$, the welfare function becomes a constant, and thus the segment size becomes irrelevant.

It has been assumed up to this point that $w(u)$ was linear in the most-preferred-good equivalent, $q/h(u)$, and that the index $\beta$ was related to the construction of the social welfare function. The results are identical, however, if it is assumed that $w(u) = [q/h(u)]^{\beta}$, which implies diminishing marginal utility, and that the social welfare function is straight utilitarian in $w(u)$; if $w(u)$ has the form $[q/h(u)]^{\alpha}$, the social welfare function has the form $W = \int w(u)^{\gamma} du$, and $\beta = \alpha + \gamma$.

It should be noted that the full optimum solution is not optimal as a second-best solution. That is, the average per capita welfare level achieved at the optimum can be attained with less resources by using the second-best solution, but this means abandoning the equity which is achieved by the full optimum. The second-best solution is itself constrained by the requirement of manifest equity, and it is this constraint that keeps the utilitarian model within bounds. Without such a constraint, the straight utilitarian model will minimize resource use for a given per capita welfare level by producing a single good and distributing it to those for whom it is the most-preferred good, giving nothing to other individuals. Concavity will inhibit the solution from going all the way in the same direction, but the tendency will be similar.

A numerical example will give some feeling for the relationship between the full optimum and the second best. By using the simplest acceptable form for the compensating function (quadratic, as shown in Appendix A) and assuming a constant value of 1.2 for $\theta$, the optimum and second-best solutions can be found explicitly. The relationships between the two solutions depend only on the assumed quadratic form and the value of $\theta$ and not on any other parameters. Using the straight utilitarian welfare function ($\beta = 1$), the differences are not large: The segment size is 10 percent larger in the second-best solution; the per capita goods quantities, 1 percent greater; the output level per good, 11 percent greater; and the resource use per capita, 0.7 percent less (when the solutions are adjusted to give identical levels of average welfare per capita). In the second-best solution, the maximum individual welfare deviation from the average is 24 percent.

## 3.12 Indivisible Goods

The basic analysis has been given in terms of goods that were noncombinable but divisible, where two varieties are not mixed together, but the chosen variety can be consumed in any quantity. This assumption is now being modified to deal with the case of goods which are still noncombinable, but in which the goods are not only specific but available only in discrete units of a size such that the typical consumer's target level of welfare would be attained by a single unit. This is a highly important category of goods in a modern society and includes many consumer durable goods, such as automobiles, houses, and refrigerators.

The indivisibility may occur because size is itself an integral part of the specification—one of the characteristics of the good—and thus the decision as to the specification of the good includes a decision as to size. A refrigerator is a good example of this kind of good. The indivisibility may also occur because the good is inherently nonadditive: 100 exact architect's models of a house to a scale of 1 in 100 do not make a house, even if the scale is in volume terms so that the replicas occupy the same real space as the house. For the purposes of analysis, the source of the indivisibility does not matter, provided each product is available in a single large package only. The possibility of "vertical" product differentiation, with products in a number of packages of different size, is not relevant here, because of the assumed uniformity.

Indivisibilities in the paradigm case make compensation impossible, since a consumer whose most-preferred specification is not that of the good actually available cannot be given a few percent more of the good, but only the package as it exists, and since there are no outside goods which can be used as alternative compensation. Thus an arbitrarily set welfare distribution can be achieved in only one way (by producing an individual package for everyone and discarding any possible scale economies), and the optimum problem with indivisibilities becomes one of balancing equity against efficiency. In this respect, it is structurally identical with the kind of second-best problem discussed earlier. In fact, indivisibilities impose the same kind of constraint on the system as does the objective of manifest equity, that all individuals will receive the same amount of the available good, but here it is because the good comes only in a single "package" size.

Equity considerations in the case of indivisible goods will call for an increase in the number of different models available, and efficiency will call for a reduction in the number. The two considerations can be balanced in accordance with a variety of criteria, as in the second-best problem.

A simple and realistic case is that in which the size of the basic unit of the good is not fixed by technological constraints but is a policy variable, indivisibility occurring because of the economies of scale which become available since the good is produced only in packages of this unit size. If $q$ is the unit size, then one solution is to choose $q$ and the number of distinct goods so as to minimize resource use, subject to attaining an average welfare level per capita on the basis of a utilitarian welfare function. The problem is then identical in structure to the second-best problem when policy requires all consumers to receive the same quantities of goods, with the general conclusion that indivisibilities will lead to a lower degree of product differentiation than would be the case at the full optimum with divisible goods. The comparison is strained, however, since the targets in the divisible and indivisible cases are different.

The effect of indivisibilities can properly be seen when there are other goods available, so that compensation can be made with outside goods that is not possible with group goods. This case is discussed in the Chapter 4.

## 3.13 Combinable Goods

In the preceding section, the working assumption that the goods of interest for the theory of product differentiation were divisible but noncombinable was relaxed to consider the effect of indivisibility. In this section, the relaxation will be made in the opposite direction, to consider goods which are both divisible and combinable.

Goods are considered combinable if their characteristics are linearly combinable, that is, if the characteristics obtained by consuming two goods together is a simple linear combination of the characteristics contained in the two goods separately. Combinability, in this sense, implies that the combinations behave like mixtures in the chemical sense and do not form new compounds. Indeed, the most obvious examples of combinable goods—kitchen spices, smoking tobaccos, college course offerings (ignoring prerequisites and other complementarities)—are simple mixtures.

If the goods are costlessly combinable, then it is obvious that a consumer whose preferred characteristics proportions are represented by some point on the spectrum can always attain the preferred point by a combination of any two goods whose specifications lie on opposite sides of that point. Thus the typical individual will be consuming two goods, not one as in the noncombinable case. With just two goods, however, every individual whose most-preferred combination lies between these goods can be given that combination, and no compensation is required. If there are economies of scale, it is obvious that the optimum solution is to produce only two goods (in the two-characteristics case), these being the most extreme goods on the spectrum, and give everyone his or her appropriate combination. Thus the optimum number of goods will be equal to the number of distinct characteristics—two in the kind of case that has been discussed to this point—and independent of any other parameters, including the degree of economies of scale, provided only that economies of scale exist.

If there is some cost to forming the combination, such as labor, time, or perhaps information as to exact proportions, then the situation is different. The consumer will then prefer a ready-made mixture of appropriate specification to the separate ingredients and will need to be compensated if supplied only with the latter. If the combination cost is sufficient, he or she will also prefer a mixture close to the desired proportions to the separate ingredients but would need some compensation if the mixture were not exactly to specification.

Thus the analysis with combination costs is very similar to, although not identical with, the noncombinable analysis. If combination costs are sufficiently high and there are scale economies available in making the combinations at the factory level, then the optimum will have properties broadly similar to those of the optimum with noncombinable goods. The resource minimization must take account of the resource costs of forming the combinations at the consumer level (if this is required) as well as at the factory level. If combination costs are low and economies of scale are high, then the solution will be similar to that of the costless combination case, with the number of products determined by the number of distinct characteristics. If the combination costs are high and the economies of scale are relatively small, then the solution will result in ready-made mixtures spaced over the spectrum rather than at the two (or more) extremes.

Thus the effects of combinability are difficult to predict in any general way, since the relationship of the consumer's combination cost to the other parameters of the situation is important. A reasonable prediction, however, is that a growth of combination costs relative to production costs, which is characteristic of modern economies with respect to household activities, will lead to a greater variety of pre-combined mixtures.

## 3.14 A Taste for Variety

It has been assumed hitherto that individuals have a most-preferred specification for goods in the group and that their interest is confined to the extent to which the best available good differs from this single ideal specification. In many cases (food, clothing, entertainment), variety itself may be an essential part of enjoyment. This factor does not possess a most-preferred specification, but implies only that the individual also gains from the presence of goods of other specifications.

There are potentially many ways of modeling a taste for variety, with almost no a priori considerations that might narrow the field, other than simplicity appropriate to the general model being considered here. One obvious approach is a stochastic one—to assume that the individual picks today's desired specifications from a known distribution and that his or her potential welfare is diminished to the extent that the chosen specification is not available. The following assumptions are necessary:

1. If the individual's choice is not available, he or she can be compensated by a best available good in an appropriate amount, given by a compensating function with the same general properties as in the deterministic case.

2. An individual's daily choice is given by a rectangular or single-peaked distribution which is continuous on the specification axis and symmetrical, the center of which can be regarded as the most-preferred good.

3. The most-preferred goods in the above sense are uniformly distributed along the spectrum, and all distributions are identical, except as to the location of the most-preferred good.

If these assumptions are met, then uniformity and a uniform distribution of welfare will lead to a distribution of *expected welfare* with the same properties of the distribution of actual welfare in the ordinary model. Expected value will give the same results as before, because there is no real weight given to variety, unless the variance appears in the welfare function.

Formal modeling will be confined here to another approach, in which the number of goods available is a positive externality, so that the individual's welfare always increases when the number of goods increases, whatever the particular most-preferred good. It will be shown that this leads to the same result as reducing the degree of economies of scale, in both the full optimum and the second-best solution, and seems to accord with what few intuitions come forward in this analysis.

It is assumed that individual welfare functions are of the form $w = w(q, n)$, where $q$ is the quantity of the actual good consumed (in units of most-preferred-good equivalents) and $n$ is the total number of different goods available. Thus there is a trade-off, for the individual, between having more of a specific good and having more variety potentially available. Since increased quantity and variety of goods both call for increased resources, there is a trade-off at the policy level as well.

The trade-off ratio for the individual is given by

$$\frac{dq}{dn} = \frac{\partial w/\partial n}{\partial w/\partial q}.$$

It will be assumed that the elasticity equivalent of this trade-off (which will be negative in sign) can be taken as a constant for the individual. By the usual uniformity assumption, it will have the same value over all individuals, so that

$$\frac{n}{q}\frac{dq}{dn} = -\alpha.$$

Now the number of goods is inverse to the segment size, so the trade-off between quantity and segment size is

$$\frac{\Delta}{q}\frac{dq}{d\Delta} = \alpha. \tag{3.30}$$

Now consider the determination of the full optimum. In the ordinary analysis, the quantity allocated to any individual is given by $q_o h(u)$, where $q_o$ is a constant determined only by the target welfare level. In this case, the level of $q_o$ necessary to attain the target level depends on the number of products and thus the segment size. As before, the aim is to minimize per capita resource use, given by Eq. (3.7),

$$v(\Delta) = \frac{1}{2\Delta} F[2qH(\Delta)],$$

except that $q$ is now a function of $\Delta$ instead of a constant.

Differentiating with respect to $\Delta$ gives

$$\frac{dv}{d\Delta} = \frac{qh(\Delta)F'}{\Delta} + \frac{H(\Delta)F'}{\Delta}\frac{dq}{d\Delta} - \frac{F}{2\Delta^2}. \tag{3.31}$$

After making the substitutions for the cumulative compensation elasticity ($e_H = h\Delta/H$), the degree-of-economies-of-scale parameter ($\theta = F/2QF'$), and the variety trade-off elasticity [$\alpha = (\Delta/q)(dq/d\Delta)$], this becomes

$$\frac{dv}{d\Delta} = \frac{qH(\Delta)F'}{\Delta^2}[e_H(\Delta) + \alpha - \theta]. \tag{3.32}$$

Thus the optimum condition becomes

$$e_H(\Delta) = \theta - \alpha.\qquad(3.33)$$

By comparing this with the standard optimum condition, $e_H(\Delta) = \theta$, it can be seen that $\alpha$ produces exactly the same effect as a reduction in the degree of economies of scale, tending to increase the optimum degree of product differentiation, as expected. Note that an interior optimum will exist only if $\alpha$ is small, since such an optimum is possible only if $\alpha < (\theta - 1)$. This seems to pose few problems, since it can be assumed that a 1 percent increase in quantities of goods actually consumed far outweighs a 1 percent increase in the number of products available and thus that $\alpha$ will be a very small number.

The role of $\alpha$ in the second-best solution is basically the same as in the optimum solution. Assume all relationships are of the constant-elasticity kind, and that the elasticity of $w$ with respect to $n$ is given by $\gamma$. The relationships between quantity and segment size can then be shown to be given by

$$\alpha = \frac{\Delta}{q}\frac{dq}{d\Delta} = \frac{\gamma}{\beta},\qquad(3.34)$$

where $\beta$ is the same index as in Eq. (3.18). The relationship above is then the trade-off for the individual.

The trade-off between $q$ and $\Delta$ required to maintain a constant level of average welfare per capita (equivalent to Eq. 3.23) is given by

$$\frac{dq}{d\Delta} = \frac{q}{\beta\Delta}(1 + \gamma - e_z).\qquad(3.35)$$

Following through the same process of minimizing resource use per capita for a target level of welfare per capita as shown in the earlier steps (Eqs. 3.24 through 3.26), but using the value of $dq/d\Delta$ from above, the second-best solution is found to be

$$1 - e_z = \beta(\theta - 1) - \gamma$$

or

$$1 - e_z = \beta[(\theta - \alpha) - 1],\qquad(3.36)$$

since $\gamma = \beta\alpha$, from Eq. (3.34).

Note that this solution has a form identical with that of the regular second-best solution, except that $\theta$ is replaced by $\theta - \alpha$, exactly as in the optimum. The relationship between the optimum and second-best solutions is left unchanged, but there will be more product differentiation in both cases.

A taste for variety, therefore, can easily be handled within the general framework of the analysis. Such a taste does not lead to any major change in conclusions, but merely results in a greater degree of product differentiation.

## 3.15 Analysis in Many Dimensions

Although the analysis to this point, and almost all the analysis which follows, is cast in terms of a linear spectrum and thus deals with two distinct characteristics only, the general principles of analysis and the general conclusions are applicable to models in any number of dimensions in which the assumption of uniformity holds for a Euclidean distance measure.

Uniformity in the multidimensional case is taken to mean that the compensating ratio for any individual with respect to any good is a function only of the distance in some appropriate metric between the points representing the specifications of the available and most-preferred goods and that the compensating ratio is the same for all individuals at the same distances from goods, whether the goods are the same or different.

If uniform density, as well as uniformity, is assumed, it can be taken that an optimal partitioning of a finite number of goods among all individuals will be such that the hyperspace is partitioned into cells of identical shape and size. The actual shape, which is a major problem of spatial analysis,[6] is not important. The size of the cells is given by some convenient measure such as the radius of the smallest hypersphere which contains the cell.

The cumulative compensation is no longer a simple integral of the compensating function, however, since the number of individuals at a distance $u$ from the center of the cell is no longer a linear function

6. See Lösch (1954), for example, for the two-dimensional spatial case.

of $u$, assuming a uniform density over the spectral space. Suppose for the moment that the spectrum was in two dimensions (corresponding to three characteristics) and that the cells were circles. Then the population at a distance between $u$ and $u + du$ from the center would be proportional to the area of a ring of radius $u$ and width $du$, or $2\pi\, u\, du$, and the cumulative compensation would be given by

$$H(u) = 2\pi \int_0^u uh(u)\, du. \tag{3.37}$$

For a three-dimensional spectrum with spherical cells, the corresponding value would be

$$H(u) = 4\pi \int_0^u u^2 h(u)\, du, \tag{3.38}$$

and for an $n$-dimensional spectrum (corresponding to $n + 1$ characteristics),

$$H(u) = C \int_0^u u^{n-1} h(u)\, du, \tag{3.39}$$

where $C$ is a constant which depends on the dimensions only.

The cells cannot be hyperspheres, since space cannot be partitioned in this way, but must be regular polyhedroids of some kind. This introduces an extra complication, since the volume integral must now be calculated by considering successively larger polyhedroids, with the population corresponding to a distance $u$ (measured by the radius of the enclosing hypersphere) given by the surface area of the polyhedroid. This is proportional to the surface area of the corresponding hypersphere, and only changes the constant in Eq. (3.39). The real problem is that different points on the surface are not all at the same distance from the center, and thus a uniform compensating ratio cannot be applied. The true compensating function must be replaced in Eq. (3.39) by a modified function $\hbar(u)$ which gives the average compensation over the polyhedroid surface. The modification will depend only on the shape of the cell and the properties of $h(u)$ itself. Given these complications, it will remain true that $H(u)$ is a well-defined function of $u$ only, for specified cell shape and dimensions, and can be expected to have the same general properties as in the line-spectrum case, except that $H'(u)$ is no longer equal to $h(u)$.

It is easy to show that the optimizing problem can be carried through essentially unchanged and that the optimum conditions have the form

$$e_H(\Delta) = \theta. \qquad (3.40)$$

These are identical with those of the line-spectrum analysis, except that $e_H$ must be defined as $uH'(u)/H(u)$ and not as $uh(u)/H(u)$.

The general properties of the optimum will be essentially the same as in the simpler case, with the optimal degree of product differentiation influenced in the same way by the same factors.

 Chapter 4

# Optimum Differentiation II: The Effect of Outside Goods

## 4.1 Introduction

IN THIS CHAPTER the analysis of the optimum is extended beyond the confines of the simple paradigm case to a group embedded in a larger economy—the output of the rest of the economy being the "outside goods" of the chapter title.[1] This extension is a major step, and turns an interesting but very special case into a true general equilibrium model, simplified though it may be by the extension of the uniformity concept to cover relationships with the rest of the economy.

The structure of the optimum problem remains the same as in the paradigm case, that is, the minimization of resource use for a given target distribution of welfare, but the resources now become those of the whole economy, and account must be taken of the resource use outside the group as well as within it. It will be shown that it is generally efficient to compensate those for whom the available good is not of most-preferred specification by giving them a mixture of additional outside goods and of the available group good, so that the events within the group affect the quantities of outside goods required and thus the resource use outside the group.

1. The "outside good" could be leisure.

Although the initial analysis is in general terms, it becomes desirable to parameterize the relationships between the group and the rest of the economy in order to see clearly the effect of these relationships on such system properties as the optimal degree of product differentiation. This is carried out in terms of two parameters, one representing the degree of substitutability between outside goods in general and group goods as a whole, the other representing the relative importance of the group in the total economy.

As in the paradigm analysis, the optimum conditions are derived and examined for existence and second-order properties, and the effect of the various parameters, including those parameters representing relationships between the group and the rest of the economy, is studied. The feasibility of compensation is examined in the wider setting, and second-best solutions are derived for situations in which compensation is infeasible. Various modifications of the basic assumptions, such as indivisibilities, are examined as in the more restricted setting of the paradigm case.

## 4.2 Outside Compensation

In the paradigm case, all compensation is necessarily *inside* compensation; that is, compensation takes the form of goods from within the group itself. Consumers receiving not their most-preferred good but the next-best available good are compensated by receiving more of that best available good than they would have received if the good had been their most-preferred good.

In moving beyond the paradigm case to the more realistic setting in which there are other goods in the economy than simply those that can be considered to belong to the group, the possibility of *outside* compensation is introduced. Consumers not receiving their most-preferred good can be compensated with an additional amount of the best available group good (as in the paradigm case), with additional amounts of goods from outside the group altogether, or with some combination of the two. A consumer whose favorite beer is not available, for example, might be given a little more of the next-best (to the individual) available brand but might also be compensated by being given some cheese perhaps or even some small cash compensation, or some combination.

The optimum problem is now expanded considerably, since the total resource use in both the group and the outside goods must be taken into account. What proportion of the compensation should be given in group goods and what proportion in outside goods is itself a matter subject to efficiency criteria, and the optimum problem with outside goods consists in determining the optimal compensation mix along with the number, specification, and allocation of goods within the group. It is expected—and this expectation will be fulfilled—that the introduction of outside goods will change the optimal degree of product differentiation, as compared with that in the paradigm case, at least in most circumstances.

The economy outside the group can be sufficiently represented by a single good. This can be viewed as an aggregate of all nongroup goods since it will be assumed that compensation effects arising from the group will have only a negligible effect on relative quantities of goods within the aggregate.[2] Thus the total economy consists of the infinite spectrum of potential group goods plus the single aggregate outside good. In a market economy, the single aggregate good can be identified with real income spent outside the group.

Introduction of outside goods places the optimal-product-differentiation analysis in a general-equilibrium setting. Through the door opened by the introduction of outside goods, all kinds of links between the group and the rest of the economy can be developed.[3]

It is convenient, but not essential, to suppose that the outside goods are produced under constant returns to scale if the group is a major sector. If the group is small relative to the whole economy, it can be assumed that variations due to compensation effects arising

2. Since separability of the group has been assumed throughout (see Chapter 2), there are no cross-effects between goods in the group and individual outside goods. There are, however, income effects between the group and outside goods, so the composition of the aggregate could be affected by events within the group if income elasticities vary among outside goods.

3. None of the analyses in this book has been formally developed into full general equilibrium models by adding a resource supply relationship and a formal budget constraint. The optimum structures (and later the market equilibria) are, however, continuous in the relevant variables, and there should be little difficulty in closing the system.

from the group are simply too small to affect the marginal resource cost of outside goods, whatever the scale properties.

Solution of the problem of optimal product differentiation with outside goods involves the following:

1. determination of the optimal division of compensation between inside (group) goods and outside goods;
2. determination of the number of different group goods to be produced;
3. determination of the optimal partitioning of consumers among the group good; and
4. determination of the optimal specifications of the group goods.

By extending the idea of uniformity over the preference spectrum to cover outside goods, it is possible to handle steps 3 and 4 with relative ease, which leaves the difficult task of solving steps 1 and 2 somewhat easier than it would otherwise be. The difficulty in the analysis that follows is not so much in setting out formal optimal conditions as in relating these to the structure of the economy.

## 4.3 Uniformity with Outside Goods

In the paradigm case, where there were no outside goods, the simplifying working assumption of "uniformity" over the preference spectrum required only to be expressed in terms of the properties of the compensating function $h$. In that context, the assumption was that the quantity of the available good which was considered equivalent by the consumer to a unit of his most-preferred good was:

1. the same for all consumers whose most-preferred goods were the same;
2. the same for all quantities of good, at least over the range of variation required by the analysis; and
3. the same for all consumers whose most-preferred goods were the same "distance" from the available goods, even when the consumers were at different points on the spectrum and supplied with different available goods.

From the above specifications of uniformity, it follows that, if $q^*$ is some quantity of the most-preferred good for some consumers and

$q$ is the quantity of an available good, differing in specification from the most-preferred good by $u$, so that $q = q^*h(u)$, then the consumer is indifferent between receiving $q^*$ of his most-preferred good and $q$ of the available good. The compensating function $h(u)$ is, of course, a function of $u$ only. Thus if quantity $q$ of some good is supplied to a consumer whose most-preferred good differs in specification by distance $u$, the value $x(u) = q/h(u)$ can be referred to as the *most-preferred-good equivalent* of quantity $q$ of that available good for that consumer. The same quantity of a given available good will have different preferred-good equivalents for different individuals depending on the specification distance between the available good and their respective most-preferred goods, the difference being determined by the compensating function.

To extend the uniformity concept to the situation in which there are outside goods available, it is first assumed that the uniformity properties with respect to goods within the group are identical with those in the paradigm case and that all interrelations between goods within the group are expressed in terms of the compensating function $h(u)$, even when outside goods are present. In addition, it is assumed that there is uniformity over the spectrum as to the preference relations between most-preferred group goods and outside goods, in the sense that the welfare or utility function in terms of most-preferred group goods and outside goods, $w(x, y)$, where $x$ is the quantity of most-preferred good and $y$ is the quantity of the outside good, has the same form for all consumers at all points in the spectrum. That is, if consumers from different points of the spectrum are given equal quantities of their respective most-preferred goods and an equal quantity of the outside good, their marginal rates of substitution between the two will be identical.

It is further assumed that the above relationships between inside and outside goods can be compounded with the intragroup relationships, so that, if an individual is supplied with quantity $q$ of some available good instead of his or her most-preferred good, the functional relationship $w = w(x, y)$ holds in the same form as above, where $x$ is now the most-preferred good equivalent of the quantity of available good, given by $x = q/h(u)$.

If the preference spectrum is uniform in this sense, then it is obvious that the optimal mix between inside and outside compensation will be, like the internal compensation in the paradigm case, a function only of the difference in specification between a consumer's most-preferred good and the best available good. It is also obvious that the following properties, analogous to those of the paradigm case, will hold at the optimum:

1. The optimal specification of the good to be provided to each set of consumers will be centered in that segment of the spectrum if the welfare density is uniform over each segment.

2. The optimal segments will be of the same size if the welfare density is uniform over the spectrum.

3. The total quantities of both the group good and the outside good to be supplied to each segment at the optimum will be the same over all segments if the welfare density is uniform.

By provisionally confining the treatment to the case of a uniform welfare density, the analysis can be carried out in terms of equal symmetrical segments, with the optimization confined to the determination of the compensation mix and the segment size.

## 4.4 The Optimal Compensation Mix

If consumers are to be compensated with the least use of resources, then there is some optimal mix of compensation from group goods and from outside goods that will achieve this. Solution for the optimal compensation mix must be determined prior to the solution for the optimal degree of product differentiation, since the latter must be based on efficient compensation.

Since the welfare functions of individuals are independent of each other, with no externalities or cross-effects, the optimal compensation mix for an individual whose most-preferred good is at distance $u$ from the available good can be solved as an isolated problem. Optimal compensation for such an individual will be that mix of the available good and the outside good which enables the individual to attain a given level of welfare with the minimum resource cost.

Let $q$ be the quantity of available good to be supplied to the individual and $y$ the quantity of outside good. Then the resource cost of supplying those quantities is given by $\delta V$, where

$$\delta V = qF' + y\bar{F}', \qquad (4.1)$$

with $F'$ and $\bar{F}'$ the marginal resource costs of producing the available and outside goods, respectively, which can be regarded as constant with respect to the goods provided to a single individual.

Noting that $x$, the most-preferred-good equivalent of $q$, is given by $x = q/h(u)$, Eq. (4.1) can be written in terms of most-preferred-good equivalent for the individual in question as

$$\delta V = xhF' + y\bar{F}'. \qquad (4.2)$$

The optimum compensation mix is then found as the solution to the problem,

$$\min_{x,y} \delta V \text{ subject to } w(x, y) = \bar{w}.$$

The solution is, of course,

$$h\frac{w_y}{w_x} = \frac{\bar{F}'}{F'}. \qquad (4.3)$$

That is, the marginal rate of substitution between the outside-good equivalent and the most-preferred-good equivalent of the available group good multiplied by the compensating ratio must equal the ratio of the marginal resource costs of the outside good and the available good. When $u = 0$, so that the available good is the most-preferred good for that individual, $h = 1$, and the optimal condition has the traditional form; that is, the marginal rate of substitution between actual goods equals their marginal resource cost ratio.

If all individuals are optimally compensated, then, since the marginal resource cost ratio is the same for all individuals being supplied with the same available good and the form of the welfare function is the same for all individuals (by the uniformity assumption), the left-hand side of Eq. (4.3) must be constant over the segment being supplied with the particular available good; that is, the left-hand side must be invariant with respect to $u$. Taking logarithms and differentiating with respect to ln $u$, this implies

$$\frac{d}{d\,(\ln\,u)}\left[\ln h(u) - \ln\left(\frac{w_x}{w_y}\right)\right] = 0$$

or

$$e_h = \frac{d\left[\ln\left(\frac{w_x}{w_y}\right)\right]}{d\,(\ln\,u)}, \tag{4.4}$$

where $e_h = d(\ln h)/d(\ln u) = uh'/h$ is the elasticity of the compensating function. Note that this is not the elasticity of *cumulative* compensation ($e_H$) which was used extensively in Chapter 3.

Relationship (4.4) establishes a unique relationship between $w_x/w_y$ and the distance $u$ along the segment in terms of the properties of the compensating function. Given the desired distribution of welfare over the segment, $w(x, y)$ is also determined uniquely as a function of $u$. Thus the welfare level and the marginal rate of substitution are both determined, so that $x(u)$ and $y(u)$ are determined. Since $q(u) = h(u)x(u)$, $q(u)$ is determined, and thus the pattern of distribution of both the available good and the outside good is fully determined.

Thus $q$ and $y$ can be written as functions of $u$ only, given the properties of the welfare functions and the distribution of welfare, where $q(u)$ and $y(u)$ represent the total allocations of available and outside good going to individuals having most-preferred goods with specifications which differ from the specification of the available good by the distance measure $u$. Associated with these are their elasticities, defined by

$$e_q(u) = d\,(\ln q)/d\,(\ln u) = uq'/q \tag{4.5a}$$

and

$$e_y(u) = d\,(\ln y)/d\,(\ln u) = uy'/y, \tag{4.5b}$$

and the corresponding cumulative values (quantities allocated to all individuals at distance up to $u$), defined by

$$Q'(u) = q(u), \quad Q(0) = 0 \tag{4.6a}$$

and

$$Y'(u) = y(u), \quad Y(0) = 0. \tag{4.6b}$$

Finally, extensive use will be made of the elasticities of the cumulative values,

$$e_Q(u) = d (\ln Q)/d (\ln u) = uq/Q \tag{4.7a}$$

$$e_Y(u) = d (\ln Y)/d (\ln u) = uy/Y. \tag{4.7b}$$

If the welfare distribution is uniform, the functions $q(u)$ and $y(u)$, together with the cumulative values and elasticities derived from them, will be the same for all segments. Furthermore, it is possible to derive some general properties of the functions in the uniform welfare case. Consider the relationship given by Eq. (4.4), which implies that the marginal rate of substitution between most-preferred-good equivalents and outside goods $(w_x/w_y)$ increases with $u$. Given the usual assumptions for welfare functions (strict quasi-concavity), this implies that the ratio $x/y$ must decrease with $u$ and thus that $x$ decreases and $y$ increases if $w(x, y)$ is kept constant, as it is under uniform distribution of welfare. Thus $y(u)$ is an increasing function of $u$ in the uniform welfare case, so that $y' > 0$, $e_y > 0$, $Y$ is convex, and $e_Y \geqq 1$ (Lemma 1a, Appendix B). Although $x(u)$ is a decreasing function of $u$ with $x' < 0$, $q(u)$ may be either increasing or decreasing since $q = hx$, $q' = h'x + hx'$, and $h' > 0$. Thus $e_q$ may be positive or negative; $Q$ convex or concave; and $e_Q$ greater than, less than, or equal to, unity. It will later be shown that the condition determining whether $q(u)$ is increasing or decreasing can be expressed in terms of the elasticity of substitution between group goods and outside goods.


## 4.5 The Optimum with Outside Goods

It is appropriate at this stage to derive the conditions for optimal product differentiation in the presence of outside goods, even though the full significance of these relationships can only be extracted after further analysis designed to reveal the part played by the degree of substitutability between inside and outside goods.

It is assumed that the preference spectrum is uniform in the sense discussed previously, that there is a uniform density, and that the conditions for the optimal division of compensation between inside and outside goods are satisfied. For the same reasons as in the paradigm case, the optimal segments will be of equal size, the good to be provided to each will have its specification at the center of the segment, and the total quantities of the inside and outside goods required to bring all consumers in the segment up to the uniform target welfare level will be the same for all segments and given by $2Q(\Delta)$ and $2Y(\Delta)$, where $2\Delta$ is the segment width and the cumulative functions $Q(u)$ and $Y(u)$ are defined by Eqs. (4.7) and (4.8).

As in the paradigm case, the optimal segment width will be that which minimizes the "per capita" resource use over the segment (actually, resource use per unit of segment width) in achieving the target welfare levels. In this case, however, the resources used for outside goods must be taken into account as well as those used for the group goods. Since all segments are to be provided with the same outside good, the production properties for outside goods depend on the total output over all segments. Let $R$ be the range of the spectrum, so that the number of segments of width $2\Delta$ is equal to $R/2\Delta$, then the total quantity of outside good will be $RY/\Delta$, its resource requirement $\bar{F}(RY/\Delta)$, and per capita resource use in the outside good will be $[\bar{F}(RY/\Delta)]/R$.

Thus the per capita resource requirement over a segment is equal to

$$v = \frac{F(2Q)}{2\Delta} + \frac{\bar{F}(RY/\Delta)}{R}, \tag{4.8}$$

where $F$ and $\bar{F}$ are the input functions of the group and outside goods and $Q$ and $Y$ are functions of $\Delta$.

By taking the derivative of $v$ with respect to $\Delta$ and substituting $\theta = F/2QF'$ (the degree of returns to scale parameter in the production of group goods) and the elasticities $e_Q = q\Delta/Q$ and $e_Y = y\Delta/Y$, the following equation is derived:

$$\frac{dv}{d\Delta} = \frac{1}{\Delta^2}[(e_Q - \theta)QF' + (e_Y - 1)Y\bar{F}']. \tag{4.9}$$

Note that the degree of economies of scale in the production of outside goods does not appear in this equation.

Now $2QF'$ and $2Y\bar{F}'$ are the "values," at marginal resource cost shadow prices, of the total inside and outside goods, respectively, supplied to the segment. If $m$ is the proportion of the total shadow price value which is supplied as a group good, then

$$m = \frac{QF'}{QF' + Y\bar{F}'}$$

and

$$1 - m = \frac{Y\bar{F}'}{QF' + Y\bar{F}'} . \tag{4.10}$$

Equation (4.9) can then be put in the form

$$\frac{dv}{d\Delta} = \frac{1}{T\Delta^2} [m(e_Q - \theta) + (1 - m)(e_Y - 1)], \tag{4.11}$$

where $T = QF' + Y\bar{F}'$.

The optimum condition $dv/d\Delta = 0$ can then be written in any one of three equivalent forms,

$$m(e_Q - \theta) = -(1 - m)(e_Y - 1) \tag{4.12a}$$

$$e_Q + \frac{1 - m}{m} (e_Y - 1) = \theta \tag{4.12b}$$

$$me_Q + (1 - m)e_Y = m\theta + (1 - m). \tag{4.12c}$$

Note the third form. The left-hand side is the weighted average of the elasticities of $Q$ and $Y$, with weights proportional to their importance in overall consumption, whereas the right-hand side is the weighted average of the degree of economies of scale in the production of group goods and unity, with the same weights. When $m = 1$, there are no outside goods, $e_Q = e_H$, and the result is precisely the same as in the paradigm case, to which it has been reduced. It will be shown in the next section that the paradigm result can also be obtained when outside goods exist and are consumed, provided there is zero substitution between these and group goods.

The question of second-order conditions and existence cannot be handled at this stage but must await further analysis of the exact effects of substitutability between inside and outside goods on the system.

It has been shown that the degree of economies of scale in the production of outside goods does not affect the optimum conditions (Eqs. 4.9 to 4.12), provided the outside good is not itself differentiated.[4] The existence of scale economies in outside goods affects the resource level required to attain given target welfare levels, but not the decision as to the degree of product differentiation within the group. Note that this implies that the *absolute* degree of economies of scale in the group good, not the degree of economies of scale relative to those in the economy as a whole, determines the degree of product differentiation.

## 4.6 Substitution Effects

The conditions for optimal product differentiation depend on the properties of the elasticities of the cumulative quantity functions for the group and outside goods, $e_Q$ and $e_Y$, in conjunction with the economies of scale properties of the technology and the relative importance of the group in the total economy. The properties of the quantity functions are determined by the conditions for the optimal compensation mix and the distribution of welfare and depend ultimately on the properties of the welfare function and the compensating function. function.

Since the form of the compensating function has been assumed to be the same whether outside goods are present or not, the effect of outside goods and of different relationships between group goods and outside goods is felt through the properties of the welfare function, in particular, through the degree of substitutability between group goods and outside goods. This degree of substitutability will

---

4. Differentiated outside goods present no intractable problems, provided that there is no correlation between an individual's position on one preference spectrum and his position on another and, in particular, that the collection of individuals having most-preferred goods in some small subsegment of the group spectrum have most-preferred outside goods which cover the whole of the outside-goods spectrum.

be parameterized by the *elasticity of substitution*, a parameter widely used in production function theory,[5] but somewhat less commonly used for utility or welfare functions.

If $F(x_1, x_2)$ is any function of the two variables $x_1$ and $x_2$, the elasticity of substitution $\sigma$ is defined as

$$\sigma = - \left[ \frac{d \ln (x_1/x_2)}{d \ln (F_1/F_2)} \right]_{F(x_1, x_2) = \bar{F}}$$

that is, the elasticity of the ratio of the two variables with respect to the marginal rate of substitution between them when the variations are restricted to a movement along a contour of the function $F$. The more substitutable the variables, the greater the variation in their proportions for a given change in the marginal rate of substitution and thus the greater the value of $\sigma$, which has been defined in such a way as to be nonnegative when $F$ is quasi-concave. If the contours of $F(x_1, x_2)$ are straight lines, the marginal rate of substitution (the slope of the contour) is the same for all ratios of the variables, and $\sigma$ is infinite, whereas if the variables can only be used in fixed proportions, the value of $\sigma$ is zero.

Since the welfare function is in the form $w = w(x, y)$, where $x$ is the most-preferred-good equivalent of the available good and $y$ is the quantity of outside good, the elasticity of substitution in this case has the form

$$\sigma = - \left[ \frac{d \ln (x/y)}{d \ln (w_x/w_y)} \right]_{w = \bar{w}} . \tag{4.13}$$

Assuming throughout that $w$ is constant, so that the condition need not be specifically noted, this implies that

$$\frac{d \ln (w_x/w_y)}{d \ln (x/y)} = - \frac{1}{\sigma}$$

or, in terms of differentials,

$$d \ln (w_x/w_y) = - \frac{1}{\sigma} d \ln (x/y)$$

$$= - \frac{1}{\sigma} (d \ln x - d \ln y). \tag{4.14}$$

5. See standard microeconomic texts, for example, Lancaster (1974) or Henderson and Quandt (1971).

The condition for the optimal compensation mix is given by Eq. (4.4) in the form

$$e_h = \frac{d\ln\,(w_x/w_y)}{d\ln\,u}\,.$$

Substituting from Eq. (4.14) gives

$$e_h = -\frac{1}{\sigma}\left(\frac{d\ln\,x}{d\ln\,u} - \frac{d\ln\,y}{d\ln\,u}\right)$$

$$= -\frac{1}{\sigma}\,(e_x - e_y), \tag{4.15}$$

where $e_x$ and $e_y$ are the elasticities of $x(u)$ and $y(u)$ with respect to $u$.

A uniform distribution of welfare implies that $w = w[x(u), y(u)] = w(u)$ is constant with respect to $u$, the position of the individual in the segment. In logarithmic terms, this implies that

$$\frac{d\ln\,w(u)}{d\ln\,u} = 0$$

or

$$\frac{\partial\ln\,w}{\partial\ln\,x}\,e_x + \frac{\partial\ln\,w}{\partial\ln\,y}\,e_y = 0 \tag{4.16}$$

By denoting the elasticities of the welfare function with respect to its arguments, $\partial(\ln w)/\partial(\ln x)$ and $\partial(\ln w)/\partial(\ln y)$, by $\omega_x$ and $\omega_y$, respectively, Eq. (4.16) can be written in the form

$$\omega_x e_x + \omega_y e_y = 0. \tag{4.17}$$

Equations (4.15) and (4.17), which express the conditions that the compensation mix be optimal and that the welfare distribution be uniform, can now be solved to give the properties of the quantity functions $x(u)$ and $y(u)$ [expressed as the elasticities $e_x(u)$ and $e_y(u)$] in terms of $\omega_x$, $\omega_y$, $\sigma$, and $e_h$, as follows:

$$e_x = -\sigma\,\frac{\omega_y}{\omega_x + \omega_y}\,e_h \tag{4.18a}$$

$$e_y = \sigma\,\frac{\omega_x}{\omega_x + \omega_y}\,e_h\,. \tag{4.18b}$$

Note that, unless $\sigma = 0$, $e_x$ and $e_y$ have opposite signs. The optimal allocation will be such that individuals whose most-preferred goods are more distant in specification from the available good (larger $u$) will receive a smaller most-preferred good equivalent of the group good ($e_x > 0$) and a larger allocation of the outside good ($e_y > 0$).

To express the allocation in terms of the actual quantity of available good instead of its most-preferred-good equivalent, it can be noted that $q = hx$, so that

$$e_q = e_x + e_h .\qquad(4.19)$$

Now

$$\omega_x = \frac{d \ln \ w}{d \ln \ x}$$

$$= \frac{x w_x}{w}$$

$$= \frac{q w_x}{h w}$$

and

$$\omega_y = \frac{y w_y}{w} ,$$

so that, from Eq. (4.3),

$$\frac{\omega_x}{\omega_y} = \frac{q w_x}{h y w_y}$$

$$= \frac{q F'}{y \bar{F}'} .$$

Now $F'$ and $\bar{F}'$ are the marginal resource costs of producing the available and outside goods, respectively, so that $\omega_x / \omega_y$ is the ratio of the "values" of group and outside goods supplied to the individual at distance $u$ from the available good, in terms of marginal resource cost shadow prices. Let the proportion of the total value of goods, at marginal resource cost prices, which is given to this individual as the available good be $\mu(u)$. Then

$$\mu(u) = \frac{\omega_x(u)}{\omega_x(u) + \omega_y(u)}\qquad(4.20a)$$

and

$$1 - \mu(u) = \frac{\omega_y(u)}{\omega_x(u) + \omega_y(u)} . \tag{4.20b}$$

The use of Eqs. (4.19), (4.20a), and (4.20b) in Eqs. (4.18a) and (4.18b) then gives the fundamental equations determining the quantities of the two goods $q(u)$ and $y(u)$, in elasticity terms, as

$$e_q(u) = \{1 - [1 - \mu(u)]\sigma\}e_h(u) \tag{4.21a}$$

$$e_y(u) = \mu(u)\sigma e_h(u). \tag{4.21b}$$

In principle, $\sigma$ may vary along the contours of the welfare function and thus may vary with $u$ when the allocation is optimal. It is convenient, however, to be able to parameterize the system in terms of the elasticity of substitution and thus it will be assumed that the welfare function has a *constant elasticity of substitution* over the range of variation in the analysis. Since it has already been assumed that the form of the welfare function is the same for all individuals, this implies that there is a single value for the elasticity of substitution which applies to all individuals, whatever the relationship between their most-preferred good and the available good. This does not imply that the proportions in which group goods and outside goods are optimally allocated will be the same for all individuals, because Eq. (4.3) shows that the marginal rates of substitution between group and outside goods will vary with the compensating ratio and thus with the position of the individual in the segment. Although $\sigma$ is constant over individuals, $\mu$ is not.

It is obvious from Eq. (4.21b) that $e_y$ is always positive (unless $\sigma = 0$), so that $y(u)$ is an increasing function of $u$ and the amount of outside good allocated to an individual always increases with his or her distance from the center of the segment. On the other hand, it is equally obvious from Eq. (4.21a) that $e_q$ may be positive or negative, depending on the value of $\sigma$ relative to $1 - \mu$. If the elasticity of substitution is relatively low [$\sigma < 1/(1 - \mu)$], then $e_q > 0$, $q(u)$ is an increasing function of $u$, the cumulative function $Q(u)$ is convex, and the elasticity of the cumulative function $e_Q$ is greater than unity. If the elasticity of substitution is relatively high [$\sigma > 1/(1 - \mu)$], then $e_q < 0$, $q$ is a decreasing function of $u$, $Q$ is a concave function, and $e_Q < 1$ for $u > 0$. Thus, at low elasticity values, the quantity of the available group good allocated to the individual increases with his or her distance from the center of the segment, and at high elasticity values, the quantity decreases.

When $\sigma = 0$, $e_q = e_h$, and $e_y = 0$, so that the behavior of the system is the same as in the paradigm case, even though $\mu$ may not be unity. The allocation of outside good is the same for all individuals (this is the implication of $e_y = 0$, which does not necessarily imply that $y = 0$), and all compensation is given in terms of the available group good, as in the paradigm case.

The effect of the parameters $\sigma$ and $\mu$ on the elasticities of the cumulative quantities $Q$ and $Y$ can easily be determined by the use of Lemma 2b (Appendix B). Since

$$\partial e_q / \partial \sigma = -(1 - \mu)e_h < 0$$

and

$$\partial e_y / \partial \sigma = \mu e_h > 0,$$

the lemma immediately gives

$$\partial e_Q / \partial \sigma < 0 \tag{4.22a}$$

$$\partial e_Y / \partial \sigma > 0, \tag{4.22b}$$

so that an increase in the elasticity of substitution decreases the elasticity of the cumulative quantity function for the group good and increases it for the outside good. An increase in $\mu$, the relative importance of the group in the economy, can easily be shown to increase the elasticities of both $Q$ and $Y$.

## 4.7 Existence of a Product-Differentiated Optimum

The optimum degree of product differentiation was found in Section 4.5 by minimizing the resource use per unit of spectrum width, with all individuals being fully compensated, so that the welfare distribution remains constant as the number of goods (represented by the segment width) varies. The condition for an interior optimum is that $dv/d\Delta = 0$, where $dv/d\Delta$ is given by Eq. (4.11), which can be written in the form

$$\frac{dv}{d\Delta} = \frac{1}{mT\Delta^2}[G(\Delta) - \theta(\Delta)], \tag{4.23}$$

where

$$G(\Delta) = e_Q(\Delta) + \frac{1 - m}{m} [e_Y(\Delta) - 1]. \tag{4.24}$$

The argument $\Delta$ is inserted to emphasize the fact that $G$ is a function of $\Delta$ only, through $e_Q$ and $e_Y$, when the parameters $m$ (the relative importance of the group in the economy) and $\sigma$ (the elasticity of substitution between group goods and outside goods) are treated as constant system parameters. The degree-of-returns-to-scale parameter is also a function of $\Delta$ only, since it is either a constant or a function of $Q$ only, and the latter is a function of $\Delta$ only, once the system parameters are given.

An interior optimum is only one possible solution, of course. The segment half-width $\Delta$ is constrained below and above—below by its essential nonnegativity and above by the half-range of the spectrum, since the largest possible segment is one covering the range of the spectrum.

Thus there are two possible boundary optima in addition to the possible interior optimum: a lower-boundary optimum at $\Delta = 0$ with an infinite number of products in the group and an upper-boundary optimum with a single group good. The lower-boundary optimum will occur if $dv/d\Delta \geqq 0$ at $\Delta = 0$, and the upper-boundary optimum if $dv/d\Delta < 0$ at $\Delta = \Delta_{max}$. The optimum will be an interior one with a finite number of goods if $dv/d\Delta = 0$ and $d^2v/d\Delta^2 > 0$ at $\Delta$ such that $0 < \Delta < \Delta_{max}$.

It is the purpose of the present section to determine whether an optimum always exists, and under what conditions it will be an interior optimum or an upper- or lower-boundary optimum. The following results will be shown to hold under the conditions being assumed in this work:

1. An optimum always exists, is unique, and is either of the interior or upper-boundary type. A lower-boundary optimum cannot occur, so that the optimal number of goods in the group is finite.

2. An interior optimum with many products will always occur for a sufficiently small degree of initial economies of scale, that is, if $\theta(0)$ is sufficiently close to unity.

3. A single-good optimum (upper boundary) is always possible for economies of scale which remain sufficiently large over the range

of output possible for a single group good in the economy under examination.

4. It is never optimal to produce a group good at minimum average resource cost, even if the technology gives such a minimum. If the group is in a configuration such that all group goods are being produced at minimum average resource cost, it will always be optimal to increase the product variety even though each of the larger number of goods will then be produced at above minimum average cost.

The first result is easy to prove, but the remaining results require some special analysis. For the first result, it can be noted that the elasticity $e_X$ of any cumulative function $X(u)$ is necessarily unity at $u = 0$ since

$$X(u) = X(0) + uX'(\lambda u)$$

for some $\lambda$ such that $0 < \lambda < 1$ (Taylor's theorem) and $X(0) = 0$ for a cumulative function, so that

$$e_X(u) = uX'(u)/X(u) = X'(u)/X'(\lambda u),$$

and thus $e_X(u) \to 1$ as $u \to 0$. In the present case, $e_Q(0) = e_Y(0) = 1$, so that $G(0) = 1$, from Eq. (4.24). But it is assumed throughout this work that $\theta(0) > 1$ (there are initial economies of scale), so that $dv/d\Delta < 0$ at $\Delta = 0$, from Eq. (4.23), and a lower-boundary optimum cannot occur.

The other results depend on proving that $G(\Delta) > 1$ for all $\Delta > 0$. It was shown in the previous section that $e_Y > 1$ for all $\Delta > 0$ but that $e_Q$ might be greater or less than unity, according to whether the elasticity of substitution is relatively low or relatively high. Thus $G(\Delta)$ is certainly greater than unity for an elasticity of substitution sufficiently low to give $e_Q > 1$, but $G(\Delta)$ will be greater than unity for high values of the elasticity of substitution only if it can be shown that the excess of $e_Y$ over unity, when weighted by the factor $(1 - m)/m$, more than counterbalances the deficiency of $e_Q$ below unity. To prove this is clearly not an easy matter.

The properties of $e_Q$ and $e_Y$ are derived from the properties of the cumulative quantity functions $Q$ and $Y$, which are derived in turn from the properties of the uncumulated or density functions $q$ and $y$. The latter are determined by the differential equations, Eqs. (4.21a) and (4.21b):

$$e_q(u) = \{1 - [1 - \mu(u)]\sigma\}e_h(u)$$
$$e_y(u) = \mu(u)\sigma e_h(u).$$

In these equations, the elasticity of substitution $\sigma$ has been taken to be a system parameter, but the number $\mu(u)$, which is the proportion of the value of the group good to the total value of all goods provided to the individual at distance $u$ from the center of the segment, varies with $u$ in a determinate manner.

The symbol $\underline{\mu}$ is used to denote the minimum value of $\mu(u)$ in the range $0 \leqq u \leqq \Delta$, and $\bar{\mu}$ denotes the corresponding maximum value. Then, if $\underline{x}$ is defined by $e_{\underline{x}} = \underline{\mu}e_h$ and $\bar{x}$ by $e_{\bar{x}} = \bar{\mu}e_h$, it is obvious from the differential equations above that

$$e_{\underline{x}} \leqq e_y \leqq e_{\bar{x}}$$

for all $u$ such that $0 \leqq u \leqq \Delta$ and thus from Lemma 2a (Appendix B) that

$$e_{\underline{X}} \leqq e_Y \leqq e_{\bar{X}}$$

for all $\Delta$, where $X$ is the cumulated value of $x$. Since $\bar{\mu} \to \underline{\mu}$ as $\Delta \to 0$, $e_{\bar{X}} \to e_Y \to e_{\underline{X}}$ as $\Delta \to 0$. From these relationships and application of the mean value theorem to the integration involved in deriving $Y$ from $y$, it can be deduced that there is some $x(u)$ of the form defined by

$$e_x(u) = \mu\sigma e_h(u)$$

such that

$$e_X(\Delta) = e_Y(\Delta),$$

where $\mu = \mu(\Delta)$ is constant for a given $\Delta$ and such that $\underline{\mu} \leqq \mu \leqq \bar{\mu}$. A similar type of argument can be given for $e_q$.

Now $m$, the proportion of the total value of goods which is supplied as group goods over the whole segment, is clearly a number with the property $\underline{\mu} \leqq m \leqq \bar{\mu}$, and it is also true that $\underline{\mu}$, $\bar{\mu}$, $\mu$, and $m$ all converge towards the same value as $\Delta \to 0$. Thus it will be assumed that, if $\Delta$ is sufficiently small, the differential equations of Eqs. (4.21a) and (4.21b) can be replaced by the differential equations having constant parameters $\sigma$ and $m$:

$$e_q = [1 - (1 - m)\sigma]e_h \qquad (4.25a)$$

$$e_y = m\sigma e_h . \qquad (4.25b)$$

The functions $q(u)$ and $y(u)$ defined by Eqs. (4.25a) and (4.25b) can be regarded as *surrogates* for the true functions defined by Eqs. (4.21a) and (4.21b), whose *cumulative* properties coincide with those of the true functions. It is obvious that the surrogate functions will be greater than the true functions over part of the segment and less than the true functions over the remainder, unless the two are equal everywhere. From this point on, it will be assumed that $q$ and $y$ are the surrogate functions, unless it is specifically noted to the contrary.

From Eq. (4.25a), $e_q \geqq 0$, provided $\sigma \leqq 1/(1 - m)$ and $e_y > 0$ for $\sigma > 0$, so that, from Lemma 1a (Appendix B), $e_Q(\Delta) \geqq 1$ for all $\Delta > 0$ and $e_Y(\Delta) > 1$ for all $\Delta > 0$. When $\sigma = 0$, $e_q > 0$ and $e_y = 0$, so that $e_Q > 1$ and $e_Y = 1$ for all $\Delta > 0$. Thus $G(\Delta) > 1$ for all $\Delta > 0$ when $\sigma$ is in the range

$$0 \leqq \sigma \leqq 1/(1 - m)$$

and, in particular, for all values of $\sigma$ up to and including unity.

For values of $\sigma$ greater than $1/(1 - m)$, the value of $G(\Delta)$ can be determined by using Lemmas 3a and 3c of Appendix B. For $q$, the multiplier $\gamma$ of the lemmas has the value $1 - (1 - m)\sigma$, from Eq. (4.25a), so that Eq. (B3.1) becomes

$$e_Q - 1 = [1 - (1 - m)\sigma](e_H - 1) \qquad (4.26a)$$
$$+ [1 - (1 - m)\sigma][-(1 - m)\sigma]\phi_q .$$

For $y$, the multiplier $\gamma$ has the value $m\sigma$, so that Eq. (B3.1) becomes

$$e_Y - 1 = m\sigma(e_H - 1) + m\sigma(m\sigma - 1)\phi_Y , \qquad (4.26b)$$

where $\phi_q$ and $\phi_y$ are functions of $\Delta$ such that both are zero at $\Delta = 0$ and positive when $\Delta > 0$. From Lemma 3c, the two functions can be treated as equal, to a high degree of approximation, and replaced by the single function $\phi$. Inserting the values of $e_Q$ and $e_Y$ given by Eqs. (4.26, a and b) into Eq. (4.24) gives

$$G(\Delta) = e_H(\Delta) + (1 - m)\sigma(\sigma - 2)\phi(\Delta). \qquad (4.27)$$

Since $e_H > 1$ for $\Delta > 0$ and $\phi \geqq 0$, it is certainly true that $G(\Delta) > 1$ for $\Delta > 0$ and $\sigma \geqq 2$. It has already been shown that $G(\Delta) > 1$ for $\Delta > 0$ and $\sigma \leqq 1$, so the required relationship has been demonstrated for all values of $\sigma$ except those in the range $1 < \sigma < 2$.

In the expression given in Eq. (4.27), $e_H$ is independent of $\sigma$, since it is the elasticity of the cumulative compensating function, and $\phi$ can be taken to be independent of $\sigma$ by Lemma 3c of Appendix B. Thus

$$\frac{\partial G}{\partial \sigma} = 2(1 - m)(\sigma - 1)\phi \tag{4.28}$$

and

$$\frac{\partial^2 G}{\partial \sigma^2} = 2(1 - m)\phi > 0, \tag{4.29}$$

so that the value of $G(\Delta)$ is a minimum for any $\Delta$ when $\sigma = 1$. But it has already been shown that $G(\Delta) > 1$ at $\sigma = 1$, and thus $G(\Delta) > 1$ for all $\Delta > 0$ and all values of $\sigma$.

Thus an interior optimum, which will occur if and only if $G(\Delta) = \theta(\Delta)$ for some $\Delta$, or an upper-boundary optimum, which will occur if and only if $G(\Delta) < \theta(\Delta)$ at $\Delta = \Delta_{\max}$, can occur only at a value of $\theta$ which is greater than unity. Since $\theta$ is the ratio of the average to marginal resource cost, the optimum cannot be where average cost is a minimum, because $\theta = 1$ at that output. Nor can the optimum be at a point beyond that of minimum average resource cost, since $\theta < 1$ for such a point. Thus result 4 has been proved.

To complete the proof, it will be shown that $G'(\Delta) > 0$ for all $\Delta > 0$. Differentiating Eq. (4.24) gives

$$G'(\Delta) = e_Q' + \frac{1 - m}{m} e_Y'. \tag{4.30}$$

The sign of $G'$ is not immediately obvious, since $e_Y' > 0$ for all $\Delta > 0$, but the sign of $e_Q'$ depends on the value of $\sigma$. However, by using the relationship given by Eq. (B3.2) in Lemma 3a of Appendix B, together with Lemma 3c, and proceeding along lines similar to those used in proving $G$ to be greater than unity, it can be shown that

$$G'(\Delta) = e_H'(\Delta) + (1 - m)\sigma(\sigma - 2)\phi'(\Delta), \tag{4.31}$$

where $\phi'(\Delta) > 0$ for $\Delta > 0$ (Lemma 3b). As with $G(\Delta)$, it can then be shown that $G'(\Delta)$ has a minimum with respect to $\sigma$ at $\sigma = 1$. But at $\sigma = 1$, $e_q = me_h > 0$, which implies that $e_Q' > 0$ from Lemma 1a of Appendix B, whereas $e_Y$ is also equal to $me_h$ and $e_Y' > 0$. Thus $G'(\Delta) > 0$ for all $\Delta > 0$ when $\sigma = 1$ and a fortiori when $\sigma > 1$ or $\sigma < 1$.

The properties of the function $G(\Delta)$ are now clear. Whatever the value of the elasticity of substitution, $G = 1$ at $\Delta = 0$, $G > 1$ for all $\Delta > 0$, and $G$ always increases with $\Delta$. The degree of returns to scale $\theta(\Delta)$, treated as a function of $\Delta$ through its dependence on $Q(\Delta)$, commences at some initial value $\theta(0) > 1$ and either remains constant or decreases with $\Delta$, since it is assumed throughout that $\theta$ is a nonincreasing function of output. The graph of $G(\Delta)$ thus commences below the graph of $\theta(\Delta)$ and rises toward it, the latter graph remaining level or falling. Thus either the graphs intersect to give an interior optimum or the graph of $G$ remains lower than that of $\theta$ when $\Delta$ reaches its maximum value, given the range of the spectrum. Either an interior or an upper-boundary optimum is assured and is unique, since both curves are monotonic.

Since $G(\Delta)$ is continuous and $G(0) = 1$, for any value of $\Delta$ there is a value of $\theta(0) > 1$ such that an interior optimum occurs at this value of $\Delta$ or a smaller one. On the other hand, since $\Delta$ has a finite maximum, there is some initial value of the degree of returns to scale which, together with a sufficiently small decline in returns to scale with output, will give an upper-boundary optimum.

At an interior optimum with $G = \theta$, the second-order conditions can be derived from Eq. (4.23) as

$$\left(\frac{d^2v}{d\Delta^2}\right)_{G=\theta} = \frac{1}{mT\Delta^2}\,(G' - \theta') > 0. \tag{4.32}$$

Since $\theta' \leqq 0$ and $G'$ has been shown to be positive, the second-order conditions are clearly satisfied.

Note that both the existence conditions and the second-order conditions could also be satisfied if the degree of returns to scale increased with output, provided that $\theta$ increased (with $\Delta$) at a lesser rate than $G$.

An optimum exists, as has just been shown, for all values of $\sigma$ from zero (which corresponds to the paradigm case) to infinity. This can be contrasted with the results derived later from the analysis of market behavior, where it is shown that there is a market solution only for a restricted range of elasticities of substitution and, in particular, that there is no stable market solution for elasticities of substitution less than unity.

## 4.8 The Effect of Substitution on Differentiation

Much of the interest in introducing outside goods into the analysis lies in finding out how the optimal degree of product differentiation is affected as a result. It is obvious that some effect on the optimal degree of product differentiation is to be expected when there are outside goods, as compared to the paradigm case, since the optimum conditions differ in the two cases. It is also to be expected that the extent of the variation from the paradigm case will depend on the values of the structural parameters $\sigma$ and $m$, since the outside-goods case becomes identical with the paradigm case as either $\sigma \to 0$ or $m \to 1$.

It will be shown that the relationship between the degree of product differentiation with outside goods and in the paradigm case does indeed vary as the structural parameters vary. This variation is not, however, of a simple monotonic kind and has some very interesting properties. Primary attention is focused on the elasticity of substitution, the effect of this parameter on the optimal degree of product differentiation being as follows:

1. The optimal degree of product differentiation with outside goods is the same as in the paradigm case at two different values of the elasticity of substitution: (a) at zero and (b) at a certain "crossover value" $\sigma_0$.

2. The degree of product differentiation with outside goods is less than the paradigm value for $0 < \sigma < \sigma_0$ and greater than the paradigm value for $\sigma > \sigma_0$.

3. The optimum degree of product differentiation does not vary

monotonically with the value of $\sigma$, but declines initially to reach a minimum at $\sigma = 1$, then rises.

4. The crossover value $\sigma_o$ lies close to 2.

These relationships are illustrated in Figure 4.1.

By assuming initially that $\theta$ is a constant parameter corresponding to a technology with a homogeneous production function and no fixed resource cost element, the paradigm optimum is the solution to the equation

$$e_H(\Delta) = \theta,$$

from Eq. (3.9), and the optimum with outside goods is given by

$$G(\Delta) = \theta,$$

from the preceding section. Since both $e_H$ and $G$ are increasing functions of $\Delta$, $G(\Delta) > e_H(\Delta)$ for all $\Delta$ would imply that

$$G(\Delta_P) > e_H(\Delta_P) = \theta = G(\Delta),$$

and thus $\Delta_P > \Delta$, where $\Delta_P$ is the optimum segment size in the paradigm case, $\Delta$ is the optimum size in the case with outside goods, and $\Delta_P > \Delta$. The degree of product differentiation would be greater (segment size smaller) with outside goods than in the paradigm case when $G > e_H$ for all $\Delta$ and less than in the paradigm case when $G < e_H$ for all $\Delta$.

From Eq. (4.27), $G$ and $e_H$ are related as follows:

$$G(\Delta) = e_H(\Delta) + (1 - m)\sigma(\sigma - 2)\phi(\Delta).$$

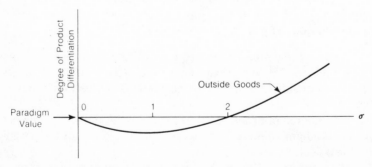

**Figure 4.1.** The optimum degree of product differentiation as a function of the elasticity of substitution, $\sigma$.

Since $\phi(\Delta) > 0$ for all $\Delta > 0$, $G = e_H$ for all $\Delta$ when $\sigma = 0$ or $\sigma = 2$, $G < e_H$ for all $\Delta$ when $0 < \sigma < 2$, and $G > e_H$ for all $\Delta$ when $\sigma > 2$. Thus the value 2 corresponds to the crossover value $\sigma_0$ in the statement given previously and result 2 is proved.

The reason for the statement (result 4) that $\sigma_0$ lies "close to" the value 2 rather than being equal to it is that the derivation of Eq. (4.27), through the use of Lemmas 3a and 3c of Appendix B, involves some approximation. There are terms omitted in the derivation which are only of the fourth order but nevertheless prevent the result from being treated as exact. Inspection of the full expressions reveals that the exact value of $\sigma_0$ will vary somewhat with system parameters (the parameter $m$, in particular), but such variations are of the fourth order or smaller.

The relationships given by Eqs. (4.28) and (4.29), derived in the previous section, show that $G(\Delta)$ has a minimum for any value of $\Delta$ when $\sigma = 1$. This might seem sufficient to prove result 3, but it is not, since it does not show the minimum to occur at the *exact* value $\sigma = 1$, because of the approximation discussed above. Since unit elasticity of substitution is a "natural" critical value, which $\sigma = 2$ is not, it might be expected that the result is exact. To prove it is requires a different approach.

Consider Eq. (4.21a), which determines the quantity function $q(u)$:

$$e_q(u) = \{1 - [1 - \mu(u)]\sigma\}e_h(u).$$

Note that this is the equation for the *true* function $q(u)$, not the surrogate function given by Eq. (4.25a) and involves no approximations or special assumptions. Now the special characteristic of unit elasticity of substitution is that, when individuals are optimally compensated, the ratio of the values of group and outside goods supplied to all individuals will be the same. That is, the proportion of the value of group goods to total goods [the parameter $\mu(u)$] is a true constant under unit elasticity and is necessarily equal to $m$, the average over all individuals. Thus Eqs. (4.25a) and (4.25b) become *exact* equations for the *true* functions in this case.

Putting $\sigma = 1$ in Eqs. (4.25a) and (4.25b) gives

$$e_q(u) = m e_h(u)$$

and

$$e_y(u) = me_h(u).$$

This implies that $e_Q(u) = e_Y(u)$ and that $Q(u)$ and $Y(u)$ bear a constant ratio to each other.

It is shown, in the derivation of Lemma 2b of Appendix B, that the following result holds for any function $x(u)$ such that $x(0) > 0$ and $x'(0) = 0$, where $x(u)$ also depends on some parameter $\sigma$:

$$\frac{\partial e_X}{\partial \sigma} = \frac{e_X}{X} \int_0^\Delta X \frac{\partial}{\partial \sigma} \left(\frac{x'}{x}\right) du. \tag{4.33}$$

This is an exact result, obtained by integrating by parts and making appropriate manipulations.

The function $q(u)$ satisfies the conditions when $\sigma \leqq 1$ and, since $e_q = uq'/q$ and $e_h = uh'/h$ by definition of the elasticities, Eqs. (4.25a) and (4.25b) can be written as

$$\frac{q'}{q} = [1 - (1 - m)\sigma] \frac{h'}{h} \tag{4.34a}$$

and

$$\frac{y'}{y} = m\sigma \frac{h'}{h}, \tag{4.34b}$$

so that

$$\frac{\partial}{\partial \sigma} \left(\frac{q'}{q}\right) = -(1 - m) \frac{h'}{h} \tag{4.35a}$$

and

$$\frac{\partial}{\partial \sigma} \left(\frac{y'}{y}\right) = m \frac{h'}{h}. \tag{4.35b}$$

Substituting $q(u)$ for $x(u)$ in Eq. (4.33) and using Eq. (4.35a) then gives

$$\frac{\partial e_Q}{\partial \sigma} = -(1 - m) \frac{e_Q}{Q} \int_0^\Delta Q \frac{h'}{h} du. \tag{4.36}$$

Substituting for $y(u)$ gives, in a similar way,

$$\frac{\partial e_Y}{\partial \sigma} = m \frac{e_Y}{Y} \int_0^\Delta Y \frac{h'}{h} \, du$$

$$= -\frac{m}{1-m} \frac{\partial e_Q}{\partial \sigma} \tag{4.37}$$

after using the relationships between $e_Q$ and $e_Y$ and $Q$ and $Y$ when $\sigma = 1$.

Differentiation of Eq. (4.24) with respect to $\sigma$ gives

$$\frac{\partial G}{\partial \sigma} = \frac{\partial e_Q}{\partial \sigma} + \frac{\partial e_Y}{\partial \sigma}$$

And when $\sigma = 1$ the function is equal to zero, from Eq. (4.37). Thus the minimum at $\sigma = 1$ is exact.

The analysis to this point has been based on the assumption of a constant degree of returns to scale. If the degree of returns to scale varies with output, there is an obvious difficulty in making any comparison between a situation in which there are no outside goods (the pure paradigm case) and one in which there are outside goods, unless the two situations are normalized in some way for size. One way of doing this is to assume that the comparisons are made between situations in which the outputs of group goods are essentially the same, in which case the results hold as given. Another is to consider an economy in which the elasticity of substitution is initially zero and then increases to map out the effect of outside goods. In this case, if the overall size of the economy (output of all goods) is held roughly constant, the output of group goods will fall as the elasticity of substitution increases. At the former crossover value $\sigma_o$, the degree of economies of scale will be greater than in the paradigm case because output is smaller, so that the relationships at that value will be given by

$$G(\Delta) = \theta(\Delta) > \theta(\Delta_P) = e_H(\Delta_P).$$

Since $G = e_H$ for all $\Delta$ at this elasticity, $\Delta > \Delta_P$, and the optimum with outside goods will give less than the paradigm degree of product differentiation. The crossover value will be shifted to the right (see

Figure 4.1), and there will be a larger range of elasticity values for which the optimum with outside goods gives less product differentiation than in the paradigm case.

Finally, it is worth noting the effect of the parameter $m$ on the degree of product differentiation. Differentiation of Eq. (4.27) gives

$$\frac{\partial G}{\partial m} = -\sigma(\sigma - 2)\phi. \tag{4.38}$$

This implies that $G$ increases with $m$ when $\sigma$ is in the range $0 < \sigma < \sigma_0$ and decreases with $m$ when $\sigma > \sigma_0$. That is, the *divergence* between the degree of product differentiation with outside goods and in the paradigm case diminishes with $m$, as shown in Figure 4.2. This is consistent with the fact that as $m \to 1$, the outside-goods case and the paradigm case become essentially the same since, although there may be potential substitutability with outside goods, these goods are not available.

## 4.9 Second- and Third-Best Solutions

The inherent problems associated with fully compensated solutions are of precisely the same kind in the economy with outside goods as they are in the paradigm case, and therefore need not be repeated here. For the same reasons as in the paradigm case, it is appropriate to discuss second-best solutions in which compensation is ruled out

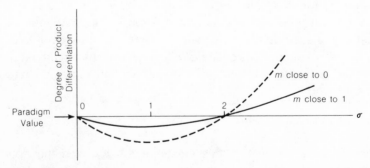

**Figure 4.2.** Effect of relative group importance ($m$) on the optimum degree of product differentiation.

by some constraint such as equal distribution of goods over the spectrum, and thus in which arbitrarily set welfare distributions cannot necessarily be attained.

Suppose that the constraint is that there should be manifest equality in distribution for political reasons. That is, there must be equality in some observable physical sense and not only in unobservable welfare, even if the distributing authority were omniscient in this respect. In the paradigm case, individuals receive only one good, and thus equality in observable distribution means the same quantity of that good for all. In the present case, there are both group goods and outside goods, and manifest equality of distribution might be considered to have been achieved under at least two different distribution systems:

1. Each individual receives the same quantities of both his best available good and the outside good as every other individual.
2. Individuals can choose their preferred mix of inside and outside goods, but the total resource value of the mixtures must be the same for all. This is equivalent to an equal distribution of money incomes when all goods are sold at prices proportional to marginal resource costs.

If the elasticity of substitution between group goods and outside goods is unity, all consumers will choose group goods and outside goods in the same proportions when given that choice, and thus the solutions for uniform physical distribution of both goods and uniform money incomes with free choice will coincide when each is devised optimally.

If the elasticity of substitution is not unity, however, the optimal mix of inside and outside goods will vary with the distance of the individual's best available group good from his most-preferred specification. In this case, it is obvious that a more uniform distribution of welfare can be achieved from the same resources by uniform money incomes and free choice than by uniform physical distribution of goods. The uniform-money-income constraint can be regarded as leading to a *second-best* solution, uniform physical distribution to a *third-best* solution.

As in the paradigm case, equity in welfare terms can be achieved (with either distribution scheme) by infinite product differentiation at the cost of maximal resource use.

The second-best criterion to be used here will be essentially the same as in the paradigm case. That is, the target will be average per capita welfare based on a utilitarian social welfare function, and the second-best solution will be that which minimizes resource use per capita when the distribution scheme is one that distributes equal resource entitlements (income) but permits the individuals to choose their optimal mix of inside and outside goods at marginal resource cost prices.

Formal analysis will be confined to the case of unit elasticity of substitution, where the second- and third-best solutions coincide because all individuals will consume the inside and outside goods in the same proportion even when permitted to choose those proportions. When $\sigma = 1$, the welfare function takes on the Cobb-Douglas form,

$$w = A \left(\frac{q}{h}\right)^a y^{1-a}.$$

Now it is well known that the proportions of expenditures on the two goods when the utility function is of this form are constant and given by $a$ and $1 - a$. Thus $a$ can be identified with the parameter $m$, and the welfare function can be written as

$$w = A h^{-m} q^m y^{1-m}. \tag{4.39}$$

If $k$ is the income and $p$ is the price ratio of group to outside goods, then $q = mk/p$ and $y = (1 - m)k$, so that the above can be rewritten as

$$w = h^{-m} A k p^{-1} m^m (1 - m)^{1-m}. \tag{4.40}$$

Everything on the right-hand side except the factor $h^{-m}$ is the same for all individuals, so that welfare considered as a function of $u$, the distance of the individual from the available good, is proportional to $(h(u))^{-m}$. If $k$ is a variable, then everyone's welfare is proportional to $k$, and individual welfare can be taken to be proportional to $h^{-m}k$.

Write $z = h^{-m}$ so that $e_z = -me_h$, and associate with $z$ its integral $Z$ and the cumulative elasticity $e_z = uz/Z$. The average welfare level over a segment of width 2Δ can then be shown to be $kZ/\Delta$. Since this is to be held at a constant target level, the required variation in $k$ as $\Delta$ varies is given by

$$\frac{dk}{d\Delta} = \frac{k}{\Delta}(1 - e_z).$$ (4.41)

Let us suppose that income is measured in terms of the outside good as numeraire, with the price of the group goods (all group goods will have the same price in the uniform model) given by $p$ in terms of the outside good. Over a segment of width 2Δ, the required quantities of the group good (2Q) and the outside good (2Y) will be given by

$$2Q = \frac{2mk\Delta}{p}$$ (4.42a)

and

$$2Y = 2(1 - m)k\Delta.$$ (4.42b)

Thus the per capita resources required to achieve the target average per capita welfare corresponding to income level $k$ will be given by

$$v = \frac{1}{2\Delta} F\left(\frac{2mk\Delta}{p}\right) + \frac{(1 - m)k}{\Delta} \bar{F}'.$$ (4.43)

By differentiating with respect to $\Delta$, substituting for $dk/d\Delta$ (from above) and also for $\theta = pF/2mkF'\Delta$, and noting that prices must be proportional to marginal resource costs so that $p = F'/\bar{F}'$, the following equation is obtained

$$\frac{dv}{d\Delta} = \frac{kF'}{p\Delta}[(1 - e_z) - m(\theta - 1)].$$ (4.44)

Thus the condition for the second-best solution with unit elasticity of substitution is given by

$$1 - e_z = m(\theta - 1)$$ (4.45a)

or

$$\frac{1}{m}(1 - e_z) + 1 = \theta.$$ (4.45b)

Note that when $m = 1$, the condition given by Eq. (4.45a) becomes identical with the condition given by Eq. (3.26) for the second best in the paradigm case, as it should.

It is important to relate the second-best solution to the full optimum. Since $e_z = -me_h$, Lemma 3a (Appendix B) gives

$$e_z - 1 = -m(e_H - 1) + m(1 + m)\phi, \tag{4.46}$$

where $\phi$ is a positive function of $u$ which is substantially independent of $m$. Denote the left-hand side of Eq. (4.45b) by $G_z$, so that the optimum has the form $G_z = 0$. Then, by Eq. (4.46),

$$G_Z = e_H - (1 + m)\phi. \tag{4.47}$$

If $G$ denotes the weighted sum of the elasticities as it appears in the regular optimum condition (Eq. 4.15b) then, from Eq. (4.36), when $\sigma = 1$,

$$G = e_H - (1 - m)\phi, \tag{4.48}$$

where, for the same value of $u$ (or $\Delta$), the values of $e_H$ and $\phi$ are identical with those in Eq. (4.47). From Eqs. (4.47) and (4.48),

$$G - G_Z = 2m\phi. \tag{4.49}$$

Since $\phi$ is positive, $G > G_z$ and $G \to G_z$ as $m \to 0$. Denote, as usual, the segment half-width at the full optimum by $\Delta^*$ and that at the second best by $\Delta$. Then, from the second-best condition (Eq. 4.45b) and the full optimum condition (Eq. 4.15b), the inequality $G > G_z$ implies that

$$G_Z(\Delta^*) < G(\Delta^*) = \theta = G_Z(\Delta) \tag{4.50}$$

if $\theta$ is constant.

By inspection of Eq. (4.45b) and noting that $Z$ is concave so that $e_z' < 0$, it is obvious that $G_z$ is an increasing function of its argument, so that Eq. (4.50) implies that $\Delta > \Delta^*$. Thus the relationship between the second-best and full optimum solutions can be stated as follows:

1. The degree of product differentiation at the second-best solution is less than at the full optimum for $\sigma = 1$, the value at which the full optimum gives the lowest degree of product differentiation.

2. The less the importance of the group in the total economy (measured by the parameter $m$), the closer the second-best solution to

the full optimum, the difference between the two becoming negligible when the group is very small relative to the economy as a whole.

The second statement has obvious importance for policy-making.

If the straight utilitarian welfare function of the form $W = \int w\, du$, used in the analysis above, is replaced by a concave function of the form $W = \int w^{\beta}\, du$, where $\beta \leq 1$, it is easily seen that the second-best solution is precisely as before, except that $m$ is everywhere replaced by $\beta m$. The factor $\beta$ does not appear, however, in the full optimum condition, and it can be shown that Eq. (4.49) is replaced by

$$G - G_z = (1 + \beta)m\phi. \tag{4.51}$$

Thus the second-best solution becomes closer to the full optimum as $\beta$ becomes smaller ($W$ becomes more concave) but always remains quite distinct unless $m \to 0$. Concavity does not, therefore, affect the general pattern to any important extent.

The conclusions reached above apply for the particular case of unit elasticity of substitution. It can be shown, however, that if consumers have identical incomes and choose their optimal compensation mix at the same marginal cost ratio, the behavior is the same as under regular market demand conditions, analyzed in detail in Chapter 5. Borrowing ahead from that chapter, it follows directly from Eq. (5.34) that

$$e_w = -e_h + \frac{1}{1 - \sigma} e\mu,$$

where $e_w$ is the elasticity of welfare with respect to $u$ when all consumers have identical incomes, and thus corresponds to $e_z$ as used above. By substituting for $e_\mu$ from Eq. (5.30b), it can be shown that

$$e_z = -\mu e_h.$$

This is the same form as in the unit-elasticity-of-substitution case, except that $\mu$, which varies with $u$, replaces the constant $m$. Note that $\sigma$ does not appear explicitly, although it does affect the path of $\mu$. Since it is assumed that the average proportion of income spent on group goods, $m$, is constant as $\sigma$ varies, the "average" value of $\mu$ is constant, and thus the replacement of $e_z = -me_h$ by $e_z = -\mu e_h$ makes only a small change in the value of $e_z$ if the segments are small. Thus the second-best solution with a value of $\sigma$ other than unity will not differ greatly from the solution when $\sigma = 1$.

Since the second-best solution gives less product differentiation than the full optimum when $\sigma = 1$ and varies little with $\sigma$ and since the full optimum gives greater product differentiation for values of $\sigma$ other than unity, it would appear that the second-best solution gives less product differentiation than the full optimum at all values of $\sigma$.

## 4.10 Indivisible Goods

In an economy having the structure of the paradigm case, with no outside goods, the presence of indivisibilities will prevent the attainment of arbitrary target welfare levels for consumers in general (and a uniform welfare distribution in particular), since inside compensation is not possible and outside compensation not available. Policy concerning product differentiation then involves a direct trade-off between equity and efficiency, and the analysis is basically the same as the second-best solution, except that the constraint is structural rather than imposed.

The same problem does not arise when there are outside goods, provided the elasticity of substitution between group goods and outside goods is not zero. In this case, those consumers receiving the single fixed unit of a good which is not their most-preferred good can be compensated with additional outside goods. Thus any welfare distribution can be attained, including a uniform welfare distribution, and there is an efficiency problem to be solved. The optimum problem is to compensate with outside goods and find the degree of product differentiation in the group that minimizes resource use overall.

The unit size of the indivisible good will be denoted by $q_o$. Then the most-preferred-good equivalent for a consumer whose most-preferred good is distance $u$ in specification from the available good is given by $q_o/h(u)$. With a uniform preference spectrum and uniform welfare density, the required quantity of outside good, $y$, for consumers at distance $u$ from the available good is then given by

$$w \left[ \frac{q_o}{h(u)}, y(u) \right] = \bar{w}. \tag{4.52}$$

The optimizing step required to determine $y(u)$ in the divisible case is absent here since compensation must necessarily be in outside goods only, and thus there is no optimal compensation mix to be determined. (It is assumed that the levels and required maximum compensation are such that it will never be optimal to give a consumer two units of the indivisible good rather than compensate entirely in outside goods.)

Differentiating the condition that $w$ be constant with respect to $u$ gives

$$y'(u) = \frac{w_1 q_0}{w_2 h(u)} \frac{h'(u)}{h(u)} .$$ (4.53)

It is reasonable to assume that the unit size, $q_0$, is such that one unit is the exact optimal quantity for some consumers.[6] For these consumers,

$$\frac{\partial W/\partial q}{\partial W/\partial y} = \frac{W_1}{W_2 h} = \frac{F'}{\bar{F}'} ,$$ (4.54)

where $F'$ and $\bar{F}'$ are the marginal resource costs for the group and outside goods, respectively. For these particular consumers, the expression $w_1 q_0 / w_2 hy$ gives the ratio of the values, at marginal resource cost shadow prices, of the group and outside goods supplied to them. These are the only consumers, of course, for whom the marginal resource costs are the true shadow prices. Thus for the consumers in question, if $\mu$ denotes the shadow price value of group goods as a proportion of the shadow price value of all goods,

$$q = q_0 \quad \text{and thus} \quad e_q = 1,$$ (4.55a)

$$e_y = \frac{\mu}{1 - \mu} e_h .$$ (4.55b)

If the goods were divisible, the expressions for $e_q$ and $e_y$ would be given by Eq. (4.21):

$$e_q = [1 - (1 - \mu)\sigma] e_h$$

$$e_y = \mu \sigma e_h .$$

---

6. If the technology requires a single size, but does not determine the exact size, there is a second optimum problem to determine $q_0$. This problem, which is not considered here, is solved *after* determining the optimum degree of product differentiation and the optimum outside compensation as functions of an arbitrary $q_0$.

Now if $\sigma$ had the particular value $\sigma = 1/(1 - \mu)$, these would give exactly the same two relationships as those given for the special consumers in the indivisible case.

Thus for consumers whose most-preferred good differs from the available good by a specification distance $\bar{u}$ such that the unit quantity of the available good is also the optimal quantity, the expressions determining $q$ and $y$ are the same as in the divisible case when the elasticity of substitution has the particular value $\sigma = 1/(1 - \mu)$. The same identity in the relationships will not hold for other consumers. However, if the special consumers are "average," in the sense that the proportion of the group good to the total for them (given by the parameter $\mu$) is the mean proportion of the group good to the total (denoted by $m$) and if the elasticity of substitution has the value $\sigma = 1/(1 - m)$, then the behavior of the functions $q$ and $y$ over all consumers can be considered to be, on the average, very close in the divisible and indivisible cases.

That is, the optimal degree of product differentiation with indivisible goods will be very close to that for divisible goods in the particular case for which $\sigma = 1/(1 - m)$, and, for convenience, will be assumed to be the same. Since the optimum with indivisible goods is independent of $\sigma$, whereas that for divisible goods varies with $\sigma$ in a well-defined way which has been already established, the relationships between the two optima at different elasticity values can be mapped out.

If $m = \frac{1}{2}$, then $1/m = 1/(1 - m) = \sigma_o = 2$, and, from the earlier results, the degree of product differentiation with divisible goods is equal to the paradigm value at $\sigma = 2$, greater than this value for $\sigma > 2$, and less than this value for $\sigma < 2$. The degree of product differentiation with indivisible goods is the same as that with divisible goods at $\sigma = 2$ in this case, and thus indivisibilities lead unambiguously to reduced product differentiation when $\sigma > 2$ and increased product differentiation when $\sigma < 2$, as compared to divisible goods.

When $m \neq 1 - m$, the results are less clear-cut. If $m > \frac{1}{2}$, so that $1/(1 - m) > 1/m$, then $1/(1 - m) > 2$. Thus the degree of product differentiation with indivisibilities corresponds to that at $\sigma = 1/(1 - m) > 2$ with divisible goods and so is greater than the paradigm value. As a result, the effect of indivisibilities is certainly to increase the degree of product differentiation at low elasticities ($\sigma < 2$) and to decrease it at very high elasticities, but there is a region for which the direction of the effect is uncertain. If $m < \frac{1}{2}$, then the effect of indivisibilities is certainly to decrease product differentiation at all elasticities greater than 2, and for elasticities near unity, but to leave the effect uncertain when elasticities are either very low or less than but close to 2.

Indivisibilities may increase or decrease the degree of product differentiation at the optimum, therefore, depending on the elasticity of substitution. In general, the degree of product differentiation will be lowered at high elasticities and increased at elasticities near unity, with the effect in the remaining ranges being uncertain.

The presence of indivisibilities requires more resources to attain given welfare targets than would be the case in their absence, owing to the inability to optimize the compensation mix. In a sense, the solution with indivisibilities is a kind of second best, but with a structural constraint rather than an imposed one. The solution is not, however, the same as for the second-best solution with a "manifest equity" constraint, because the constraint properties are quite different. In the indivisibilities analysis, the group good is distributed uniformly, but the outside good is adjusted to give full compensation, whereas in the second-best solution given here, full compensation is not possible. It is possible, however, to conceive of a situation in which the imposed constraint in the second-best could be of the same kind as the structural constraint in the indivisibility case, namely, that the group good is to be distributed uniformly but that full outside compensation is possible. "Manifest equity" would be confined to the group good (schooling, for example), and compensation would be permissible if paid in outside goods only. In these circumstances, the solution would be of the same kind as in the indivisibilities case.

# ⬚⬚◌ Chapter 5

# Market Demand

## 5.1 Introduction

THIS IS A technical chapter, the purpose of which is to set out the properties of market demand for an economy with properties similar to those assumed in the discussion of optimal product differentiation. It is a necessary preliminary to the chapters which follow, in which the structures of market equilibria are derived under conditions of variable product specification, diversity of preferences, and economies of scale.

The demand for products within a group will obviously depend on prices, incomes, and the properties of substitution with respect to outside goods. Analysis of these factors, although modified for the rather specific form assumed for the utility function, is conventional enough. But the demand for group products also depends on their specifications and on the specifications of other goods in the group, and the analysis of the effects of specification and differences in specification on demand necessarily breaks new ground.

The demand properties will be synthesized from the assumed properties of individual utility or welfare functions and alternate assumptions as to the distribution of incomes. It is obviously impossible simply to assert, "let the demand function possess such and such properties." In fact, it will become apparent that the demand curves

**140**

*cannot* be either linear[1] or of constant elasticity,[2] two assumptions widely made in the analysis of market behavior and which lead to special conclusions as to the properties of market equilibrium, unless the distribution of income over the consumer spectrum is tailored precisely to generate those properties.

## 5.2 The Structure of Demand

The basic context within which market demand will be analyzed will be essentially the same as that within which the conditions for socially optimal product differentiation were established. That is, it is assumed that there is an infinite spectrum of potential products, of which only a finite number are actually available, that consumer preferences vary continuously over the spectrum (in the sense that every point on the spectrum corresponds to the most-preferred good of some individuals), and that, in general, there exist alternatives to goods within the group which can be simplified to a single aggregate outside good. Uniformity of the preference spectrum will be assumed to hold in the same sense as before, namely, that the behavior of an individual is determined fully by (a) parameters and variables common to all individuals and (b) the distance, in terms of an appropriate measure, between the specification of the individual's most-preferred good and the specification of the available good.

The central analysis will be for a consumption technology characterized by group goods which are divisible but noncombinable, as in the optimal analysis, so that an individual buys only one of the goods from the group. This will later be modified to take account of indivisibility.

As in conventional demand theory, each individual makes de-

1. As, for example, in Negishi's well-known general equilibrium analysis of monopolistic competition. Negishi's demand curves are, however, "perceived" demand curves and not necessarily the true curves (see Negishi, 1960).

2. But demand for the group as a whole may have constant elasticity, in which case the demand curve for a monopolist having control of all the group goods would be of the constant elasticity kind (see Chapter 9).

cisions on the basis of his or her income and the prices of the goods—parameters which he or she accepts as exogenous—and adjusts market choices as to what, and how much, to buy in order to maximize personal welfare or utility, subject to the constraints. In addition, the individual here takes into account the specifications of the available group goods. The individual is assumed to be fully informed as to the relevant parameters—prices, income, and specifications—and to know his or her own preferences.[3]

The individual faces a two-stage decision process:

1. *Which?*—that is, which of the group goods to buy.

2. *How Much?*—that is, how to divide expenditures between the chosen group good and the outside good.

It is the first of these stages which is special to the present analysis. Once the individual has decided which of the group goods to buy, the division of expenditure between this and the outside good is determined in essentially the same way as in conventional demand theory, modified by some simplifying features of the model being used here. Since it is assumed throughout this work that the group goods share no characteristics with the outside good, the choice between group goods is quite independent of the relative quantities of group goods and outside goods actually consumed, and thus the *which?* decision is independent of, and occurs before, the *how much?* decision.

Corresponding to the two-stage decision by the individual is a two-part determination of the aggregate market demand for a particular good:

1. *The market width*—that is, what portion of the total spectrum of consumers will buy this good rather than some other good.

2. *The market depth*—that is, how much of the good will be purchased, on average, by those consumers who buy it.

Since the individual decisions are separable, the market width can be determined separately from the market depth.

The purpose of demand theory is not primarily to set up conditions which show how much of each good will be purchased but to

---

3. Demand under conditions of imperfect information is discussed in Chapter 8.

use the conditions to show how the quantities will change in response to changes in the market variables such as prices and incomes—to which must be added changes in specifications in this analysis. It will be shown that the decision as to which group good to purchase, and thus the determination of market width, depends only on prices of group goods *relative to each other* and on specifications, and not at all on incomes or prices of group goods relative to outside goods. On the other hand, decisions as to how much to buy depend only on incomes and the prices of group goods *relative to outside goods* and not directly on the prices of group goods relative to each other. Specifications have some effect on the relative quantities of group goods and outside goods, however.

The effect of price changes on the quantity of a group good that will be purchased is more complex than in ordinary demand theory, because of the switching from one group good to another. It is convenient to distinguish four separate elements in the overall effect:

1. *An inside-substitution effect*. Resulting from the change in market width due to a change in the price of the good relative to adjacent group goods. It will occur whatever the changes (or lack of them) in real incomes and whether or not the price of the good changes relative to that of the outside good.

2. *A specification effect*. All consumers pay the same price for the good, but consumers at the market fringe derive less welfare per dollar than those near the center, because of the difference in specification between the available good and their most-preferred good. A change in the market width of itself, therefore, changes the average real incomes of consumers in the market (unless there is compensation for specification) and leads to changes in the quantities purchased.

3. *An outside-substitution effect*. The pure effect of a change in the relative price of the group good as compared with the outside good on the quantity of the group good purchased.

4. *An income effect*. The effect of the real income change (if any) due to the change in the price of the good when income is not adjusted to compensate.

The two last effects, the outside-substitution effect and the income effect, are essentially the same as in traditional demand theory. They will have counterparts in the demand for the outside good itself.

The first two effects are essentially internal to the group, although the specification effect has some influence on the demand for the outside good.

Perhaps the best way to appreciate the significance of the various effects is to note the circumstances under which each would vanish. The inside-substitution effect vanishes if the relative prices of group goods do not change, for example, if the prices of all group goods were raised in the same proportion. If the price of the outside good remained the same, there would then be outside-substitution effects, but no inside-substitution effects. On the other hand, if the price of one of the group goods were increased in the same proportion as the outside price while other group prices remained fixed, there would be no outside-substitution effect for that good (but there would be for other group goods), although there would be an inside-substitution effect. The income effect would vanish if consumers were given a sufficient change in their money incomes to enable them to attain the same utility level after the price change as before.

The specification effect is more complex. It would certainly vanish if there were infinite product differentiation such that all consumers could buy their most-preferred good. It would also vanish if group goods were perfect substitutes for each other, so that there was no loss of real income owing to the specification of the good actually available. These cases are extreme and of no real interest. In the succeeding analysis, the specification effect is defined as that effect which vanishes when individuals are fully compensated for not having their most-preferred good available—the type of compensation on which the optimum analysis was based.

In conventional demand theory, it is usual to consider price changes within two contexts, *compensated* demand (a context in which income is adjusted to make the income effect vanish) and *uncompensated* demand (in which money income is held constant). In the product-differentiation model, there are two forms of compensation: compensation for specification (as in the optimum analysis), which implies an adjustment of income based on the difference in specification between most-preferred and available goods; and price compensation, in which (as in conventional analysis) the income adjustment depends on the price change. Thus it is necessary to specify clearly what form of compensation is implicit in a compensated demand function. The term *fully compensated* will be used to mean that there is compensation for both price and specification, so that all individuals remain at the same welfare level as specifications or prices change.

The demand analysis that follows is not in the most general form, but is based on structural simplifications that permit the effect of various aspects of the system to be clearly seen. As in the optimum analysis, a uniform distribution of real income (welfare) is assumed when demand is compensated, and a uniform distribution of nominal income is assumed when demand is uncompensated. Relationships with outside goods are parameterized through the elasticity of substitution and the relative importance of the group by using a constant-elasticity-of-substitution form of the uniform utility function, as in the optimum analysis with outside goods.

## 5.3 Market Width

The market width is determined by examining the decision of the individuals as to which good they should choose from the group, only one good being chosen by each individual since the goods are assumed to be noncombinable. The relevant information for the individual consists of the specifications and prices of the various goods, and it will be assumed that the spectrum of goods is unidimensional, as in a group defined by two characteristics.

Consider a part of the spectrum in which there are two[4] adjacent available goods, the $j$th and $(j + 1)$th, with specifications given by parameters $b_j$ and $b_{j+1} (> b_j)$. Now consider an individual whose most-preferred good has specification $x$ in the range $b_{j+1} > x > b_j$. Which good will the individual choose if the prices of the goods are $P_j$ and $P_{j+1}$, respectively? (Assume he or she will choose one of these two goods.)

---

4. The description as given is for a linear spectrum (two characteristics) in which each good has two goods adjacent to it. For more than two characteristics, which gives a spectrum in two or more dimensions, the possible number of adjacent goods rises rapidly with the dimensionality. See Archibald and Rosenbluth (1975).

From the properties of the compensating function, one unit of the $j$th good is equivalent, for this individual, to $1/h(x - b_j)$ units of the unavailable most-preferred good, whereas one unit of the $(j + 1)$th good is equivalent to $1/h(b_{j+1} - x)$ units of the most-preferred good. Thus, for a dollar spent on good $j$, the consumer obtains the equivalent of $1/P_j h(x - b_j)$ units of most-preferred good, and for a dollar spent on good $(j + 1)$, the consumer obtains a "most-preferred-good equivalent" of $1/P_{j+1} h(b_{j+1} - x)$ units. Thus the individual will choose the $j$th or $(j + 1)$th good according to whether $1/P_j h(x - b_j)$ is greater or less than $1/P_{j+1} h(b_{j+1} - x)$.

Since the preference spectrum and the compensating function are continuous, there will be some consumer whose most-preferred-good specification, $\bar{x}$, is such that he or she is indifferent between buying good $j$ or good $j + 1$ at those prices. This consumer is the *dividing consumer* for goods $j$ and $j + 1$ at prices $P_j$ and $P_{j+1}$, and the corresponding value of $\bar{x}$ is given by the *dividing condition*:

$$P_j h(\bar{x} - b_j) = P_{j+1} h(b_{j+1} - \bar{x}). \qquad (5.1)$$

From the uniformity properties, it follows immediately that any consumer at $x$ such that $\bar{x} > x \geqq b_j$ will also buy good $j$ and any consumer at $x$ such that $b_{j+1} \geqq x > \bar{x}$ will buy good $j + 1$. Thus the location of the dividing consumer gives the point in the spectrum which constitutes the common boundary between the market for the $j$th good and for the $(j + 1)$th good. The market for the $j$th good will be fully defined when the boundary between it and the $(j - 1)$th good (point $\underline{x}$) is determined in a similar way by the lower dividing condition. Obviously, this market is a continuous closed segment of the spectrum with $\bar{x}$ and $\underline{x}$ as boundary points.

Note that the dividing conditions, and thus the width of the market for the $j$th good, depend only on the following factors:

1. the price of the good relative to those of the two adjacent goods;

2. the specification of the good relative to the specifications of the two adjacent goods; and

3. the properties of the compensating function.

Once the good has been chosen, the quantities of the good that individuals purchase, which determine the depth of the market, play no part in determining the width of the market, nor do the prices or specifications of goods which are not the *adjacent* goods to good $j$—unless the prices of adjacent goods are so high relative to the prices of more-distant goods that consumers who do not buy good $j$ itself will buy good $j + 2$, for example, in preference to good $j + 1$. In this case, good $j + 1$ is effectively priced out of the market, and good $j + 2$ becomes the relevant adjacent good to good $j$.

Note that the upper and lower market boundaries are determined separately and independently. As far as inside effects are concerned, the market for good $j$ consists of two separate half-markets, one determined by the relationship of the price and specification of the good to those of the upper adjacent good ($j + 1$) and the other by the relationship of these factors to those of the lower adjacent good ($j - 1$). In many important contexts, the market for a good will be *symmetric*, with the relative price and differences in specification being the same with respect to each of the adjacent goods, but the two half-markets are, in principle, quite separate. With a multidimensional spectrum there will, of course, be more complex relationships with other goods in the spectrum, but the special relationship between adjacent portions of the markets for two goods will remain.[5]

## 5.4 Changes in Market Width

Since the market width depends on relative prices and specifications of a particular good as compared with those of the upper and lower adjacent goods, it will be affected by a change in any one of the six variables $P_{j-1}$, $P_j$, $P_{j+1}$, $b_{j-1}$, $b_j$, or $b_{j+1}$. Since the half-markets are independent,[6] it is sufficient to concentrate on one of these at a time, and since the dividing condition depends only on relative prices, it

5. In the multidimensional case, each consumer faces a sequential decision process which ends with a final choice between two goods. Suppose good A has $k$ goods adjacent to it. Then a consumer who finally chooses A must first decide which of the $k$ adjacent goods he would choose if he did not choose A and then decide between this good and A on the same principles as given in the analysis.

6. In the multidimensional analysis there will be more than two subdivisions of the total market, and these will not be as firmly separated from each other as in the linear spectrum case.

is sufficient to consider changes in $P_j$ with prices of adjacent goods constant. Furthermore, owing to the uniformity assumption, it is only the differences in specification between adjacent goods which count, so that it is sufficient to consider changes in $b_j$ with the specifications of adjacent goods constant.

Concentrating on the upper market boundary, consider first the effect of a change in $P_j$ on the position of this boundary. The boundary is defined by the upper dividing condition,

$$P_j h(\bar{x} - b_j) = P_{j+1} h(b_{j+1} - \bar{x}),$$

and the effect of $P_j$ is found by differentiating through this condition. Before doing so, it is convenient to change the notation somewhat. By writing $2\bar{\Delta} = b_{j+1} - b_j$ and $\bar{u} = \bar{x} - b_j$, the dividing condition appears in the form

$$P_j h(\bar{u}) = P_{j+1} h(2\bar{\Delta} - \bar{u}), \tag{5.2}$$

where $2\bar{\Delta}$ is the distance between the specifications of the $j$th and $(j + 1)$th goods and $\bar{u}$ is the distance of the upper market boundary from the specification of good $j$ itself. Because of uniformity of the spectrum, all functions depend only on these differences between points on the spectrum and not on absolute locations. The bars on the variables will now be dropped since they are no longer necessary for identification.

From Eq. (5.2),

$$\ln h(u) - \ln h(2\Delta - u) = \ln P_{j+1} - \ln P_j,$$

so that, if $P_{j+1}$ remains constant,

$$\frac{du}{d(\ln P_j)} = -[\underline{h}'(u) + \underline{h}'(2\Delta - u)]^{-1}, \tag{5.3}$$

where the notation $\underline{h}(x)$ is used for $\ln h(x)$ and $\underline{h}'(x) = d(\ln h)/dx = h'/h$.

If the elasticity of the half-market width with respect to price is denoted by $s(\Delta, u)$, then

$$s(\Delta, u) = -\frac{du}{u \, d(\ln P_j)} \tag{5.4}$$

$$= [u \, \underline{h}'(u) + u \, \underline{h}'(2\Delta - u)]^{-1}. \tag{5.5}$$

This last expression can be written in terms of the elasticity of compensation $e_h(u)$, since $e_h(u) = u\,d[\ln h(u)]/du = u\underline{h}'(u)$, to give

$$s(\Delta, u) = \left[ e_h(u) + \frac{u}{2\Delta - u} e_h(2\Delta - u) \right]^{-1}. \tag{5.6}$$

The expression $s(\Delta, u)$ plays a very important part in the properties of demand. It is the elasticity of market width with respect to price and thus expresses the degree of shift between one good and another when the relative prices of the two goods change. Note that $s(\Delta, u)$ is determined by the values of $\Delta$ and $u$ and the properties of the compensating function only. If individuals are insensitive to specification, then $h(u) = 1$ for all $u$, $e_h(u) = 0$ everywhere, and $s(\Delta, u)$ is infinite for all $\Delta$ and $u$, which expresses the fact that all goods are perfect substitutes and the consumers will always switch to the cheapest. On the other hand, if goods of different specifications have no substitutability, so that $e_h(u)$ is infinite for all $u > 0$, then $s(\Delta, u)$ is zero for all $\Delta$ and all $u$.

Although $s(\Delta, u)$ expresses substitution properties between goods in the group, it is not itself the elasticity of substitution between adjacent goods. The elasticity of substitution gives the change in the relative quantities of the two goods as a result of changes in their relative prices and depends on the quantities of the goods per unit of market width (the market depth) as well as on the widths of the markets. The elasticity of substitution is the product of the elasticity $s(\Delta, u)$ and another elasticity expressing market depth.

The position of the market boundaries for the $j$th good are obviously affected by a change in the specification of the good as well as by a change in its price. A shift in the specification by an amount $\delta b_j$ will reduce the spacing between that good and one of the adjacent goods by $\delta b_j$, so that $\Delta$ (the half-spacing) is reduced by $\frac{1}{2}\delta b_j$. The spacing between the $j$th good and the other adjacent good will be increased by a like amount.

Taking logs in Eq. (5.2) and noting that prices are held constant gives

$$\ln h(u) - \ln h(2\Delta - u) = \text{constant}.$$

Variations in $b_j$ affect $\Delta$, so that $u$ must vary to satisfy the equation.

It is easily found that

$$\frac{\partial u}{\partial b_j} = \pm \frac{\underline{h}'(2\Delta - u)}{\underline{h}'(u) + \underline{h}'(2\Delta - u)} \tag{5.7}$$

$$= \pm su(\Delta, u)\underline{h}'(2\Delta - u), \tag{5.8}$$

where the plus sign refers to the change in the boundary toward which the specification has moved and the minus sign refers to the other boundary.

## 5.5 The Market-Width Elasticity

The elasticity $s(\Delta, u)$, which was introduced in the previous section, is the elasticity of market width with respect to price and will appear in all demand expressions except those in which the relative prices of goods within the group remain constant. Because of its importance, it is useful to summarize its properties before proceeding further.

From inspection of Eq. (5.5), it is obvious that:

1.   the properties of $s(\Delta, u)$ depend only on the properties of the compensating function and are independent of other parameters of the system and also independent of the distribution of consumers and incomes over the spectrum, provided the distribution remains continuous.

2.   $s(\Delta, u) > 0$ for all $\Delta$ and $u$, provided $h'$ remains finite.

3.   $s(\Delta, 0)$ is infinite for all $\Delta$.

When $u = \Delta$, $2\Delta - u = \Delta$, so that (from Eqs. 5.5 and 5.6):

4.   $s(\Delta, \Delta) = \frac{1}{2}\Delta \underline{h}'(\Delta) = \frac{1}{2}e_h(\Delta)$. $\tag{5.9}$

Then, taking derivatives gives:

5.   $\dfrac{\partial s(\Delta, u)}{\partial \Delta} = -2s^2 u \underline{h}''(2\Delta - u)$. $\tag{5.10}$

The value of this function is less than zero, at least for sufficiently small $\Delta$, since $\underline{h}''[= (hh' - h'^2)/h^2]$ is certainly positive near the origin (see Appendix A).

6.   $\dfrac{\partial s(\Delta, u)}{\partial u} = -s^2\{[\underline{h}'(u) + \underline{h}'(2\Delta - u)]$

$$+ u[\underline{h}''(u) - \underline{h}''(2\Delta - u)]\}. \tag{5.11}$$

The sign of $\partial s/\partial u$ is obviously indeterminate, in general, but when $u = \Delta$, $\underline{h}''(u) = \underline{h}''(2\Delta - u)$ and $\underline{h}'(u) = \underline{h}'(2\Delta - u)$, so that:

7. $\left[ \dfrac{\partial s(\Delta, u)}{\partial u} \right]_{u=\Delta} = -2s^2\underline{h}'(\Delta) < 0 \qquad \text{if } \Delta > 0.$     (5.12)

In general, $s(\Delta, u)$ is a function of two distances, the half-spacing between the goods and the width of the half-market. These two distances may happen to be equal, and will be equal when the prices of the adjacent goods are the same. An important situation in the analysis of succeeding chapters is that in which the prices of adjacent goods always remain equal (although the common price may change), so that $u = \Delta$. The function $s$ then becomes a function of the single variable $\Delta$ and will be written as $s^*(\Delta)$ when it is important to make the distinction. Then, from Eq. (5.9):

8. $s^*(\Delta) = s(\Delta, \Delta) = \frac{1}{2}e_h(\Delta).$     (5.13)

And the above function has as the derivative:

9. $s^{*\prime}(\Delta) = -2s^{*2}e_h{}'(\Delta).$     (5.14)

The value of the derivative is less than zero since $e_h{}'$ is taken to be positive for all $u > 0$ (see Appendix A or Chapter 2).

Note that the market-width elasticity is certainly greatest when the market width is smallest (property 3), and when the market boundary is at the midpoint between the specifications of the goods, the elasticity is certainly declining with increased market width. However, the relationship between the elasticity and market width, except at these special points, depends on the third-derivative properties of $h(u)$ and thus cannot be characterized in general. The elasticity declines as the spacing between goods increases, however, from properties 5 and 9.

## 5.6 Market Demand in the Paradigm Case

The paradigm case, in which the economy consists of the group only, with no outside goods, provides a useful introduction to the more general and realistic case in which outside goods are present. If there are no outside goods, the individual has essentially only one decision: which of the group goods to buy. This decision having been made, all the individual's income will then be spent on that good, and thus the quantity bought (which gives market depth) is determined by real income. Obviously, there can be no outside-substitution effect in this case, but by changing the contexts, the inside-substitution effect, the specification effect, and the income effect can all be identified.

Consider either half-market, for which the relevant adjacent good differs in specification from the good being considered by a distance $2\Delta$, and the boundary of which is at distance $u$ from the specification of the good. The total quantity of the good that will be demanded is given by

$$Q = \int_0^u q(v) \, dv, \tag{5.15}$$

where $q(v)$ is the quantity that will be purchased by those consumers with most-preferred good distant $v$ from the specification of the available good. The form of $q(v)$ will depend on the context and will be left general for the moment.

The effect of a price change on the demand for this good, when the price of the adjacent good remains fixed, is given by

$$\frac{\partial Q}{\partial \ln P} = q(u) \frac{\partial u}{\partial \ln P} + \int_0^u \frac{\partial q}{\partial \ln P} \, dv$$

$$= -q(u)s(\Delta, u)u + P \int_0^u \frac{\partial q}{\partial \underline{P}} \, dv, \tag{5.16}$$

from Eq. (5.4).

Elasticity of demand is defined as

$$E = -\frac{P}{Q} \frac{\partial Q}{\partial P} = -\frac{1}{Q} \frac{\partial Q}{\partial \ln P}. \tag{5.17}$$

Then, by using the notation $e_Q = uq/Q$, Eq. (5.16) becomes

$$E = se_Q - \frac{P}{Q} \int_0^u \frac{\partial q}{\partial P} \, dv, \tag{5.18}$$

where arguments have been dropped from the various functions since no confusion can arise.

There are four contexts in which elasticity can be measured, which correspond to the cases on which there is or is not compensation for specification and is or is not compensation for price. A "hat" will be used to indicate absence of compensation for specification, and the subscript "np" will indicate absence of compensation for price.

1. *Fully compensated demand.* In this context, individuals are fully compensated for both specification effects and price effects. Assuming uniformity of the welfare distribution, each consumer is given an income such that he or she can buy that quantity of the available good that will bring him or her to the uniform level. That is, the quantity for each individual will be that allocated to him or her in the optimum analysis of the paradigm case, $q_o h(v)$, where $h$ is the compensating function. In this case, $\partial q/\partial P$ is zero everywhere, and the elasticity properties of $q$ with respect to $u$ are those of the cumulated compensating function ($e_Q = e_H$), and thus

$$E = se_H. \tag{5.19}$$

Since demand is fully compensated and there are no outside goods, $se_H$ can be identified as the *inside-substitution effect*.

2. *Compensation for price only.* This is taken to be the context in which "real" income (the quantity of available good that can be purchased), rather than individual welfare, is uniform. The quantities purchased are invariant as to price, since individuals are compensated for price changes but are not compensated for the unavailability of their most-preferred goods. Since $q$ is constant at $q_o$, $\partial q/\partial P = 0$ and $q' = 0$, so that $e_Q = 1$. The elasticity of demand is then given by

$$\hat{E} = s$$

$$= se_H - s(e_H - 1). \tag{5.20}$$

Since $se_H$ has been identified as the inside-substitution effect, there is no outside-substitution effect, and there has been full compensation for price, the term

$$-s(e_H - 1)$$

can be identified as the *specification effect*. Since $e_H \geqq 1$, this is always nonpositive.

*3. Uncompensated demand.* In this context, all individuals receive the same money income, so that there is no compensation either for specification or for price changes. If the uniform money income is denoted by $c$, then $q = c/P$ and $\partial q/\partial P = -c/P^2$. Then $Q = \int_0^u q\, dv = cu/P$, and

$$-\frac{P}{Q}\int_0^u \frac{\partial q}{\partial P}\, dv = 1.$$

In this case, $q' = 0$, so that $e_Q = 1$ and thus

$$\hat{E}_{np} = s + 1$$

$$= se_H - s(e_H - 1) + 1. \tag{5.21}$$

The term "+ 1" at the end can now be identified as the *income effect* since all other nonzero effects have been accounted for.

*4. Demand compensated for specification only.* In this context, individuals receive money incomes which depend on their distance from the available good, so that all individuals can attain the same welfare level, although this level will change with price. The appropriate money income will obviously be given by $c = c_0 h(v)$, so that $q = c_0 h/P$. In this case, $q$ is proportional to $h$, so that the elasticity of the $q$ function (with respect to $v$) will be the same as that of the compensating function, and $e_Q = e_H$.
Also

$$Q = \int_0^u q(v)\, dv$$

$$= \frac{c_0}{P}\int_0^u h(v)\, dv$$

$$= \frac{c_0 H}{P},$$

and

$$\int_0^u \frac{\partial q}{\partial P}\, dv = -\frac{c_0}{P^2}\int_0^u h(v)\, dv$$

$$= -\frac{c_0 H}{P^2},$$

so that

$$E_{np} = se_H + 1. \tag{5.22}$$

In this case, as it should, the elasticity of demand is composed only of the inside-substitution effect and an income effect, with no specification effect.

The relationships between the elasticities in the four contexts can be seen by displaying them in tabular form, where the inside-substitution and specification effects have been combined:

|  | *Compensated for specification* | *Uncompensated for specification* |
|---|---|---|
| Compensated for price | $E = se_H$ | $\hat{E} = s$ |
| Uncompensated for price | $E_{np} = se_H + 1$ | $\hat{E}_{np} = s + 1$ |

Since $e_H > 1$ if $\Delta > 0$, it is immediately obvious that:

1.   if there is a compensation for price, the elasticity is higher if there is also compensation for specification than if there is no such compensation.

2.   if there is compensation for specification, the elasticity is higher if price is uncompensated than if it is compensated.

In other words, compensation for specification and compensation for price have opposite effects on the elasticity. The relationship between the fully compensated elasticity $E$ and the completely uncompensated elasticity $\hat{E}_{np}$ is not, therefore, directly apparent. However, it is shown later, in Chapter 7 (Section 7.7), that the inequality

$$se_H < 1 + s$$

holds when the market boundary is midway between the two goods (the adjacent goods have the same price), and the inequality can be expected to hold for some variation away from this point. Thus it will generally be true that $E < \hat{E}_{np}$, and this will certainly be so when the price of the good under examination is the same as that of the adjacent good.

The above elasticities, it should be noted, are for a half-market in one direction. The elasticity of demand over the whole market is the weighted average of the elasticities in the half-markets, with weights proportional to the proportions sold in each half. In a symmetric context, when the specification of the good is centered between the specifications of adjacent goods and the prices of the adjacent goods are the same (but not necessarily equal to the price of the good itself), then the half-markets are identical.

## 5.7 The Choice Between Inside and Outside Goods

Before proceeding to establish the demand relationships for a group good in the presence of outside goods, it is necessary to examine the properties of the individual's decision concerning the division of his or her income between the chosen group good and outside goods. As in traditional demand theory, this decision is presumed to be such as to maximize the individual's personal welfare, subject to a budget constraint in which income and prices are taken as fixed parameters at the time of decision.

As in the optimum analysis, it is highly desirable to simplify the relationships between the group and the outside goods to the minimum number of parameters, so that the effect of those relationships can most clearly be seen. For this reason, it is assumed that outside goods can be represented by a single aggregate outside good—identified, in the case of market demand, with money expenditure on goods outside the group—and that the individual welfare function can be well represented over the range of variations of the analysis by a function of the constant-elasticity-of-substitution kind, also as in the optimum analysis. It is assumed, as in Chapter 4, that the arguments of the welfare function are the *most-preferred-good equivalent* of available good $(q/h)$ and the quantity of aggregate outside good $y$.

If $f(x_1, x_2)$ is a function which is homogeneous of the first degree and possesses constant elasticity of substitution $\sigma$, it is well known that it has the functional form[7]

---

7. This form first appeared in the literature as the CES (Constant Elasticity of Substitution) production function, the properties of which were derived in Arrow, Chenery, Minhas, and Solow (1961). For a textbook treatment, see Henderson and Quandt (1971, Sections 3–6).

$$f(x_1, x_2) = [ax_1^{(\sigma-1)/\sigma} + (1-a)x_2^{(\sigma-1)/\sigma}]^{\sigma/(\sigma-1)},$$

where $a$ is a parameter representing the relative weights of the variables.

Thus, if it were homogeneous of the first degree, the welfare function would have the form

$$w\left(\frac{q}{h}, y\right) = [aq^{(\sigma-1)/\sigma}h^{(1-\sigma)/\sigma} + (1-a)y^{(\sigma-1)/\sigma}]^{\sigma/(\sigma-1)}. \quad (5.23)$$

The analysis in this chapter is unchanged if the function $w$, as given above, is replaced by $T(w)$, where $T$ is any positive, monotonically increasing function of $w$, but it is convenient to work with Eq. (5.23), which simplifies the arithmetic by avoiding the introduction of factors $T'$ which later cancel. Under the uniformity assumption, the same functional form will hold for all individuals, individuals differing only in their most-preferred goods and thus in the value of $h$ which appears in Eq. (5.23).

The outside good will be treated as the numeraire for price and income, so that the individual budget constraint has the form

$$Pq + y = I. \quad (5.24)$$

Although the income $I$ is fixed for an individual making a specific market decision, it may vary over individuals or with price in accordance with the type of compensation (if any) specified in a given context.

The individual will choose the quantities of the group and outside goods so as to maximize $w$, subject to the budget constraint, and thus his or her choice will satisfy the traditional condition that the marginal rate of substitution between the goods should equal the price ratio, or

$$\frac{\partial w/\partial q}{\partial w/\partial y} = P.$$

For the form of the welfare function given in Eq. (5.23) or any monotonic transform of this, the relationship becomes

$$\frac{a}{1-a} h^{(1/\sigma)-1}q^{-1/\sigma}y^{1/\sigma} = P. \quad (5.25)$$

Solving for the variables $q$ and $y$ between Eq. (5.25) and the budget-constraint equation (Eq. 5.24) gives the *individual demand functions* for $q$ and $y$

$$q = IP^{-1}(1 + Ah^{\sigma-1}P^{\sigma-1})^{-1}, \tag{5.26}$$

$$y = IAh^{\sigma-1}P^{\sigma-1}(1 + Ah^{\sigma-1}P^{\sigma-1})^{-1}, \tag{5.27}$$

where

$$A = \left(\frac{a}{1-a}\right)^{-\sigma}.$$

If $\mu(u,P)$ denotes the proportion of income spent on the group good at price $P$ by a consumer whose most-preferred good is at a distance $u$ from the available good, then

$$\mu(u, P) = \frac{Pq}{I} = (1 + Ah^{\sigma-1}P^{\sigma-1})^{-1}. \tag{5.28}$$

Since $q = \mu I/P$ and $y = (1 - \mu)I$, it is convenient to work initially with the properties of $\mu$, since $\mu$ and $I$ are independent because of the homothetic form (Eq. 5.23) of the welfare function.

Using primes to denote derivative with respect to $u$, differentiation of the logarithm of Eq. (5.28) with respect to $u$ gives:

$$\frac{d(\ln \mu)}{du} = \frac{\mu'}{\mu} = -\frac{(\sigma - 1)Ah^{\sigma-2}P^{\sigma-1}h'}{1 + Ah^{\sigma-1}P^{\sigma-1}}. \tag{5.29}$$

Substituting $Ah^{\sigma-1}P^{\sigma-1} = (1 - \mu)/\mu$ from Eq. (5.28) gives

$$\frac{\mu'}{\mu} = -(1 - \mu)(\sigma - 1)\frac{h'}{h} \tag{5.30a}$$

or

$$e_\mu = -(1 - \mu)(\sigma - 1)e_h. \tag{5.30b}$$

Inspection of Eq. (5.28) shows that $P$ appears in a form which is structurally identical with that of $h$, so the properties of $\mu$ as a function of $P$ are expressed by

$$\eta_\mu = -(1 - \mu)(\sigma - 1), \tag{5.31}$$

where the notation $\eta_x$ means the elasticity of $x$ with respect to $P$, a notation that will be used henceforth, together with the standard notation of $e_x$ for the elasticity of $x$ with respect to $u$. There is no $\eta$ on the right-hand side of Eq. (5.31) since $\eta_P = 1$.

Taking logarithms and differentiating the equations determining $q$ and $y$ in terms of $\mu$, $I$, and $P$ with respect to $u$ then gives

$$e_q = -(1 - \mu)(\sigma - 1)e_h + e_I, \tag{5.32a}$$

$$e_y = \frac{\mu}{1 - \mu}(1 - \mu)(\sigma - 1)e_h + e_I, \tag{5.32b}$$

and

$$\eta_q = -(1 - \mu)(\sigma - 1) + \eta_I - \sigma, \tag{5.33a}$$

$$\eta_y = \frac{\mu}{1 - \mu}(1 - \mu)(\sigma - 1) + \eta_I. \tag{5.33b}$$

(Some obvious cancellations have been left unmade in order to exhibit the structural relationships between the equations.)

The full demand properties can be derived from these last four relationships once the type of compensation (if any) has been determined. The compensation context then provides the appropriate expressions for $e_I$ and $\eta_I$, completing the system.

## 5.8 Compensated Demand with Outside Goods

This section is concerned with market demand under conditions of full compensation, that is, when incomes are adjusted both for the individual's position on the spectrum relative to the specification of the available goods and also for price changes, so that welfare remains uniform over individuals and constant over price changes. It is an important case, in spite of its apparent unrealism, because it provides the context in which market equilibrium can be compared with the full optimum under conditions which are identical except for market structure.

Using the relationships in Eqs. (5.25) and (5.28) and the definition of the constant $A$ given in Eq. (5.27), the welfare function (Eq. 5.23) can be expressed in terms of $\mu$ and $I$ rather than $q$ and $y$. After working through the substitutions, the welfare function emerges in the form

$$w = IP^{-1}h^{-1}\mu^{1/(1-\sigma)}.$$ (5.34)

Full compensation implies that $I$ varies such that $w$ remains constant, so that

$$I = cPh\mu^{1/(\sigma-1)},$$ (5.35)

where $c$ is constant for a given welfare level.

Logarithmic differentiation then gives

$$e_I = e_h + \frac{1}{\sigma - 1}e_\mu$$

$$= \mu e_h,$$ (5.36)

from Eq. (5.30b), and

$$\eta_I = 1 + \frac{1}{\sigma - 1}\eta_\mu$$

$$= \mu,$$ (5.37)

from Eq. (5.31). Substituting these expressions in Eqs. (5.32a) and (5.33a), derived in the previous section, the fundamental differential equations for compensated demand are given by

$$e_q = [1 - (1 - \mu)\sigma]e_h,$$ (5.38)

$$\eta_q = -(1 - \mu)\sigma.$$ (5.39)

Note that $q' < 0$ for all values of $u > 0$ if $\sigma > 1/[1 - \max_u \mu(u)]$, and thus $Q$ is concave for high values of $\sigma$ and convex for low values.

Note that the equation determining $e_q$ is identical with Eq. (4.21a) in the optimum analysis with outside goods, as far as form is concerned. In both cases, the proportions of group to outside goods satisfy the same efficiency condition—that the marginal rate of substitution be equal to the appropriate price ratio. In the market demand case however, the price ratio might not be that of the optimum (equal to the ratio of marginal resource costs), which will lead to a different value of $\mu$ in the two cases and different values of $q'/q$, even though the form of the relationships is the same.

Total demand over the half-market is given, as in the paradigm demand case, by

$$Q = \int_0^u q \, dv,$$

where $q$ is given by the equations just derived. Thus the demand elasticity is determined, as in the paradigm case, by

$$E = se_Q - \frac{P}{Q} \int_0^u \frac{\partial q}{\partial P} \, dv. \tag{5.40}$$

From the results obtained earlier in the section,

$$\int_0^u \frac{\partial q}{\partial P} \, dv = \int_0^u - (1 - \mu)\sigma \frac{q}{P} \, dv$$

$$= -\frac{\sigma}{P} \left[ Q - \int_0^u \mu q \, dv \right].$$

Consider $\int \mu q \, dv$. From the mean value theorem, this is equal to $\bar{\mu} \int q \, dv = \bar{\mu} Q$, where $\bar{\mu}$ is some value of $\mu(v)$ within the range of integration. It will be assumed that the "mean value" $\bar{\mu}$ is not significantly different from $m$, the true average proportion of expenditure on the group good to total expenditure [$= PQ/(PQ + Y)$], so that

$$\int_0^u \frac{\partial q}{\partial P} \, dv = -(1 - m)\sigma \frac{Q}{P}, \tag{5.41}$$

and thus

$$E = se_Q + (1 - m)\sigma. \tag{5.42}$$

Since demand is fully compensated, the two terms in the expression for $E$ are both pure substitution terms, the first being the inside-substitution effect, and the second, the outside-substitution effect. The outside-substitution effect vanishes when either $m = 1$ (the paradigm case) or $\sigma = 0$ (outside goods are not substitutable for group goods). In both cases, $q'/q = h'/h$, so that $e_Q = e_H$, and the results coincide fully with those of the paradigm case.

By writing $\alpha = (1 - m)\sigma$, with $\alpha$ the outside-substitution effect, $q'/q$ can be written, from Eq. (5.38), as

$$e_q = (1 - \alpha)e_h,$$

so that

$$\frac{\partial}{\partial \alpha} e_q < 0.$$

But this implies that $\partial e_Q / \partial \alpha < 0$, from Lemma 2b of Appendix B. Thus the inside- and outside-substitution effects are partial substitutes for each other; that is, the larger the outside-substitution effect, the smaller the inside-substitution effect. This is because, with better substitutability between inside and outside goods, more individuals at the market fringes will buy outside goods rather than inside goods and the proportional change in sales of the inside good for a given change in the market width will be less. The market-width change itself is determined by $s$, which depends on the properties of $h$ only and is thus independent of the degree of substitutability between inside and outside goods.

Note that the outside-substitution effect becomes greater (and the inside-substitution effect smaller), the larger the elasticity of substitution and the smaller the importance of the group in total expenditure.

## 5.9 Uncompensated Demand

Uncompensated demand is taken to be demand under conditions in which there is no compensation for specification. On the matter of compensation for price, it is possible to be somewhat flexible. Rigidly fixed money incomes are out of place in a context, such as that considered here, where the setting is one of simplified general equilibrium, so that a change in the value of total sales due to a price change must be expected to lead to some degree of change in total incomes in the same direction. On the other hand, perfect compensation for price changes in the absence of compensation for specification is not possible, in general, since such compensation requires that incomes be adjusted by $\mu$ times the percentage change in price, where $\mu$ varies from one individual to another.

The difficulty will be solved by introducing a degree-of-price-compensation parameter, defined as follows. Denote the mean proportion of total expenditure devoted to the group goods by $m$, as usual. Then let the proportional change in incomes be given by $\gamma m$ times the proportional change in price, where $\gamma$ is the degree-of-price-compensation parameter. If $\gamma = 0$, there is no price compensation at all (fixed money income). If $\gamma = 1$, this will be regarded as "full" price compensation, although it is not *perfect* price compensation, because it is the same for everyone.

Thus uncompensated demand will be defined by the income-adjustment properties

$$\eta_I = \gamma m$$

and

$$e_I = 0.$$

If these are inserted in Eqs. (5.32a) and (5.33a) for $e_q$ and $\eta_q$, the resulting equations for uncompensated demand become

$$e_{\hat{q}} = -(1 - \mu)(\sigma - 1)e_h, \tag{5.43}$$

and

$$\eta_{\hat{q}} = -[(\sigma - \gamma m) - (\sigma - 1)\mu], \tag{5.44}$$

where "hats" are used to distinguish uncompensated values like $\hat{q}$ from their fully compensated equivalents ($q$). Note that $q'$ is greater than or less than zero according as $\sigma$ is greater than or less than 1, so that $Q$ is convex for $\sigma < 1$, concave for $\sigma > 1$. Then, from the above equations,

$$\int_0^u \frac{\partial \hat{q}}{\partial P}\, dv = -\frac{1}{P}\left[ (\sigma - \gamma m)\hat{Q} - (\sigma - 1) \int_0^u \mu \hat{q}\, dv \right]. \tag{5.45}$$

As in the analysis of the compensated version, it will be assumed that only a negligible error is introduced by writing $m\hat{Q}$ for $\int \mu \hat{q}\, dv$, so that

$$-\frac{P}{\hat{Q}} \int_0^u \frac{\partial \hat{q}}{\partial P}\, dv = (1 - m)\sigma + (1 - \gamma)m.$$

As before,

$$\hat{E} = -\frac{P\hat{q}}{\hat{Q}}\frac{\partial u}{\partial P} - \frac{P}{\hat{Q}}\int_0^u \frac{\partial \hat{q}}{\partial P}\,dv$$

$$= se_{\hat{Q}} + (1 - m)\sigma + (1 - \gamma)m, \tag{5.46}$$

where $e_{\hat{Q}}$ is the elasticity of the uncompensated quantity function $\hat{Q}$.

Equation (5.46) is not in final form, however, since the first term is not the inside-substitution effect, which is given by $se_Q$, where $e_Q$ is the elasticity of the compensated quantity function $Q$. The final form, with the various components of the elasticity of demand correctly labeled, is

$$\hat{E} = \underset{\substack{\text{(Inside-}\\\text{substitution}\\\text{effect)}}}{se_Q} \underset{\substack{\text{(Specification}\\\text{effect)}}}{- s(e_Q - e_{\hat{Q}})} + \underset{\substack{\text{(Outside-}\\\text{substitution}\\\text{effect)}}}{(1 - m)\sigma} + \underset{\substack{\text{(Income}\\\text{effect)}}}{(1 - \gamma)m}. \tag{5.47}$$

Comparison of the expressions for $q'/q$ and $\hat{q}'/\hat{q}$ shows that

$$e_q - e_{\hat{q}} = \mu e_h > 0, \tag{5.48}$$

so that $e_Q > e_{\hat{Q}}$ (Lemma 2a, Appendix B). Thus the specification effect is always negative and diminishes as the relative importance of the group in total expenditure diminishes. The income effect, on the other hand, is always positive, and it, too, diminishes as the relative importance of the group decreases.

The reason for the negativity of the specification effect, which may not seem obvious, is as follows. If individuals are not compensated for specification, then those individuals at the fringes of the market, who have the greatest distance between the available good and their most-preferred good, will suffer the greatest loss of compensation. Thus the quantity they will buy is less, relative to individuals near the market center, than would be the case with compensation for specification. Lack of compensation, therefore, reduces the quantities bought at the market fringe relative to the quantities bought at the center, so that a small change in the market width causes a smaller proportional change in aggregate purchases than when demand is compensated for specification, which reduces the elasticity of demand compared with the compensated value.

The parameter $\gamma$ represents the degree of price compensation. If $\gamma = 0$, there is no compensation, and the income effect is given by $m$; as $\gamma$ approaches 1, there is full compensation and the income effect vanishes. It is possible, in principle, to have overcompensation for price ($\gamma > 1$) with a negative income effect, but it will be assumed throughout that $\gamma$ lies in the range $0 \leqq \gamma \leqq 1$.

The effect of the structural parameters $\sigma$ and $m$ can be seen quite clearly. If $\sigma = 0$, the outside-substitution effect vanishes, but the other effects remain ($e_Q$ becomes equal to $e_h$ in this case). If $m = 1$, the outside-substitution effect again vanishes (there are no outside goods), and $e_Q$ again becomes equal to $e_h$, giving the paradigm case. As $m$ becomes very small, both the income and specification effects become very small, but the two substitution effects increase. The increase in the outside-substitution effect is obvious. The increase in the inside-substitution effect is less obvious and occurs because $\partial e_q / \partial m > 0$, which implies $\partial e_Q / \partial m > 0$, from Lemma 2b of Appendix B.

Comparison of the compensated and uncompensated elasticities from Eqs. (5.42) and (5.46) gives

$$E - \hat{E} = (e_Q - e_{\hat{Q}})s - (1 - \gamma)m.$$

Since $e_Q > e_{\hat{Q}}$, the first term is always positive, so that if there is full price compensation the last term vanishes and $E > \hat{E}$. That is, when there is compensation for price, additional compensation for specification increases the elasticity. If there is not full price compensation, however, the two terms are of opposite sign, and the relationship between the elasticities is not immediately apparent.

For the paradigm case discussed earlier in the chapter, it was shown that the fully compensated elasticity was less than the completely uncompensated elasticity. When there are outside goods, this relationship no longer holds. It can be shown that $E < \hat{E}$ if $\gamma = 0$ and $\sigma \leqq 1/(1 - m)$, but the relationship may go in any direction if $0 < \gamma < 1$ and $\sigma > 1/(1 - m)$, so that no general statement can be made as to the relationship between completely compensated elasticity and elasticity which is uncompensated for specification and incompletely compensated for price.

## 5.10 Properties of the Demand Elasticity

The demand elasticity, whether compensated or uncompensated, is seen to be composed of three types of basic building blocks: the market-width elasticity $s$, the elasticity of quantity with respect to market width $e_Q$ (or $e_{\hat{Q}}$), and the structural parameters $m$ and $\sigma$, which appear explicitly in the outside-substitution and income terms. Now the market-width elasticity $s = s(\Delta, u)$ is a function of the spacing between the good and the next adjacent good ($2\Delta$) and the width of the half-market $u$. The quantity elasticity is a function of $u$ and of the two structural parameters. Both parameters, of course, derive their properties from those of the compensating function. The outside-substitution and income terms involve the structural parameters only and do not depend on $\Delta$, $u$, or the compensating function.

Thus the elasticity can be considered to be determined by two variables $\Delta$ and $u$, two structural parameters $m$ and $\sigma$, and the properties of the compensating function. Only the variables $\Delta$ and $u$ can be changed by the behavior of actors in the market; the remaining parameters are considered fixed (subject to comments below on the role of $m$) for a given economy.

The variable $u$—the width of the particular half-market being examined—is a variable determined by decisions in the market, but is not a direct-decision variable. The direct-decision variable is typically the price of the product, which does not appear explicitly in the elasticity expression or even implicitly in the various functional components of the elasticity in the forms derived here. But the price is the direct determinant of $u$ since, given the spacing between the goods and the properties of the compensating function, the dividing condition (Eq. 5.2) gives $u$ as a function of price. Thus in relating the properties of elasticity to the behavior of decision-makers in the market, it is appropriate to take the price, rather than the width of the market, as the relevant variable.

In the sections that follow, therefore, an analysis will be made of the effects on the elasticity of demand of four influences:

1. the effect of the spacing between goods, with relative prices held constant;
2. the effect of price changes, with the spacing between goods held constant;
3. the effect of changes in the elasticity of substitution $\sigma$; and
4. The effect of changes in the relative importance of the group in the economy, represented by the parameter $m$.

A comment on the treatment of $m$ as a structural parameter is in order at this point. The size of $m$, an average over all the individuals in the market, is determined by the individual proportions of total expenditure going to group goods. The individual proportions, denoted by $\mu$ in the preceding analysis, are variables that depend not only on the specification of the consumer's most-preferred good relative to the available good but also on $\sigma$ and $P$, as shown by Eqs. (5.30) and (5.31). But $\mu$ also depends on the parameter $a$ in the welfare function (Eq. 5.23), a parameter that has not been used explicitly as a parameter of the system. In a *comparative static context*, where economies with different structures are being compared, it is implicitly assumed that the parameter $a$ is varied in such a way as to keep $m$ the same as between economies with different values of $\sigma$ when the effect of $\sigma$ alone is being analyzed.

Within a single economy, when price is varied as part of a market process, the effect of $P$ on $m$ cannot be ignored. Indeed, part of the effect of price in such a context is almost inevitably to cause variations in the division of expenditure between group goods and outside goods, the exception being when the elasticity of substitution is unity.

Contrary, perhaps, to initial expectations, none of the four influences on the elasticity—$\Delta$, $P$, $m$, or $\sigma$—is such that its effects can be derived either simply or with full generality. This is true even of the elasticity of substitution, the influence of which might seem to be intuitively obvious. There are two sources of difficulty, one being that the structural parameters have opposite effects on the group terms and the outside terms and that the market variables have opposite effects on the two components ($s$ and $e_Q$) of the group terms, the other being that the effects depend on the properties of the group substitution parameter $s(\Delta, u)$.

It was shown in Eq. (5.11) that the way in which $s(\Delta, u)$ varies with $u$ depends on third-derivative properties of the compensating function, no presumptions concerning which have been made in the analysis. On the other hand, when the price of the good and the adjacent good are equal, so that the market boundary is at the midpoint between the two goods and $u = \Delta$, then $s(\Delta, \Delta) = s^*(\Delta) = \frac{1}{2}e_h(\Delta)$, from Eq. (5.13). The derivative of the effects of the variables and parameters is based on the properties at $u = \Delta$, and the results therefore hold if the prices of adjacent goods are approximately equal, but not necessarily if they are very different, unless additional assumptions are made as to the compensating function properties.


## 5.11 Effect of the Structural Parameters

It has previously been pointed out that the effect of variations in the two structural parameters, $\sigma$ and $m$, on the elasticity of demand cannot easily be determined, because the inside- and outside-substitution terms are affected in opposite ways, and thus the overall effect depends on the relative magnitudes of the two. It will be shown, however that the outside-substitution effect is the dominant factor when the value of $\Delta$ is sufficiently small and that the following statements can be made.

For a sufficiently close spacing between adjacent goods:

1. Both the compensated and uncompensated demand elasticities increase when the elasticity of substitution between group goods and outside goods increases.

2. The compensated demand elasticity decreases as the importance of the group in the economy increases, and the same holds true for the uncompensated demand elasticity when the elasticity of substitution is greater than unity.

3. When the elasticity of substitution is less than unity, the effect of the relative importance of the group on the elasticity uncompensated for specification will depend on the degree of price compensation.

Consider the compensated elasticity. From Eq. (5.42), with $u = \Delta$,

$$E = s^* e_Q + (1 - m)\sigma,$$

for which

$$\frac{\partial E}{\partial \sigma} = s^* \frac{\partial e_Q}{\partial \sigma} + (1 - m). \qquad (5.49)$$

Now

$$e_q = [1 - (1 - \mu)\sigma]e_h,$$

from Eq. (5.38), so that

$$\frac{\partial}{\partial \sigma} e_q = -(1 - \mu)e_h < 0. \qquad (5.50)$$

From Lemma 2b (Appendix B) this implies that $\partial e_Q/\partial \sigma < 0$, so that the two terms in the expression for $\partial E/\partial \sigma$ have opposite signs, as already stated. This same lemma, however, can be used to give the magnitude of $\partial e_Q/\partial \sigma$, since in the proof it is shown that, after changing the notation,

$$\frac{1}{e_Q} \frac{\partial e_Q}{\partial \sigma} = \frac{1}{Q} \int_0^\Delta Q \frac{\partial}{\partial v} \left( \frac{q'}{q} \right) dv$$

$$= -\frac{1}{Q} \int_0^\Delta Q(1 - \mu)\underline{h}' \, dv,$$

where $\underline{h} = \ln h$.

From the mean value theorem,

$$\int_0^\Delta Q(1 - \mu)\underline{h}' \, dv = (1 - \bar{\mu}) \int_0^\Delta Q\underline{h}' \, dv,$$

where $\bar{\mu}$ is some value of $\mu$ in the range of integration. Also, since $Q$ and $\underline{h}'$ are both increasing functions of $v$,

$$0 < \int_0^\Delta Q(v)\underline{h}'(v) \, dv < Q(\Delta)\underline{h}'(\Delta) \, \Delta. \qquad (5.51)$$

Then, from these relationships,

$$s^*(\partial e_Q/\partial\sigma) > -s^* e_Q(1 - \bar{\mu})\underline{h}'\Delta$$

$$> -\tfrac{1}{2}e_Q(1 - \bar{\mu}) \tag{5.52}$$

since $s^* = \tfrac{1}{2}e_q = \tfrac{1}{2}\underline{h}'\Delta$.

As $\Delta \to 0$, $e_Q \to 1$ and $\bar{\mu} \to m$, so that

$$0 > s^*(\partial e_Q/\partial\sigma)_{\Delta=0} > -\tfrac{1}{2}(1 - m), \tag{5.53}$$

and therefore

$$1 - m > (\partial E/\partial\sigma)_{\Delta=0} > \tfrac{1}{2}(1 - m). \tag{5.54}$$

Thus $\partial E/\partial\sigma > 0$ for $\Delta$ sufficiently close to zero.

The result is identical for the uncompensated elasticity $\hat{E}$ since the expression for $\partial\hat{E}/\partial\sigma$ is identical with that for $\partial E/\partial\sigma$, except that $\partial e_{\hat{Q}}/\partial\sigma$ replaces $\partial e_Q/\partial\sigma$, since $\partial(\hat{q}'/\hat{q})/\partial\sigma = \partial(q'/q)/\partial\sigma$.

Now consider the effect of the parameter $m$ on the compensated elasticity $E$. This is given by

$$\frac{\partial E}{\partial m} = s^* \frac{\partial e_Q}{\partial m} - \sigma. \tag{5.55}$$

By using the same kind of arguments as those given above and assuming changes in $m$ involve equiproportional changes in all the $\mu$ values, it can be shown that

$$0 < s^* \frac{\partial e_Q}{\partial m} < \tfrac{1}{2}e_Q \frac{m}{\bar{\mu}} \sigma \tag{5.56}$$

$$< \tfrac{1}{2}\sigma \qquad \text{as } \Delta \to 0,$$

so that

$$-\sigma < (\partial E/\partial m)_{\Delta=0} < -\tfrac{1}{2}\sigma. \tag{5.57}$$

The effect in changes in $m$ on the uncompensated elasticity is more complex. Now, from Eq. (5.46),

$$\hat{E} = s^* e_{\hat{Q}} + (1 - m)\sigma + (1 - \gamma)m,$$

so that

$$\frac{\partial\hat{E}}{\partial m} = s^* \frac{\partial e}{\partial m} \hat{Q} + (1 - \sigma) - \gamma. \tag{5.58}$$

Also, from Eq. (5.43),

$$e_{\hat{q}} = -(1 - \mu)(\sigma - 1)e_h,$$

and therefore

$$\frac{\partial}{\partial m} e_{\hat{q}} = (\sigma - 1)e_h, \tag{5.59}$$

the sign of which depends on the relationship of $\sigma$ to unity.
If $\sigma > 1$, then proceeding as before gives

$$0 < s^{\star} \frac{\partial e_{\hat{q}}}{\partial m} < \tfrac{1}{2}(\sigma - 1)e_{\hat{q}} \frac{m}{\bar{\mu}} \tag{5.60}$$

$$< \tfrac{1}{2}(\sigma - 1) \qquad \text{as } \Delta \to 0,$$

and thus

$$-(\sigma - 1) - \gamma < (\partial \hat{E}/\partial m)_{\Delta = 0} < -\tfrac{1}{2}(\sigma - 1) - \gamma \tag{5.61}$$

$$< 0 \qquad \text{for all } \gamma.$$

If $\sigma < 1$, the inequalities are reversed and the final inequality is

$$(1 - \sigma) - \gamma > (\partial \hat{E}/\partial m)_{\Delta = 0} > \tfrac{1}{2}(1 - \sigma) - \gamma. \tag{5.62}$$

Clearly, $\partial \hat{E}/\partial m$ is positive if $\gamma \leqq \tfrac{1}{2}(1 - \sigma)$ and negative if $\gamma \geqq (1 - \sigma)$, with indeterminance for intermediate values.

## 5.12 Intergood Spacing

The goods spacing, or difference in specification between adjacent goods, is the market variable of particular interest in this analysis because of the emphasis on product differentiation. It is a market variable because firms are free to choose the specifications of the goods they produce, and thus the space between their good and the next good on the spectrum.

The effect of the goods spacing on the elasticity of demand is summarized in the following statement:

The elasticity of demand is strictly positive, approaches infinity as the spacing between adjacent goods approaches zero, and is bounded below by the value

$$E_{\min} = (1 - m)\sigma + (1 - \gamma)m,$$

where the second term is zero if the elasticity is fully compensated. The value of the elasticity varies inversely with the goods spacing in a smooth manner (a) if the elasticity of substitution is greater than $1/(1 - m)$ for compensated demand or greater than unity for uncompensated demand or (b) for goods spacing no greater than some well-defined value $2\Delta_o$ in all other cases.

Consider the compensated and uncompensated elasticities, from Eqs. (5.42) and (5.46), respectively:

$$E = se_Q + (1 - m)\sigma,$$

$$\hat{E} = se_{\hat{Q}} + (1 - m)\sigma + (1 - \gamma)m.$$

If the prices of the adjacent goods are approximately equal, $s$ is approximately equal to $s^* = \frac{1}{2}\Delta h'(\Delta)$, from Eq. (5.13).

First of all, it is obvious that the elasticity is strictly positive since the term $se_Q$ (or $se_{\hat{Q}}$) is strictly positive and the remaining terms are nonnegative. Now as $\Delta \to 0$, $h'(\Delta) \to 0$, so that $s^* \to \infty$, and thus $E$ becomes infinite. On the other hand, $h'(\Delta)$ is an increasing function of $\Delta$ (because the compensating function is convex), so that $\Delta h'(\Delta)$ increases without limit as $\Delta$ increases, and thus $s^* \to 0$ for large $\Delta$. Thus the first (group-substitution and specification effect) term in the expressions for $E$ and $\hat{E}$ may become negligible with large spacing, but the outside terms do not and thus provide the lower bound for the elasticity. Note that at high elasticities of substitution, $Q$ is concave and $e_Q$ is a decreasing function of $\Delta$, so the first term certainly approaches zero as $\Delta$ becomes very large in this case.

It is obvious from the above arguments that $se_Q$ and $se_{\hat{Q}}$ are decreasing functions of $\Delta$ if $Q$ and $\hat{Q}$ are concave, that is, if $\sigma \geq 1/(1 - m)$ for compensated demand or $\sigma \geq 1$ for uncompensated demand, and thus that the elasticity of demand varies inversely with the goods spacing under such circumstances.

If $Q$ (or $\hat{Q}$) is convex, however, then $e_Q$ (or $e_{\hat{Q}}$) is an increasing function of $\Delta$, and it is not obvious whether the elasticity of demand increases or decreases when $\Delta$ increases, since $e_Q$ may increase at a rate faster or slower than that at which $s*$ decreases. It is necessary to carry out further analysis when $\sigma$ is in the low range.

If $Q$ is strictly convex, because $\sigma < 1/(1 - m)$, the results of Lemma 1a (Appendix B) can be used. The relevant results are

$$e_Q < q/q_o,$$

$$e_Q' < q'/q_o,$$

so that

$$\frac{dE}{d\Delta} = e_Q \frac{ds*}{d\Delta} + s* e_Q'$$

$$< \frac{q}{q_o} \left( \frac{ds*}{d\Delta} + s* \frac{q'}{q} \right). \tag{5.63}$$

By using the relationship $q'/q \leqq h'/h = \underline{h}'$ (which is always true) and the following properties from Eqs. (5.13) and (5.14),

$$s* = \tfrac{1}{2} \underline{h}' \Delta$$

$$ds*/d\Delta = -2s*^2(\underline{h}' + \underline{h}''),$$

it is easy to show that

$$\frac{dE}{d\Delta} < \frac{q}{q_o} \left[ \frac{1}{2\underline{h}'\Delta^2} (\underline{h}'\Delta - 1) - 2s*^2\underline{h}'' \right]. \tag{5.64}$$

Since $\underline{h}'' > 0$ (logarithmic convexity of the compensating function), $dE*/d\Delta$ is negative if $\underline{h}'\Delta < 1$, that is, if $h'\Delta < h$. Now $h'\Delta$ is of the order of $\Delta^2$ if $\Delta$ is close to zero, whereas $h$ is close to unity at this value. Thus $dE/d\Delta$ for $\Delta$ in the range $0 \leq \Delta \leq \Delta_o$, where $\Delta_o$ is such that $h'(\Delta_o)\Delta_o = h(\Delta_o)$. Clearly $\Delta_o$ is at a finite distance from the origin. For a compensating function with constant convexity (quadratic), it can be shown that the value of $\Delta_o$ is such that $h(\Delta_o) = 2$. Obviously, a distance along the spectrum such that it requires two units of the available good to equal one unit of the most-preferred good could even be considered a "large" distance.

The analysis given above holds equally for the uncompensated elasticity $\hat{E}$, the only difference being that the factor outside the bracket in Eq. (5.64) is $\hat{q}/\hat{q}_o$.

## 5.13 The Effect of Price on Elasticity

Price does not appear explicitly in the elasticity expressions, but changes in price affect the market variable $u$ and also the parameter $m$, which has been treated as constant (by adjustments of the parameter $\underline{a}$ in the welfare function) with respect to changes in the other parameter $\sigma$. Comparisons of the system at different values of $\sigma$ are comparative, static comparisons of different economic structures, and juggling to preserve the constancy of $m$ is justified. It is not possible to treat $m$ as constant when price changes, since changes in the $\mu$ values (which determine $m$) are an essential part of the adjustment to price changes.

The story is complicated, but it will be shown that:

1. An increase in price increases the elasticity of demand when the elasticity of substitution between group and outside goods is relatively high, that is, if $\sigma \geqq 1/(1 - m)$ for compensated demand or $\sigma \geqq 1$ for uncompensated demand.

2. An increase in price lowers the elasticity of demand if (a) the elasticity of substitution is less than unity and (b) there is full (or near-full) price compensation, whether there is compensation for specification or not.

3. In other cases, that is, for compensated demand with the elasticity of substitution in the range $1 < \sigma < 1/(1 - m)$ or uncompensated demand with the elasticity of substitution less than unity and little price compensation, an increase in price may either increase or decrease the elasticity of demand.

To demonstrate these properties, note that if $E$ is any elasticity, whether compensated or not, then the effect of a price change is given by

$$P \frac{\partial E}{\partial P} = P \frac{\partial E}{\partial u} \frac{\partial u}{\partial P} + P \frac{\partial E}{\partial m} \frac{\partial m}{\partial P} . \tag{5.65}$$

It is convenient to divide this overall effect, in accordance with the two terms above, into the "$u$-effect" and the "$m$-effect". The $u$-effect involves only the term or terms in the elasticity expression involving $s$ or $e_Q$, that is, the inside-substitution and specification terms, while the $m$-effect involves all terms.

Consider first the compensated elasticity. Differentiation of Eq. (5.42) with respect to $u$ gives

$$\frac{\partial E}{\partial u} = s e_Q' + e_Q \frac{\partial s}{\partial u}. \tag{5.66}$$

Now if the prices of adjacent goods are approximately equal, so that $u = \Delta$, then $\partial s/\partial u = 0$ (Eq. 5.12). The expression $s$ will be written $s^*$ to make it clear that the assumption about approximate price equality has been made. Equation (5.66) then becomes

$$\frac{\partial E}{\partial u} = s^* e_Q'. \tag{5.67}$$

By using the value of $\partial u/\partial P$ from Eq. (5.5), the $u$-effect is given by

$$P \frac{\partial E}{\partial u} \frac{\partial u}{\partial P} = -s^{*2} e_Q'. \tag{5.68}$$

The sign of this expression is determined by the sign of $e_Q'$, which depends on whether $Q$ is concave or convex:

1. If $\sigma > 1/(1 - m)$, $e_Q' < 0$ and the $u$-effect is positive.
2. If $\sigma < 1/(1 - m)$, $e_Q' > 0$ and the $u$-effect is negative.

The $m$-effect is composed of two factors, one of which, $\partial E/\partial m$, has already been shown to be always negative (Eq. 5.57). The other is given by Eq. (5.31), after substituting $m$ for $\mu$

$$P \frac{\partial m}{\partial P} = -m(1 - m)(\sigma - 1).$$

This factor is negative or positive according to whether $\sigma$ is greater or less than unity. Thus the $m$-effect is positive if $\sigma > 1$, negative if $\sigma < 1$.

Putting the two effects together gives that $\partial E/\partial P$ is positive if $\sigma \geq 1/(1 - m)$, negative if $\sigma \leq 1$, and may be of either sign if $1 < \sigma < 1/(1 - m)$.

Now consider the uncompensated elasticity. The $u$-effect is the same as for the compensated elasticity, except that $e_Q'$ is replaced by $\acute{e}_Q'$, which is positive or negative according to whether $\sigma$ is less or greater than unity rather than the value $1/(1 - m)$. Thus the $u$-effect in the uncompensated case is positive if $\sigma > 1$ and negative if $\sigma < 1$.

In the $m$-effect for the uncompensated elasticity, the expression for $\partial m/\partial P$ is the same as in the compensated case, its sign determined by whether $\sigma$ is greater or less than unity. But the expression for $\partial E/\partial m$ is now of uncertain sign, as shown in Eqs. (5.61) and (5.62). If $\sigma > 1$, then $\partial E/\partial m$ is definitely negative and the $m$ effect is certainly positive, as is the $u$-effect, so that $\partial E/\partial m$ is positive. But if $\sigma < 1$, the sign of $\partial E/\partial m$ depends on the degree of price compensation. If there is almost full compensation for price, then $\partial E/\partial m$ is negative, and both the $u$-effect and the $m$-effect are negative, which makes $\partial E/\partial P$ negative.

## 5.14 Demand for Indivisible Goods

Assume initially that the indivisibility is "large," so that a consumer will buy one unit of the good or none at all. Then the choice situation is (a) which of the group goods to buy, if any at all is purchased, and (b) whether to buy the good or not. The choice between group goods will be made on the same basis as for divisible goods; namely, the consumer will buy the good giving the greatest quantity of "most-preferred-good equivalents" per dollar. Whether this best choice among the available group goods is then worth buying at all depends on whether the total welfare obtained by buying the good and spending the rest of the income on the outside good is at least as great as the welfare obtained from spending all the income on the outside good.

It will be assumed that the units have been chosen so that the price of the outside good is unity, that income $I$ is measured in units of outside good, and that the price of the best available group good is $P$. The most-preferred-good equivalent of a unit of this good is then $1/h(u)$, where $u$, as usual, is the distance of the available good from the most-preferred good in terms of specification. Thus the group good will be purchased if

$$w(1/h, I - P) > w(0, I) \tag{5.69}$$

and will not be purchased if the inequality is reversed, with equality giving a marginal case of indifference.

Since $w(1/h, I - P)$ is a decreasing function of both $h$ (and thus $u$) and $P$, the good will not be purchased by consumers for whom the distance $u$ is greater than some distance $\bar{u}(P)$, which depends on $P$, and will not by purchased by any consumers at all if $w(1, I - P) > w(0, I)$ since the smallest value of $h$ is unity. Assuming that $w(1, I - P) < w(0, I)$, so that the good has some buyers, the market width will be determined by one of two considerations:

1. If the spacing between adjacent goods is sufficiently great, the marginal consumer will be indifferent between buying the good and spending all his or her income on the outside good and will prefer the latter to buying the adjacent good. In this case, the market boundary will be determined by the relation given by Eq. (5.69).

2. If the spacing between adjacent goods is sufficiently small, the marginal consumer will switch to the adjacent good, preferring a unit of either adjacent good to spending all his or her income on the outside good. In this case, the market boundary will be determined by the regular dividing condition (Eq. 5.1).

In the first case, the demand spectrum will have "holes" consisting of sets of consumers not buying any of the group goods, between which will be sets of consumers buying one of the goods. The demand for an individual good will essentially be isolated from that for other goods in the group, with no inside-substitution effects. In the second case, the demand for the good will consist entirely of inside-substitution effects. Since all consumers will buy the same quantity of the good (one unit), $e_Q = 1$, and the demand elasticity will be given by

$$E = \hat{E} = s. \tag{5.70}$$

Since there are no income or specification effects, the compensated and uncompensated elasticities are equal. The elasticity of demand can be calculated in the first case by taking the equality in Eq. (5.69) and differentiating with respect to $P$ to find how the market boundary changes. The resulting expression cannot be directly related to that in Eq. (5.70), and the elasticity may be greater or less than in the second case.

If the indivisibilities are "small," so that consumers may choose more than one unit of the good, the demand conditions take on a relatively complex form, with an inner circle of consumers who each purchase $k$ units of the good, a ring who purchase $k - 1$ units, and so on, and an outer boundary where consumers either switch from buying $s$ units of the good to $t$ units of the adjacent good (where $s$ may or may not equal $t$) or switch from buying one unit of the good to buying none of any group good.

The analysis of the indivisible case in later chapters will be confined to the "large" indivisibility case.

Chapter 6

# Perfect Monopolistic Competition

## 6.1 Introduction

THE MARKET STRUCTURE that will be analyzed in this chapter is the most competitive structure that is possible under conditions of continuously variable product specification, economies of scale, and a continuous spectrum of consumer preferences. It is appropriate to use the traditional term "monopolistic competition" for this structure because it possesses some of the fundamental properties of the configuration to which Chamberlin originally applied the term and also has similarities to the Hotelling model of spatial competition, to which the same term has come to be applied.

It has been common to treat monopolistic competition as a special form of "imperfect competition," but the latter term is quite inappropriate for the structure being examined here. Imperfection surely connotes some flaw which, if removed, leaves perfection. The essential feature of monopolistic competition, in the sense in which the term is used here, is that, although it is not perfect competition, it is the "most perfect" competition that can be attained in an economy of the kind being examined. The three elements that prevent the structure from becoming that of traditional perfect competition—variable specification, economies of scale, and diverse preferences—are not "flaws" in the system rising out of restrictive practices by firms but fundamental and embedded properties of the economy

**179**

which possesses them. On the contrary, the absence of variable specification, for example, would itself be a flaw. If all products in a group were legally restricted to a uniform specification, and provided economies of scale were to the U-shaped cost-curve variety, a structure conforming to traditional norms of perfect competition[1] might be generated, but it would not be an optimal structure, nor would it be the structure generated by a free market. It is for these reasons that the term "perfect monopolistic competition" is used for the structure discussed here and the term "imperfect monopolistic competition" for the cases discussed in Chapter 8 in which there are true imperfections such as incomplete information.

The market structure under discussion is defined on the demand side by the market demand properties set out at length in Chapter 5. Demand may be compensated (primarily for purposes of comparison with the optimum) or uncompensated, but the distinction is not important for most of the general analysis, and the demand properties will be represented by the elasticity of demand $E$ and the quantity function $Q$, which are interpreted specifically as referring to compensated or uncompensated demand when the distinction is necessary. The general context is that of a uniform spectrum, with a uniform distribution of real income (compensated demand) or money income (uncompensated demand). It will be found necessary, however, to make certain modifications of both uniformity and uniform density at the ends of the spectrum to avoid the "end-firm problem", discussed later in the chapter.

On the supply side, the structure is defined by the existence of profit-maximizing firms having cost structures with the same general properties as in the optimal analysis, that is, with positive but nonincreasing economies of scale, and selling their product at the same price to all customers. The competitive relationship among the firms is defined as follows:

1. Each firm produces a single good but is free to choose and vary the specification of that good without cost, prior to commencing a production run.

1. That is, there will be a homogeneous product, and the equilibrium will be such that price is equal to both marginal and average cost.

2. Each firm manipulates the variables under its direct control so as to maximize its profit but takes the behavior of other firms as exogenous.

3. There is no collusion among firms.

4. There are no restrictions on entry into the group, and there is always a supply of firms willing to enter whenever profits are expected to be positive. Firms can and do exit costlessly when profits are negative. (Normal returns to capital, entrepreneurship, and management are costs.)

5. Firms possess full information on the properties of market demand,[2] and it is assumed that buyers possess full information as to the specifications and prices of goods sold by firms in the group.

It is *not* assumed that each good is produced only by a single firm, since there is no restriction on the firm's choice of the specification of the good it produces. It will be proved as a proposition that, indeed, no firm will choose to produce a good to the same specification as that produced by another firm, but it is not introduced as an assumption. Since this proposition underlies the assertion that the failure to achieve perfect competition is structural and not due to implicit lack of "competition" among firms, it is important that it be shown to be a consequence of the structure and not be explicitly assumed at the beginning.

The assumption that each firm produces a single good can be regarded as superfluous or essential, according to the definition of the firm. If a "firm" means a production unit rather than a strategy unit, then it is single-product by definition since there is no joint production. The no-collusion assumption then rules out two production units being operated as a single strategy unit, but if a firm is a strategy unit, it is necessary to make the assumption explicit.[3]

2. Note that the demand curves here are real demand curves, not "perceived" or "conjectural" demand curves as in the traditional general equilibrium analysis of monopolistic competition represented by Negishi (1960) or Arrow and Hahn (1971). The model here shows that the pessimism expressed by Roberts and Sonnenschein (1977) as to the existence of equilibrium with true demand curves is unjustified, since the conditions which give a viable equilibrium will be shown to be eminently reasonable ones. There are, however, clear restrictions on viability.

3. Common ownership with separate management leaves the conglomerate as a collection of separate single-product firms in the sense used here. True multiproduct firms with single management are discussed in Chapter 9.

The five assumptions defining the monopolistic-competition structure are similar to those underlying the Chamberlin analysis, except for two crucial differences. In the Chamberlin model, it is essential to the analysis that no two firms produce the same product (a proposition that cannot be derived in that model and must be assumed), and there is no satisfactory explanation as to how firms determine the specifications of their products. The Chamberlin analysis implicitly assumes that firms vary the specifications of their goods so that with every new entrant the firms redistribute themselves evenly over the spectrum—a result that will be derived here and not assumed.

Variable specification, in the sense of position along the spatial spectrum, is an essential feature of the Hotelling model and more recent neo-Hotelling versions. However, the nature of transport costs in these spatial models leads to linearity in the implicit compensating function (as discussed in Chapter 2), and this property, together with the lack of provision for smooth substitution between group goods and outside goods, leads to important differences in predicted market properties as compared to the characteristics model. Comparison between the two models is given later in the chapter.

Two phases of market equilibrium will be examined in the analysis which follows. One, which might be termed the "medium run" phase, is the equilibrium that will be established when the number of firms in the group is given and these firms adjust the variables under their control (specification and price) under the behavior assumptions laid out above. Such an equilibrium will be a *Nash equilibrium,*[4] a situation in which every firm will find it optimal to maintain its current behavior, given the current behavior of the other firms. Such an equilibrium will be sustained if it can be shown that the appropriate first- and second-order conditions for profit maximization with respect to both price and specification can be satisfied.

4. Technically, a Nash equilibrium is a joint strategy that cannot be blocked by any one-person coalition; that is, it is a solution in which no individual player can gain by any change of strategy that does not involve a coalition with one or more other players. The term has come to be widely used in economics to describe an equilibrium in which no individual firm or individual (depending on the context) can gain by any change in behavior which does not involve collusion with others (see Nash, 1950). The basic concept of such an equilibrium goes back, of course, to Cournot.

The second equilibrium phase, appropriately termed the "long run" phase, is the Nash equilibrium that is established among the number of firms the group will contain when there is free and willing entry and free and costless exit. This long-run equilibrium establishes the equilibrium degree of product differentiation that will be generated by the market, and it is the long-run equilibrium that will be compared with the optimum.

It can be emphasized again that the long-run monopolistic-competition equilibrium is the most "competitive" solution that the market can generate. It is the noncollusive outcome of competitive, profit-maximizing firms operating without discrimination in a market of perfectly informed consumers with complete freedom of entry.

## 6.2 Nash Equilibrium

The first problem to be investigated is that of the existence and specification of a Nash equilibrium when the number of firms is given. The following structural properties of such an equilibrium will be shown:

Under conditions of a uniform preference spectrum and a uniform distribution of real or money income, with certain end-of-spectrum modifications, the Nash equilibrium for a fixed number of firms such that all firms can at least break even is characterized by:

1. an equal spacing over the spectrum between the specifications of goods produced by adjacent firms;
2. the same prices for all goods;
3. the same quantities of all goods, the same marginal and average costs for all firms, and the same elasticities in all markets;
4. a price given by the relationship $P = R(\Delta)F'$, where $R(\Delta) = E(\Delta)/(E(\Delta) - 1)$, $E$ being the elasticity of demand, $F'$ the marginal cost, and $2\Delta$ the spacing between adjacent goods.

Take any firm which is not an end firm, say the $i$th. Its profit function is given by

$$\pi_i = (\bar{Q}_i + \underline{Q}_i)P_i - F(\bar{Q}_i + \underline{Q}_i), \tag{6.1}$$

where $P_i$ is its price and $\bar{Q}_i$ and $\underline{Q}_i$ are the quantities sold in its upper and lower half-markets. The boundaries of its market at price $P_i$ are at distances $\bar{u}_i$ (upper half-market) and $\underline{u}_i$ (lower half-market) from the market center, defined by the specification $b_i$ of the good produced by the firm. The specifications of the adjacent goods are at distances $2\bar{\Delta}_i$ and $2\underline{\Delta}_i$ from $b_i$.

The firm has two variables at its disposal, the price $P_i$ and the specification $b_i$. With the subscript $i$ dropped for simplicity, the effect on profit of variations in $P$ is given by

$$\frac{\partial \pi}{\partial P} = \bar{Q} + P \frac{\partial \bar{Q}}{\partial P} - F' \frac{\partial \bar{Q}}{\partial P} + \underline{Q} + P \frac{\partial \underline{Q}}{\partial P} - F' \frac{\partial \underline{Q}}{\partial P}$$

$$= \left( \frac{P}{\bar{R}} - F' \right) \frac{\partial \bar{Q}}{\partial P} + \left( \frac{P}{\underline{R}} - F' \right) \frac{\partial \underline{Q}}{\partial P}, \tag{6.2}$$

where $R = E/(E - 1)$ and the upper and lower bars identify variables associated with the upper and lower half-markets.

The effect of specification on profit is given by

$$\frac{\partial \pi}{\partial b} = (P - F') \left[ q(\bar{u}) \frac{\partial \bar{u}}{\partial b} + q(\underline{u}) \frac{\partial \underline{u}}{\partial b} \right]. \tag{6.3}$$

The condition for profit maximization with respect to specification will be analyzed first. From Eq. (5.8) of Chapter 5,

$$\frac{\partial \bar{u}}{\partial b} = - \frac{h'(2\bar{\Delta} - \bar{u})}{h(2\bar{\Delta} - \bar{u})} s(\bar{\Delta}, \bar{u}) \, \bar{u},$$

$$\frac{\partial \underline{u}}{\partial b} = \frac{h'(2\underline{\Delta} - \underline{u})}{h(2\underline{\Delta} - \underline{u})} s(\underline{\Delta}, \underline{u}) \, \bar{u}.$$

The relationship between $u$ and $\Delta$, for either half-market, depends on the relative price of the firm's good and the adjacent goods. If both adjacent goods have the same price *and* if $\bar{\Delta} = \underline{\Delta}$, then $\partial \bar{u}/\partial b = -\partial \underline{u}/\partial b$, whatever the price of the firm's good relative to the adjacent goods, since then $\bar{u} = \underline{u}$. In this case, $q(\bar{u}) = q(\underline{u})$ also, so that $\partial \pi/\partial b = 0$.

Thus a sufficient condition for satisfaction of the first-order profit-maximizing condition when the firm's two adjacent competitors[5]

---

5. The description here is based on the two-characteristics case, in which no firm has more than two adjacent competitors. The number of adjacent competitors increases

charge the same price is that the specification of the firm's good be chosen to be midway between the specifications of the competitors, whatever the price charged by the firm itself.

The midpoint solution is not always the only solution to the first-order specification condition, however. When the prices of the two adjacent competitors are the same *and* the firm's own price is the same as both—the very conditions already posited as the equilibrium configuration—then $\partial \bar{u}/\partial b = \frac{1}{2}$ and $\partial \underline{u}/\partial b = -\frac{1}{2}$. This follows immediately from noting that the market boundary is always at the midpoint between the specifications of adjacent goods when the prices are the same, so that any specification shift moves the market boundary by half the amount of the shift. In this case, therefore, the right-hand side of Eq. (6.3) will be zero for any $\bar{u}$ and $\underline{u}$ such that $q(\bar{u}) = q(\underline{u})$, and the first-order condition is satisfied.

Now $q(u)$ is either a constant or a one-to-one mapping of $u$ into $q$ for which $q(\bar{u}) = q(\underline{u})$ only if $\underline{u} = \bar{u}$, giving the midpoint solution as before. It is the constant-$q$ case that may provide a different solution, therefore. From Eqs. (5.38) and (5.43), $q' = 0$ if and only if one of the following is true:

1. Demand is compensated for specification and $\sigma = 1/(1 - \mu)$. This can be *exactly* true only at one value of $\mu$, and, from Eq. (5.30), $\mu$ varies with $u$ unless $\sigma = 1$, in which case $\sigma \neq 1/(1 - \mu)$ since $\mu > 0$.

2. Demand is uncompensated for specification and $\mu = 1$ (no outside goods) or $\sigma = 1$. This is a possible case.

Thus if demand is uncompensated and there are either no outside goods or outside goods with unit elasticity of substitution, then the first-order condition for profit maximization with respect to specification is satisfied at all goods spacings when the prices of all goods are the same. If the price of the firm's good differs from the prices of adjacent goods, even when the two adjacent goods have the same

rapidly with the dimensionality of the characteristics space, a relationship that has been partly explored by Archibald and Rosenbluth (1975). The potential complexity of the relationship between the number of adjacent competitors and dimensionality is apparent from the location-theory literature when this moves from location on a line to location in a plane (see Lösch, 1954, and Eaton and Lipsey, 1976).

price, this relationship does not hold, however, since then $\partial u/\partial b$ is no longer a constant but varies with $\Delta$.

Whether the above case gives a true Nash equilibrium cannot be determined without investigation of the second-order conditions, so a final judgment must be deferred until later.

Assume now that the prices of the adjacent firms are the same and that the target firm chooses the optimal specification at midpoint. Then its market is symmetrical, with both half-markets identical, and Eq. (6.2) becomes

$$\frac{\partial \pi}{\partial P} = 2 \left( \frac{P}{R} - F' \right) \frac{\partial Q}{\partial P} . \tag{6.4}$$

The first-order condition for profit maximization with respect to price is then

$$P = RF'. \tag{6.5}$$

This is, of course, merely the standard condition that marginal revenue equal marginal cost, since

$$\frac{P}{R} = P \left( 1 + \frac{1}{E} \right)$$

can be immediately identified as the marginal revenue. The expression $R$ will be referred to as the *marginal revenue ratio*. It is simply a transformation of the demand elasticity and is thus a function of the price $P$, the goods spacing $\Delta$, and the structural parameters.

Provided the end-of-spectrum modifications discussed in Section 6.4 are assumed, so that all firms are identical in structure, the above conditions will hold for all firms, and thus the properties outlined earlier for the Nash equilibrium are consistent with satisfaction of the first-order conditions for profit maximization with respect to both price and specification for all firms. The second-order conditions are nontrivial, however, and will be taken up in a later section.

The proposition that no two firms will produce the same good is suggested by the above analysis, but not proved. This, too, will be taken up in a later section.

## 6.3 Entry–Exit Equilibrium

It has been shown that if the number of firms in the group is given (and thus the number of product differentiates), there is a Nash equilibrium for that number of firms with respect to the choices of both price and specification by each individual firm. To establish the equilibrium degree of product differentiation, it is necessary to establish the equilibrium number of firms when there is unrestricted entry into the group.

It is assumed that the entry of firms occurs in accordance with the following conditions:

1. A Nash equilibrium is established among whatever number of firms are initially in the group.

2. If the profit per firm at this equilibrium is positive, there will always be new potential entrants. They will, however, enter one (or very few) at a time, allowing the Nash equilibrium to be reestablished for each new number of firms.

3. Entry will cease when the profit per firm at equilibrium is zero. The number of firms (products) at this point is then the equilibrium degree of product differentiation.

4. If profits per firm are negative, firms will leave the group (one or a few at a time) until profit per firm is zero and again there is equilibrium.

Under the above conditions it will be shown that

1. Profit per firm declines monotonically as the number of firms increases, provided profits are nonnegative or, at worst, losses are small.

2. The equilibrium degree of product differentiation under monopolistic competition will be shown to be given by the market width $2\Delta$ such that, when equilibrium prices are established for the individual firms, the relationship $R(\Delta) = \theta(2Q(\Delta))$ holds, where $R(\Delta)$ is the marginal revenue ratio and $\theta(2Q(\Delta))$ is the degree of economies of scale.

The number of firms is represented indirectly by $2\Delta$, the equilibrium market width for the number of firms. Obviously, $\Delta$ is inversely proportional to the number of firms, and a smaller value of $\Delta$ corresponds to a higher degree of product differentiation.

At the Nash equilibrium, profit per firm is given by

$$\pi^*(\Delta) = 2PQ(\Delta) - F[2Q(\Delta)]$$
$$= 2R(\Delta)Q(\Delta)F'[2Q(\Delta)] - F[2Q(\Delta)] \qquad (6.6)$$

after using the equilibrium condition for the firm. Now $\theta = F(2Q)/2QF'(2Q)$, by definition, so that

$$\pi^* = (R\theta^{-1} - 1)F. \qquad (6.7)$$

Profit per firm is positive if $R\theta^{-1} > 1$, that is, if $R > \theta$, and is zero, the equilibrium condition, if

$$R = \theta. \qquad (6.8)$$

Variation of $\pi^*$ with the number of firms and thus with $\Delta$ is given by

$$\frac{d\pi^*}{d\Delta} = \left( \theta^{-1}\frac{dR}{d\Delta} - 2R\theta^{-2}\theta'\frac{dQ}{d\Delta} \right) F$$

$$+ 2(R\theta^{-1} - 1)F'\frac{dQ}{d\Delta}. \qquad (6.9)$$

Now $dQ/d\Delta$ is certainly positive, and $\theta'$ is taken, as usual, to be nonpositive. Provided firms are making no losses, $R\theta^{-1} - 1 \geqq 0$. Thus all terms except $\theta^{-1}(dR/d\Delta)$ are known to be positive or non-negative.

The marginal revenue ratio $R$ is defined as

$$R = E/(E - 1), \qquad (6.10)$$

so that, if $\alpha$ is any parameter or variable,

$$\frac{\partial R}{\partial \alpha} = - \frac{1}{(E - 1)^2}\frac{\partial E}{\partial \alpha} \qquad (6.11)$$

and $\partial R/\partial \alpha$ always has a sign opposite to that of $\partial E/\partial \alpha$. Since it was shown in Chapter 5 (Section 5.12) that $dE/d\Delta$ is negative, it follows that $dR/d\Delta$ is positive.

Thus $\pi^*$ declines when $\Delta$ decreases, that is, when the number of firms increases.

Since $dR/d\Delta$ is strictly positive, it is permissible for the expression $(R\theta^{-1} - 1)$ to be marginally negative and still have $d\pi^*/d\Delta$

positive. Thus there is no unstable behavior at the zero-profit boundary.

The group equilibrium condition, $R = \theta$, is simply the combination of the individual firms's equilibrium condition

### Marginal Revenue = Marginal Cost

and the zero-profit condition

### Price = Average Cost.

This is easily seen by noting that $\theta$ is the ratio of average to marginal cost and that $R$ is the ratio of price to marginal revenue.

To complete the picture of monopolistic-competition equilibrium, it remains to be established under what conditions the second-order conditions for the individual firm are satisfied and under what conditions the group equilibrium exists. The latter problem can be tackled immediately, the former is deferred to the next section.

Since $E$ is infinite when $\Delta = 0$, $R(0) = 1$ and $dR/d\Delta$ is positive. Thus the graph of $R$ against $\Delta$ is an upward-sloping curve, commencing from the value $R(0) = 1$. If $\theta$ is constant and small enough or if $\theta' < 0$ and $\theta_{max}$ is small enough, a solution will exist at some positive value of $\Delta$, since it is assumed throughout that $\theta(0) > 1$. Thus there will be an equilibrium with a finite number of different products, at least for a sufficiently small degree of scale economies.

In the classic case of firms with U-shaped cost curves, where $\theta$ is above unity at zero output and falls to unity at minimum average cost output, the equilibrium will necessarily be where $\theta > 1$, that is, at an output less than that giving minimum average cost. This is identical to the so-called "excess capacity" result of Chamberlin, a result that has been debated in recent years and is discussed in more detail later in the chapter.

Two kinds of difficulty may arise if $\theta$ is relatively large. One is that the equilibrium value of $\Delta$ may exist, but at a value so large as to call for only one or very few firms so that the many-firm structure implicit in monopolistic competition cannot exist. At even larger values, there may be no intersection at all with the graph of $R$. It was shown in Chapter 5 that the demand elasticity is bounded below, so that the marginal revenue ratio is bounded above. If $\theta_{min}$ is greater than this upper boundary the industry will not be profitable, even for a single firm. A fuller discussion of the viability of the monopolistic-competition structure is given later, after examination of the second-order conditions and other relevant matters.


## 6.4 The End-Firm Problem

The first-order conditions for monopolistic competition have been derived on the assumption that all firms face situations which are structurally identical. The firms at the ends of the spectrum do not face the same situation as other firms, however, because they have no adjacent competitors between them and the extreme points of the spectrum, and thus have a monopoly in one of their half-markets.

Boundary problems of this kind arise frequently in modeling phenomena in all the sciences, and there are only three possible approaches. One is to avoid having boundaries at all, by assuming infinite spaces (common in location theory) or by other ingenious means. It has become popular, for example, to remove the boundaries in neo-Hotelling models by assuming the linear space to be the circumference of a circle, like a ring road.[6] The circular solution is obviously quite inappropriate in the characteristics model, since it makes no sense to assume that a consumer is almost indifferent between a good having characteristic A only and one having characteristic B only, while he or she finds great difference between a good with characteristic A only and one with 90 percent characteristic A and 10 percent characteristic B. Nor is the infinite spectrum approach fruitful (although it would be possible to recast the analysis in this form), since it would seem that the range of diversity in preferences is an important structural parameter of the economy.

The second approach is to presume that the boundary effects are an important feature of the model and to build them in even if the analysis is changed in a major way as a result. A case in point is the original Hotelling spatial analysis with its prediction of a clustering

6. See Salop (1976). The circular-road solution appears to have been introduced by Chamberlin (1953).

of firms toward the center of the spectrum, which is, unfortunately, the feature of the model that has been best remembered. This prediction follows entirely from the existence of the end-firm problem and results in the properties of the model being almost entirely determined by its boundary properties. This can be regarded as entirely realistic or as a case of the tail wagging the dog, according to one's judgment as to how important events near the boundary are compared to events in the interior. In the spatial model, it might be quite appropriate to let boundary conditions dominate in modeling Main Street in a small town, quite inappropriate in modeling location along a coast-to-coast highway.

In the characteristics model, it would seem inappropriate to have the properties of the system unduly influenced by properties at the end of the spectrum, and thus by the most atypical individuals. Thus the third possible approach will be used here—to assume whatever special properties are necessary at the spectrum ends to guarantee that the end firms face a situation comparable to that of other firms, provided those special properties are not inconsistent with commonsense expectations. A falloff in density of consumers near the ends would seem to accord with common sense, for example, whereas a rise in density near the ends would not.

Consider any one of the end firms, and assume that the system as a whole satisfies the first-order conditions for equilibrium which were set out in the two previous sections. The end firm will have two half-markets, one in which all the variables will have the same values as in the half-markets of the interior firms, and another which extends to the end of the spectrum with no competition from any other firm. The necessary end-of-spectrum modifications are those that will ensure that this end firm is in equilibrium at the same price and at the same distance from the nearest interior firm as would be the case for other firms and that it makes zero profit under these circumstances.

There are three first-order conditions that the firm must satisfy: the conditions of profit maximums with respect to both specification and price and the zero-profit condition (average cost equals price). Denoting values of variables in the end half-market by overbars and those in the interior half-market by unmarked symbols, the first two conditions are, from Eqs. (6.2) and (6.3), respectively,

$$\frac{\partial \pi}{\partial P} = \left( \frac{P}{\bar{R}} - F' \right) \frac{\partial \bar{Q}}{\partial P} + \left( \frac{P}{R} - F' \right) \frac{\partial Q}{\partial P} = 0, \tag{6.12}$$

$$\frac{\partial \pi}{\partial b} = (P - F') \left( \bar{q}(\bar{u}) \frac{\partial \bar{u}}{\partial b} + q(u) \frac{\partial u}{\partial b} \right) = 0. \tag{6.13}$$

Now the second term in Eq. (6.12) vanishes since the values are those for the regular firms, and thus the first term must vanish also. Since it can be assumed that $\partial \bar{Q}/\partial P \neq 0$, this implies that $P = \bar{R}F'$ and thus that $\bar{R} = R$, since $P$ and $F'$ are the same in both half-markets. Since $R$ is simply a transform of the elasticity $E$, this implies that $\bar{E} = E$, the well-known result that a firm is in equilibrium in two markets at the same price only if the elasticities in both markets are the same.

Consider the condition set forth in Eq. (6.13). Since the boundary of the half-market toward the interior is at the midpoint between the specifications of the end firm and the adjacent interior firm (since both sell at the same price), $\partial u/\partial b = \frac{1}{2}$, as shown in Section 6.2. For the end half-market, $\partial \bar{u}/\partial b = -1$ since the position of the end of the spectrum is fixed. It is assumed that the end firm being investigated is that at the top end (highest value of specification parameter) and that the other end firm has the signs of $\partial u/\partial b$ and $\partial \bar{u}/\partial b$ reversed. Thus Eq. (6.13) implies that

$$\bar{q}(\bar{u}) = \frac{1}{2}q(u).$$

Finally, consider the zero-profit condition, which has the form $R = \theta$ as for the other firms, since it has been shown that $\bar{R} = R$. If $\theta$ is a constant (homogeneous production), this condition will be satisfied automatically. But if $\theta$ varies with output, as will be taken to be the general case, then $\theta$ will have the same value as for other firms (necessary to give $R = \theta$) only if the production of the regular firms is given by $2Q$ and that of the end firm by $(Q + \bar{Q})$, which requires that $\bar{Q}(\bar{u}) = Q(u)$.

Thus the conditions that must be satisfied in the end half-market, by adjustment of spectrum properties if necessary, are

$$\bar{q}(\bar{u}) = \tfrac{1}{2} q(u),$$ (6.14a)

$$\bar{Q}(\bar{u}) = Q(u),$$ (6.14b)

$$\bar{E} = E.$$ (6.14c)

Since $Q$ and $\bar{Q}$ are the integrals of $q$ and $\bar{q}$, it is obvious that Eqs. (6.14a) and (6.14b) cannot simultaneously be true if the functions $q$ and $\bar{q}$ are identical, as they are over the main part of the spectrum under the assumed uniform density of either welfare (for compensated demand) or income (for uncompensated demand). However, if the average density over the tail of the spectrum is lower than elsewhere and $\bar{u}$ is greater than $u$, it is possible to satisfy both conditions simultaneously.

The elasticities $E$ and $\bar{E}$ cannot, however, be equalized by differences in average density, since they are independent of absolute quantities. These elasticities need further consideration. The special feature of the elasticity $\bar{E}$ for the end half-market, is that it contains no inside-substitution terms, since there is no width-of-market effect, and that it consists entirely of outside-substitution and income terms. Assume that demand is compensated for a slightly simpler analysis (the results follow equally for uncompensated demand), then the expressions for the two elasticities are given (from Eq. 5.42) by

$$E = se_Q + (1 - m)\sigma$$ (6.15a)

$$\bar{E} = (1 - \bar{m})\bar{\sigma},$$ (6.15b)

where $\sigma$ is the elasticity of substitution between group goods and outside goods, $m$ is the proportion of total expenditure which is on group goods, and $se_Q$ is the inside-substitution effect, which is essentially positive.

Obviously, $E > \bar{E}$ if $m = \bar{m}$ and $\sigma = \bar{\sigma}$. Now if $\bar{u} \neq u$, as assumed above, then there will be some difference between $m$ and $\bar{m}$ unless $q$ and $\bar{q}$ are constants (as with unit elasticity of substitution), but this effect will be relatively small. The most obvious way in which $E$ and $\bar{E}$ might be made equal is by assuming some change in the elasticity of substitution at the end of the spectrum. The requisite change is one in which $\bar{\sigma} > \sigma$.

Thus the required end-firm conditions (Eqs. 6.14a–c) can be satisfied by an end-of-spectrum modification in which:

1. the average density of consumers is lower at the very ends of the spectrum than for the spectrum generally, over which it is assumed to be constant.

2. the average value of the elasticity of substitution is higher for consumers at the very ends of the spectrum than elsewhere, being assumed to be constant other than at the ends.

Both these conditions can be satisfied by a continuous falloff in density of appropriate shape and on appropriate continuous rise in the elasticity of substitution, over a distance which need not be greater than the distance of the end firm from the end of the spectrum.

Do these end-of-spectrum modifications pass the common-sense test? The density falloff surely does, and it is even more reasonable than assuming that the density remains constant right to the end and then falls to zero. The elasticity-of-substitution rise is also reasonable, since it can be argued that individuals with preferences at the end of the spectrum have only a marginal interest in the goods in the group and thus may find outside goods relatively better substitutes than would individuals with preferences in the interior of the spectrum.

Thus it will be assumed that the required modifications of uniformity and uniform density at the very ends of the spectrum have been made when general cases are analyzed, so that there are no end-firm problems and all firms can be treated alike. Although the exact forms of the end modifications hold only for the particular equilibrium configuration for which they were designed, it will be assumed that the usual comparative static analysis can be carried out without any significant problems arising.

It should be noted that the spacing between the end firms and the end of the spectrum will be greater than half the spacing between adjacent firms, and this is the only equilibrium variable that will reveal the existence of an end effect.

## 6.5 The Second-Order Conditions

The properties of the monopolistic-competition equilibrium have been defined entirely in terms of the first-order conditions for profit maximization, assuming that it can be shown that these conditions do, indeed, give a true maximum under acceptable restrictions on the structure of the system. The point has now arrived at which the second-order conditions must be examined to determine whether the provisional assumption was justified.

Profit is a function of the two variables, price and specification, and the condition that it has a strong maximum with respect to joint variations in both variables is

$$d^2\pi = \frac{\partial^2\pi}{\partial P^2}\, dP^2 + \frac{\partial^2\pi}{\partial P\partial b}\, dP db + \frac{\partial^2\pi}{\partial b^2}\, db^2 < 0 \tag{6.16}$$

for all combinations of $dP$ and $db$ such that at least one is nonzero.

Necessary and sufficient conditions for the satisfaction of Eq. (6.16) are

$$\frac{\partial^2\pi}{\partial P^2}, \frac{\partial^2\pi}{\partial b^2} < 0 \tag{6.17a}$$

and

$$\left(\frac{\partial^2\pi}{\partial P\partial b}\right)^2 < \left(\frac{\partial^2\pi}{\partial P^2}\right)\left(\frac{\partial^2\pi}{\partial b^2}\right). \tag{6.17b}$$

For a weak maximum, the strict inequalities in Eqs. (6.16) and (6.17a and b) are replaced by weak inequalities.

The task is simplified somewhat by noting that if Eq. (6.17a) is satisfied by strict inequalities, then Eq. (6.17b) is necessarily satisfied if

$$\frac{\partial^2\pi}{\partial P\partial b} = 0,$$

and if either $\partial^2\pi/\partial P^2$ or $\partial^2\pi/\partial b^2$ is zero, then even the weak condition cannot be satisfied if

$$\frac{\partial^2\pi}{\partial P\partial b} \neq 0.$$

These relationships will prove to be sufficient to establish the basic propositions as to the stability (second-order properties) of the monopolistic-competition equilibrium, which can be stated as follows:

1. The necessary and sufficient condition for strong stability of the monopolistic-competition equilibrium with respect to both price and specification is that there be outside goods having an elasticity of substitution with respect to group goods in the high range, that is, $\sigma \geq 1/(1 - m)$ for compensated demand or $\sigma > 1$ for uncompensated demand.

2. The equilibrium is stable with respect to price over a wider elasticity range than that for which it is stable with respect to both price and specification.

3. If demand is uncompensated for specification and either (a) there are no outside goods (the paradigm case) or (b) there are outside goods, but the elasticity of substitution with respect to these is unity, and the first-order conditions with respect to specification are satisfied by all goods spacings, but the equilibrium is unstable except when goods are evenly spaced over the spectrum, in which case the equilibrium may be, at best, weakly stable.

Investigation of the effects of variation in specification begins with the relationship, from Eq. (6.3),

$$\frac{\partial \pi}{\partial b} = (P - F') \left[ q(\bar{u}) \frac{\partial \bar{u}}{\partial b} + q(\underline{u}) \frac{\partial \underline{u}}{\partial b} \right],$$

so that

$$\frac{\partial^2 \pi}{\partial b^2} = (P - F') \left[ q'(\bar{u}) \left( \frac{\partial \bar{u}}{\partial b} \right)^2 + q'(\underline{u}) \left( \frac{\partial \underline{u}}{\partial b} \right)^2 \right.$$

$$\left. + q(\bar{u}) \frac{\partial^2 \bar{u}}{\partial b^2} + q(\underline{u}) \frac{\partial^2 \underline{u}}{\partial b^2} \right]. \qquad (6.18)$$

At equilibrium, prices of all goods are the same, so that, as shown in Section 6.2,

$$\partial \bar{u}/\partial b = -\tfrac{1}{2}, \quad \partial \underline{u}/\partial b = \tfrac{1}{2}, \quad \text{and} \quad \partial^2 \bar{u}/\partial b^2 = \partial^2 \underline{u}/\partial b^2 = 0.$$

As a consequence, Eq. (6.18) simplifies to

$$\frac{\partial^2 \pi}{\partial b^2} = \tfrac{1}{4}(P - F')[q'(\bar{u}) + q'(\underline{u})]. \qquad (6.19)$$

Whatever the specification of the good, and thus whatever the relationship between $\bar{u}$ and $\underline{u}$, the derivatives $q'$ will both be negative if $Q$ is concave, positive if $Q$ is convex, and zero if $Q$ is linear with $q$ constant. Thus the equilibrium is unstable ($\partial^2\pi/\partial b^2 > 0$) for convex $Q$, that is, if $\sigma < 1/(1 - m)$ for compensated demand or $\sigma < 1$ for uncompensated demand. For the uncompensated paradigm case, $q' = 0$ everywhere, and thus $\partial^2\pi/\partial b^2$ is always zero.

Thus it is necessary for a strong maximum, and sufficient for the satisfaction of the particular condition $\partial^2\pi/\partial b^2 < 0$, that $Q$ be concave, with $q' < 0$. From Eqs. (5.38) and (5.43), the requirement is satisfied if $\sigma \geqq 1/(1 - m)$ for compensated demand or $\sigma > 1$ for uncompensated demand.

If demand is uncompensated for specification and either $\sigma = 1$ or there are no outside goods (paradigm case), then $q' = 0$ and $\partial^2\pi/\partial b^2 = 0$, so that a weak maximum is a possibility in this case, subject to the remaining conditions being satisfied

The mixed partial derivative is obtained by differentiating Eq. (6.3) (reproduced above) with respect to $P$:

$$\frac{\partial^2\pi}{\partial P\partial b} = (P - F')\left[\frac{\partial q(\bar{u})}{\partial P}\frac{\partial\bar{u}}{\partial b} + \frac{\partial q(\underline{u})}{\partial P}\frac{\partial\underline{u}}{\partial b}\right.$$

$$\left. + q(\bar{u})\frac{\partial^2\bar{u}}{\partial b\partial P} + q(\underline{u})\frac{\partial^2\underline{u}}{\partial b\partial P}\right] . \quad (6.20)$$

At the equilibrium configuration of uniform prices, $\partial\bar{u}/\partial b = -\frac{1}{2}$ and $\partial\underline{u}/\partial b = \frac{1}{2}$, as before. Also, in this case it can be shown that

$$\frac{\partial^2\bar{u}}{\partial b\partial P} = -\frac{h(\bar{\Delta})h''(\bar{\Delta}) - [h'(\bar{\Delta})]^2}{4[h'(\bar{\Delta})]^2} \quad (6.21a)$$

$$\frac{\partial^2\underline{u}}{\partial b\partial P} = \frac{h(\underline{\Delta})h''(\underline{\Delta}) - [h'(\underline{\Delta})]^2}{4[h'(\underline{\Delta})]^2} , \quad (6.21b)$$

where $2\bar{\Delta}$ and $2\underline{\Delta}$, are the distances to the upper and lower adjacent goods and the values $\bar{u} = \bar{\Delta}$ and $\underline{u} = \underline{\Delta}$ have been incorporated because the prices of all goods are the same.

From these relationships and inspection of Eq. (6.20), it is obvious that:

1. if there is uniform spacing between goods, then $\bar{\Delta} = \underline{\Delta}$ and the

terms inside the bracket on the right-hand side of Eq. (6.20) consist of pairs having the same magnitude but opposite signs, so that $\partial^2\pi/\partial P\partial b = 0$.

2. if $\underline{\Delta} \neq \bar{\Delta}$ (uneven spacing), then the terms in Eq. (6.20) do not cancel and $\partial^2\pi/\partial P\partial b \neq 0$ (its sign does not matter, only its nonvanishing property).

For compensated demand, or for uncompensated demand with $\sigma \neq 1$, the first-order conditions implies equal spacing and thus that $\partial^2\pi/\partial P\partial b = 0$. For uncompensated demand with $\sigma = 1$ or the uncompensated paradigm case, the first-order condition $\partial\pi/\partial b = 0$ is satisfied at all spacings when prices are uniform, but $\partial^2\pi/\partial P\partial b = 0$ only at uniform spacing, and otherwise $\partial^2\pi/\partial P\partial b \neq 0$. Since it has been shown that, in this case, $\partial^2\pi/\partial b^2 = 0$, the uncompensated unit elasticity and paradigm cases are definitely unstable except at the same uniform goods spacing as in the other cases. At the uniform spacing, Eqs. (6.17a) and (6.17b) are satisfied by equalities and not strict inequalities, so that the equilibrium is, at best, weakly stable.

For compensated demand with $\sigma > 1/(1 - m)$ or uncompensated demand with $\sigma > 1$, then $\partial^2\pi/\partial b^2 < 0$ and $\partial^2\pi/\partial P\partial b = 0$, so that, since it will be shown below that $\partial^2\pi/\partial P^2 < 0$ under these same conditions, the equilibrium satisfies the conditions for a strong maximum and is thus stable.

Satisfaction of the second-order conditions is thus confined to equilibria with uniform spacings only, so that the effect of price need only be investigated in the symmetric market case (Eq. 6.4):

$$\frac{\partial\pi}{\partial P} = 2\left(\frac{P}{R} - F'\right)\frac{\partial Q}{\partial P} .$$

From this, the second-order derivative is

$$\frac{\partial^2\pi}{\partial P^2} = 2\left(\frac{1}{R} - \frac{P}{R^2}\frac{\partial R}{\partial P} - 2F''\frac{\partial Q}{\partial P}\right)\frac{\partial Q}{\partial P}$$

$$+ 2\left(\frac{P}{R} - F'\right)\frac{\partial^2 Q}{\partial P^2} . \qquad (6.22)$$

Note that the argument of $F$ and $F'$ is $2Q$, not $Q$.

At equilibrium the second term on the right-hand side of Eq.

(6.22) vanishes, which gives

$$\frac{\partial^2 \pi}{\partial P^2} = \frac{2}{R}\frac{\partial Q}{\partial P}\left(1 - 2RF''\frac{\partial Q}{\partial P} - \frac{P}{R}\frac{\partial R}{\partial P}\right)$$    (6.23)

when $\partial \pi/\partial P = 0$. The sign of $\partial^2\pi/\partial P^2$ is certainly not obvious, since it was shown in Chapter 5 that the sign of $\partial E/\partial P$, and hence $\partial R/\partial P$, depends on the parameters. The value for $F''$ may also have any sign since both rising and falling marginal cost is consistent with the existence of economies of scale. Furthermore, the conditions that determine the sign of $\partial E/\partial P$—the elasticity of substitution and the compensation properties—are quite independent of the technology properties that determine the sign of $F''$.

Limits can, however, be placed on $F''$ from the assumed properties of the economies of scale and from the equilibrium conditions. Since $\theta = F/2QF'$, by definition, $F' = F/2Q\theta$, so that

$$F'' = \frac{F'}{2Q\theta} - \frac{F}{4Q^2\theta} - \frac{F\theta'}{2Q\theta^2}$$

$$= \frac{F'}{2Q}\frac{1-\theta}{\theta} - F'\frac{\theta'}{\theta}$$    (6.24)

after substituting $F = 2QF'\theta$ and again noting that the argument of $F$, $F'$, and $\theta$ is $2Q$.

Thus

$$2RF''\frac{\partial Q}{\partial P} = \frac{P}{Q}\frac{\partial Q}{\partial P}\frac{1-\theta}{\theta} - 2P\frac{\theta'}{\theta}\frac{\partial Q}{\partial P}$$

$$= E\frac{\theta-1}{\theta} + 2QE\frac{\theta'}{\theta}$$    (6.25)

after using the equilibrium condition of the firm $(P = RF')$ and substituting for $E = -(P/Q)(\partial Q/\partial P)$.

Now $R = E/(E-1)$, and if firms do not make losses, $R \geq \theta$, so that $E(\theta-1)/\theta \leq 1$. Noting that $\partial Q/\partial P$ is essentially negative, Eq. (6.23) then implies

$$\frac{\partial^2 \pi}{\partial P^2} \leq -\frac{2}{R}\frac{\partial Q}{\partial P}\left(2QE\frac{\theta'}{\theta} + \frac{P}{R}\frac{\partial R}{\partial P}\right),$$    (6.26)

with equality if $R = \theta$.

The factor outside the bracket on the right-hand side of Eq. (6.26) is positive, so $\partial^2\pi/\partial P^2$ is negative if the contents of the bracket are negative. Since $\theta' \leqq 0$, it is obviously sufficient for the bracket to be negative, and thus the second-order condition $\partial^2\pi/\partial P^2 < 0$ to be satisfied, if $\partial R/\partial P$ is negative. From Eq. (6.11), $\partial R/\partial P$ is negative if $\partial E/\partial P$ is positive, and from Chapter 5, $\partial E/\partial P$ is certainly positive if $\sigma > 1/(1 - m)$ when demand is compensated or if $\sigma > 1$ when demand is uncompensated. Thus under the same conditions which guarantee that $\partial^2\pi/\partial b^2$ is negative, $\partial^2\pi/\partial P^2$ is also negative. Thus the condition, $\sigma > 1/(1 - m)$ or $\sigma > 1$, according to whether demand is compensated or not, is sufficient to guarantee satisfaction of all the second-order conditions for a maximum and is necessary to guarantee that both $\partial^2\pi/\partial b^2$ is negative and $\partial^2\pi/\partial P\partial b$ is zero.

Note that, as specified in the earlier statement, the condition for stability with respect to price alone ($\partial^2\pi/\partial P^2 < 0$) is less stringent than that for stability with respect to both price and specification. This follows from the fact that the elasticity conditions given above are sufficient but not necessary for the negativity of $\partial R/\partial P$, and if $\theta' < 0$, the right-hand side of Eq. (6.26) can be negative even if $\partial R/\partial P$ is positive, that is, even if $\sigma$ is less than the values 1 or $1/(1 - m)$ necessary to give stability with respect to specification. Thus a *fixed-specification* model will be stable over a larger range of values than the variable-specification model set out here.

## 6.6 Uniqueness of Product

In the preceding analysis it was shown that, under conditions of uniformity and uniform income distribution (real or money, according to whether demand is compensated or not), the only stable equilibrium for monopolistic competition is one in which the specifications of the goods produced are distributed evenly over the spectrum. The possibility that this condition is satisfied by a configuration in which there are several firms producing each of the goods has not yet been definitively ruled out, and it is the purpose of this section to show that such clustering will not occur.

The proposition to be demonstrated can be stated as follows:

A stable Nash equilibrium will be characterized by the property that no two firms will produce a product of the same specification, so that every firm's product is unique.

The proposition will be proved by showing that, under the conditions necessary to give a stable equilibrium, whenever two firms produce the same good, at least one can gain by varying the specification away from that of the other firm.

Consider a configuration that conforms to the general equilibrium requirement that goods be distributed evenly over the spectrum but in which some goods are produced by two or more firms. Since the goods are distributed evenly over the spectrum, the prices of all goods must be the same, and, of course, the prices charged by each firm when more than one sell the same good must also be the same. Consider some good for which there are two sellers, the joint market for which is divided in proportions $\lambda$ and $1 - \lambda$. If the spacing between the goods is $2\Delta$, then the quantities sold by the two firms are $2\lambda Q(\Delta)$ and $2(1 - \lambda)Q(\Delta)$, respectively.

Now suppose the firm having the share $\lambda$ changes the specification of its good by an amount $2\delta$ away from that of its rival, in either direction. On the "away" side (away from the rival), the firm's good is now at a distance $2(\Delta - \delta)$ from the nearest adjacent good, and since all prices are the same, its market boundary will be at half this distance, or $\Delta - \delta$. On the other, or "near," side, the minimarket of width $2\delta$ will be shared equally by both the firms originally selling the same product. Thus the firm which has moved will have total sales at its new specification equal to

$$Q(\Delta - \delta) + Q(\delta).$$

Now the stability conditions require that $q' \leqq 0$, that is, that $Q$ is at least weakly concave. But concavity of $Q$ implies that

$$Q(\Delta) \leqq Q(\Delta - \delta) + Q(\delta). \tag{6.27}$$

Thus the firm increases its sales if $\lambda \leqq \frac{1}{2}$ and $Q$ is strictly concave [a strict inequality in Eq. (6.27)] or if $\lambda < \frac{1}{2}$ and $Q$ is weakly concave (linear), and its sales are unchanged if $\lambda = \frac{1}{2}$ and $Q$ is linear. Since price is unchanged and average cost is falling ($\theta > 1$), the firm increases its profit if it has either no more than half the original market and $A$ is strictly concave or less than half the original market and $Q$ is linear (a borderline case for stability). With exactly half the original market and linear $Q$, the firm neither gains nor loses by the move.

The second firm, assumed to remain at the original place, finds its market width to be $\Delta$ (the original value) on one side and $\delta$ on the other, so its sales become $Q(\Delta) + Q(\delta)$. This is clearly greater than its original sales, $2(1 - \lambda)Q(\Delta)$, if $\lambda \geqq \frac{1}{2}$, whatever the concavity properties of $Q$.

Thus, whatever the original division of the market, a move that results in the two firms producing goods of different specifications always results in a gain for at least one of the firms and, if the market is split evenly and $Q$ is strictly concave, in gains to both firms. Note that variable specification removes the "cutthroat" price competition which would exist with fixed specification.[7] Neither firm can hope to gain the whole of the original market by undercutting the other firm on price, since either firm can always regain at least half the market by a specification change.

The move described above is, of course, merely an initial move and does not represent a final equilibrium situation, which will be achieved only when all clusters of firms have dispersed and when the configuration is that of firms all producing a unique good with specifications distributed evenly over the spectrum.

Finally, consider the configuration which is possible when the cost curves are U-shaped with a minimum average cost at an output which is very small compared to the total market for goods within the group. Then it is possible to have $k$ firms producing each of $n$ goods, each firm producing at minimum average cost, and to have a structure similar to that of perfect competition. Each firm producing the good is merely one of a large number producing the same good and thus faces a perfectly elastic demand if specification is taken as fixed. Thus $R = 1$ for each firm, and the equilibrium conditions with respect to price (Eq. 6.5) and entry (Eq. 6.8) can be satisfied at the perfectly competitive equilibrium $P = F'$ and $\theta = 1$. This configuration is unstable with respect to specification, however, for the same reasons as given for the two-firm case. Any one of the $m$ firms can gain sales

---

7. See Kaldor (1935), Lerner and Singer (1937), Sweezy (1939), and Smithies (1941).

by moving to a different specification, as argued above. Since average cost is not falling, this does not necessarily imply an increase in profit at the old price; however, by moving to a different specification, the firm reduces the elasticity of its demand from infinity to some finite value, and, for the same output level as before, can thus raise its price while keeping average cost near the minimum level. Thus a firm can always gain by moving out of the cluster, and the equilibrium with minimum average cost at a low output level will consist of a large number of products (of the order of $nk$ different specifications) rather than $n$ clusters of $k$ firms.

## 6.7 Product Differentiation in the Market

Since each firm produces a unique product under monopolistic competition, the degree of product differentiation corresponds to the number of firms at full equilibrium. For a fixed range of preferences over the spectrum, the degree of product differentiation is inverse to the size of $\Delta$, the equilibrium half-spacing between the specifications of adjacent goods.

The degree of product differentiation is determined by the full equilibrium condition (Eq. 6.8),

$$R = \theta.$$

Since $R$ depends on the structural parameters $\sigma$ and $m$, as well as on the market variables, it is obvious that the degree of product differentiation attained in the market cannot be determined from group properties alone, but depends on the relationship between the group and the rest of the economy. The degree of product differentiation in the market will be shown to have the following properties:

The market equilibrium degree of product differentiation depends on the technology and intragroup substitution properties and on the relationships between the group and the rest of the economy. In particular, the degree of product differentiation will be lower:

(*a*) the higher the degree of economies of scale ($\theta$);

(*b*) the higher the elasticity of substitution between group goods and outside goods ($\sigma$); and

(*c*) the less important the group in the total economy ($m$).

Consider a parameter $\alpha$ that may affect either the demand conditions or the degree of returns to scale, or both. Differentiation of the equilibrium condition $R = \theta$ gives the effect of a change in such a parameter as

$$\frac{d\Delta}{d\alpha} = \frac{\dfrac{\partial \theta}{\partial \alpha} + 2\theta' \dfrac{\partial Q}{\partial \alpha} - \dfrac{\partial R}{\partial \alpha}}{\dfrac{\partial R}{\partial \Delta} - 2q\theta'}, \tag{6.28}$$

noting that $\theta = \theta(2Q)$. The denominator on the right-hand side is clearly positive, since $\theta' \leqq 0$ and $\partial R/\partial \Delta > 0$, so that the sign of $d\Delta/d\alpha$ is the sign of the numerator.

If $\alpha$ affects only the degree of returns to scale (a pure technology or cost change), and affects it positively, then $d\Delta/d\alpha$ is positive and the degree of product differentiation is lowered, giving result (a) above.

If $\alpha$ is a parameter that does not affect $\theta$ directly, as is true of the two structural parameters $\sigma$ and $m$, then the first term in the numerator on the right-hand side of Eq. (6.28) vanishes and the sign of $d\Delta/d\alpha$ is the same as the sign of

$$2\theta' \frac{\partial Q}{\partial \alpha} - \frac{\partial R}{\partial \alpha}.$$

Since $\theta' \leqq 0$, this is unambiguous in sign if the sign of $\partial Q/\partial \alpha$ is the same as that of $\partial R/\partial \alpha$. Now the sign of $\partial R/\partial \alpha$ is itself opposite to that of $\partial E/\partial \alpha$, so that

$$d\Delta/d\alpha > 0 \quad \text{if } \partial Q/\partial \alpha \leqq 0 \text{ and } \partial E/\partial \alpha > 0,$$

$$d\Delta/d\alpha < 0 \quad \text{if } \partial Q/\partial \alpha \geqq 0 \text{ and } \partial E/\partial \alpha < 0.$$

Taking the parameter $\sigma$ first, it was shown in Chapter 5 (Eq. 5.54) that $\partial E/\partial \sigma > 0$. Thus $d\Delta/d\sigma > 0$ if it can be shown that $\partial Q/\partial \sigma < 0$. Now

$$\frac{\partial q}{\partial \sigma} = \int_0^u \frac{\partial q'}{\partial \sigma} \, dv + \frac{\partial q(0)}{\partial \sigma}$$

and, since $\partial q(0)/\partial\sigma = 0$,

$$\frac{\partial q}{\partial\sigma} > 0 \quad \text{if } \frac{\partial q'}{\partial\sigma} > 0$$

$$< 0 \quad \text{if } \frac{\partial q'}{\partial\sigma} < 0 \qquad \text{for all } v.$$

Similarly, since $Q(0) = 0$, it can be shown that

$$\frac{\partial Q}{\partial\sigma} > 0 \quad \text{if } \frac{\partial q}{\partial\sigma} > 0$$

$$< 0 \quad \text{if } \frac{\partial q}{\partial\sigma} < 0.$$

Thus the sign of $\partial q'/\partial\sigma$ (the same as that of $\partial e_q/\partial\sigma$) gives the sign of $\partial Q/\partial\sigma$. But from Eq. (5.50), $\partial e_q/\partial\sigma < 0$, so that $\partial Q/\partial\sigma < 0$, and thus $d\Delta/d\sigma > 0$. An increase in the elasticity of substitution increases $\Delta$ and reduces the degree of product differentiation, result b above.

The simple economic interpretation of the above relationship is as follows. A higher elasticity of substitution results in a higher demand elasticity for each good at the original spacing, and thus a lower ratio of price to marginal revenue. If firms continue to equate marginal cost (which is unchanged) with marginal revenue, price will now be below average cost and firms will make losses. There will be a reduction in the number of goods until the elasticity of demand (which falls as the market width increases) has dropped sufficiently to give a new equilibrium with zero profits.

It was shown in Chapter 5 that $\partial E/\partial m$ is negative if demand is compensated but $\sigma \geqq 1$. Since there is no stable market solution if demand is uncompensated and $\sigma < 1$, it can be taken that $\partial E/\partial m < 0$. Then $d\Delta/dm < 0$ if it can be shown that $\partial Q/\partial m > 0$.

By the same kind of argument as in the case of $\sigma$, it can be shown that $\partial Q/\partial m$ has the sign of $\partial e_q/\partial m$. From Eqs. (5.38) and (5.43), $\partial e_q/\partial m > 0$ for compensated demand, and $\partial e_q/\partial m \geqq 0$ for uncompensated demand if $\sigma \geqq 1$, as must be the case for a stable equilibrium. Thus $\partial Q/\partial m \geqq 0$, which implies that $d\Delta/dm < 0$ and therefore that the degree of product differentiation becomes less if $m$ becomes smaller, giving result c above.

## 6.8 The Size of the Market

Exactly the same kind of distinction needs to be made here as was made in Chapter 3 between the breadth of the market and the depth of the market. The breadth of the market (that is, for the whole group, not for an individual firm) is given by the range of diversity in preferences. Since the equilibrium conditions determine the equilibrium market segment size for the individual firm, the total number of different products (firms) is found by dividing the equilibrium segment size into the range. An increase in the range will increase the number of products, but not the product density (number of products per unit distance along the spectrum).

As in the conditions for the optimum, the equilibrium conditions for monopolistic competition represent a relationship between two elasticities, the elasticity of demand and the elasticity of the input function. Thus a change in the depth of the market (represented by $q_o$, the scale parameter in the quantity demanded) will have no effect on the equilibrium segment size unless the size of one of the elasticities is affected. Now the elasticity of demand, $E$, is not affected in any way by variations in $q_o$, but the elasticity of the input function, $\theta$, may be affected if $\theta$ is a function of output. Since $\theta = \theta(2Q)$,

$$\frac{\partial \theta}{\partial q_o} = 2\theta' \frac{Q}{q_o},$$

and this is negative if $\theta$ is sensitive to output ($\theta' < 0$). Thus $d\Delta/dq_o$ is negative, and an increase in the depth of the market will increase the degree of product differentiation if the degree of returns to scale is a function of output.

Note that these results imply that two markets of identical "size," measured by the total quantity of goods $\Sigma(2Q_i)$ (there is no aggregation problem since all goods have the same price), may have different equilibrium numbers of product differentiates in the group, even though the production technologies and relationships with outside goods are identical in both cases. This can occur if one market is broader but less deep than the other and $\theta$ is a constant. On the other hand, if $\theta$ is sensitive to output, the markets may have the same number of goods, and if the markets differ in size, the larger number of products may occur in either the larger or the smaller market, depending on how the breadth and depth effects are related to each other.

The size of the market may be critical in determining whether a good is produced at all or whether it can be produced under conditions which give sufficient firms for the monopolistic-competition structure to be viable if the economies of scale vary with output. The question of viability is taken up in the next section, in which it is shown that the market may not produce goods in the group if the economies-of-scale parameter $\theta$ is above some critical level. If the economies of scale are the result of a fixed cost plus constant or increasing marginal cost, then the market is always viable if it is large enough. Thus it is possible to have two economies basically identical in everything but size such that a particular group of goods appears on the market only in the larger economy.

## 6.9 The Viability of Monopolistic Competition

As is apparent from the earlier analysis of the second-order conditions, a stable Nash equilibrium does not necessarily exist in the market for all structural relationships between the group and the rest of the economy. The second-order conditions place a minimum value on the elasticity of substitution and a requirement that there be outside goods, but these will be shown to be only part of the total restrictions necessary to guarantee the existence and stability of a market equilibrium. There are upper limits on the elasticity of substitution as well.

There are three types of conditions that must be satisfied in order to have a viable market solution with the properties of monopolistic competition:

1. conditions necessary for a Nash equilibrium to be stable, if such an equilibrium exists;
2. conditions necessary to ensure that there is some configuration in which the firm or firms can operate without making a loss; and
3. conditions necessary to ensure that the equilibrium number of firms is large enough to justify the assumption of noncollusion and give the required "competitiveness" of monopolistic competition.

The first set of conditions have been derived in the discussion of the second-order requirements and need only be assembled together with the other conditions at the appropriate stage. The second set of conditions, which relate to the viability of *any* market structure, need to be investigated.

It was shown in Chapter 5 that the elasticity of demand has a lower bound, given by the sum of the outside-substitution and compensation terms. However wide the market area of any firm, the elasticity of demand it faces is always greater than the value

$$E_{\min} = (1 - m)\sigma + (1 - \gamma)m, \tag{6.29}$$

where the parameter $\gamma$ represents the degree of price compensation and is unity for fully compensated demand and zero for completely uncompensated demand. The existence or absence of compensation for specification is irrelevant since the "inside" terms in the elasticity expression do not appear in the expression for the lower bound.

Since $R = E/(E - 1)$, the existence of a lower bound for $E$ implies the existence of an upper bound for $R$ given by

$$E_{\max} = 1 + \frac{1}{(1 - m)\sigma + (1 - \gamma)m - 1}. \tag{6.30}$$

Now $R$ is the marginal revenue ratio, the ratio of price to marginal revenue. The degree of economies of scale parameter $\theta$ is the ratio of average cost to marginal cost. At the maximum-profit point for the firm (marginal revenue = marginal cost), the firm makes no loss only if average revenue is at least as great as average cost, that is, if $R \geqq \theta$. Now suppose $\theta$ is either fixed or, if it declines with output, has some minimum value $\underline{\theta}$. Then if $R_{\max} < \underline{\theta}$, there is no firm, however large its market, that can make a profit, and thus even a monopolist will not operate in the industry, because the elasticity of demand is always so high that the spread between price and marginal revenue is insufficient to cover the spread between average cost and marginal cost.

Thus there is no viable market solution of any kind (ruling out price discrimination) unless the parameters are such as to satisfy the condition

$$R_{\max} \geqq \underline{\theta}. \tag{6.31}$$

From (6.30) this can be shown to imply

$$\sigma \leqq \sigma_U = \left(\frac{1}{1-m}\right)\left(\frac{\underline{\theta}}{\underline{\theta}-1}\right) - (1-\gamma)m, \qquad (6.32)$$

where $\sigma_U$ indicates the upper limit of $\sigma$.

As $m \to 1$, $\sigma_U$ becomes infinite and there is effectively no upper limit on $\sigma$ when outside goods become insignificant. As $m \to 0$, the important case in which the group is very small relative to the total economy, then

$$\sigma_U \to \frac{\underline{\theta}}{\underline{\theta}-1}.$$

In general, for compensated demand,

$$\sigma_U = \frac{\underline{\theta}}{(1-m)(\underline{\theta}-1)}. \qquad (6.33)$$

If cost curves are U-shaped, then $\underline{\theta} = 1$ and $\sigma_U$ is infinite. However, if the minimum average cost output is large relative to the size of the market, there may be an effective minimum value for $\theta$ which is greater than unity, and thus viability problems may emerge. As indicated in the previous section, a group may have a viable market solution when the market is large, and no solution when it is small.

It should be noted that the value $E_{min}$ (and thus $R_{max}$) is derived by allowing the market width to become infinite (see Chapter 5), and thus, for a finite spectrum, the effective maximum value for $R$ will be less than the value given as $R_{max}$, and the viability problems will thus be greater.

Less dramatic than the total failure of the market when $\sigma > \sigma_U$ is that high values of $\sigma$, although less than $\sigma_U$, may result in the dissolution of the group as such, leaving it uncertain whether the structure that remains (which may be perfectly viable) should be considered to be one of "monopolistic competition." Note that the stability conditions require that the quantity function $Q$ be concave, and the higher the value of $\sigma$, the greater the degree of concavity. This means that the quantity purchased per individual falls with increasing distance from the market center, because the available good becomes progressively less good as a substitute for the unavailable most-preferred good while the substitutability of outside goods remains the same. Thus the higher the value of $\sigma$, the less important are the purchases by individuals at the market fringes relative to the average per capita purchases over the whole market.

The result of this effect is that changes in the market width have a relatively small impact on the firm's sales as compared to that of substitution by outside goods by buyers near the market center. Thus the firm becomes more oriented toward the relationship between its product and outside goods than toward its relationships with its nominal rivals within the group. Among other things, the firm's profitability becomes less sensitive to the specification of its good, and its pricing policy more dominated by absolute price (in terms of outside goods) and less dominated by price relative to other group goods. The resulting structure becomes more like that of a number of isolated monopolists, each the sole supplier of a particular good, and less like a group of competitors supplying similar goods. Since the metamorphosis from a competitive structure to isolated monopolists occurs gradually but steadily as the elasticity of substitution increases, it is a matter of judgment at what point the term "monopolistic competition" becomes inappropriate.

Finally, since the degree of product differentiation declines as the elasticity of substitution increases, high elasticities of substitution imply fewer firms and thus the possibility that an oligopolistic structure will emerge, rather than one of monopolistic competition. The tendency toward oligopoly is, however, dampened by the effect just described, in which the rivalry between firms within the group becomes subordinate to competition with outside goods. It is not by any means certain, therefore, that few firms means a true oligopoly situation, if the small number of firms is due to a high elasticity of substitution with respect to outside goods.

An oligopoly situation may emerge, however, if the number of firms is small even though the elasticity of substitution is not large, because the degree of economies of scale is large. In this case, intragroup substitutability remains high, and the potential gains from removing rivals and expanding the sales of the firm's good are very high, giving conditions conducive to oligopolistic behavior. As long as there is free entry and, in particular, as long as product specification is potentially variable, the degree of oligopolistic rivalry is far less than suggested by analyses based on fixed specifications.

The general conclusions as to viability can be summarized as follows:

1. A stable market equilibrium is possible only if the elasticity of substitution between group goods and outside goods lies within the limits

$$\frac{1}{1-m} \leqq \sigma \leqq \left(\frac{1}{1-m}\right)\left(\frac{\theta}{\theta-1}\right) \tag{6.34a}$$

for compensated demand or

$$1 \leqq \sigma \leqq \left(\frac{1}{1-m}\right)\left(\frac{\theta}{\theta-1}\right) - m \tag{6.34b}$$

for uncompensated demand. If the group can be considered to be of negligible size relative to the economy as a whole ($m \rightarrow 0$), the condition becomes

$$1 \leqq \sigma \leqq \frac{\theta}{\theta-1} \tag{6.34c}$$

for both compensated and uncompensated demand. The parameter $\theta$ is the smallest degree of scale economies possible when the market is supplied by a single good. The lower limit may be unity or less, in which case $\sigma$ is unbounded above.

2. Some market solutions may be viable, but the monopolistic-competition structure itself may not be, if the above viability conditions are met but either the elasticity of substitution or the degree of returns to scale is relatively high.

3. There is always a viable and stable monopolistic-competition solution for a group which is of negligible importance relative to the economy as a whole and has U-shaped cost curves, with minimum average cost output ($\theta = 1$) small relative to the size of the market, and for which the elasticity of substitution with respect to outside goods is greater than unity.

## 6.10 A Note on the Spatial Model

A considerable amount of the recent work on monopolistic-competition theory has been in terms of spatial models of the neo-Hotelling kind.[8] As point out in Section 2.18, there are obvious similarities between a model in which firms and consumers are located spatially, with transport costs, and a model in which the specification of products actually produced and specifications preferred by consumers are located on a spectrum in characteristics space, with a utility or welfare loss related to spectrum distance. However, as was also pointed out, there are important differences between the standard spatial model and the model used here. The critical differences are:

1. The pure spatial models assume constant transport costs per quantity unit per distance unit (per ton-mile or equivalent). This leads to an implicit compensating function which is linear in the distance between the locations of the consumer and the good, instead of the nonlinear, strictly convex compensating function which forms the basis of this analysis. As shown in Chapter 6, the linearity property of the spatial model leads to neutral stability of the monopolistic-competition equilibrium with respect to specification (that is, location), where the general model is unstable under otherwise similar circumstances.

2. The smooth substitutability between group goods and outside goods, which is of such importance in the general model, is absent in the spatial models. Outside goods do not appear explicitly in such models at all, but they do appear implicitly, through the assumed existence of some fixed reserve price or valuation such that the consumer will not buy the group good at all if the price (including transport costs) exceeds the valuation. The substitution is discontinuous, however, since it is assumed that the consumer will buy a fixed quantity (typically a single unit) for all inclusive prices less than the valuation and none at all for all prices which exceed the valuation.

There are other differences between the typical spatial models and the general model given in this work, such as the differences in

8. See Salop (1976) for a recent survey of such models.

the approach to welfare rankings, but the linearity of the implicit compensating function and the absence of smooth substitution in the spatial models are by far the most important differentiating features.

Owing to these special properties of the spatial model, a firm has a finite market area even if there are no other firms in the space, the outer limits being where the price of the product plus transport cost is just equal to the valuation level. Thus it is possible to have a solution in which there are several firms in the group but in which there is effectively no interaction between adjacent firms. If the maximal markets for adjacent firms overlap, there is a part of the market in which there is potential rivalry and a part which is pure monopoly, leading to a kinked demand curve for each firm. Thus there are equilibria of distinct kinds in the spatial model, instead of a smooth succession of equilibrium positions as the parameters of the system are varied continuously. One of these equilibria can justifiably be called monopolistic competition—the equilibrium that occurs when the relationship between the cost structure of the firms, the transport costs, and the valuation level, is such that firms make positive profits when operating as monopolists with maximal market areas. In this case, enough firms will enter to assure the overlapping of market areas and thus monopolistic competition rather than isolated monopolies.

A spatial monopolistic-competition equilibrium in the above sense is most closely analogous to the paradigm case with compensation for price (since quantity demanded per person is constant) but not for specification, among the various cases of the general model. It is not surprising, therefore, that the analysis of the spatial model results in the conclusion that the degree of product variety generated is greater than optimal, since it will be shown in Chapter 7 that this conclusion holds for the paradigm case of the general model when demand is uncompensated for specification and a suitable welfare index is used. It will also be shown in Chapter 7, however, that the market does not necessarily generate more-than-optimal product variety when there is smooth substitutability for outside goods—a result that cannot be reached by applying the spatial-model conclusions to the more general model.

## 6.11 The "Excess Capacity" Debate

The best-known result of Chamberlin's original analysis of monopolistic competition, and a result that follows also from the model analyzed here, is that the monopolistic-competition equilibrium will always be such that firms are producing at outputs less than their least average cost outputs. If "capacity" is *defined* as the least average cost output, then the equilibrium is such that there is "excess capacity."

Chamberlin's result has been attacked over the years, especially by Demsetz,[9] but has also been defended.[10] The reasons behind the attack, and thus behind the whole debate, stem from attaching a normative implication to the notion of excess capacity. The implied argument is that production at minimum average cost is optimal, and thus that excess capacity is nonoptimal. To a considerable extent, the debate has been rendered moot by the analysis given here, which shows that there will be "excess capacity" at the optimum configuration (as shown in Chapters 3 and 4) and thus that no normative significance can be attached to production at minimum average cost. The real question, and a much more difficult one, is whether there is more or less excess capacity under monopolistic competition than is optimal, a problem to which the next chapter is devoted.

Much of the debate is clouded by the basic imprecision of Chamberlin's original attempts to describe what is meant by product differentiation without the firm quantitative basis provided by the characteristics approach. This leads Demsetz to assume that a consumer can have a choice between an "undifferentiated" product at a competitive (minimum average cost) price and a "differentiated" product at a higher price. Such a choice has no meaning in a context of clearly defined product differentiation, since a consumer can choose only between a product of one specification and a product of a different specification. A good cannot of itself be "undifferentiated" or "differentiated," since these terms refer to the relationship between the goods in the group. The group either has a single good, in which case it is undifferentiated, or several goods, in which case it is

9. See Demsetz (1959, 1964, 1972).

10. For representative views, see Archibald (1967), and Barzel (1970).

differentiated. If the group happened to be organized into two parallel structures, one consisting of many firms producing to a single specification and the other of firms each producing a good of unique specification, the equilibrium is found by aggregating the two into a single unit, in which case, as has already been shown, the cluster of firms which all produce the same good will dissolve, and the monopolistic-competition equilibrium will prevail.

The Demsetz analysis fails to take note of the essential feature of monopolistic competition—variety in preferences of individuals. In the parallel-structure case, only those consumers for whom the "competitive" subindustry's good is to their most-preferred specifications will choose on price alone. Other consumers will willingly pay a higher price for a good which is closer to their most-preferred specification, and it is the behavior of the monopolistic-competition subindustry, not the competitive subindustry, that will dominate the industry as a whole.

Other aspects of the debate are concerned with advertising and other selling costs. Such costs have not appeared in this chapter, since it has been assumed that there is perfect information, and indeed, the objective of this chapter has been to show that the structure of monopolistic competition does *not* depend on poorly informed consumers, but that it is the natural structure under conditions of economies of scale, freely variable product specifications, and perfect information. Implicit in some of the arguments, including Chamberlin's (which is ambiguous on the true nature of product differentiation), is that monopolistic competition is often concerned with differentiation that is somehow not "real," but forced on the consumer by clever salesmanship. In Chapter 8, where monopolistic competition is considered under conditions imposed by various imperfections in the market, this phenomenon is treated as "pseudodifferentiation."

The analysis given here should terminate the debate definitively. The following conclusions are made:

1. Monopolistic competition certainly leads to "excess capacity," if that term simply means output below the minimum average cost level.

2. This conclusion does not depend on the existence of selling costs of any kind but does depend on the ability of firms to vary their

product specifications freely and on the existence of variety in consumer preferences.

3. Since the optimum configuration also leads to "excess capacity" in the same sense, the existence of such excess does not *of itself* carry normative implications. Indeed, it will be shown in the next chapter that monopolistic competition may sometimes lead to *less* excess capacity than the optimum, but this does not make monopolistic competition better than the optimum.

## 6.12 Indivisibility, Quality, and Stratification

If goods are indivisible, rather than divisible as assumed previously in the chapter, the analysis becomes more complex, and different types of equilibria are possible. Indivisibility also introduces the problem of differentiation in quality, or vertical differentiation, rather than the pure horizontal differentiation that has been analyzed to this point.

As shown in Chapter 5, the demand curve for indivisible goods exhibits a kink at some point because there are two possible sources of customers for any one product: those that have chosen not to buy any group good because of the price relative to outside goods and the all-or-nothing nature of the choice and those that are buying an adjacent group good. Suppose that initially a particular group good is offered at a price which attracts some customers (those for whom it is close to most-preferred specifications), but that, given indifference in specification from the adjacent good and its price, none of these customers would regard the adjacent good as anything near a substitute. Thus the customers are taken entirely from consumers whose effective choice is to buy a unit of the good or do without and buy more outside goods. At this price, the producer of the good in question is effectively a monopolist, gaining or losing customers to outside goods as the price is varied but insulated from the actions of other group firms. The firm's market is surrounded by a border of potential customers who currently buy neither this good nor the adjacent good but will buy this good if the price is lowered. Beyond these are other potential customers who currently buy the adjacent good but will switch if this good's price is lowered sufficiently. In the upper price range, demand is determined entirely by the monopoly demand curve, and in the lower price range, entirely by substitution with respect to the adjacent good. The intersection of the two separate portions of the demand curve will occur at that price at which the marginal customer is indifferent in the choice between buying the single unit of this good, a single unit of the adjacent good, or buying neither and consuming more outside goods.

The relationships determining the two portions of the curve are given by Eqs. (5.69) and (5.70) of Chapter 5. Although no generalizations can be made about the relative elasticities of the two portions of the curve over the whole range, it can be assumed that the lower portion (representing substitution for the adjacent good) is more elastic *at the intersection* than the upper portion, since the lower portion provides one more degree of freedom to consumers making their choice at this point. Thus the two curves do not have the same slope at the intersection point, and there is a kink. Note that the kink is opposite in direction to that of the traditional oligopoly diagram, in which the upper portion is more elastic at the intersection that the lower portion.

If there is uniformity and a uniform density of consumers, it is obvious that the indivisible case will, like the divisible case, always possess symmetric equilibria with all firms behaving alike. Assuming a uniform spacing of firms, consider an individual firm with the adjacent firms all at the same distance and selling their products at the same prices. (It is assumed that the indivisibility is technical and that the unit size is the same for goods of all specifications.) The marginal revenue curve of such a firm, which is discontinuous, is shown in Figure 6.1. The right-hand portion of the curve lies above the left-hand portion at the discontinuity because the left-hand, or monopoly, segment corresponds to the lower elasticity.

The individual equilibrium of such a firm will depend on where its marginal cost curve cuts the marginal revenue curve, whether on the left- or right-hand portion. If, as in the case of $MC_1$ in the diagram, the intersection $X_1$ lies on the left-hand portion, the firm is a monopolist, and its equilibrium is unaffected by marginal changes in either the spacing between firms or the prices of other firms. On the other

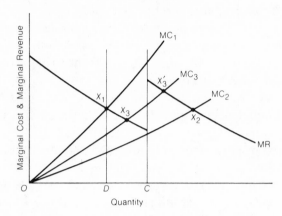

**Figure 6.1.** Relationship between marginal cost (MC) and marginal revenue (MR) when goods are indivisible.

hand, if the marginal cost curve is like $MC_2$, the firm is in direct competition with its neighbors. Note that the marginal cost curve necessarily cuts at least one of the two portions if it is rising, the case that will be discussed here. (A falling marginal cost curve may pass through the gap between the two portions, giving a different situation.) There is a third possibility, corresponding to $MC_3$, in which the marginal cost curve intersects both portions of the marginal revenue curve, at $X_3$ and $X_3'$.

Consider the last case, which is isolated in Figure 6.2. Which of the two points $X_3$ and $X_3'$ will the firm choose? The answer is easily obtained by investigating what the firm gains or loses by increasing output from $OQ_3$ (corresponding to $X_3$) to $OQ_3'$ (corresponding to $X_3'$). The additional revenue is given by the area under the marginal revenue curve between $Q_3$ and $Q_3'$, and the additional cost by the area under the marginal cost curve between the same points. Clearly, there is an excess of extra revenue over extra cost, given by the shaded triangular area $X_3MX_3'$, so that the firm will always choose point $X_3'$ as its equilibrium.

Consider initially the case in which the marginal cost curve is represented by $MC_1$ and the equilibrium of the firm by $X_1$. Whether this is a viable equilibrium or not depends on whether price is at least as great as average cost, a relationship that is independent of events depicted in the diagram since it depends on the level of the fixed cost. If price does not cover average cost in this case, the group good will not be produced at all, since other firms will face identical situations and none will be able to break even. If price at least covers average cost, the firm will at least break even and will stay in business.

In the particular case under discussion, there will initially be "holes" in the market spectrum, representing sets of consumers who buy none of the group goods because outside goods are preferable given the distance of the available goods from their most-preferred specification. Since each consumer is buying a single unit (if any) of the good, a product's market width and quantity sold are directly proportional to each other. Thus the horizontal axis in Figure 6.1 can be used to measure market widths. Since all firms are behaving alike, it is obvious that the distance from the good in question to the next adjacent good is equal to twice the distance $OC$ in the figure and that the half-market width of the good is $OD$ (and a similar half-market width exists for the adjacent good), so that the market "hole" is of width twice $DC$. If existing firms are making profits, it might be presumed that other firms will enter until, after adjustments, there are no gaps left in the spectrum, but each firm is still a monopolist on its own turf.

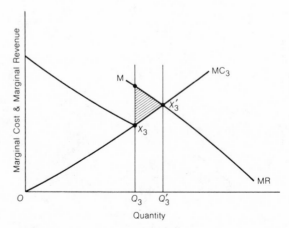

**Figure 6.2.** Case in which the marginal cost (MC) curve intersects both portions of the marginal revenue (MR) curve. See text for details.

But as firms move closer together in order to close up the gaps, the right-hand portion of the marginal revenue curves in Figure 6.1 move to the left, as shown in Figure 6.3. That is, the closer together the firms, the smaller the distance $OC$ between the market center and the kink point, shown moving from $OC$ to $OC'$ in Figure 6.3. To fill all the gaps with all firms behaving as monopolists, the half-market widths would have to be equal to the distance $OD$, which would require that $OC$ be equal to $OD$. Before this situation could be reached, however, the kink point would have moved far enough to the left to have the marginal cost curve intersecting both parts of the marginal revenue curve, and the equilibrium for the firm would move to a point like $X_3'$ in Figure 6.2, which corresponds to market interaction between adjacent firms rather than monopoly behavior. Note that until this double intersection takes place, the profits of the firms already in the group do not change as new entry takes place, and thus the existence of profits in the initial state will inevitably lead to the double-intersection case.

The equilibrium configuration in the indivisibility case will, therefore, always consist of firms related by a monopolistic-competition structure and not of firms behaving as isolated monopolists and thus will have the same general pattern as with divisible goods. The

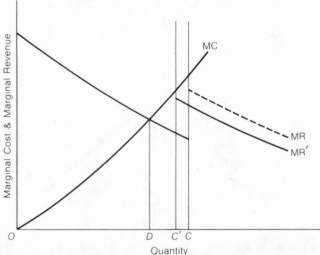

**Figure 6.3.** Effect of reducing difference in specification between adjacent goods.

equilibrium will be determined in the same way as for divisible goods, except that the demand elasticity is now simply equal to the market-width elasticity $s$ [from Eq. (5.70)] rather than the expression $se_Q +$ $(1 - m)\sigma + m$ (for the uncompensated case). Since $e_Q > 1$ and the remaining terms in the regular elasticity are all positive, the elasticity is clearly less in the indivisible case than with divisible goods. Since $E$ is lower for a given value of the equilibrium half-market width $\Delta$, $R$ is higher, and the equilibrium relationship $R = \theta$ will occur at a smaller value of $\Delta$ when goods are indivisible than when they are divisible. *There will be a greater degree of product differentiation with indivisible goods than with equivalent divisible goods.*

Indivisibility introduces the possibility of *vertical* product differentiation, of making a good in more than one "package" size. Vertical differentiation is irrelevant for divisible goods, since characteristics bundles of any magnitude can be obtained by varying quantity. For most of the analysis, it has been assumed that there is a uniform density of consumers and a uniform distribution of income (or welfare, if demand is fully compensated) over the spectrum. If this is interpreted to represent an *equal* distribution of income over individuals, then there is no scope for vertical differentiation. If it is technically possible to make the product in more than one unit size, only one of these sizes will be chosen, since all consumers will want the same size.

Vertical differentiation becomes relevant, in general, only when there are unequal incomes such that there are relatively richer consumers who would prefer a large unit at higher cost over a small unit and relatively poorer ones whose preference will be for the smaller but cheaper unit. By "large" and "small" here is meant the absolute size of characteristics content and not necessarily physical size, so it is more appropriate to refer to the distinction as that between lower and higher "quality."

The market context in which vertical product differentiation becomes most relevant is that of monopoly, where the monopolist can assess the demand for goods of different degrees of quality and choose the number of distinct quality variants that maximize profits, given the technology constraints on quality variation and the cost structure. The analysis becomes highly complex if the monopolist can simultaneously differentiate in two directions, horizontal (different characteristics proportions) and vertical (different package sizes or qualities).

In the monopolistic-competition setting, it is possible to consider a simplified version of vertical differentiation by confining the analysis to a market stratified into a finite number of "layers." First of all, it should be noted that uniform population density across the spectrum, together with a uniform distribution of income across the spectrum, does not *necessarily* imply equality of incomes across the population. The same combination is possible if there are unequal incomes but the distribution of incomes over individuals is the same at all points of the spectrum. Suppose the income distribution consists of a proportion $\lambda$ of "ordinary" consumers having equal incomes $I_o$ and a proportion $1 - \lambda$ of "rich" consumers having equal incomes $I_r(> I_o)$. The market is then stratified into two spectra of consumers, the ordinary and the rich, with total income divided between the strata in proportions $\lambda I_o/(\lambda I_o + (1 - \lambda)I_r)$ and $(1 - \lambda)I_r/(\lambda I_o + (1 - \lambda)I_r)$.

Each stratum will have a uniform population density and a uniform distribution of income and will be assumed to show uniformity of preferences. Now if it is technically feasible to produce goods in smaller and larger indivisible units or of lower and higher quality, it is possible that two unit sizes or quality levels will be produced, one for each stratum. (It is always possible that the relationship between costs and size or quality level is such that the rich consumers still prefer to buy the same good as the ordinary consumers.) When goods are produced at two quality levels under these circumstances, the two strata of the market are substantially independent and can be analyzed separately, the analysis of each being essentially the same as the ordinary analysis of the unstratified market. There will be a monopolistic-competition equilibrium for each stratum, with its own solution as to the number of product differentiates, giving a simplified version of two-way product differentiation (vertical and horizontal).

The relationship between the degrees of product differentiation in the two strata will depend on the technology and the relative numbers of consumers in the two income groups. The very existence of technological indivisibilities implies some difference between the production conditions for goods of smaller unit size or lower quality and those of larger unit size or higher quality, so it is difficult to make any generalizations. If, as is often assumed to be the case, higher quality goods require a higher proportion of handcraftmanship than do lower quality goods, the degree of economies of scale would be lower for the high quality goods, which would tend to lead toward more differentiation among those goods. But the size of the market would also be smaller, which would tend to give a greater degree of economies of scale, if economies of scale fall with output, and would result in an opposite tendency. If the higher-quality goods are entirely hand-made, there will be no economies of scale, and these goods will show infinite product differentiation (i.e., be custom-made).

Chapter 7

# The Market and the Optimum

## 7.1 Introduction

IN EARLIER CHAPTERS of the book, the conditions for the optimal degree of product differentiation were established in terms of the structural properties of the group and the relationship of the group to the economy in which it is embedded. In the preceding chapter, the conditions for equilibrium under perfect monopolistic competition— the most "competitive" market structure possible with variable product specification and economies of scale—were examined in terms of the same system properties as in the optimum analysis. Now has come the point at which the two can be compared in order to determine the relationship between the market solution and the optimum, with special reference to the degree of product differentiation.

The traditional comparison, based on the Chamberlin model, reaches the conclusion that monopolistic competition leads to a greater-than-optimal degree of product differentiation, in the sense that individual monopolistic-competition firms will each produce at a lower-than-optimal output level because each firm will show "excess capacity" and thus there will be more firms for a given market size. As already pointed out in Chapters 3, 4, and 6, this traditional answer is based on a major error in analysis since it assumes that the optimum is the perfect-competition solution with output at the minimum average cost level (a U-shaped cost curve being essential to the Chamberlin model). However, as the analysis of the optimum given earlier has shown, the optimal output, even with U-shaped cost curves, is not at the point of minimum average cost but at a lower output where average cost is still falling, so that there is "excess capacity" at the optimum. Thus the mere demonstration that equilibrium under monopolistic competition occurs at some point on the falling section of the average cost curve does not suffice to show that this market form leads to a greater-than-optimal degree of product differentiation.

To prove the traditional proposition correctly would require a demonstration that, although both the monopolistic-competition and the optimum output levels per firm fall on the downward-sloping portion of the average cost curve, the monopolistic-competition equilibrium point lies to the left of the optimum point. Clearly this is a more difficult proposition to prove, even if it is true, than seems to be the case in traditional analysis.

It will be shown here that monopolistic competition leads to a greater-than-optimal degree of product differentiation in a significant class of cases—those for which the elasticity of substitution with respect to outside goods is relatively low—but it will also be shown that there exists a class of cases (high substitution elasticities) for which monopolistic competition leads to a less-than-optimal degree of product differentiation.[1] Thus the traditional result does not hold in general.

The comparison that is being made is appreciated most easily if it is assumed that the distribution of goods under the optimum regime is handled by giving every consumer an appropriate money income, charging marginal resource cost prices for both the group and outside goods, and allowing the individual to buy the goods out of his or her income. If each consumer's money income is properly computed, so that he or she can attain the target welfare level in this way, the consumer will choose the optimal mix of group and outside goods, and the result will be exactly the same as with physical

1. Spence (1976b) showed that monopolistic competition would lead to less-than-optimal product differentiation if there were *complementary* goods. Spence's basic model and his welfare criterion differ from those used here, and complementarities are not considered in this work.

distribution of the goods. The crucial property of the optimum regime is that the specification of the goods to be produced is computed by use of the optimum condition given by Eq. (4.15) and is not left to private firms.

In the comparison model of monopolistic competition with full compensation, the same principle of income distribution is used, that is, income distribution is *not* left to the market, so that each individual is given whatever money income is required to enable him or her to attain the same welfare level as at the optimum, but by buying the goods under the conditions generated by the market. The difference between this and the optimum case is that the decisions as to what goods to produce are left to the private firms operating under the conditions of perfect monopolistic competition. Thus the difference between the two cases being compared is that of pure structure only—the optimum regime in one case, the market equilibrium in the other—whereas welfare, and its distribution, is identical in both.

It will become apparent that the elasticity of substitution is extremely important in determining the relationships between the degrees of product differentiation in the two cases. The problems and techniques of comparison also differ at different elasticity values, so the results cannot be obtained as a single proposition.

Since the full optimum, with compensation for individuals not receiving goods of their most-preferred specification, may be infeasible for reasons set out in Chapter 3, a second comparison is made between the market and the optimum, that is, between the market equilibrium with uncompensated demand and the second-best solution. This comparison, which is somewhat more restricted than that between the compensated market equilibrium and the full optimum, shows that monopolistic competition leads to a greater degree of product differentiation than the second-best optimum, over a rather wider range of parameter values than those for the full optimum.

After the comparisons of the market and the optimum, consideration is given to policy measures designed to manipulate the market into producing the optimum or second-best solutions.

Note that monopolistic competition is not treated here as "imperfect" competition, but as the natural market form under the conditions of the model. As pointed out in the previous chapter, "perfect" competition will not operate in a context of variable product specification and economies of scale: A firm will never choose to produce a product identical with that of their competitors. Monopolistic competition is the most competitive market form under the circumstances—it is the Nash equilibrium of fully informed, noncollusive players in a frictionless environment with open entry into the group. No structure can be more competitive than that.


## 7.2 The Paradigm Case

The paradigm case, in which the economy consists of group goods only and no outside goods, was introduced into this study because of the simplicity of deriving its optimal properties and the ease with which those properties can be appreciated intuitively. An obvious first step in comparing the market and the optimum, therefore, would seem to be to make the comparison for the paradigm case.

There is a problem, however. As already made clear, a valid comparison between the market and the optimum requires that demand be fully compensated in the market case. But it was shown in the previous chapter that monopolistic competition in the compensated paradigm case cannot satisfy the second-order conditions for a stable equilibrium with respect to choice of specification. Thus the compensated paradigm case is not viable as a market structure.

In spite of this, the paradigm comparison will be made, a comparison that calls for a suspension of disbelief for the time being. The analysis will proceed as though the first-order equilibrium conditions for monopolistic competition are indeed associated with a viable market structure. The reasons for this unusual procedure are (a) that the analysis is simplest for the paradigm case and yet of the same style as that for the more complex cases, (b) that a key result proved in this section is used later and would have to be derived in any case, and (c) that the paradigm case is the fundamental standard of comparison by which the effects of the elasticity of substitution between group goods and outside goods on the optimal degree of product differentiation are measured. It is also relevant because the author concluded in an earlier study (Lancaster, 1975) that the market leads necessarily to a greater-than-optimal degree of product differentiation. This conclusion was based on this one comparison, although it is now seen to be not only a special case but to be based on a nonviable market structure.

Treating the monopolistic-competition equilibrium as though it were a stable state of the market, the comparison with the optimum leads to an unambiguous result:

A monopolistic-competition equilibrium would, in the paradigm case, result in a greater-than-optimal degree of product differentiation.

Note that the result, and the caveats associated with it, holds for an economy in which there are outside goods but zero elasticity of substitution between these and group goods, as well as for the paradigm case proper, in which there are no outside goods.

The proof, like many others throughout the study, requires some restriction on the maximum permissible degree of economies of scale.

The optimum half-spacing between goods will be denoted by $\Delta^*$, and the half-spacing under monopolistic-competition equilibrium by unstarred $\Delta$. Then the two conditions determining these values are given by Eqs. (3.9) and (6.8),

$$e_H(\Delta^*) = \theta^* \qquad \text{(Paradigm optimum),}$$

$$R(\Delta) = \theta \qquad \text{(Monopolistic competition),}$$

where the two values of $\theta$ are distinguished because, if $\theta$ is sensitive to output and the outputs differ, then the $\theta$ values will differ.

In the monopolistic-competition equilibrium condition, the marginal revenue ratio $R$ (the ratio of price to marginal revenue) is equal to $(1 - E^{-1})^{-1} = E/(E - 1)$, where $E$ is the demand elasticity. Since comparisons with the optimum are always made in terms of fully compensated demand, the value of $E$ in the paradigm case is given by Eq. (5.19) from Chapter 5:

$$E = s(\Delta)e_H(\Delta).$$

From Eq. (6.10), the marginal revenue ratio $R$ is equal to $E/(E - 1)$,

so that

$$R = \frac{se_H}{se_H - 1}$$

$$= e_H \left( e_H - \frac{1}{s} \right)^{-1}, \tag{7.1}$$

where the arguments have been dropped for simplicity. Obviously,

$$R > e_H \quad \text{if} \quad e_H - (1/s) > 1 \tag{7.2a}$$

$$< e_H \quad \text{if} \quad e_H - (1/s) < 1. \tag{7.2b}$$

Since $e_H$ is the elasticity of cumulative compensation $H$, which is convex, Lemma 1a (Appendix B) gives

$$e_H(u) < h(u)$$

$$< 1 + uh'(u) \quad (\text{since } h \text{ is convex and } h(0) = 1)$$

$$< 1 + h(u)\frac{uh'(u)}{h(u)}. \tag{7.3}$$

Now the compensation elasticity $e_h(u)$ is given by

$$e_h(u) = uh'(u)/h(u), \tag{7.4}$$

so that Eq. (7.3) can be written

$$e_H(u) < 1 + h(u)e_h(u). \tag{7.5}$$

From Eq. (5.13),

$$s(u) = \tfrac{1}{2}e_h(u). \tag{7.6}$$

Thus, from Eqs. (7.5) and (7.6),

$$e_H - \frac{1}{s} < 1 + (h - 2)e_h. \tag{7.7}$$

Since $e_h > 0$, a sufficient condition for $e_H - (1/s)$ to be less than unity is that $h < 2$. The condition is not necessary in Eq. (7.5), because of the inequality.

Consider the economic meaning of the restriction $h(u) < 2$. Since $h$ is the compensating function, $h(u) = 2$ would imply that $u$, the distance of the consumer's most-preferred good from the actual good, was sufficiently great for the consumer to require 2 units of the actual good to be compensated for one unit of the unavailable most-preferred good. It seems reasonable to consider this a "large" distance on the spectrum, and thus a restriction on segment width so that no consumer was distant enough from the best available good to give $h(\Delta) \geqq 2$ is consistent with the "large" number of products required for monopolistic competition. Accepting the restriction $h(\Delta) < 2$, a restriction that occurs elsewhere in the analysis, then $e_H(\Delta) - 1/s(\Delta) < 1$, and thus

$$R(\Delta) > e_H(\Delta). \tag{7.8}$$

Suppose initially that $\theta$ is a constant and does not vary with output, so that $\theta^*$ (at the optimum) $= \theta$ (at monopolistic-competition equilibrium). Then, from the paradigm optimum condition (Eq. 3.9), the monopolistic-competition equilibrium condition (Eq. 6.8), and the inequality given by Eq. (7.8),

$$e_H(\Delta) < R(\Delta) = \theta = \theta^* = g(\Delta^*). \tag{7.9}$$

But $e_H$ is an increasing function of its argument, so that $e_H(\Delta) < e_H(\Delta^*)$ implies $\Delta < \Delta^*$ and thus the degree of product differentiation is greater at the monopolistic-competition equilibrium than at the optimum.

The argument has so far been based on assumption that $\theta$ is a constant. However, it can be shown to hold if $\theta$ depends on the output level, provided (as always) that $\theta' \leqq 0$. It is essential to show that the conclusion holds for variable $\theta$ in the paradigm case, in particular, since without outside goods (or with $\sigma = 0$) the monopolistic competition is unstable with respect to price unless $\theta' < 0$.

Suppose that the introduction of variable $\theta$, with $\theta' < 0$, resulted in the previous conclusion being upset, and led to the opposite inequality $\Delta \geqq \Delta^*$. Then, since quantity is an increasing function of $\Delta$ and $\theta$ is a decreasing function of quantity, this would imply that $\theta \leqq \theta^*$. The chain of inequalities would then be as follows

$$e_H(\Delta) < R = \theta \leqq \theta^* = e_H(\Delta^*),$$

which leads to the conclusion that $\Delta < \Delta^*$ and thus contradicts the original supposition. Thus the same conclusion must hold for variable $\theta$ as for fixed $\theta$.

## 7.3 Outside Substitution

It was shown in Chapter 4 that as the elasticity of substitution between group goods and outside goods increases from $\sigma = 0$ (the paradigm case), the optimal degree of product differentiation declines from that in the paradigm case to reach a minimum level at $\sigma = 1$, then rises to equal the paradigm level again at a value $\sigma = \sigma_o$, after which it remains higher than the paradigm level. It was shown in the previous section that the market degree of product differentiation would be higher than optimal in the paradigm case ($\sigma = 0$) if this were viable in the market, and it was shown in Chapter 6 that the degree of product differentiation in the market declines steadily as the elasticity of substitution increases. This implies that the degree of product differentiation in the market will certainly be higher than optimal for sufficiently low values of the elasticity of substitution and that, if the market results in less-than-optimal differentiation, this will occur at high elasticity values.

In this section, it will be shown that:

1. The degree of product differentiation generated by the market would be greater than optimal for values of the elasticity of substitution in the range by $\sigma \leqq \text{Min}(\sigma_o, 1/(1 - m))$.

2. There is a "crossover value," $\sigma^*$, of the elasticity of substitution such that the market gives the optimal degree of product differentiation if $\sigma = \sigma^*$, greater-than-optimal differentiation if $\sigma < \sigma^*$, and less-than-optimal differentiation if $\sigma > \sigma^*$.

3. Since $\sigma^* > \text{Min}(\sigma_o, 1/(1 - m))$ and the market is always viable for $\sigma \geqq 1/(1 - m)$ when demand is compensated as here (up to some upper limit $\bar{\sigma}$), there is a viable range for the market in which it gives greater-than-optimal product differentiation, provided the group is small relative to the whole economy.

4. It is shown that $\sigma^* < \sigma_U$, where $\sigma_U$ is a value of the elasticity of substitution beyond which it is certain that the market is not viable. Thus there is the possibility that there exists of a range of values of

the elasticity of substitution for which the market gives less-than-optimal product differentiation.

5. In summary, the market can be expected to give greater-than-optimal differentiation in the lower part of the range of values of the elasticity of substitution for which it is viable and less-than-optimal differentiation in the higher part of the range.

To prove these propositions, it will first be shown that the market degree of product differentiation is greater than the paradigm optimum level for $\sigma = 1/(1 - m)$, which implies that the market (if viable) would give more than the paradigm optimum degree of product differentiation for all $\sigma \leqq 1/(1 - m)$.

The fully compensated elasticity of demand is given by Eq. (5.42) as

$$E = se_Q + (1 - m)\sigma,$$

where $e_Q$ is the compensated quantity elasticity derived ultimately from the differential equation determining $q = Q'$, given by Eq. (5.38):

$$e_q = [1 - (1 - m)\sigma]e_h,$$

where $m$, the average proportion of expenditure on group goods has been substituted for $\mu(u)$, the proportion for an individual distance $u$ from the available good. Now if $\sigma = 1/(1 - m)$, $e_q = 0$, so that $q$ is a constant and $e_Q$ is equal to unity. The elasticity value for this case then becomes

$$E = s + 1. \tag{7.10}$$

The marginal revenue ratio $R$ is given by Eq. (6.10):

$$R = E/(E - 1)$$

$$= 1 + \frac{1}{s}. \tag{7.11}$$

The monopolistic-competition equilibrium condition (Eq. 6.8) then becomes

$$1 + \frac{1}{s(\Delta)} = \theta. \tag{7.12}$$

It was shown in the preceding section that

$$e_H - \frac{1}{s} < 1,$$

provided the segment size is sufficiently small to guarantee $h(\Delta) <$ 2. As already argued, this is not unduly restrictive, so that the condition is accepted, and thus

$$e_H(\Delta) < 1 + \frac{1}{s(\Delta)} . \tag{7.13}$$

Suppose initially that $\theta$ is a constant, and denote the paradigm optimum segment width by $2\Delta^*$ and the monopolistic-competition segment width by $2\Delta$. Then, from Eqs. (7.12), (7.13), and the paradigm optimum condition (Eq. 3.9),

$$e_H(\Delta) < 1 + \frac{1}{s(\Delta)} = \theta = e_H(\Delta^*), \tag{7.14}$$

so that

$$\Delta < \Delta^*, \tag{7.15}$$

and the degree of product differentiation in the market with $\sigma = 1/(1 - m)$ is greater than that at the paradigm optimum.

Note that the same inequality (Eq. 7.13) is used to prove that the market degree of product differentiation is greater than that of the paradigm optimum at both $\sigma = 0$ and $\sigma = 1/(1 - m)$. This does not mean that the market degree of differentiation is the same, because the inequality appears somewhat differently in the two cases. It can easily be shown that the difference $R - e_H$ is given by

$$R - e_H = \frac{e_H}{e_H - (1/s)} \left(1 + \frac{1}{s} - e_H\right) \quad \text{for } \sigma = 0$$

$$R - e_H = 1 + \frac{1}{s} - e_H \quad \text{for } \sigma = 1/(1 - m),$$

so that $R - e_H$ is greater, and the gap between the market and the paradigm optimum wider, at $\sigma = 0$ than at $\sigma = 1/(1 - m)$.

It was shown in Chapter 4 that the degree of product differentiation at the optimum with outside goods was less than the paradigm optimal value for $\sigma < \sigma_o$, where $\sigma_o$ has a value close to 2. The above result thus shows that the market degree of product differentiation is greater than that of the optimum with outside goods for $\sigma < \min(\sigma_o, 1/(1 - m))$, which proves the first proposition given at the beginning of the section, at least for a constant $\theta$.

If $\theta$ is variable, the same kind of argument as in the preceding section can be used to show that this cannot upset the direction of the inequality, and thus that the result is unchanged.

To prove the second proposition, that there always exists a value of $\sigma$ high enough to give less-than-optimal product differentiation in the market, it will be shown that there is always some value of $\sigma$, greater than $1/(1 - m)$, above which the market degree of product differentiation is less than that at the paradigm optimum. Since it was shown in Chapter 4 that the optimal degree of product differentiation is always greater than the paradigm value for $\sigma > \sigma_o$, this is sufficient to establish the proposition.

The fully compensated elasticity of demand

$$E = se_Q + (1 - m)\sigma,$$

together with the relationship $R = E/(E - 1)$, gives the value of the marginal revenue ratio in the general case as

$$R = \frac{se_Q + (1 - m)\sigma}{se_Q + (1 - m)\sigma - 1}$$

$$= 1 + \frac{1}{se_Q + (1 - m)\sigma - 1}. \tag{7.16}$$

From Eq. (5.13), $s = \tfrac{1}{2}e_h$. Using this relationship, and writing $\beta = (1 - m)\sigma - 1$, Eq. (7.16) can be written in the simplified form

$$R = 1 + \frac{2e_h}{e_Q + 2\beta e_h}. \tag{7.17}$$

The differential equation determining $q$ (and ultimately $e_Q$) is Eq. (5.38),

$$e_q = [1 - (1 - m)\sigma]e_h$$

$$= -\beta e_h \tag{7.18}$$

after substituting $\beta = (1 - m)\sigma - 1$. Since it is assumed that $m$, and thus $\beta$, can be treated as a constant, the result of Lemma 3a of Appendix B can be used. Since $\sigma > 1/(1 - m)$ is the range being examined, $-\beta < 0$, and the relevant result of the lemma is

$$e_Q - 1 > -\beta(e_H - 1). \tag{7.19}$$

Using Eq. (7.19) in Eq. (7.17) gives

$$R < 1 + \frac{2e_h}{1 + \beta(1 + 2e_h - e_H)}. \tag{7.20}$$

Now consider the difference $R - e_H$. From above, this is limited by the inequality

$$R - e_H < 1 - e_H + \frac{2e_h}{1 + \beta(1 + 2e_h - e_H)}. \tag{7.21}$$

Note that $1 + 2e_h - e_H = 1 + (1/s) - e_H$ has previously been shown to be positive, provided distances within the segment are such that $h < 2$, a restriction that is accepted here. Now the functions $e_h(u)$ and $e_H(u)$ are derived directly from the compensating function $h(u)$ and are quite independent of the parameters $m$ and $\sigma$ appearing in the factor $\beta$, which can be treated as an exogenous parameter that can be varied at will without affecting $e_h$ or $e_H$. (The only restriction on $\beta$ is that it must be positive, since this property was used in deriving Eq. (7.19).)

If $\beta$ is very small, the right-hand side of Eq. (7.21) is very nearly equal to $1 + 2e_h - e_H$, and thus the upper limit on $R - e_H$ is positive. This is consistent with the earlier result that $R - e_H$ is positive when $\sigma = 1/(1 - m)$, corresponding to $\beta = 0$.

The right-hand side of Eq. (7.21) can be shown to be positive if $\beta < 1/(e_H - 1)$ and negative if $\beta > 1/(e_H - 1)$. Substituting for $\beta$ in terms of $\sigma$, it follows that

$$R - e_H < 0 \quad \text{if} \quad \sigma \gtreqless \frac{e_H}{(e_H - 1)(1 - m)}. \tag{7.22}$$

Thus for sufficiently large values of $\sigma$, $R(\Delta) < e_H(\Delta)$. Together with the monopolistic-competition equilibrium condition and the paradigm condition, this implies that

$$e_H(\Delta) > R(\Delta) = \theta = e_H(\Delta^*), \tag{7.23}$$

so that

$$\Delta > \Delta^*, \tag{7.24}$$

and the degree of product differentiation in the market is certainly less than that at the paradigm optimum for $\sigma \geqq \hat{\sigma}$, where

$$\frac{1}{1-m} \leqq \hat{\sigma} \leqq \frac{e_H}{(e_H - 1)(1-m)} . \tag{7.25}$$

Now, from Chapter 4, the optimum with outside goods shows more product differentiation than the paradigm optimum for $\sigma > \sigma_o$, so that the market gives less-than-optimal product differentiation for $\sigma > \max(\sigma_o, \hat{\sigma})$.

Thus the market gives greater-than-optimal product differentiation if $\sigma < \min[\sigma_o, 1/(1-m)]$ and less-than-optimal product differentiation if $\sigma > \max(\sigma_o, \hat{\sigma})$, where $\hat{\sigma} \geqq 1/(1-m)$, so that, from consideration of continuity, there is a crossover value $\sigma^*$ of the elasticity of substitution at which the market gives the optimal degree of product differentiation.

Clearly, the crossover will occur at a lower value for the elasticity of substitution (a) the larger the economies of scale parameter $\theta$ (and thus the larger the equilibrium segment width $\Delta$), the larger the value of $e_H(\Delta)$, and the smaller the ratio $e_H/(e_H - 1)$ or (b) the less important the group in the economy, and thus the smaller the factor $1/(1-m)$.

Note that as $m$ approaches unity (the group becomes very important), $1/(1-m)$ becomes very large and crossover elasticity also becomes very large. As $m \to 1$, the crossover point becomes infinite and the market always gives greater-than-optimal differentiation, as in the paradigm case, to which the general case then converges. If the group is very small relative to the economy, however, $1/(1-m) \to 1$, and thus the crossover elasticity lies in a realistic range.

The question of market viability needs to be considered, however, since it was shown in Chapter 6 that the market cannot be viable (because no firm can ever break even) for substitution elasticities greater than a well-defined value $\sigma_U$. From Eq. (6.33), this value is given by

$$\sigma_U = \frac{\underline{\theta}}{(\underline{\theta} - 1)(1-m)}, \tag{7.26}$$

where $\underline{\theta}$ is the minimum value of $\theta$ (or 1 if $\theta_{\min} < 1$).

The structural similarity of this expression to the equation determining the upper limit of $\hat{\sigma}$ (Eq. 7.25) is striking. It is even more so when it is noted that $e_H(\Delta^*) = \theta > \underline{\theta}$, where $\Delta^*$ is the paradigm optimum half-space between goods, so that, if $e_H(\Delta^*)$ is written $e_H{}^*$ for simplicity,

$$\sigma_U > \frac{e_H{}^*}{(e_H{}^* - 1)(1 - m)} \tag{7.27}$$

since $\underline{\theta}/(1 - \underline{\theta}) > \theta/(1 - \theta)$. This is identical with Eq. (7.22), except that, in the latter, $e_H(\Delta)$ corresponds to the equilibrium market segment width and not the paradigm optimum segment width $\Delta^*$.

Since it has already been shown that $\Delta > \Delta^*$, and since $e_H/(e_H - 1)$ is a decreasing function of the segment width,

$$\sigma^* < \hat{\sigma} \leqq \frac{e_H}{(e_H - 1)(1 - m)}$$

$$< \frac{e_H{}^*}{(e_H{}^* - 1)(1 - m)} < \sigma_U. \tag{7.28}$$

This inequality shows that a range of elasticity values, $\sigma^* \leqq \sigma < \sigma_U$, always exists for which it is possible that the market is viable and gives less-than-optimal product differentiation. However, $\sigma_U$ is an upper limit, beyond which it is certain the market is *not* viable, not a lower limit, below which it would be certain the market *is* viable. Thus it is always possible that the market is not viable above some elasticity value less than $\sigma^*$, and the untraditional case, in which the market gives less-than-optimal differentiation, may not appear.

Figure 7.1 illustrates the relationships among the degree of product differentiation in the market, at the optimum with outside goods, and at the paradigm optimum, showing the relationships between the critical values $\bar{\sigma}$ and $\sigma^*$ for two ranges of $m$.

## 7.4 The Market as a Second Best

Since the market solution, as represented by perfect monopolistic competition, has already been established to be nonoptimal (except possibly at a single value of the elasticity of substitution) even if there were some *deus ex machina* to compensate for both specification

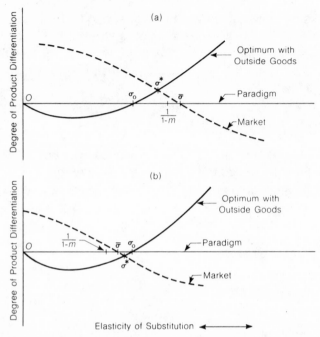

**Figure 7.1.** Relationship between market and optimum degrees of product differentiation for different values of system parameters: Case (a): $\sigma_o < \sigma^* < 1/(1 - m)$; Case (b): $1/(1 - m) < \sigma^* < \sigma_o$.

and price so that the same uniform target welfare levels were attained in the market as at the optimum, it is of considerable interest to compare the market solution with the second-best solutions derived in Chapter 4. Since second-best solutions are based on the absence of compensation for specification, they can be directly compared with realistic market solutions, in which such compensation is also absent.

It is useful first to summarize the relationships already established between the degrees of product differentiation that will occur under different conditions:

1. It was shown in the previous section that the degree of product differentiation in the market is certainly greater than at the full optimum for all values of the elasticity of substitution up to some value $\sigma^*$ which is greater than min ($\sigma_o$, $1/(1 - m)$). Since $\sigma_o$ was shown in

Section 4.8 to be very close to 2, it follows that the degree of product differentiation in the market is certainly greater than that of the full optimum when $\sigma = 1$.

2. It was shown in Section 4.9 that the degree of product differentiation for the second-best solution is certainly less than at the full optimum when $\sigma = 1$ and that the degree of product differentiation for the second-best solution shows little sensitivity to the value of $\sigma$.

3. It was shown in Section 6.7 that the market degree of product differentiation decreases as the elasticity of substitution increases.

4. The relevant comparison between the market and the full optimum is when demand is fully compensated in both cases, and the relationships given above are based on this assumption. On the other hand, the relevant comparison between the market and the second-best solution is with demand uncompensated in the market, as it is in the second-best configuration. Since it was shown in Chapter 5 (Section 5.9) that the compensated elasticity may be greater or less than the uncompensated elasticity, the degree of product differentiation in the market with compensated demand may be greater or less than with uncompensated demand.

If the market degree of product differentiation were at least as great with uncompensated as with compensated demand, then conclusions 1, 2, and 3 above would imply that the market degree of product differentiation is greater than the second best whenever the market degree of differentiation is greater than the full optimum. Since no such relationship between the compensated and uncompensated market solutions can be established, it is necessary to make a direct comparison between the uncompensated market equilibrium and the second-best solution. This comparison will be made for unit elasticity of substitution, which is the borderline case for a stable market, but the value for which the second-best solution was derived earlier.

For an economy with outside goods for which the elasticity of substitution is unity, the second-best solution satisfies the condition given by Eq. (4.45a) in Chapter 4,

$$1 - e_z = m(\theta - 1), \tag{7.29}$$

where $Z$ is the cumulative value of the function $z(u)$ defined by $z(u) = [h(u)]^{-m}$, or $e_z = -me_h$. Since $z' = -mh^{m-1}h' < 0$, Lemma 1c of

Appendix B gives the inequality

$$e_z > 1 + e_z$$

$$> 1 - me_h. \tag{7.30}$$

With the optimal half-spacing between goods at the second-best solution denoted by $\hat{\Delta}$, Eqs. (7.29) and (7.30) imply that

$$e_h(\hat{\Delta}) > \frac{1 - e_z(\hat{\Delta})}{m} = \theta - 1. \tag{7.31}$$

From Eq. (5.46) of Chapter 5, the uncompensated demand elasticity, which is the appropriate case for comparison with the second-best solution, is given by

$$\hat{E} = se_{\hat{Q}} + (1 - m)\sigma + (1 - \gamma)m,$$

where $\gamma$ is a parameter representing the degree of compensation for price (there is no compensation for specification) and $e_Q$ is the elasticity of the cumulative quantity function. When $\sigma = 1$, the uniform distribution of money incomes implies that all consumers buy the same quantity of the group good, so that $e_{\hat{Q}} = 1$. Thus the demand elasticity for $\sigma = 1$ with no price compensation ($\gamma = 0$) becomes

$$\hat{E} = s + 1. \tag{7.32}$$

The marginal revenue ratio $R = E/(E - 1)$ becomes, in this case,

$$R = 1 + \frac{1}{s}. \tag{7.33}$$

At equilibrium all firms will charge the same price, so that the market-width elasticity has the value given in Eq. (5.9) of Chapter 5,

$$s = \frac{1}{2e_h},$$

and Eq. (7.33) becomes

$$R = 1 + 2e_h. \tag{7.34}$$

Denote the market equilibrium segment half-width by $\Delta$, so that the market equilibrium condition $R = \theta$ in this case has the form

$$1 + 2e_h(\Delta) = \theta,$$

or

$$2e_h(\Delta) = \theta - 1. \tag{7.35}$$

If $\theta$ is a constant, as in the case of a homogeneous production function, Eqs. (7.31) and (7.35) can be combined directly to give

$$e_h(\Delta) > \theta - 1 = 2e_h(\hat{\Delta}). \tag{7.36}$$

Since $e_h$ is an increasing function, this implies that $\Delta > \hat{\Delta}$, i.e., that the degree of product differentiation in the market is greater than that for the second-best solution. Because of the factor 2 on the right-hand side, the inequality is a strong one, and thus market differentiation is much greater than that given by the second-best solution.

It is necessary to consider the case of a variable $\theta$, with $\theta' < 0$, since the U-shaped cost curve has been considered typical of monopolistic competition. Suppose that the effect of variable $\theta$ is to upset the original conclusion and give less product differentiation in the market than at the second-best solution. Then the output per good would be higher in the market, and the degree of economies of scale would be lower than at the second best. Denote the value of $\theta$ at the second best by $\hat{\theta}$ and the market value by unmarked $\theta$, so that $\hat{\theta} > \theta$. From Eqs. (7.31) and (7.35), the relationships given in Eq. (7.36) would be replaced by

$$e_h(\hat{\Delta}) > \hat{\theta} - 1 > \theta - 1 = 2e_h(\Delta), \tag{7.37}$$

from which it would follow that $\hat{\Delta} > \Delta$ as before, which contradicts the hypothesis that the degree of product differentiation in the market is less than that at the second-best solution. Thus a variable degree of economies of scale cannot upset the original result.

It has been shown that the market degree of product differentiation is definitely greater than that of the second-best solution at unit elasticity of substitution. Now the second-best degree of differentiation varies little with the elasticity of substitution, but the market degree of differentiation decreases as the elasticity of substitution becomes higher, so that the existence of a high elasticity range in which there is less than a second-best degree of product differentiation in the market remains a possibility. Comparison with the full-optimum case suggests that this range will be smaller than the corresponding range for the full optimum, since the degree of differentiation curve for the full optimum rises to meet the falling curve for the market (See Figure 7.1), whereas the degree of differentiation curve for the second-best solution is relatively flat.

When there is no compensation for specification, as at the second-best and in the comparable market equilibrium, the degree of product differentiation has a special significance which it does not possess when there is compensation for specification: It carries implications concerning equity. The lower the degree of product differentiation, the larger the segments of the spectrum being supplied with each good, and thus the greater the difference in welfare levels between consumers at the segment centers and those at the edges, since money incomes are taken to be uniform over the spectrum. Thus the degree of equity increases with the degree of product differentiation when there is such compensation for specification. At the full optimum, where there is such compensation, and in the compensated market equilibrium, equity is maintained, by definition, for all degrees of product differentiation, and this effect does not occur.

Thus, although the realistic uncompensated market equilibrium leads, in general, to greater-than-optimal (second-best) product differentiation and thus to inefficiency, there is some trade-off in the form of greater equity. For the greater part of the range of values of the elasticity of substitution for which the market is viable it seems possible, therefore, to make the following statement:

The market solution is less efficient but more equitable than the simple utilitarian second-best optimal solution.

Two points should be noted in relation to the above statement. The first is that, as in the comparison between the market and the full optimum, the effects of price distortion between group and outside goods under monopolistic competition have been ignored. The second is that "equity" refers only to the distribution of real incomes over the spectrum owing to specification effects and is not related in any way to the notion of equity in the distribution of money incomes over individuals or to the distribution of incomes between wages and profits. In this model, it has been assumed that the distribution of money income is uniform and that the perfect-monopolistic-competition equilibrium generates no pure profits, so that the specification effects are the only potential source of inequity.

If there exists some range at high substitution elasticities for which the market gives less product differentiation than the second-best solution, then there is no trade-off between equity and efficiency. In this case, the market clearly gives the worst of both worlds: It is less efficient and less equitable than the second best.

## 7.5 Price Distortion

In comparing the market with the optimum, the emphasis in this work is on differences in the degree of product differentiation, since it is the analysis of product differentiation which represents the primary original contribution of the book. The "monopolistic" element of monopolistic competition—that firms choose their actions to equate marginal cost with marginal revenue instead of marginal cost with price—does however lead to price-distortion effects. Although these effects are of the same kind as in the traditional analysis of imperfect competition generally, some specific comments seem called for.

There are no price distortions within the group, at least with the uniform density across the spectrum that has been assumed in the models discussed here, since all goods in the group will sell at the same price in both the market equilibrium and under either the full-optimum or second-best configurations. Distortions within the group occur because of the different numbers and specifications of the goods offered in the market as compared with the optimum and not because the consumers face inappropriate relative prices of group goods.

The price-distortion effects are confined to the relationships between group goods and outside goods. If the latter are produced within a structure of perfect competition which leads to marginal-cost pricing, then the group goods (which are priced above marginal cost) are relatively too expensive, and the optimum relationship between the two sets of goods would call for more group goods and less outside goods than at the market equilibrium prices. These effects have been largely eliminated in the previous comparisons between the market and the optimum by assuming that the parameter $m$, which represents the expenditure on group goods as a proportion of total expenditure, is the same in both.

To the extent that the degree of returns to scale is a function of output, the market solution will result in a higher degree of economies of scale than would the optimum under the same conditions, *taking account of price effects alone*. This, in turn, would tend to decrease the market degree of product differentiation relative to the optimum, again with respect to relative price effects alone. In the lower elasticity-of-substitution range, for which the market degree of product differentiation would otherwise be greater than optimal, the effect of the price distortions is partly to counter this tendency. In the high-elasticity range, where the market degree of product differentiation is already less than optimal (if this range exists in a particular case), the effect of price distortions is to increase the difference between the market and optimal degrees of product differentiation.

Thus there is interaction between the price distortion and other effects, which leads to some modification of previous conclusions, primarily in reducing somewhat the range of elasticity-of-substitution values for which the market gives greater-than-optimal differentiation and increasing the range for which the market gives less-than-optimal differentiation. These interactions disappear, however, if the degree of economies of scale in the production of group goods is unaffected by the output level.

## 7.6 Contexts for Policy-making

In approaching the problems of policy-making—and policy is taken to include the decision to leave the market alone, as well as intervention in some form—there are various initial considerations that provide the context in which final policy decisions must be made. Since these are scattered at various points through the preceding analysis, it is important to bring them together here in a coherent relationship to each other.

*1. Markets may be less viable than commonly believed.* As shown in Chapter 6, the market may simply not produce any goods at all in some group for which it can be shown to be optimal to have goods produced. This can occur if the elasticity of substitution between the group and outside goods is relatively high and the degree of economies of scale is also relatively high. Such a combination can result in the elasticity of demand being too high to give a sufficient margin of price over marginal revenue to match the margin of average cost over marginal cost resulting from the economies of scale, and even a monopolist could not make a profit. This is an old problem in the theory of public utilities, but its application is very much wider, and the problem may arise in any industry showing economies of scale of any kind.

The problem is obviously most acute when the economies of scale are due to true increasing returns to scale, so that the degree of economies of scale is constant or is bounded below. The problem will not arise if the economies of scale are due to a fixed cost and marginal cost is rising, which gives a U-shaped cost curve, so that $\theta \leqq 1$ and $\bar{\sigma}$ is infinite, provided the minimum average cost is at an output well within the total output level of the group. In this case, the goods will be produced when the market is of sufficient size, but not if it is too small.

If the elasticity of substitution between the group goods and outside goods is too low rather than too high, then the monopolistic-competition equilibrium may be unstable, and it certainly will be if there are increasing returns to scale. As in the high-elasticity case, a U-shaped cost curve will improve the chances of a viable equilibrium.

The possibility of market failure is not, therefore, confined to special cases like public goods or public utilities but can appear in ordinary consumer goods. A laissez-faire policy must take into account the possibility that some goods may not be produced at all by the market, even though their production would be socially optimal.

2. *Monopolistic competition is not a market aberration.* It is commonly believed that the divergence of markets from the perfect-competition pattern in some kind of pathological state, differences in viewpoint being primarily about the appropriate treatment. Noninterventionists believe that the markets will cure themselves homeopathically in the long run, interventionists that radical antitrust surgery

and other measures are required, but both proceed as if the well-known optimal properties of perfect competition were widely attainable.

It has been shown here that perfect monopolistic competition is the natural final state that will be achieved in the absence of collusion and entry barriers and in the presence of vigorous entrepreneurship and full information (precisely the conditions that are supposed to bring about perfect competition) if there are variable specifications of goods, diversity of preferences, and average costs which fall initially, even for a very small output range.

Policy, therefore, cannot be based on attempts to induce free entry and thus bring about perfect competition or on a belief that the system will approach perfect competition of its own accord but must be based on recognizing that the market solution under the most competitive circumstances will be that of monopolistic competition. Since the monopolistic-competition equilibrium does not possess the optimal properties of perfect competition, a policy of leaving the market alone is appropriate only if the losses from market suboptimality are considered to be less than the potential costs of intervention.

3. *The structure of an industry is not sufficient guide for policy.* It has been made abundantly clear in the preceding analysis that the relationship of the market equilibrium to the optimum cannot be determined from the intragroup properties alone but depends in a very essential way on the structural relationships between the group and the rest of the economy. As between two groups with identical internal structures, one may give a market solution with a greater-than-optimal degree of product differentiation, the other a solution with less-than-optimal differentiation, since the elasticities of substitution between the group and the rest of the economy may differ in the two cases or the relative importance of the groups in the economy may be different. Thus policy cannot be based on a detailed analysis of the structure of the group without the additional information as to its relationship to the rest of the economy.

4. *The divergence of the market from the optimum is not unidirectional.* If the divergence of market equilibria from the optimum is always in the same direction, then an interventionist at least knows

the direction in which he will intervene. Antitrust policy has been built on the belief in such unidirectional divergence and that it is always better to have more firms than fewer firms, except in special cases. But it has been shown that the market may give too few goods or too many goods, so that even the direction of optimal intervention is not certain.

However, since the realistic alternative to the market is the second-best solution rather than the full optimum, it seems likely that the market produces too many goods unless the elasticity of substitution with respect to outside goods is very high. Note that if the divergence from the optimum is accepted as being generally toward too many goods, then the direction of intervention should be toward fewer firms—the "rationalization" rather than the "antitrust" approach.

The apparent paradox that barriers to entry may promote optimality illustrates the other facet of the lack of unidirectional divergence from optimality: The market diverges from the optimum in more than one way, and the direction of divergence may differ according to the criterion. In monopolistic competition, the fewer the firms, the fewer the goods, and thus (within some range) the closer to the optimum—as measured in terms of the degree of product differentiation. On the other hand, the fewer the firms, the higher the ratio of price to marginal cost, and thus the greater the divergence from the optimum—as measured by the degree of price distortion (the traditional criterion, and the basis for much antitrust reasoning).

5. *Policy normally involves an equity-efficiency choice.* The full optimum discussed in detail in the earlier chapters of the book is Pareto-efficient (that is, an optimum can be found for any welfare distribution), but only by the use of compensation. One of the policy options is for the government to intervene in income distribution alone, leaving the market to determine how many of which goods to be produced.

In this case, that is, the compensated demand case, in which the market solution is compared with the full optimum, the market and the optimum differ only in terms of efficiency. In all other cases, the market solution differs from the optimum in equity as well as efficiency. Insofar as equity and efficiency are both regarded as desirable, and because in many instances the market is more equitable but less efficient than the second best or other appropriate standard of comparison, policy designed to increase efficiency may reduce equity. In a product-differentiated context without compensation for specification—a form of compensation that must be considered a virtual impossibility under realistic conditions—every increase in the degree of product differentiation is more equitable, and every decrease less equitable, so that equity considerations are always present.

The one uncompensated case in which no trade-off is present is if there exists a high range of values of the elasticity of substitution for which the market gives less product differentiation than the second best. For a group in this context, the market is both less efficient and less equitable than the second-best optimum solution.

## 7.7 Optimal Intervention

It will be assumed that there are no problems of monopoly or oligopoly, such as discussed in later chapters, or of imperfect information or other "frictions" discussed in the next chapter, so that the market will reach a perfect-monopolistic-competition equilibrium in the absence of intervention, provided the parameters of the system are such as to make such a structure a viable one. Thus the discussion of optimal intervention is confined to intervention in the context of perfect monopolistic competition, which will be referred to simply as market equilibrium.

Divergence of the market equilibrium from the optimum is not unidimensional (except in terms of welfare itself), and there are three areas of potential intervention:

1. intervention with respect to income distribution, meaning here the compensation of individuals for whom the best available good is not of most-preferred specification;
2. intervention designed to achieve the optimal degree of product differentiation; and
3. intervention designed to remove the price distortion resulting from the "monopolistic" element in monopolistic competition.

The first form of intervention is not specific to the correction of market suboptimality but is required to achieve the full optimum under fully controlled production. The problems associated with this compensation for specification were discussed in some detail in Chapter 3, where it was shown that such compensation might be infeasible for administrative or political reasons. The decision of whether to compensate or not must be made before decisions about the remaining forms of intervention, since the former decision determines whether the market is to be manipulated to give the full optimum or a second-best solution.

Once the decision as to compensation has been made, the target, whether the full optimum or the second-best solution, can be achieved by the use of two policy instruments only. This is because there are two divergences from the target—in the degree of product differentiation and in the ratio of price to marginal cost—and instruments can be found which affect each. The instruments are not fully separable in their effects but can be determined sequentially as shown below.

There are two conditions satisfied by the market equilibrium. One is the profit-maximizing condition for the individual firm (Eq. 6.5),

$$P = RF',$$

and the other is the condition for the equilibrium number of firms (Eq. 6.8),

$$R = \theta.$$

Now the optimum degree of product differentiation, whether the full optimum or the second best, is determined by equating an elasticity expression to $\theta$, the measure of the degree of economies of scale. Optimal pricing is either marginal-cost pricing proper ($P = F'$) or marginal-cost-proportional pricing ($P = \lambda F'$, where $\lambda$ is the same for all industries). Thus the optimal degree of product differentiation can be achieved by confronting the firms with a degree of economies of scale $\hat{\theta}$ which is not the "natural" degree but a value manipulated to give optimal differentiation at $R = \hat{\theta}$. Optimal pricing can be achieved by making the marginal costs of the firms diverge from the marginal social cost so that $P = RF' = \hat{F}'$ (or $\lambda F'$), where $\hat{F}'$ is the manipulated marginal cost.

The parameter $\theta$ can easily be manipulated by imposing on every potential firm a fixed license fee or giving a fixed bonus independent of output. Such a fixed cost changes $\theta$ but does not affect marginal cost. Private marginal costs can be made to diverge from true marginal cost by a proportional tax or subsidy on total production costs (including the fixed-cost element). Since this changes average and marginal cost in the same proportion, it does not affect $\theta$, which is the ratio of the two.

Thus the optimum can be achieved by a combination of a fixed license or bonus and a proportional tax or subsidy on total costs. If the divergence from the optimum in terms of product differentiation is considered most likely to be in the direction of too much product differentiation (and this will be an even more likely for the second-best configuration), the usual case will require fewer firms than the market equilibrium will give, a higher apparent value of $\theta$ to the firms, and thus a fixed license fee rather than a bonus. The bonus case would arise only when the elasticity of substitution was high enough to give market differentiation of less than the optimal degree. Unless there is marginal-cost-proportional pricing with a high value of $\lambda$ at the optimum, it can be assumed that the direction of price distortion is such as to require a proportional subsidy on product costs rather than a tax.

Since the optimum is always such that the true $\theta$, the ratio of average social cost to marginal cost, is greater than unity even when cost curves are U-shaped, the combination of the license fee and proportional subsidy will necessarily result in net subsidization if there is strict marginal-cost pricing. The net subsidy over the whole group will be the same as required under an optimal regime with no market, however, since the profit per firm is assumed to be zero and is a consequence of the existence of economies of scale. The form of taxation by which the net subsidy is financed is determined in the same way, whether the market is used as an instrument of policy or production is controlled directly.

With a system of marginal-cost-proportional pricing, where the value of $\lambda$ is chosen so that total sales exactly equal the costs of production over the economy as a whole, then some industries receive net subsidies and some pay net taxes, depending on whether the value of $\theta$ in a particular industry is above or below the average for the economy.

It is obvious enough that optimal intervention, although simple in theory, poses great problems in practical application. The greatest of these is information, since the optimal license fees and subsidies can be calculated only if the optimum is first determined. There is no way of using the market itself to perform the calculations as can be done with perfectly competitive markets. The closest to being able to use the market as a computer would be if the optimal number of goods were known approximately, in which case the appropriate number of licenses could be auctioned off annually or at some regular interval. This would not solve the price-distortion problem, however.

Rule-of-thumb approaches are not very helpful, although if there is a presumption that the market will tend to generate too much product differentiation, then some degree of "entry" cost may move the number of products in the direction of the optimum. The term "entry" is placed in quotes because licenses or other barriers must not be *one-time* obstacles to entry, which, once met, would allow the firm to behave as it wishes, but continuous payments to stay in business, with continuous open entry to new firms which are willing to pay the annual fee.

Finally it should be noted that the costs and difficulties of administering optimal intervention will be most easily justified when the group is of significant size relative to the economy as a whole, and thus when the losses from a suboptimal market equilibrium are a significant part of social welfare. There is no reason to suppose that the information or other costs are lower for a group of products having very low weight in overall welfare, but the gains from intervention will obviously be lower.

## 7.7 The Case for Laissez-faire

The case for nonintervention in markets involving variable specifications and economies of scale is not based, as it is in the traditional arguments, on the potential for optimality at the market equilibrium, but on the trade-off between the inefficiency of the market and the cost of intervention. Policy-makers who choose not to intervene cannot comfort themselves that they are thereby ensuring the best of all possible worlds by simultaneously increasing economic efficiency and personal freedom while saving themselves administrative headaches, as in one well-known scenario, but must recognize that they are sacrificing efficiency for other things.

It is obvious that the case for laissez-faire is not, therefore, a general case against intervention in any markets, but a case for nonintervention in markets when such intervention is simply not worthwhile, and is thus a case to be argued on an industry-by-industry basis, even if the final conclusion is that the state of the art and the availability of information do not justify intervention in any market under current circumstances.

The strongest case for nonintervention is for groups which account for only a very small proportion of total expenditure (a negligible value of $m$ in terms of the parameters used in the preceding analysis), and for which the degree of economies of scale is relatively small. This follows from several converging considerations:

1. As $m$ (the expenditure on group goods as a proportion of total expenditure) approaches zero, the difference between the full optimum and the second best also approaches zero, as shown by Eq. (4.49), so the loss from not intervening in the income distribution becomes minimal at small values of $m$, that is, when the group is only a small part of the total economy.

2. With no compensation for specification, the difference between the welfare of an individual at the market fringe and at the center depends on the factor $[h(\Delta)]^{-m}$, as shown by Eq. (4.40). This factor becomes closer to unity (and thus to no falloff in welfare) with decreasing values of $m$ and $\Delta$, the latter being smaller when the degree of economies of scale is lower. This reinforces the above argument, that compensation problems become negligible.

3. When $m$ is small, the proportional increase in the total resource use of economy due to inefficiency in the particular industry becomes very small.

4. When $\theta$ (the degree of economies of scale) is small, the proportionate increase in resources resulting from a suboptimal degree of

product differentiation is small even over the group itself, and the price distortion is small since $\theta$ is equal to the ratio of price to marginal cost.

5. If $m$ is small, the effect of price distortion between the group and the rest of the economy will be small.

If the economy contains many such groups, each a negligible fraction of the whole economy, but collectively a significant sector, then some of the above arguments in favor of nonintervention hold, whereas others do not. It remains true that, provided there is no correlation between the position of an individual on the spectrum for one group and his or her position on the spectrum for another, the compensation problem remains negligible. In fact, it can be argued that the existence of many groups with uncorrelated spectrum positions will tend toward a uniform distribution of welfare overall by an averaging process, without any compensation within individual groups.

It also remains true that a small value of $\theta$ for all groups will minimize the loss arising from nonoptimal product differentiation and reduce the price distortion. The total effects of inefficiency losses, however, can no longer be treated as negligible.

Whereas the compensation effects tend to cancel over many groups, the other distortions do not. Even if the average degree of product differentiation was optimal owing to cancellation effects between groups with too much and too little differentiation, the losses are always in the same direction (too much resource use), whether the market errs on one side or the other.

The strongest argument in favor of nonintervention, when the individual groups are small relative to the economy, is that the information and other costs of intervention can be presumed to be much the same whether or not the group is important in the economy, whereas the gains from intervention are small if the group is small. This argument continues to hold even if the number of groups becomes large, unless there are information externalities or other economies from simultaneous intervention in different markets.

Thus there is quite a good case for leaving small groups alone, even if the small-group sector is not unimportant when aggregated, but it is a pragmatic case, based on living with suboptimality because it is too difficult to do anything about it. The case becomes weaker the more important the individual group in the economy and the greater the degree of economies of scale in the group.

There is some consolation in living with market inefficiency, in that the market is generally more equitable when it is less efficient, and a market which is important enough for the resource loss to be significant will also be important enough for the equity improvement to be significant as well.

Chapter 8

# Imperfect Monopolistic Competition

## 8.1 Introduction

The term "perfect monopolistic competition" has been used in previous chapters to denote the market structure that results from noncollusive firms operating in a context of diversity in consumer preferences, variable product specification, and some degree of economies of scale, under "perfect" conditions of full information for both individuals and firms, costless specification change, and free entry and access to technology for all potential competitors. Imperfect monopolistic competition, the subject of this chapter, denotes the market structures which result from the same context of diversity, product variation, and scale economies when the conditions are not perfect in the sense described.

Whereas perfection is a uniquely defined concept, markets can be imperfect in a wide variety of ways. This poses two kinds of problems, one of selecting appropriate, realistic, and interesting directions of deviation from the conditions of perfection, the other of devising an appropriate analysis of the particular deviation selected. The latter problem is the more difficult, since there may be no underlying presumption as to behavior under the particular conditions which constitute the market imperfection.

Three main types of divergence from perfection will be considered in this chapter, together with some special phenomena, such as

255

advertising and "pseudodifferentiation," which are associated with these divergences. The first to be considered will be that of imperfect information, potentially a large topic since it may refer to lack of complete information as to price or specification (or both) on the part of the consumers or the firms (or both) and since imperfect information on any aspect of the situation may mean anything from total ignorance, or even misinformation, to a reasonable estimate with a range of error. The emphasis will be on imperfect information to individuals as to specification of goods actually available and imperfect information to firms as to the degree of information available to individuals. The other two divergences from perfection to be examined will be the effect of costs of specification change and costs of entry.

The role of advertising will also be studied, especially the conditions under which firms will, or will not, wish to promulgate information as to the exact specifications of the goods they produce.

There will be a discussion of pseudodifferentiation, the attempt by firms to make products which are actually identical in specification appear to the consumer to be different from each other. This is a phenomenon related both to incomplete information and to costs of specification change.

To complete the analysis of monopolistic competition, there will be a study of some scenarios depicting the industry dynamics as the market converges towards the perfect-monopolistic-competition equilibrium from a disequilibrium situation under perfect conditions or from an equilibrium under imperfect conditions as the imperfections are relaxed or removed.

If there is any single conclusion which is common to the analysis of such a wide variety of imperfections, it is this:

Market imperfection leads to a lower degree of product differentiation than would occur under perfect monopolistic competition, except in one special case.

## 8.2 Imperfect Information

Information may be imperfect in many ways, including being just plain wrong. It will be assumed at this stage, however, that the basic problem is that of quantity, rather than quality, of information, so that whatever information is available is indeed information and not misinformation. Thus the discussion which follows is primarily concerned with situations in which information is incomplete or absent with respect to some data necessary for decision-making.

There are two sets of information which the individual consumer requires in order to make a fully informed choice on the market. The first set refers to the individual's personal situation and consists of his or her preference structure and income or other constraints: It will be assumed that every consumer is fully informed in regard to these.[1] The second set of information refers to the available choice situation in the market and consists of information as to the prices and specifications of all the goods available. It is with respect to this second set that incomplete information will be considered as a possibility.

There is a considerable literature on the effect of incomplete price information on the equilibrium structure and dynamic behavior of markets in which there is a given number of goods having fixed specification and in which it is assumed that those specifications are known.[2] The analysis here will be confined to the conditions of most importance and interest for the theory of product variety, those in which there is incomplete information as to the specifications of the available goods, although the prices of the goods are assumed to be known or to be more readily attainable than details of specification.

The general effect of incomplete information as to specification can be studied by taking an extreme case, which will be referred to as *ignorance*. The term must be defined carefully, however, since it is certainly something more than total lack of any information concerning the goods in the group. It is assumed, in particular, that the ignorant consumer knows that all the goods in the group *are*, in fact, in that group, that is, that he or she is aware that all goods possess the characteristics that are considered to define the group and, since the analysis is confined to horizontal product differentiation, that the goods are of equivalent "quality." The consumer's ignorance is con-

1. Although even this assumption will be relaxed at one stage in the succeeding analysis.

2. The modern analysis of market equilibria under conditions of imperfect price information commenced with Stigler (1961). See the critical survey in Rothschild (1973).

fined to knowledge of the proportions in which those characteristics are possessed by the different goods available, that is, knowledge of their positions along the goods spectrum. In other words, the consumer knows, for example, that all the goods in question are high-fidelity amplifiers, but does not know the ratio of power output to lack of distortion among the various models. This seems a realistic-enough situation.

It will be assumed that the ignorant consumer will, as is traditionally supposed in such situations, assign the available goods along the potential goods spectrum in a random fashion, so that the probability that a specific good is assigned to a point on the spectrum in the segment $(x, x + \delta)$ is a linear function of $\delta$ and independent of $x$. Given the individual's most-preferred specification (which the individual is assumed to know), all goods have equal probability of being assumed by that individual to be the available good which is, closest in specification to the most-preferred good. If the market consisted entirely of ignorant consumers and the prices of all goods were the same, then the expected values of the sales of all goods would be the same. This would be true whatever the actual locations of the goods along the spectrum. Note that this is an implicit definition of equal "quality"—that all goods have an equal probability of being purchased when all sell at the same price.

The problem in proceeding to the next step is in deciding what would be reasonable behavior on the part of ignorant consumers when prices change or differ between goods. If all goods are considered equally probable of being closest to the individual's most-preferred good, then the rational choice would be the cheapest good (asuming equal "quality"). If there were perfect price information, any good priced above the minimum would have zero sales, and if all goods were sold at the same price, the market for each would be characterized by infinite elasticity of demand with respect to its own price. This conclusion would be modified if either price information was less than perfect or some information as to specification was available, and since perfect price information and complete ignorance as to specification form an extreme combination, it will be assumed that a firm which charges less than other firms will gain customers and one that charges more will lose customers but that the elasticity is less than infinite.[3]

Note that the interrelations among the markets of the firms when all consumers are ignorant are quite different from those with perfectly informed consumers. In the fully informed case, a firm which raises its price marginally will lose sales to the *adjacent* firms only, and more distant firms will be unaffected. In the case of ignorance, however, a firm which raises its price will lose sales to *all* other firms, as in the original Chamberlin analysis. Because of this property, it is reasonable to assume that the elasticity of demand for a single good will be higher the larger the number of other goods available, for the case of ignorant consumers.

When there are outside goods, the loss in sales resulting from a price increase by a firm within the group is not simply diverted to other firms within the group but results, in part, in substitution of outside goods. Since it has already been assumed that the consumers, although ignorant as of the place of the group goods along the group spectrum, are clear as to the place of the group as a whole in their total preference pattern, it seems reasonable to suppose that the consumers see the same substitutability properties between whatever group good they buy and the outside good, in both the ignorance and full-information contexts.

Thus the properties of the demand for a single good in a context of ignorant consumers can be assumed to have the following properties:

1. The own-price demand elasticity will be high and will always be higher than that of fully informed consumers facing the same number of group goods, with the same price structure and the same elasticity of substitution for outside goods. In the extreme case, the elasticity may be infinite.

2. The elasticity of demand will increase as the number of group goods increases.

3. An alternative model which gives the same result is to assume perfect price information but uncertainty over whether the quality level of all goods is the same. Since the relevant price for decision is the price after standarization for quality, certainty concerning price per physical unit and uncertainty concerning quality have the same effect as certainty concerning quality and uncertainty concerning price per physical unit.

3. The elasticity of demand will increase as the price increases, since it can be assumed that information on large price differentials will diffuse more readily than information on small price differentials, whatever the specific nature of the imperfection in price information.[4]

4. The role of the elasticity of substitution with respect to outside goods will be the same as in the fully informed case.

5. When the price of any group good rises, with the prices of other goods remaining constant and equal to each other, some of the sales will be diverted to outside goods (unless the elasticity of substitution is zero), and the remainder will be diverted evenly across the remaining group goods.

The elasticity of demand for ignorant consumers will be denoted by $\bar{E}$. Then $\bar{E}$ has the basic properties

$$\partial \bar{E}/\partial n > 0 \tag{8.1}$$

$$\partial \bar{E}/\partial p > 0 \tag{8.2}$$

$$\partial \bar{E}/\partial \sigma > 0 \tag{8.3}$$

where $n$ is the number of goods. These relationships correspond to properties 2, 3, and 4 listed above.

Note that Eqs. (8.2) and (8.3) are similar to the properties of demand for fully informed consumers, as set out in Sections 5.13 and 5.11, respectively. The property described by Eq. (8.1) will be seen to be similar to the corresponding property for fully informed demand, $\partial E/\partial \Delta < 0$, which was derived in Section 5.12, when it is noted that the spacing between goods in the fully informed case ($2\Delta$) is inverse to the number of goods. The spacing between goods is, of course, irrelevant in the ignorance case. In all cases, the comparisons are assumed to be made with demand which is uncompensated for specification (such compensation being a meaningless concept for ignorant consumers) and for the range of parameter values over which the fully informed market is viable.

The basic differences in demand properties between ignorant and fully informed consumers lie in the greater value of the elasticity

---

4. In the uncertain quality model it is assumed that the probability of the quality difference being worth the price difference diminishes as the latter increases.

for ignorant consumers and in the effects on other firms, which are different in the two cases.

Ignorance, as defined above, can eventually be dispelled by trial and error or other forms of search for information,[5] so it is unrealistic to regard ignorance on the part of all consumers as a permanent feature of a market. There are clearly many possible states between ignorance and full information, but it is very difficult to devise a scheme for handling partial information in a complicated context in which the relevant information is that concerning combinations of several characteristics for each of a large number of goods. How can a consumer be expected to behave, for example, when he or she knows the exact specifications of $m$ of the goods but nothing about the remaining $n - m$?

There is, however, a form of partial information which is just as useful to the individual as full information. If the consumer knows (a) the specifications of the goods closest to his most-preferred good (two goods in the two-characteristics case, more in others) and (b) that none of the remaining goods has specifications lying within the region bounded by these, then he or she can make a proper choice without knowing the exact specifications of the remaining goods.[6] Information which satisfies these two criteria will be regarded as "full" information for the purposes of the analysis, since further information is irrelevant to decision-making for that individual.

It seems appropriate, therefore, to ignore information states between ignorance as previously described and modified "full" information as defined above and assume that the market consists of a mix of ignorant consumers and informed consumers, with the proportions of the two as one of the variables to be considered. Two further assumptions will be made about the informed consumers: first, that they are distributed uniformly over the spectrum, and second,

---

5. Nelson (1970) divides goods into "search goods," in which the properties can be determined by inspection before purchase, and "experience goods," the properties of which can only be determined after purchase by actual use. It is obvious that ignorance can persist much longer for experience goods than for search goods.

6. This assumes that the prices of more distant goods are not so low as to make these dominate the closer goods.

that they are fully informed as to the prices of the products between which they must actually choose and know that the prices of the remaining products are not so low as to dominate goods which are relatively closer to their most-preferred specifications.

On the other side of the market, it is assumed that the firms are fully informed as to the specifications and prices of all products in the group. The information problem facing the firms is entirely different from that of the consumers: It consists of knowing the state of information of the consumers. The firms may believe that all consumers are ignorant, that all are informed, or that the market consists of a mixture of the two types of consumer, and these beliefs may be correct or incorrect. In all cases, it will be supposed that the beliefs are the same for all firms.

The general pattern of possible equilibrium configurations can then be determined by considering different possible beliefs on the part of firms as to consumer information and then finding the market outcome for different true states of consumer information.

## Case I: All Consumers Correctly Believed To Be Ignorant

In this case, under the assumptions already made, the sales of all firms will be the same if prices are the same, whatever the specifications of the goods actually produced by the firms. Choice of specification becomes irrelevant, and firms might produce identical goods or might differentiate their products in any way. All firms will have markets with identical properties and are assumed to have identical costs, so that the equilibrium will be characterized by identical prices for all products. With free entry, the equilibrium conditions for the group will have the same form as given in Eq. (6.8) for perfect monopolistic competition: $\tilde{R} = \theta$, where $\tilde{R} = \tilde{E}/(\tilde{E} - 1)$ is the marginal revenue ratio corresponding to the demand elasticity under ignorance and $\theta$ is the degree of economies of scale.

It has been suggested above that the demand elasticity under ignorance, $\tilde{E}$, can be expected to be higher than the demand elasticity with full information, $E$, when other market variables are the same, so that $\tilde{R}$ will be less than $R$ for the same prices and number of goods. Thus if the degree of economies of scale, $\theta$, is a constant, the ignorant market cannot be in equilibrium at the same prices, with the same number of goods, as the informed market. The equilibrium configuration under ignorance must differ from that under full information in such a way as to reduce the elasticity $\tilde{E}$, so that $\tilde{R}$ increases. From Eqs. (8.1) and (8.2), this implies a lower price or a smaller number of goods than at the informed equilibrium. If marginal cost is falling (certainly true if $\theta$ is constant and greater than unity), then a smaller number of goods will imply a larger production and lower marginal cost for each, so that the required changes in price and number of goods are consistent. If the economies-of-scale parameter $\theta$ is not constant, but decreases with output ($\theta' > 0$ has been ruled out throughout the analysis), the above argument holds a fortiori. Suppose that variable $\theta$ led to the opposite result—that the number of goods under ignorance was larger than in the informed market. Then the output of each good would be smaller in the ignorance case and the economies of scale parameter would be larger, and $\tilde{R}$ would necessarily be smaller than $R$, so that the equilibrium condition could not be satisfied. Thus the number of goods at equilibrium with ignorant consumers must be less than with informed consumers, whether the degrees of economies of scale is constant or decreases with output.

Note that the equilibrium configuration under ignorance as to the specification really depends on the information as to price and has nothing to do with specification properties themselves. In the extreme case, in which there is perfect price information and consumers buy only the cheapest good, $\tilde{E}$ is infinite.[7] No monopolistic-competition equilibrium is possible under these circumstances if there are true increasing returns to scale, since $\tilde{R}$ will be unity and $\theta$ will be greater than unity. However, there is an interesting possibility if there are U-shaped cost curves, since then it is possible to have an equilibrium configuration in which the number of firms is such that price equals both average and marginal cost ($R = \theta = 1$), with production at minimum average cost level.

7. This does not hold if quality is uncertain.

*It is possible to have an imperfect-monopolistic-competition equilibrium that looks like perfect competition, although perfect monopolistic competition cannot have such an equilibrium.*

The apparent resemblance to the perfect-competition equilibrium occurs, of course, because the heterogeneity of the products is masked by ignorance, and the market behaves in the aggregate as though the goods were homogeneous.

### Case II: Consumers Incorrectly Believed To Be Ignorant

If consumers are in fact fully informed, but firms believe them to be ignorant, they may pay little attention to specification choice, so that the goods are distributed at random over the spectrum. The misadjustment of the market would then become apparent in the variation in market shares among firms. An exception would occur if either the firms produced products of identical specifications (in which case it can be assumed that the informed consumers would be distributed evenly over the goods) or the specifications happened by chance to be such that the goods were distributed evenly over the spectrum, so that the informed equilibrium gave equal market shares. A firm could always test the hypothesis that all consumers were ignorant by varying its specification; if and only if the hypothesis is true, its market share will be unaffected. Because of the simplicity of this test, it can be assumed that an incorrect belief that all consumers are ignorant cannot persist for long, and thus an equilibrium analysis of Case II is unjustified.

### Case III: Firms Correctly Believe Some Consumers To Be Informed

If firms believe that at least some consumers are informed, there is a crucial change in the structure of the situation as compared to the case in which firms believe that all consumers are ignorant. The distribution of the product specifications over the spectrum will then be determined by he distribution of preferences of informed consumers, since the sales among ignorant consumers are independent of the distribution. Since it has been assumed that the informed consumers are distributed evenly over the spectrum, the resulting distribution of goods will be one in which they are evenly spaced, just as under perfect information.

The number of goods will not necessarily be that of perfect monopolistic competition, however, since the demand properties will be a combination of the properties derived from the ignorant consumers and the informed consumers. It has been supposed that the demand for any particular good from the ignorant consumers will have higher price elasticity, other parameters being the same, than the demand from informed consumers. Thus the elasticity of the combined demand will be higher than that for a fully informed market, converging toward the latter value as the proportion of informed consumers increases. Since the direction of the changes in the elasticities with respect to the number of goods, the price, and the elasticity of substitution with respect to outside goods are the same for both the informed and ignorant segments of the market, the combined demand has the same general properties as in the perfect-monopolistic-competition case, but with a higher elasticity for all parameter values.

Thus the equilibrium in Case III will be characterized by an even distribution of products over the spectrum, a uniform price for all products, and a number of goods which will be *less* than under conditions of full information but *more* than in Case I. The higher the proportion of consumers who are informed, the closer the equilibrium degree of product differentiation to that of perfect monopolistic competition. Note that the critical difference between this and Case I occurs when *some* consumers are informed. From the ensuing structure, the configuration then converges smoothly to the full-information case as the proportion of informed consumers rises towards 100 percent.

Case IV: Firms Incorrectly Believe Some Consumers To Be Informed

If firms believe that some consumers are informed, they will distribute themselves evenly over the spectrum, as in Case III. The resulting distribution is as good as any other if, in fact, all consumers are ignorant, and thus there is no incentive for firms to behave otherwise. The firms will misjudge the elasticity of demand, estimating it to be lower than it really is, so that the price will be higher and the number of firms larger than in Case I, when the firms correctly believe that there are no informed consumers. An equilibrium is possible with the same number of goods as in the corresponding Case III equilibrium.

If firms start experimenting, however, the equilibrium will clearly be unstable. A firm which lowers its price will find that it gains more sales than it anticipated (since the true elasticity is higher than estimated), and thus its profit will increase. Competitive price reductions will eliminate firms from the group until the Case I equilibrium is reached. A firm could also experiment with its specification but would find no change in sales (which would indicate the hypothesis of informed consumers to be incorrect) and would have no incentive to make specification changes.

Thus the stable equilibrium configuration in Case IV will correspond to the same number of goods at the same prices as in Case I, but firms will not produce identical goods, as is possible in Case I. The latter conclusion follows from noting that the initial unstable equilibrium will be such that every firm produces a unique product, whereas the ensuing dynamic movement to the stable equilibrium will result in the exit of some firms. There will be no reason, however, for any of the remaining firms to change their goods away from their original specifications so that the firms which remain will produce different products. The distribution of those products over the spectrum will depend on which of the original firms have been eliminated in the dynamic changes, and there is no necessary correlation between elimination and place on the spectrum.

## Other Possibilities

Note that it is always a safe strategy on the part of firms to distribute themselves over the spectrum as if all consumers were informed, since this will be the appropriate distribution if any nonnegligible proportion of consumers are in fact informed and as good as any if all consumers are ignorant. Thus it is reasonable to assume a uniform distribution of goods over the spectrum (in an economy characterized by a uniform preference distribution), whatever the state of information of the consumers.

It has been argued above that ignorant consumers will be more sensitive to price changes than informed consumers, since they cannot be sure that the higher-priced good is closer to the specification they seek than the lower-priced good. It has also been argued that the price elasticity will tend to be higher for ignorant consumers when the number of goods is larger, on the implicit grounds that the probability of the lower-priced good being further from the desired specification than any assigned distance will decline with the number of goods. On the basis of this last argument, concerning the relationship between demand elasticity and number of goods, it is concluded that there would tend to be fewer goods provided by firms to an ignorant market than to an informed one.

This chain of argument does not, however, have the status of a formal model, and the conclusions reached are tentative ones. This is primarily because, if consumers do not know the true specifications of the goods, there is no entirely satisfactory basis for constructing a model of rational behavior with respect to price differences between the goods, and thus some kind of ad hoc behavioral pattern must be assumed. The pattern which has been chosen seems reasonable enough, but other possibilities exist.

Since the imperfect-monopolistic-competition equilibrium is not based on a full formal model, no attempt has been made to investigate stability or viability conditions in any complete fashion. Some relevant considerations should be noted, however:

1. Since the demand elasticity is taken to be higher under conditions of ignorance, the viability range changes somewhat as compared with the perfect-information case. In particular, the imperfect-information cases cease to be viable at lower minimum levels for the degree of economies of scale than under perfect conditions. With U-shaped cost curves or other production conditions giving minimum degree of scale economies at or below unity, this problem does not arise.

2. The competitive structure of the group is different for markets with ignorant consumers as compared to fully informed markets, in that the direct rivalry between adjacent firms is softened (absent if all consumers are ignorant) because sales losses are spread over all firms. The group conforms much more closely to the classic Chamberlin pattern.

3. In a largely uninformed market, firms cannot adjust to market situations by varying specifications. Thus the emphasis will be on price competition (or on advertising, to be discussed later), and the price competitiveness will be heightened by the relatively high price elasticity.

4. The incentive to restrict entry in a collusive way will be greater with ignorant consumers, since all firms will expect to lose the same proportionate share when new firms enter. With fully informed consumers, only the firms with goods having specifications close to that of a new entrant will be affected.

## 8.3 Advertising and Information

In the absence of perfect information, will such information be provided by advertising? This is the question to which the present section is devoted.

Advertising is a form of public announcement that is provided and paid for by the seller, and the volume and content of advertising is chosen strictly in the interests of the seller, unless there are outside constraints such as "ethical" restrictions or government regulations. The analysis here will be confined to "truthful" advertising, in which the information content may be considerable or negligible, but there are no factual misstatements.

Although all advertising can be considered to provide some information, if only that there is a product in the group which is sold under a certain brand name, the term "information" will be used here to refer to "hard" information, such as the price of the product or some part of its specification. Advertising which merely familiarizes consumers with a particular brand name or makes vague and unspecific statements that the product is "good" will be referred to as "informationless" advertising. An assertion that "Brand X is best," since it is regarded as devoid of content, is not considered to contravene the assumption of truthfulness. The information of special interest in this analysis is that concerning specification—information that can assist the consumer to locate the good on the product spectrum. Price information will not be examined since it will be assumed, as in the preceding section, that consumers are relatively well informed on prices but less so on specification.

Consider first the situation in which all consumers are ignorant and in which the social value of information is at its highest. Will it be in the interest of individual firms to provide the information, primarily information as to the specifications of their goods? The answer is, not necessarily, because advertising is not one-on-one communication, but a general public announcement that reaches all consumers, at least within the group who read, watch, or listen to, some specific communication medium. In the context of ignorance, the market is divided among consumers on a random basis, with some consumers buying a particular good for the right reason (because it really does have their desired specification) and others buying it for the wrong reason (because they incorrectly believe it to possess the specification they seek). Any information as to the true specification of the good may attract consumers who have been buying other goods for the wrong reason but can also lose present customers who are buying this good on the basis of imperfect information.

Suppose there were just two goods in the group, each with a specification and price such that it would gain exactly half the consumers on the spectrum if there were perfect information. Suppose that good A would have the right half of the spectrum and good B the left half under these circumstances. If consumers are ignorant, the two goods would also split the market on the basis of random choice. Advertising by A that provided the information as to its specification relative to that of B would result in A gaining the customers who had incorrectly chosen B but losing those that had previously chosen A in error. There would be a clear social gain from the information, since the welfare of half the population (those that chose the wrong good in ignorance) would be increased, but no private gain in terms of market share to firm A. Thus advertising makes no difference to sales in this case and does not justify its cost (which falls entirely on firm A) if sales is the criterion.

The two-good argument does not hold, however, when there are many goods,[8] since a firm which announces the specification of its

8. In Lancaster (1976a), the author was in error, owing to making generalizations from the two-good case.

good will not only attract those customers who would form its market under conditions of full information but also customers who would buy a different good (but close in specification) under full information. This is because the deviation of the known specification from these additional customer's most-preferred specifications is less than the *expected value of the deviation under random choice.*

This can be illustrated by a simple example. Suppose there are five goods known to be distributed evenly over the spectrum, but it is not known which good occupies which position. Consumers are distributed evenly over the five segments into which the spectrum would be divided among the firms under full information. The spectrum can be thought of us made up of five numbered boxes, 1, . . . , 5, where adjacent numbers represent adjacent segments. Each consumer knows which box contains his or her most-preferred specification once the number on the relevant box is known.

In the ignorance case, none of the numbers on the boxes are visible, and each consumer has no option but to choose at random, so that each firm has a 20 percent market share. A consumer whose preferred specification corresponds to box 1 will find that the good obtained by random choice is in the correct segment if it turns out to be box 1, one segment away if it is box 2, two segments away if it is box 3, and so on. The expected value for the number of segments difference between the good a consumer wants and the good he or she obtains is 2. The consumer whose most-preferred good is in box 2 will find the difference to be one segment if the chosen box is either 1 or 3; zero, if 2; two segments, if 4; and three segments, if 5. The expected value of the difference is 1.4 segments, not the same as that of the first consumer, because of edge effects with a small number of goods. In a similar way, the consumer whose most-preferred good is in box 3 will face an expected value of the deviation under random choice of 1.2 segments, and consumers with most-preferred goods in boxes 4 and 5 will have expected values of 1.4 and 2, respectively. The variation in the expected values among consumers does not, however, affect the distribution of sales under random choice.

Now suppose the firm producing the good in box 2 identifies itself, so that the number of this box is now visible. Each consumer now has the option of choosing box 2 or making a random choice among the others, which he knows to consist of boxes 1, 3, 4, and 5. The consumer will choose box 2 if the actual deviation of this from the desired box is less than the expected value of the deviation from random choice among the remaining boxes.[9] The relevant values are tabulated below.

| Preferred box | Deviation from box 2 | Expected value of deviation with random choice among boxes 1, 3, 4, and 5 |
|---|---|---|
| 1 | 1 | 2.25 |
| 2 | 0 | 1.75 |
| 3 | 1 | 1.25 |
| 4 | 2 | 1.25 |
| 5 | 3 | 1.75 |

Consumers with preferred boxes 1, 2, and 3 will all choose the labeled box 2, and consumers with preferred boxes 4 and 5 will make a random choice among the remaining four boxes. Thus the firm producing box 2 (firm 2) will obtain 60 percent of the total market, and the remaining four firms will obtain only 10 percent each. Obviously, firm 2 gains enormously from having made its specification known, with its market share increasing from 20 to 60 percent.

One firm having announced its specifications, it will then clearly pay the others to do so. If the firm producing the box 3 good makes this known (after firm 2 has already announced its specification), an analysis along the same lines as that given above shows that firms 2 and 3 will then each obtain 40 percent of the market, with the remaining three firms obtaining a mere 6.67 percent each, because only consumers with preferences for box 5 will now choose randomly among the unmarked boxes (1, 4, and 5). If firm 4 now announces, it can easily be shown that firms 2 and 4 each obtain 40 percent of the

9. Strictly speaking, the consumer's valuations of the actual and expected deviations, $h(u)$ and $E$ $[h(u)]$, are the relevant decision variables, rather than $u$ and $E(u)$, and the properties of the compensating function influence the choice. The general principles are illustrated by the example given, however, which is equivalent to that obtained with a linear compensating function. Nonlinearity changes the number of goods necessary for the consumer to prefer the announced good over a random choice among the remainder but does not change the general structure of the situation.

market and firm 3 obtains 20 percent, and that no consumer will prefer to choose at random among the other two firms, which then have no sales.

Once all firms have made known their specifications, the market shares become equal again at 20 percent. In terms of market shares, the firms are in the same position in the end as at the beginning, but the dynamics of the situation are such that once firms start making their specifications known, the others must follow or drop out of the market.

Note that the above result does not depend on the simplifying assumption that the firms are known to be distributed evenly over the spectrum. Consider a case in which nothing is known of the distribution of firms, so that the announcement of specification by any firm leaves unchanged the probabilities associated with random choice among the remaining firms, as in sampling with replacement. For a continuous spectrum of unit length, the expected value of the distance between the specification for a randomly drawn firm and that for a consumer with most-preferred specification between $x$ and $x + dx$ is easily shown to be given by

$$\phi(x) = x^2 - x + \tfrac{1}{2}$$

as the number of firms approaches infinity.

Suppose the firm producing a good of specification $\bar{x}$ publishes its specification. A consumer will choose this good if his or her most-preferred specification is such that the expected deviation from a random choice exceeds the actual deviation from the known good, that is, if $\phi(x) \geqq x - \bar{x}$ or $\bar{x} - x$, according to whether $x \geqq \bar{x}$ or $x \leqq \bar{x}$. The market segment for the firm which announces can be shown to be the segment (a) from 0 to $1 - (\tfrac{1}{2} - \bar{x})^{1/2}$ if $\bar{x} \leqq \tfrac{1}{2}$ or (b) from $(\tfrac{1}{2} - \bar{x})^{1/2}$ to 1 if $\bar{x} \geqq \tfrac{1}{2}$. Obviously, the firm which announces its specification gains enormously in market share, from an infinitesimal share to a finite one. The share after announcement depends on the actual specification and ranges from a minimum of 29.3 percent if $\bar{x}$ is at the end of the spectrum (0 or 1) to the whole market if $\bar{x} = \tfrac{1}{2}$.

The enormous market shares in the example occur only if one firm alone announces its specification. If the first firm announces with specification 0.5, it temporarily gains the whole market, but if the firm with specification 0.4 then identifies itself, it will obtain 45 percent of the market, leaving 55 percent for the original firm. Announcement by the firm producing the good of specification 0.6 will give it the top 45 percent of the spectrum, which leaves the 0.4 good with the bottom 45 percent and the 0.5 good with only 10 percent. If firms can decide their specification before announcing it, the announcements can be expected to start at the center of the market and spread out toward the edges.

If the diffusion of information takes time, the first firm to announce may have gained only a small part of its predicted market before other firms also announce, so that large market shares may never appear in a real situation. In any case, information will breed further information, and firms relying on their share of random choice will be pushed out of the market by firms providing information.

So far, the effect of information has been confined to that on sales or market shares. But there is a potential gain of another kind from a firm having its market share made up of customers who have chosen the product on the basis of information rather than random choice. As was shown in the previous section, the elasticity of demand will be generally higher for firms whose markets are determined randomly in a context of ignorance than for the same number of firms selling to fully informed consumers. Thus the provision of information will give the firm customers who are less sensitive to price differentials than are customers obtained on a random basis, which permits the firm to raise prices and increase profits, at least until new firms are attracted into the group. This effect holds even in the two-firm case.

In a context of ignorance, an alternative strategy for the firm is to engage in "informationless" advertising rather than provide information as to its specifications. It is not unreasonable to suppose (as the advertising profession has long presumed) that customers who are choosing randomly because they lack information as to true specifications will have their choices biased in favor of products having familiar names.[10] If familiarity is an increasing function of the volume

10. For economic theories of advertising, see, for example, Nelson (1970, 1974), Schmalensee (1972), and Rosen (1978a).

of advertising for the product and the probability of choosing a product is directly related to its familiarity, then the sales of the product on a random-choice market will be an increasing function of the volume of advertising. The optimal level of advertising will then be when the marginal selling cost (advertising) plus the marginal production cost equals the marginal revenue, as in traditional neo-Chamberlin models.

In an initial zero-information no-advertising situation, it is not apparent whether the best interests of a firm will be served by providing information, by informationless advertising, or by some mixture of the two. Either form of advertising will increase the market of the first firm to engage in it, and the initial effect will be reduced to the extent that other firms follow suit. It is not possible to give any general model which quantifies the sales effect of informationless advertising or to make any general assumptions about the cost functions for the two forms of advertising or the relative costs of the two for a given increase in market share (the data on which the firm will presumably base its choice), so that only the broad qualitative effects can be stated.

If it can be assumed that the additional cost of making an informationless advertising pitch ("Smith widgets are the best") in conjunction with providing information is relatively small, then it can also be assumed that the advertising will always include some noninformation, whether or not it also includes information. This will be especially true if there exist consumers who are ignorant as to their own most-preferred specification, a class of consumers that has not been considered up to this point. Such consumers, it can be assumed, will be choosing randomly, even after the specifications of all goods are known, and thus would provide a target for informationless advertising under full-information conditions. If such consumers predominate, the incentive to provide any information at all diminishes.

The general conclusion is that if potential customers are sophisticated, in the sense that they are aware of their own most-preferred specifications and can correctly assess the expected outcome of a random choice, there is a strong incentive for firms to provide information. The less sophisticated the potential customers, the greater the incentive for informationlessadvertising. Any provision of information—by outside bodies (such as consumer organizations) or by firms themselves as a rational strategy or under duress (such as labeling or advertising regulations imposed by regulatory bodies)— is likely to increase the incentive to provide further information.

## 8.4 Costs of Entry and of Specification Change

Other than imperfect information, the main barrier to attaining perfect-monopolistic-competition equilibrium is the existence of adjustment frictions, in the form of either costs of entry or costs of changing specifications of goods. The equilibrium of perfect monopolistic competition is assumed to be established under frictionless conditions, in which there are no barriers to entry and firms can costlessly change the specifications of the goods they produce when it is desirable for them to do so. It is the effect of costs in entering or adjusting that will be discussed in this section.

A pure entry cost will appear to the individual firm in the same way as any other fixed cost, and such a cost will be subsumed within the firm's cost function.[11] The analysis for the individual firm will be no different from that without entry costs, except that the fixed-cost element in the cost functions will be larger and thus the economies of scale greater for a given output, which leads to a smaller equilibrium number of firms and thus less product differentiation than with costless entry. It is assumed that there is no collusion or element of cartel, so that the entry cost is an expenditure on real resources which is required to establish a firm's place in the group by assembling market and production information or by making its existence known to potential customers and is not a transfer payment from new firms to established firms as in buying cartel membership. The existence of entry costs will reduce the degree of product differentiation, and thus bring the market solution closer to the optimum in those cases (assumed to be the most common) in which the market leads to a

11. In this chapter, devoted to single-product firms, entry into the group and production of a new product are synonymous. *Interproduct economies,* which enable a firm already within the group to "enter" a new product at a lower fixed cost than an outside firm, are considered in Chapter 9.

higher-than-optimal degree of product differentiation. It was argued in Chapter 7 that the imposition of entry costs by licensing would be one policy by which the market could be induced to reach an optimal solution, but only if there are no real resources used in the process of entry. With real resource costs of entry, the market might produce the optimum number of goods but would still be inefficient because of these costs if they did not respect true social costs.

Costs associated with specification change have more complex effects on market equilibrium. It should first be noted that the costs are not those of producing a good with a new specification, since design and tooling costs are assumed to form part of the fixed costs in any case, but are the costs of abandoning the production of the former good. They are the holdover fixed costs associated with setting up a good which is no longer to be produced.

Specification-change costs introduce three elements into the situation:

1. If a firm changes its specification, its fixed costs rise, so that its degree of economies of scale rises and its profits fall as compared to the same width of market prior to change. Obviously, a firm will change its specification only if its new market is sufficiently increased to cover the added fixed cost.

2. The previously assumed uniformity of costs over different firms no longer holds if, for historical reasons, some firms have changed specifications and others have not.

3. The new entrant, because it is free to choose its specification from scratch, has an advantage over an existing firm in filling a "hole" which becomes apparent in the spectrum.[12] In the extreme case, existing firms producing goods of inappropriate specification may go bankrupt and be replaced by new firms, the holdover fixed costs being borne by the firm's creditors.

The dynamics of adjustment towards equilibrium are severely affected by these elements. In the perfect-monopolistic-competition case, the existence of positive profits will induce new firms to enter, even if the firms are evenly distributed with market segments only a little larger than the zero-profit equilibrium size. This is because it

12. Interproduct economies, as discussed in Chapter 9, may give the advantage to existing firms even when there are costs of specification change.

will be optimal for the existing firms to move away from the new entrant, whatever the point of entry, because it is costless to do so. This will cause other firms to adjust their specifications, costlessly, until the market is evenly divided once again, but into smaller segments. If there are costs of specification change, a new firm will not want to enter with a specification which will require later change and will also be aware that existing firms will not lightly change their specifications to adjust to the new entrant. Thus there may exist market segments so large as to make clear positive profits for the firms supplying them, and yet there will be no new entrants into these segments, nor will adjacent firms change their specifications to gain parts of the market. Similarly, the markets of adjacent firms may differ in size, but the firm with the smaller market will not change its specification toward that of the other firm in order to obtain the fringe customers.

Since these adjustment costs act as threshold effects on the behavior of firms, the equilibrium situation may consist of firms which are not uniformly distributed over the spectrum and which show varied market sizes and profit levels. The smallest viable market segments will be those of the equilibrium size under costless adjustment (and then only for firms which have not varied their specification), so that the average segment size will tend to be greater than under perfect monopolistic competition and the average degree of product differentiation will tend to be less. There will be no unique equilibrium configuration, but a relatively wide range of possibilities which are "equilibria" in the sense that no new firms will enter and no existing firms will change their specifications. One of the possible configurations is that of the perfect-monopolistic-competition equilibrium, but this will occur only if firms have been able to enter at their optimum specifications and the group has developed with every good at its perfect equilibrium point on the spectrum.

Prices, as well as market sizes, will vary in the presence of adjustment costs since the different market sizes are associated with different demand elasticities and firms which have changed specifications will have different cost functions from those that have not. The variations in prices and market sizes will be limited since it will be worthwhile for a firm with a small market to incur the costs of specification change if the disparity is sufficiently large. The larger the costs of adjustment relative to other costs, the larger the possible degree of dispersion in prices and markets.

Specification-change costs will tend to increase the oligopolistic element in competition among firms in the group. Without such costs, when firms are producing goods to the same specification, at least one firm will always change its specification so that different goods are being produced, as shown in Chapter 6. If change is not costless, however, each firm will try to force the other to move away, leading to direct rivalry of the traditional oligopoly kind, with the usual possibility of price wars, loss selling to induce bankruptcy of the rival, and so on. These elements will be present to a lesser degree when the firms are producing goods which have different specifications, but with the specifications closer to each other than would ensue under costless change.

## 8.5 Pseudodifferentiation

Before the introduction of the characteristics approach to consumr behavior theory, there was no real framework for the analysis of product differentiation and, in particular, no framework for distinguishing products that were different in some objective sense from those merely believed to be different. Since price theory had historically been developed for a world of homogeneous products where goods either were very different (like goods from different groups in the present analysis) or were identical, the product differentiation posited by Chamberlin's original work was regarded by many economists as representing no real differences between goods but as being due to imaginary differences created in the eyes of the consumers by such devices as product names and skillful advertising. Such differentiation can be referred to as "pseudodifferentiation," and the purpose of this section is to examine whether this is a real phenomenon and under what circumstances it might occur.

Two things are immediately obvious. One is that pseudodifferentiation cannot occur under conditions of perfect information, since consumers (by definition of perfect information) certainly know whether two products are different or not. The other is that pseudo-differentiation is unlikely to arise under conditions of costless specification change, since it is as easy for a firm to make its product really different as to leave it unchanged, and it can be presumed that it is less costly to inform consumers of a real change than to try and convince them that a change has been made when it has not. Thus pseudodifferentiation will occur, if at all, under conditions of both imperfect information and costs of adjustment.

Since plain lying has been ruled out in this analysis, (if only because it is potentially useful only as a very short-run strategy by firms that do not expect to continue doing business in the same market), pseudodifferentiation must be carried out in an indirect manner, by implication or by selective emphasis. The use of different brand (or even product) names for goods which are identical is pseudodifferentiation by implication, whereas selective emphasis occurs when one firm stresses certain characteristics of the product and another firm different characteristics, although the characteristics of both are the same.

Pseudodifferentiation can, by implication, be used to create the impression that identical goods are different but is nonspecific and cannot give potential customers a sense of the goods being different in a particular way. Given two identical goods, there is no way such a technique can be used to guarantee one firm the part of the spectrum to the left and the other firm the part to the right. However, pseudodifferentiation of this kind can be assumed to generate some "brand loyalty" among customers who have found satisfaction in whichever firm's products they happened to choose and thus to reduce the elasticity of demand for each product from infinity (with identical products, perceived as such) to some finite level. This both increases the potential profits of the firms and reduces the degree of oligopolistic rivalry between them. The pseudodifferentiation as such would not change the relative market shares of the firms from what would occur under random choice, but the elasticity effects would generate the potential gains that can be expected to be an increasing function of advertising outlays, at least up to some saturation limit.

Specific pseudodifferentiation, by advertising in which different firms stress different elements of the same combination of characteristics, requires that the consumers have some knowledge of the combinations they find most preferred. Under conditions of adjustment costs, when two firms are closer together than is optimal for them, each can give consumers the impression that they are further apart on the spectrum than they really are. In the absence of adjustment costs, the firms would actually change their specifications away from each other, but when such change is costly, it may be more profitable to gain some of the effect through pseudodifferentiation.

Some form of pseudodifferentiation, either specific or nonspecific, is likely to occur under conditions of imperfect information and costs of specification changes. The techniques of pseudodifferentiation, such as the use of brand names, are perfectly consistent with real product differentiation, however, and much specific pseudodifferentiation can be expected to be associated with real product differentiation, even though it is used to make an apparent shift of the product along the spectrum. The existence of advertising, or even its form, cannot be treated as presumptive evidence that real product differentiation is absent. Indeed, pseudodifferentiation cannot succeed unless it is impossible to distinguish it from real differentiation except by physical analysis of the products.

## 8.6 In the Long Run

Provided that the technology of production, preferences and their distribution, and the prices of inputs and outside goods all remain constant, imperfect monopolistic competition will converge to perfect monopolistic competition in the long run. This is because the components of imperfection—lack of information and adjustment costs—fade over time, either by inherent attrition of because they induce actions that lead to their eventual elimination. There is no element of imperfection that is either self-reinforcing or inherently persistent.

Adjustment costs are inherently evanescent, since these are holdover fixed costs associated with goods no longer produced. These costs, which are presumed to be tooling and development costs for abandoned models, become amortized with time or become insignificant as compared to the very long-run gains from producing a good of optimal specification for the firm. The same is true of entry costs, if these represent one-shot costs incurred in establishing the firm within the group. Note that the license-fee policy to achieve optimal product differentiation is a continuous payment and is thus not subject to such fading over time, nor i the fixed-cost element in the production technology, which is presumed to be a continuous payment for "overhead" resources.

It has already been shown that imperfection of information is self-eliminating because it will be in the interests of firms to provide information (if the equilibrium number of products exceeds two) and, in any case, the experience of purchasers plus the diffusion of knowledge gained from this experience will gradually make the consumers more informed As the random element in choice diminishes, it becomes more important for firms to produce goods to a specification that guarantees them an appropriate share of the market among informed consumers, and the incentive to change specifications if necessary (even with adjustment costs) increases. The impact of "informationless" advertising will diminish as consumers become better informed, whereas "pseudodifferentiation" will become more difficult to sustain and will be replaced by real differentiation.

These considerations will only hold if the broad conditions for monopolistic compettion continue to be satisfied, with no collusion or cartelization within the group.

In a fluid economy, in which production technologies, relative prices, and preferences are changing so that the perfect-monopolistic-competition equilibrium is itself changing, the various sources of imperfection will not have time to fade before the firms are faced by new situations, so the convergence to "perfection" will remain a tendency but not a reality.

Chapter 9

# Multiproduct Firms

## 9.1 Introduction

UP TO THIS POINT in the analysis, it has been assumed that every good was produced by a different firm, so that the market consisted entirely of single-product firms. This chapter will be devoted to the study of market structures in which multiproduct firms are an important feature.

By a "multiproduct firm" is meant a firm producing more than one product *within the group*. Interindustry conglomerates which may produce a single product in each of several groups are not considered and would, indeed, be regarded as single-product firms within the group context. The term is also used to imply something more than simply common ownership of several single-product firms, in which the central ownership merely means that the profits are added. Such a case is indistinguishable from a collection of independent single-product firms in terms of its economic consequences.

Thus the emphasis is on firms which produce several products as a matter of policy and on structures in which a firm which produces several products gains some advantage over the equivalent collection of single-product firms. Such advantages might be in the exercise of monopoly or quasi-monopoly power or in production economies arising from the joint management, as well as the joint ownership, of plants producing different goods within the group.

The analysis will commence with the study of firms which possess an explicit monopoly over all goods within the group (full group monopoly) and then proceed to firms which possess explicit monopoly power over some portion of the group spectrum (island monopoly) and, finally, to firms which possess no explicit monopoly power but may be able to exercise a quasi-monopoly power or which can take advantage of interproduct economies in production.

It will be shown that firms with explicit monopoly power will still produce a variety of products, but a lesser variety than would exist with monopolistic competition, and generally a less-than-optimal variety. Multiproduct firms with no explicit monopoly power will be shown to possess no advantage over single-product firms unless they produce products which form a *bloc* of adjacent goods in the spectrum, in which case they possess some quasi-monopoly power. Finally, it will be shown that the existence of interproduct production economies will necessarily lead to a structure of multiproduct firms but that the economies will be fully passed on to consumers unless firms can achieve quasi-monopoly status by assembling product blocs.

## 9.2 Full Group Monopoly

The simplest form of the multiproduct firm is the full group monopoly, in which all the products and potential products in the group are under the control of a single firm. The firm is taken to have no rivals, actual or potential, in producing the group goods, and is free to choose how many product varieties to produce, the specifications of these, and the prices at which they are to be sold.[1]

---

1. The analysis is restricted to monopoly without price discrimination, in which each distinct product is sold to all takers at the same price. Price discrimination would be difficult or impossible to exercise in most circumstances. In the first place, the monopolist would have to identify the distance between the most-preferred and available good for each consumer by name, as in the compensation problem associated with achieving a full optimum. There are no objective criteria on which to base discrimination in the uniform model. In addition, the possibility of trade between customers would have to be ruled out. For comments on price discrimination in relation to the author's earlier (1975) analysis, see White (1977).

It is obvious from the previous analysis of monopolistic competition and the optimum, and from the well-known properties of firms operating in several markets, that, under conditions of a uniform preference spectrum and uniform market density, the specifications and prices of the individual products will be so chosen that (1) the market segments will be the same size for all goods; (2) the specifications of the goods will be centered in their market segments; and (3) all goods will be produced in the same quantities and sold at the same price, since costs will be the same for all goods.

The analysis of this case consists then in determining two variables—the common price of the various product differentiates and the number of those products. As usual, the number of products will be determined by finding the width of the market segment.

It will be shown that:

1. There is a well-behaved equilibrium for the full group monopolist only if there are outside goods ($m < 1$), the elasticity of substitution ($\sigma$) with respect to which lies within the limits

$$1 < \sigma \leq 1 + \frac{1}{(1 - m)(\theta - 1)} \; .$$

2. In addition to the limits given above on $\sigma$, the existence of a well-behaved equilibrium depends also on the exact shape of the cost curve. It is sufficient for satisfaction of the second-order conditions for profit maximization that the marginal cost be constant, and the conditions may not be satisfied if the scale economies are due to pure increasing returns to scale with falling marginal cost.

Since the monopolist will keep the relative prices between the group goods constant, owing to the uniformity of the market which has been assumed throughout, there are no inside-substitution or specification effects. A price change will be proportionally the same across all products and will lead to a quantity change which is proportionally the same across all products and is due entirely to outside-substitution and income effects. Thus the elasticity consists of the last two terms in Eq. (5.46):

$$E = (1 - m)\sigma + (1 - \gamma)m. \tag{9.1}$$

The parameter $\gamma$ represents the degree of price compensation, which can normally be taken to be zero in a market context, so that the elasticity becomes:

$$E = (1 - m)\sigma + m. \tag{9.1b}$$

Note that the elasticity here is independent of whether there is compensation for specification or not. Such compensation affects the quantity sold, but not the price elasticity, since all consumers change their purchases in the same proportion in response to a price change.

If $A$ denotes the range of the spectrum and $2\Delta$ denotes the market width for the individual good, the number of goods is equal to $A/2\Delta$. The total profit of the firm over its whole market is then given by

$$\pi(P, \Delta) = \frac{A}{2\Delta} [2PQ - F(2Q)], \tag{9.2}$$

where $Q$ is the quantity for each half-market, the markets being symmetrical. The effect of price on profit is formally similar to monopolistic competition,

$$\frac{\partial \pi}{\partial P} = \frac{A}{\Delta} \frac{\partial Q}{\partial P} \left( \frac{P}{R} - F' \right), \tag{9.3}$$

where $R = E/(E - 1)$ is the ratio of price to marginal revenue. The first-order condition for a profit maximum, $\partial \pi / \partial P = 0$, is satisfied by

$$\frac{P}{R} = F'$$

(marginal revenue = marginal cost) or

$$P = RF'.$$

Although this condition is formally the same as in monopolistic competition, the marginal revenue ratio is, of course, different. Since the elasticity here contains no intragroup effects, it is lower than in monopolistic competition, and thus $R$ is higher. Thus the ratio of price to marginal cost (the price distortion) is higher than under monopolistic competition.

It should be noted that the elasticity in the monopoly case contains no terms that are functions of the goods spacing, so that the latter affects price determination only insofar as it affects $F'$, the marginal cost, through quantity.[2]

The relationship $P = RF'$ can always be satisfied if $R$ is positive, but $R$ may not always be positive, and the equation $P = RF'$ may not necessarily give a true maximum or guarantee a nonnegative profit. Since $R = E/(E - 1)$, $R < 0$ if $E < 1$, in which case the expression

$$\frac{P}{R} - F'$$

is negative ($P \geqq 0$) and $\partial\pi/\partial P$ is positive, since $\partial Q/\partial P$ is always negative. Thus profit increases as price is raised, without limit. This is an old problem in monopoly analysis, and it is usually assumed that $E$ eventually rises above unity as price becomes high enough. Since $E$ is constant here, because of the simple structure of the system, this argument does not hold,[3] and the analysis is limited to $E > 1$. This implies a lower limit on $\sigma$, derived as follows. If

$$E = (1 - m)\sigma + m > 1$$

then

$$\sigma > 1. \tag{9.4}$$

For there to be no loss, price must be at least as great as average cost. Since marginal revenue equals marginal cost, the ratio of price to marginal revenue ($R$) must be at least as great as the ratio of average cost to marginal cost ($\theta$). Thus the no-loss condition is $R \geqq \theta$, and this imposes an upper limit on the value of $\sigma$ for which a well-behaved equilibrium exists. If

$$R = \frac{E}{E - 1} = 1 + \frac{1}{(1 - m)(\sigma - 1)}, \tag{9.5}$$

---

2. When $F'$ is constant there are no cross-effects, and this will be shown to be a sufficient condition for satisfaction of second-order conditions.

3. It is assumed that $m$, the relative importance of the group in the economy, is constant. If this restriction is dropped and total income is assumed to be constant, then $E$ less than unity implies that expenditure on the group good increases with price, so that $m$ increases. As $m \to 1$, $E \to 1$ (from below) but never rises above unity if $\sigma$ is constant.

$R \geqq \theta$ implies

$$\sigma \leqq 1 + \frac{1}{(1 - m)(\theta - 1)} . \tag{9.6}$$

This upper limit on $\sigma$ varies inversely with $\theta$. If $\theta$ is small (but $> 1$), the upper limit is not very restrictive, but if it is relatively large, the limit may result in only a narrow range of elasticities of substitution, for which there is a regular equilibrium. If $\sigma$ is above the upper limit given above, it implies that the monopoly markup is too small to cover the excess of average cost over marginal cost owing to the economies of scale. This is a standard decreasing cost problem. If the monopoly markup is insufficient to cover this gap, the monopolist will not produce any good within the group at all. Since the full group monopolist can extract the largest markup possible, other than by price discrimination (ruled out here), the group goods will not be produced by the market at all, unless it is possible to exercise price discrimination, although the optimum may call for such goods.

If the group is very small, so that $m$ can be regarded as negligible, the limits on $\sigma$ take the very simple form

$$1 < \sigma \leqq 1 + \frac{1}{\theta - 1} .$$

Now consider the problem of the most profitable number of products for the firm to offer. Differentiation of Eq. (9.2) gives

$$\frac{\partial \pi}{\partial \Delta} = - \frac{A}{2\Delta^2} [2PQ - F(2Q)] + \frac{A}{2\Delta} (2Pq - 2F'q). \tag{9.7}$$

Assuming that the price is optimal, $P = RF'$. Also, $F = 2QF'\theta$, so that

$$\frac{\partial \pi}{\partial \Delta} = - \frac{AQF'}{\Delta^2} (R - \theta) + \frac{AqF'}{\Delta} (R - 1). \tag{9.8}$$

Since $\Delta q/Q = e_Q$ (the quantity elasticity), this then becomes

$$\frac{\partial \pi}{\partial \Delta} = \frac{AQF'}{\Delta^2} [(R - 1)e_Q - (R - \theta)]. \tag{9.9}$$

Thus the first-order condition for optimal market width for each product, $\partial\pi/\partial\Delta = 0$, is satisfied if

$$e_Q(\Delta) = \frac{R - \theta}{R - 1} .$$ (9.10)

Since $R$ is constant in the monopoly case, $e_Q$ is the variable that must adjust to satisfy the equilibrium condition. Now, if the firm is producing at all, $R \geqq \theta > 1$, so that the equilibrium condition can only be satisfied if $e_Q < 1$. Since demand is taken to be uncompensated for specification, the quantity function is the uncompensated function given by the differential equation (Eq. 5.43),

$$e_q = -(1 - \mu)(\sigma - 1)e_h .$$

Provided $\sigma > 1$, $q' < 0$, $Q$ is concave, and $e_Q < 1$. Thus the condition $\sigma > 1$, which is necessary for a proper maximum with respect to price, is also a necessary condition for an interior optimum with respect to the number of products.

Note that, as in the optimal analysis, the monopolist will not operate at the minimum average cost output for any good when the cost curves are U-shaped, since $\theta = 1$ (minimum average cost) calls for a solution such that $e_Q(\Delta) = 1$. There is no such solution at $\Delta > 1$, and thus the number of products will always be great enough to ensure operation on the downward-sloping portion of the average cost curve, even if minimum average cost occurs at relatively low output levels.

The second-order conditions have not yet been explored. These turn out to be somewhat complex and are not necessarily satisfied by the restrictions imposed up to this point.

The second-order conditions for profit maximization with respect to price alone are somewhat similar to those for monopolistic competition, although simpler, since $R$ here is constant and does vary with $P$. The analysis is as follows:

$$\frac{\partial^2\pi}{\partial P^2} = \frac{A}{\Delta}\left(\frac{P}{R} - F'\right)\frac{\partial^2 Q}{\partial P^2} + \frac{A}{R\Delta}\frac{\partial Q}{\partial P}\left(1 - 2RF''\frac{\partial Q}{\partial P}\right) .$$ (9.11)

At equilibrium, the first term vanishes. Since $\partial Q/\partial P < 0$, the second-order condition $\partial^2\pi/\partial P^2 < 0$ is satisfied if the bracketed expression in the second term is positive.

It was shown in Eq. (6.25), derived in examining the second-order conditions for monopolistic competition, that

$$2RF'' \frac{\partial Q}{\partial P} = -E\left(\frac{1}{\theta} - 1\right) + 2QE\frac{\theta'}{\theta}.$$

Now if the condition for no loss is satisfied, $R = E/(E - 1) \geq \theta$. This implies that

$$-\frac{1}{E} \leq \frac{1}{\theta} - 1$$

and thus that

$$1 - 2RF'' \frac{\partial Q}{\partial P} \geq -2QE\frac{\theta'}{\theta}$$

$$\geq 0 \qquad (\text{since } \theta' \leq 0).$$

The inequality will be strong if the firm makes a positive profit ($R > \theta$) or economies of scale decline with output ($\theta' < 0$).

The second-order derivative for $\Delta$ alone, at equilibrium, is derived from Eq. (9.9) and is given by

$$\frac{\partial^2 \pi}{\partial \Delta^2} = \frac{AQF'}{2} [(R - 1)e_Q' + 2\theta'q]. \tag{9.12}$$

Since $Q$ is concave, $e_Q'$ is negative. In addition, $R - 1$ is positive and $\theta'$ is nonpositive, by assumption, so that $\partial^2\pi/\partial\Delta^2 < 0$.

Problems in fulfilling the second-order conditions arise with respect to the relationship involving the mixed derivative $\partial^2\pi/\partial P\partial\Delta$. For a maximum, the following relationship must hold:

$$\left(\frac{\partial^2\pi}{\partial P\partial\Delta}\right)^2 \leq \left(\frac{\partial^2\pi}{\partial P^2}\right)\left(\frac{\partial^2\pi}{\partial\Delta^2}\right). \tag{9.13}$$

Differentiation of Eq. (9.3) with respect to $\Delta$ gives the mixed partial derivative at the equilibrium price

$$\frac{\partial^2\pi}{\partial P\partial\Delta} = -2\frac{A}{\Delta}\frac{\partial Q}{\partial P} qF''. \tag{9.14}$$

If $F'' = 0$ (constant marginal cost), this derivative is zero and Eq. (9.13) is certainly satisfied. However, if $\theta'$ is zero (pure increasing returns to scale) so that $F''$ is not zero, and if the elasticities are such that $R$ is very close to $\theta$, then the reasoning given above as to the nonpositivity of $\partial^2 \pi / \partial P^2$ shows that this will be very close to zero and will be zero in the limiting case for which $R = \theta$. In such a case, Eq. (9.13) is not satisfied, and a proper interior maximum does not exist. Detailed pursuit of the conditions that guarantee the satisfaction of Eq. (9.13) does not seem warranted, since a sufficient condition has already been established. There will be a proper maximum if the economies of scale are derived primarily from the existence of a fixed cost and if marginal cost is relatively constant—a realistic-enough situation. Economies of scale due to pure increasing returns to scale (constant $\theta$) may, however, give a situation without an interior maximum.

## 9.3 Product Variety under Monopoly

In this section it will be shown that:

1. The degree of product differentiation under full group monopoly decreases if the degree of economies of scale increases, as with all configurations studied, but there is no general relationship between either the elasticity of substitution ($\sigma$) or the importance of the group ($m$) and the degree of product variety.

2. The degree of product variety will always be less under monopoly than under monopolistic competition.

3. The degree of product variety under monopoly will be less than optimal if there is compensation for specification so that the full optimum and monopoly can be directly compared.

4. Without compensation for specification, the degree of product variety under monopoly will be greater than appropriate for a second-best solution at low values of the elasticity of substitution and less than the second-best value for high elasticities. If the group is of negligible importance in the economy, monopoly will give less than the second-best degree of product variety.

From Eq. (9.10) it can be shown that

$$e_Q' \frac{d\Delta}{d\theta} = 1 - E. \tag{9.15}$$

Since $E > 1$ and $e_Q' < 0$ ($Q$ is concave), both of which are requirements for equilibrium, it follows that $d\Delta/d\theta > 0$. The effect of $\sigma$ on the degree of product variety is also found from Eq. (9.10) and is given by

$$e_Q' \frac{d\Delta}{d\sigma} = -\frac{\partial e_Q}{\partial \sigma} - (\theta - 1)(1 - m). \tag{9.16}$$

Now $\partial e_Q/\partial\sigma < 0$, from Eq. (5.50) of Chapter 5, and $(\theta - 1)(1 - m) > 0$, so the two terms on the right-hand side of Eq. (9.16) have opposite signs. Since the first term depends on preference properties and the second does not, their magnitudes may bear any relationship, and thus the sign of $d\Delta/d\sigma$ depends on demand properties. It can be shown that the expression for $d\Delta/dm$ has a form somewhat similar to that for $d\Delta/d\sigma$, and its sign is indeterminate for similar reasons.

Comparison of the degree of product variety between monopoly and monopolistic competition will be made by showing that if the goods spacing were that appropriate to (perfect) monopolistic competition, a monopolist would always be able to increase profit by producing fewer goods at a larger spacing. The elasticity of demand for the monopolistic competitor consists of two "outside" terms (which constitute the monopolist's whole elasticity) plus two "inside" terms which sum to $se_Q$ since demand is taken to be uncompensated for specification, as shown in Eq. (5.46) of Chapter 5. The elasticity $e_Q$ is, of course, the same quantity elasticity that appears in the above solution to the monopoly product differentiation.

Using overbars to denote monopolistic-competition values, the monopolistic-competition elasticity is given by

$$\bar{E} = E + se_Q, \tag{9.17}$$

so that $\bar{R} = \bar{E}/(\bar{E} - 1)$. Since $E = R/(R - 1)$, the expression for $\bar{R}$ can be put in the form

$$\bar{R} = R - \frac{se_Q(R - 1)^2}{se_Q(R - 1) + 1}. \tag{9.18}$$

This shows formally that $R > \bar{R}$, as argued earlier.

Assume initially that $\theta$ is a constant and suppose the monopolist is producing at the same degree of product differentiation as under monopolistic competition—it can be assumed that the monopolist has just bought out all the firms but has not commenced to implement the policy appropriate to monopoly control. The direction of movement from this structure to the equilibrium monopoly structure can then be investigated.

Since the initial situation, at goods spacing $2\bar{\Delta}$, is the monopolistic-competition equilibrium, it must satisfy the Eq. (6.8),

$$\bar{R}(\Delta) = \theta.$$

From the relationship between $R$ and $\bar{R}$ derived above, this implies that

$$R - \theta = \frac{se_Q(R - 1)^2}{se_Q(R - 1) + 1} . \tag{9.19}$$

Substituting for $R - \theta$ in Eq. (9.10) above gives

$$\frac{\partial \pi}{\partial \Delta} = \frac{AQF'}{\Delta^2} (R - 1)e_Q \left[ \frac{1 - s(1 - e_Q)(R - 1)}{1 + se_Q(R - 1)} \right] . \tag{9.20}$$

The only part of the expression which is not certainly positive is the numerator of the last factor, and it is this that must be examined.

Since the comparison between the two market structures can only be made under circumstances which make both structures viable, it must be assumed that $\sigma > 1$. Since $Q$ is concave, and logarithmically concave, use can be made of Lemma 1c (Appendix B), which shows that

$$e_Q > 1 + e_q$$

$$> 1 - (1 - m)(\sigma - 1)e_h .$$

This expression follows from Eq. (5.43) if it is assumed that the individual proportion of expenditure on the group, $\mu$, can be replaced by the average proportion, $m$, without affecting the validity of the inequality.

From the above inequality,

$$1 - e_Q < (1 - m)(\sigma - 1)e_h .$$

Also, the function $s$ is equal to $\tfrac{1}{2}e_h$, from Eq. (5.13), and $R - 1$ is given by

$$R - 1 = \frac{1}{(1 - m)(\sigma - 1)},$$

so that

$$s(1 - e_Q)(R - 1) < \frac{1}{2e_h} \frac{(1 - m)(\sigma - 1)e_h}{(1 - m)(\sigma - 1)}$$

$$< \frac{1}{2}.$$

Thus $1 - s(1 - e_Q)(R - 1) > 0$ at the monopolistic-competition-equilibrium values, so that $\partial\pi/\partial\Delta > 0$ for the monopolist at these values. The most profitable degree of product differentiation for the monopolist will therefore be less than under monopolistic competition, since the equilibrium monopoly spacing will be larger than the monopolistic-competition spacing.

The above argument has been based on a constant degree of economies of scale. Suppose that $\theta$ is variable (but, as always, $\theta' \leq 0$), so that the degree of economies of scale at the monopolistic-competition equilibrium, $\bar\theta$, differs from that at the monopoly equilibrium, $\theta$, with the latter value used in computing the events relevant to the monopolist. The monopolistic-competition equilibrium is still defined by $\bar R = \bar\theta$, so that

$$R - \theta = R - \bar\theta + (\bar\theta - \theta)$$

$$= R - \bar R + (\bar\theta - \theta).$$

Proceeding as before, it can then be shown that

$$\frac{\partial\pi}{\partial\Delta} = \{ \quad \} - \frac{AQF'}{\Delta^2}(\bar\theta - \theta), \tag{9.21}$$

where the empty braces of the first term represent the right-hand side of Eq. (9.20), the value of $\partial\pi/\partial\Delta$ when $\theta$ was assumed constant, which has already been shown to be positive. Thus

$$\frac{\partial\pi}{\partial\Delta} > -\frac{AQF'}{\Delta^2}(\bar\theta - \theta).$$

Now suppose that the effect of a variable $\theta$ results in the previous finding being reversed, so that the degree of product differentiation is no less under monopoly. This would imply that the output per firm is no greater under monopoly and, with $\theta' < 0$, that the degree of economies of scale was no less, so that $\bar{\theta} - \theta$ is nonpositive. From the above discussion, this would certainly imply that $\partial\pi/\partial\Delta > 0$ at the monopolistic-competition values and thus that the degree of differentiation is less under monopoly, which contradicts the supposition. Thus the general result—that the degree of product differentiation will be less under monopoly than monopolistic competition—holds for variable, as well as fixed, $\theta$.

Thus monopoly will be more efficient than monopolistic competition by making greater use of economies of scale but will be less equitable. For the same reason that monopoly is more efficient—greater market widths for individual goods—it will bring greater disparities in welfare between those at the market center (able to buy a good to their most-preferred specification) and those at the market fringes.

Although there will be greater price *distortion* (a higher ratio of price to marginal cost) under monopoly than under monopolistic competition, the price itself may be higher or lower under monopoly, depending on the properties of the cost function. In the monopoly situation, there will be fewer goods, each produced at a higher output level, than under monopolistic competition. If the production conditions are such as to give constant or rising marginal cost, then the marginal cost under monopoly will be no less than under monopolistic competition, and the greater price distortion in the latter case necessarily implies a higher price. But if marginal cost is falling (which is always the case if $\theta$ is a constant), then a higher ratio of price to marginal cost under monopoly can be consistent with a lower price.

The possibility of a lower price under monopoly exists because the difference between the marginal revenue ratios under monopoly and monopolistic competition ($R$ and $\bar{R}$, respectively) depends on the ratio of inside- to outside-substitution effects in the full (monopolistic-competition) elasticity expression, as can be seen from inspection of Eq. (9.12). The difference in the marginal costs between the two cases depends in part on the demand properties, which determine how $Q$ varies with market width, and in part on the production properties. Thus there is sufficient independence between the determination of the two marginal costs and the two marginal revenue ratios to give cases with lower price under monopoly conditions. This case will tend to occur when inside-substitution effects are small relative to outside-substitution effects (group goods are poor substitutes for each other) and, of course, only when marginal cost falls with output. This result is consistent with what can occur for a single-good monopoly as compared with a competitive market for the same good. Both cases can be regarded as exceptional.

It might also be noted that one well-known property of the single-good market, the restriction of output under monopoly when marginal cost is not falling, is also present in the multigood case. Since all goods in the group are sold at the same price under both monopoly and perfect monopolistic competition, the total output of the group can be found by simple summation, as $2nQ$, where $n$ is the number of goods and $2Q$ is the output of each good. If $A$ is the range of preferences, $n$ and $\Delta$ are related through the equation $2\Delta = A/n$, so that total group output is given by $AQ/\Delta$. Now

$$\frac{\partial}{\partial \Delta}\left(\frac{Q}{\Delta}\right) = \frac{Q}{\Delta^2}(e_Q - 1),$$

and $e_Q < 1$ since viable solutions occur only when $Q$ is concave. Thus $Q/\Delta$ falls when $\Delta$ rises. The difference between $Q$ in the monopoly case and under monopolistic competition is due to (a) the larger value of $\Delta$ with monopoly and (b) the effect of price differences. If marginal cost is not falling, so that the price is no lower under monopoly, then both these effects are in the same direction—toward a lower total output under monopoly.

To compare the behavior of monopoly with the full optimum, it is necessary to suspend disbelief (and worries about viability) by assuming that the monopoly operates in a setting in which there is some authority which compensates for specification behind the scenes, so that the relevant demand elasticities are those for fully compensated demand. The basic property for the compensated quantity elasticity is given by Eq. (5.38), with the average proportion of expenditure on the group good, $m$, substituted for $\mu$,

$$e_q = [1 - (1 - m)\sigma]e_h,$$

From this equation, by the use of Lemma 3a of Appendix B, can be derived the expression for $e_Q$, to a high degree of approximation,

$$e_Q = 1 + [1 - (1 - m)\sigma](e_H - 1)$$

$$- (1 - m)\sigma[1 - (1 - m)\sigma]\phi, \qquad (9.22)$$

where $\phi > 0$ is relatively insensitive to the other parameters.

Since $E = (1 - m)\sigma$ for fully compensated demand in the monopoly case, the monopoly equilibrium condition (Eq. 9.10), which can be written in the form $(E - e_Q)/(E - 1) = \theta$, becomes

$$\hat{e}_H - (1 - m)\sigma\hat{\phi} = \hat{\theta} \qquad (9.23)$$

after making use of Eq. (9.22). The "hats" are used to identify this as the monopoly case.

In Chapter 4, it was shown (Eq. 4.27) that the optimum condition could be written in the form

$$G = e_H{}^* + (1 - m)\sigma(\sigma - 2)\phi^* = \theta^*, \qquad (9.24)$$

where the stars identify values at the optimum.

If $\theta$ is constant so that $\hat{\theta} = \theta^*$, the relationship between $\hat{e}_H$ and $e_H{}^*$ is given from Eqs. (9.23) and (9.24) as

$$\hat{e}_H - e_H{}^* = (1 - m)\sigma[\hat{\phi} + (\sigma - 2)\phi^*]. \qquad (9.25)$$

But, from Lemma 3a of Appendix B, $\hat{\phi} = \phi^*$, to a close approximation, so that

$$\hat{e}_H - e_H{}^* = (1 - m)\sigma(\sigma - 1)\phi^*, \qquad (9.26)$$

to a close approximation. Since $\phi^* > 0$, $\hat{e}_H > e_H{}^*$ if $\sigma > 1$, and $\hat{e}_H = e_H{}^*$ only at $\sigma = 0$ or $m = 1$ (no outside goods, or outside goods are not substitutes at all) or at $\sigma = 1$, at which value monopoly is not viable. Since $e_H(\Delta)$ is an increasing function, this implies that $\hat{\Delta} > \Delta^*$ and there is less-than-optimal product variety under monopoly. The same type of argument as has been used previously can be used to show that this result is not affected if $\theta$ is variable, with $\theta' < 0$, instead of being constant.

In comparing the monopoly configuration with the second-best configuration, the demand is uncompensated for specification or income, which gives a more realistic case. Proceeding as above, but using the uncompensated values for $e_q$ (from Eq. 5.43) and $E$ (from Eq. 9.1b), it can be shown that the monopolistic-competition equilibrium can be written in the form

$$\hat{e}_H - (1 - m)\sigma\hat{\phi} - m\hat{\phi} = \hat{\theta}. \tag{9.27}$$

From Eq. (4.47) of Chapter 4, the second-best condition in equivalent form is given by

$$e_H{}^* - (1 + m)\phi^* = \theta^*. \tag{9.28}$$

Assuming $\hat{\theta} = \theta^*$ and using the approximation $\hat{\phi} = \phi^*$, Eqs. (9.27) and (9.28) together imply that

$$\hat{e}_H - e_H{}^* = [(1 - m)\sigma - 1]\phi^*, \tag{9.29}$$

so that $\hat{e}_H$ is greater than or less than $e_H{}^*$ according to whether $\sigma$ is greater than or less than $1/(1 - m)$. Thus monopoly gives more than second-best-optimal product variety over the viable range $1 < \sigma < 1/(1 - m)$ and less-than-optimal variety if $\sigma > 1/(1 - m)$. As the group becomes insignificant relative to the total economy, $m \to 0$, and monopoly gives less-than-optimal variety over the whole viable range. The results hold if $\theta$ is variable.

## 9.4 Island Monopoly

The preceding analysis covered the situation in which a firm has, for whatever reason, a true monopoly over all the actual and potential products within the group. A more restricted situation is that in which the firm has a monopoly over all actual or potential products in some segment of the group spectrum but outside that segment faces the same market conditions as any other firm. It will be assumed that firms other than the monopolist have no privileged position in the market (at least not in the immediate vicinity of the monopolist's segment) and that they behave as firms in monopolistic competition unless the monopolist's behavior is such as to upset a monopolistic-competition equilibrium. Thus the picture is that of a firm with monopoly power over a segment of the spectrum, surrounded by non-monopolistic firms like an island.

It will be assumed that the monopolist behaves as a "quiet" monopolist, choosing strategies so as to leave the surrounding monopolistic competition undisturbed and thus evoking no reactions of an oligopolistic kind. To do this, the monopolist must ensure that the firms immediately adjacent to his segment of the market find their half-markets on the monopolist's side identical in all respects to their half-markets on the monopolistic-competition side. If this is done, then the market situation has the following properties:

1. The island monopolist can remain completely silent, in the sense of preserving a Nash equilibrium situation among the surrounding firms, if and only if the market segment is staked out with boundary goods sold at the same price as the monopolistic-competition goods and with specifications chosen to give the same distance from the nearest nonmonopoly goods as between any two adjacent monopolistic-competition goods. These "boundary stakes" can be regarded as dummy monopolistic-competition goods, which look to the monopolistic competitors like true monopolistic-competition goods.

2. Within the boundary goods described above, the firm is free to operate at will, provided that the prices of whatever goods it chooses to produce in the interior of its segment lie above a minimum price profile. This profile is well defined, falling from the monopolistic-competition price at the edges to a minimum value at the center of the segment.

3. If the surrounding firms are in monopolistic-competition equilibrium (zero profits), the island monopolist can always make positive profits if it controls a segment at least as great as twice the equilibrium market width of a monopolistic competitor, while still remaining "silent." If the monopolist is the first firm to enter, it can make positive profit with monopoly control over a segment of any width, however small.

Consider first the "silence" condition (condition 1). It is obviously a necessary condition for the adjacent firms to be unaffected that the monopolist's boundary goods are of such price and specification that the adjacent firm's half-market on the monopolist's side is of the same size as its other half-market. There is a continuous relationship between price and specification of the boundary good that will achieve this, not merely a single price and specification. If the equilibrium price and half-spacing in the monopolistic-competition surround are $\bar{P}$ and $\Delta$, respectively, and the monopolist's boundary good is distant $2\delta$ from the adjacent good and sold at price $P$, then the edge of the nonmonopolist's market is given by the dividing condition (Eq. 5.2)

$$\bar{P}h(u) = Ph(2\delta - u),$$

where $u$ is the distance of the half-market edge from the nonmonopoly good. The nonmonopolist's market area is preserved, therefore, by any combination of $P$ and $\delta$ such that

$$Ph(2\delta - \Delta) = \bar{P}h(\Delta)$$

Obviously, $P = \bar{P}$ and $\delta = \Delta$ is one of these combinations.

But preservation of the market area is only one necessary condition. The other is that the elasticity of demand is the same in both halves of the nonmonopolist's market. Now the elasticity of demand is a function of the spacing between the two adjacent goods (Chapter 5) and will only be the same in both half-markets if the monopolist's boundary good and the adjacent good on the other side are equidistant from the firm's good. Thus both necessary conditions (which together are sufficient) are satisfied only by $\delta = \Delta$ and $P = \bar{P}$, so that the monopolist's boundary goods must "look" like the monopolistic-competition goods, in terms of both price and distance from adjacent goods, when viewed from outside the monopoly segment.

Within the boundaries, the firm's freedom to operate is limited only by the requirement that none of the interior goods intrude beyond the boundary goods. That is, if there is an interior good at distance $2\delta$ from the boundary good (not from the adjacent nonmonopoly good) and $u$ is the half-market width for this good, then $u$ should not exceed $2\delta$, since $u > 2\delta$ would imply that the interior good was being sold beyond the boundary. If the price of the interior good relative to the boundary good is $p$, then the lowest permissible value of $p$ is that for which $u = 2\delta$. From the dividing condition, this is given by

$$p_{\min} = \left[ \frac{h(2\delta - u)}{h(u)} \right]_{u=2\delta} = 1/h(2\delta) \qquad (9.30)$$

since $h(0) = 1$.

Since $h(u)$ is an increasing convex function, the lower price profile falls from unity at the edges of the segment to a least value at the center. Note that there is no upper limit on the price of interior goods since if the price is so high that consumers at the segment center do not buy the good, the good they buy instead will always be the monopolist's boundary good because it is closer than, and its price the same as, any nonmonopoly good. Thus the effects of high prices of interior goods will never spill beyond the boundary.

Now consider the proposition that the monopolist can always make a positive profit. Suppose that the monopolist enters by buying out monopolistic competitive firms. The firm must then buy out at least three adjacent firms to obtain a monopolistic segment at least twice the width of the monopolistic competition market segment. If the monopolist takes over $m$ adjacent firms ($m \geqq 3$) and ceases production of all but its two boundary goods, the consumers who previously purchased those goods will now either buy the boundary goods or shift to outside goods. The sales of the boundary goods will necessarily increase beyond the levels under monopolistic competition, and thus the average cost will be lower. Since the monopolistic-competition price is equal to the average cost at monopolistic-competition output levels, the same price will exceed average cost at the new output, and thus the monopolist will make a positive profit. Note that it is assumed that the monopolist can restrict entry into his sector after buying up the former individual firms, otherwise new entries would restore the former monopolistic-competition equilibrium, and the monopolist would simply be the owner of two different monopolistic competitors, no longer adjacent.

If the monopolist is first on the scene, but with true monopoly power only a segment of the spectrum, he can do better than above. He can set up his "boundary" goods each at a distance $\Delta$ from the end of his segment, where $2\Delta$ is the equilibrium market width under monopolistic competition, and wait for the monopolistic-competition equilibrium to become established around him. The only point within the monopolist's market area at which it would be profitable for a new firm to enter is within the monopoly segment, where entry is not possible. Thus the monopolist's two boundary goods each have a market area larger than those of the monopolistically competitive firms by an amount equal to half the width of the monopoly segment.

The above demonstration of the ways in which the monopolist can always make a profit do not necessarily represent the appropriate policies for making the *maximum* profit. Having set the boundary goods, the monopolist can maximize profits by appropriate choice of the prices and specifications of the goods to be produced within his private segment, with the option of producing only the boundary goods as a possible choice. As will be seen in the succeeding analysis, determination of the appropriate choice is an extraordinarily difficult problem in its general form, although a real monopolist confronting a situation in which the parameters were specific could always solve the problem by ad hoc methods, simulation, or even computerized enumeration.[4]

It was shown above that a monopolist who took over $m$ adjacent firms could always move to a positive-profit position by ceasing to produce goods that are not boundary goods. This strategy will always give positive profit (as compared with zero profit for the original firms as monopolistic competitors), but not necessarily the maximum profit.

The problem to be investigated here is whether the monopolist will make even greater profit if he also produces *interior* goods (goods in his monopoly segment other than boundary goods), and, if so, under what conditions. The general structure of the problem and the nature of the solution can be grasped by a study of the case in which a monopolist who produces only the boundary goods (sold at the monopolistic-competition price) considers the potential profitability of producing a single interior good.

The price and distance from the nearest competitor of the boundary goods are determined by the surrounding monopolistic-competition equilibrium. The equilibrium price and half-spacing will be denoted by $\bar{P}$ and $\Delta$, respectively. The distance between the two boundary goods will be denoted by $4\delta$, and the price of the interior good (if produced) by $P$. In the initial situation, with no interior good,

4. The complexity of the next stage of the analysis, the only case in which market areas for individual goods are not assumed to be equal and symmetrical, points up the reason for basing the primary analysis on a uniform spectrum.

the firm's profit for two goods $(\pi_{2G})$ is given by

$$\pi_{2G} = 2\bar{P}\,\bar{Q}(\Delta) + \bar{Q}(2\delta) - 2F\,\bar{Q}(\Delta) + \bar{Q}(2\delta), \qquad (9.31)$$

where the $Q$ values are barred to indicate that they represent the quantity functions corresponding to price $\bar{P}$.

Now consider the total profit with three goods, the two boundary goods and a single interior good. The boundary goods remain at price $\bar{P}$ in order to remain in equilibrium with the surrounding monopolist competition, but the price of the interior good, $P$, is a variable to be determined by the monopolist. Since the monopolist's market situation is symmetrical, it is obvious that the specification of the interior good will be chosen to be at the midpoint between the boundary goods. If the half-market width of the interior good is denoted by $u$, then the firm's profit with three goods is given by

$$\pi_{3G} = 2\bar{P}[\bar{Q}(\Delta) + \bar{Q}(2\delta - u)] + 2PQ(u)$$
$$- 2F[\bar{Q}(\Delta) + \bar{Q}(2\delta - u)] - F[2Q(u)]. \qquad (9.32)$$

The unbarred $Q$ values are quantity functions for price $P$.

It is convenient to break down the change in profit in going from two to three goods into the revenue change and the cost change. The revenue terms are the first term of Eq. (9.31) and the first two terms of Eq. (9.32), so that the revenue change from introducing the interior good, $R_3 - R_2$, is given by[5]

$$R_3 - R_2 = 2PQ(u) - 2\bar{P}[\bar{Q}(2\delta) - \bar{Q}(2\delta - u)]. \qquad (9.33)$$

Suppose initially that the interior good is sold at price $\bar{P}$, so that $u = \delta$. Then the revenue change has the simple form

$$R_3 - R_2 = 2\bar{P}[2\bar{Q}(\delta) - \bar{Q}(2\delta)]. \qquad (9.34)$$

Now the preexisting monopolistic-competition equilibrium could only be viable if the quantity function $\bar{Q}$ was concave. Since $\bar{Q}(0) = 0$, strict concavity implies that $2\bar{Q}(\delta) > \bar{Q}(2\delta)$, so that the introduction of the third good necessarily increases revenue if the good is sold at

---

5. Note that $R_i$ here refers to total revenue from $i$ goods and the notation is not related to the use of $R$ elsewhere for the marginal-revenue ratio.

the monopolistic-competition price, except in the borderline case of weak concavity for $\bar{Q}$, in which case revenue is unchanged.

The change in total costs from introduction of the third good is given, in the general case, by

$$C_3 - C_2 = 2F[\bar{Q}(\Delta) + \bar{Q}(2\delta - u)] + F[2Q(u)]$$
$$- 2F[\bar{Q}(\Delta) + \bar{Q}(2\delta)] \qquad (9.35)$$

and, when $P = \bar{P}$, by

$$C_3 - C_2 = 2F[\bar{Q}(\Delta) + \bar{Q}(\delta)] + F[2\bar{Q}(\delta)]$$
$$- 2F[\bar{Q}(\Delta) + \bar{Q}(2\delta)]. \qquad (9.36)$$

Since $u$ is necessarily less than $2\delta$, the output of the interior and boundary goods in the three-good case are each less than the output of the boundary goods in the two-good case, so that average costs are higher. If $P = \bar{P}$, the total output of goods in the three-good case is higher than with two goods (the source of the increase in revenue discussed above), so that total cost certainly rises with the introduction of an interior good, when it is sold at the competitive price.

Thus any increase in profit from the introduction of the third good, when it is sold at the monopolistic-competition price, can only occur if the increase in revenue is sufficient to outweigh the increase in cost. In this case, the difference in profit between the two cases has the form

$$\pi_{3G} - \pi_{3G} = 2\bar{P}[2\bar{Q}(\Delta) - \bar{Q}(2\delta)] - 2F[\bar{Q}(\Delta) + \bar{Q}(\delta)]$$
$$- F[(2\bar{Q}(\delta)] + 2F[\bar{Q}(\Delta) + \bar{Q}(2\delta)]. \qquad (9.37)$$

Whether this is positive or negative depends, even in this simplified case, on the relationship between the properties of the $Q$ and $F$ functions and the relationship between the magnitudes of $\Delta$ and $\delta$. Some idea of the pattern of possibilities can be obtained by simplifying even further, assuming that the cost function has the form of a fixed cost plus a linear variable cost (constant marginal cost).[6]

By putting $F(Q)$ in the form $F(Q) = F_o + mQ$, Eq. (9.37)

---

6. Constant marginal cost, it will be noted, also guarantees satisfaction of second-order condition.

reduces to

$$\pi_{3G} - \pi_{2G} = 2(\bar{P} - m)[2\bar{Q}(\delta) - \bar{Q}(2\delta)] - F_o. \tag{9.38}$$

Since $\bar{P} - m > 0$ and $2\bar{Q} > \bar{Q}(2\delta)$, since it is assumed that $\bar{Q}$ is strictly concave (viability), the introduction of a third good increases profit in this case if the first term is larger than the fixed cost for a single good. Now the monopolistic-competition equilibrium implies that

$$2(\bar{P} - m)\bar{Q}(\Delta) = F_o, \tag{9.39}$$

since this is the zero-profit condition with the cost function in question. Thus the introduction of the third good is profitable at monopolistic-competition prices if

$$2\bar{Q}(\delta) - \bar{Q}(2\delta) > \bar{Q}(\Delta). \tag{9.40}$$

The left-hand side of the inequality increases with (a) the degree of concavity of $\bar{Q}$, which depends ultimately on the elasticity of substitution between group goods and outside goods, and (b) the value of $\delta$ for a given degree of concavity. The higher the elasticity of substitution, the lower the value of $\delta$ at which it will be profitable to introduce a third good. Provided the elasticity of substitution is greater than unity (so that $\bar{Q}$ is strictly concave), it is always profitable to introduce a third good if the magnitude of $\delta$ is large enough relative to the magnitude of $\Delta$ and unprofitable if $\delta$ is sufficiently small. It is obvious from Eq. (9.40) that it cannot be profitable to produce the third good and sell it at the monopolistic-competition price unless $\delta > \Delta$. Since $4\delta$ is the width of the monopoly segment, this segment must be at least twice the width of the equilibrium competitive segment ($2\Delta$). In general, profitability requires that $\delta$ be much greater than $\Delta$, and thus that the monopoly segment be much more than twice the monopolistic-competition market width.

It has been assumed above that the interior good, if produced, is sold at the monopolistic-competition price. But the firm is free to choose the price which is most profitable, which need not be the price of the other goods in the market (and of its own boundary goods). To investigate the most profitable price for the interior good, the profit expression in the three-good case (Eq. 9.32) can be differentiated with respect to the interior-good price to give

$$\frac{\partial \pi}{\partial P} = 2 \left[ (\bar{P} - \bar{F}') \frac{\partial \bar{Q}(2 - u)}{\partial P} \right.$$

$$\left. + (P - F') \frac{\partial Q(u)}{\partial P} + Q(u) \right], \quad (9.41)$$

where $\bar{F}'$ and $F'$ are the marginal costs for the boundary and interior goods, respectively.

The effect of the change in $P$ on $\bar{Q}(2\delta - u)$ differs from that on $Q(u)$. The former is the quantity function for the boundary goods, the price of which does not change, so that the effect of $P$ is entirely through changes in $u$, that is, through shifts of consumers between the interior and boundary goods. The quantity function for the interior good, $Q(u)$, is actually shifted by a change in $P$, owing to outside-substitution effects, so that the price change causes shifts both between the interior good and the boundary good and between the interior and outside goods. (Outside goods are, as elsewhere, goods which are not in the group which forms the market under consideration.)

Allowing for the effects of the price change, Eq. (9.41) can be written as

$$\frac{\partial \pi}{\partial P} = 2 \left\{ [(P - F')q(u) - (\bar{P} - \bar{F}')\bar{q}(2\delta - u)] \frac{\partial u}{\partial P} + Q(u) \right.$$

$$\left. + (P - F') \left( \frac{\partial Q}{\partial P} \right)_{os} \right\}, \quad (9.42)$$

where $q(x) = Q'(x)$ and the last term represents outside-substitution (OS) effects.

Rather than attempting to examine the conditions which give $\partial \pi / \partial P = 0$, it is easier to examine the sign of $\partial \pi / \partial P$ at $P = \bar{P}$. At the monopolistic-competition price, since the interior and boundary goods have the same price, the market segment between the two is divided in half, so that $u = \delta$ and $\bar{q}(2\delta - u) = q(u) = q(\delta)$. Thus, from

Eq. (9.42),

$$\left(\frac{\partial \pi}{\partial P}\right)_{P=\bar{P}} = 2 \left[ (\bar{F}' - F')q(\delta) \frac{\partial u}{\partial P} \right.$$

$$\left. + (P - F') \left(\frac{\partial Q}{\partial P}\right)_{\mathrm{os}} + Q(u) \right]. \qquad (9.43)$$

In the right-hand side of Eq. (9.43), the second term is necessarily nonpositive and the third term necessarily nonnegative, whereas the first term may have any sign, depending on the relationship between $\bar{F}'$ and $F'$, although $\partial u/\partial P$ is essentially negative since $u$ is the half-market width of the interior good. Thus the sign of $\partial \pi/\partial P$ is not determined without further specification.

If production is subject to constant marginal cost, as was assumed in the case discussed earlier, then the first term in Eq. (9.43) vanishes, and the sign of $\partial \pi/\partial P$ is determined by the last two terms. From the definition of elasticity, $\partial Q/\partial P = -QE/P$, where $E$ is the elasticity of outside substitution.[7] Thus the two final terms in Eq. (9.43) can be written

$$Q + (P - F') \left(\frac{\partial Q}{\partial P}\right)_{\mathrm{os}} = \left[ 1 - \left(1 - \frac{F'}{P}\right) E \right] Q. \qquad (9.44)$$

At $P = \bar{P}$ (the monopolistic-competition price), $P = \bar{R}F'$, where $\bar{R}$ is the marginal revenue ratio under monopolistic competition, given by $\bar{R} = \bar{E}/(\bar{E} - 1)$, $\bar{E}$ being the demand elasticity for a monopolistic competitor. Substitution of this relationship in Eq. (9.44) and substitution of Eq. (9.44) in Eq. (9.43) gives

$$\left(\frac{\partial \pi}{\partial P}\right)_{P=\bar{P}} = 2 \left(1 - \frac{E}{\bar{E}}\right) Q. \qquad (9.45)$$

Since $\bar{E}$ contains outside-substitution terms which are identical with $E$ plus intragroup substitution terms which are positive, $\bar{E} > E$, so that the right-hand side of Eq. (9.45) is positive. Thus it is always profitable for the island monopolist to charge a higher price for the interior good

---

7. That is, $E$ is the elasticity of demand without intragroup substitution—the same as the elasticity of demand for a full group monopoly.

than for the boundary goods, provided marginal cost is constant. If marginal cost is rising, inspection of the equation in its original form (Eq. 9.43) will show that the result also holds in this case, since $\partial u/\partial P$ is negative.

It is obvious that, if possession of a monopoly segment larger than that occupied by two monopolistic competitors makes it profitable to produce a single interior good, then extending the monopoly further will make it profitable to produce two interior goods, and so on. Once the monopoly segment is wide enough, the interior becomes so insulated from the surrounding monopolistic competition that the monopolist can behave as if he were a full group monopolist with a restricted spectrum width, except near the edges of the segment. The analysis of the group monopolist then applies, with the spacing between the interior goods and the optimal price for those goods having the same values as under group monopoly. As shown earlier, for this interior subsegment to be isolated, it is sufficient that the distance from each extreme good within it to the nearest monopolistic-competition good be related to the price of the interior good in a way that satisfies the lower price profile restriction. This restriction applies only if the price of interior goods is less than that of the surrounding monopolistic competition. If the price is higher, as will be the case with constant or rising marginal cost, the boundary goods prevent consumers in the monopolist's segment from spilling beyond the boundaries of the segment.

Note that, since viability of the monopolistic competition implies an elasticity of substitution for which the quantity function is concave, the price of interior goods is limited by outside-substitution properties, and thus the interior is fully insulated.

Thus the behavior pattern of the island monopolist is clear. By using the boundary goods as dummy monopolistic competitors, he can maximize profit over his segment without repercussions from other firms.

If the monopoly segment is relatively narrow, the monopolist may produce these boundary goods but, although they are sold at the monopolistic-competition price, he still makes a positive profit through lowered costs due to economies of scale. If the monopoly segment is wider, the monopolist may produce one or more interior goods, the prices of which may be higher or lower than in the surrounding market, depending on whether the production process shows rising or falling marginal cost. If the monopoly segment is sufficiently wide, the interior can be treated as if it were a group monopoly, with the same goods spacing and prices as in such a monopoly. In the last case, there may be intermediate goods between the boundary goods and the true interior goods, with prices and spacings intermediate between the true interior goods and the boundary goods.

In all cases, the exact pattern of the monopolist's prices and specifications will depend on the shape of the cost function $F(Q)$, the properties of the quantity function $Q(u)$, the substitution properties with respect to outside goods, and the size of the monopoly segment relative to the market segments under monopolistic competition.

## 9.5 Multiproduct Nonmonopoly Firms

In this section, attention will be given to market structures which are characterized by multiproduct firms even though there are no formal or overt barriers to entry within the group. This is a very important class of structures, which includes some of the major industries in the United States and other economies with a private-enterprise sector. Industries which conform to the pattern include automobiles, pharmaceuticals, publishing, domestic appliances, and certain kinds of food processing, to mention but a few.

The simplest explanation of the existence of multiproduct firms is a historical one, based on the dynamics of monopolistic competition. A technological breakthrough, such as the development of the automobile or radio, which opens up a new potential group of products, will start with an empty spectrum. Firms which produce products in the group will initially make positive profits, and there will be plenty of scope for new entrants. It was assumed in the analysis of monopolistic competition that every entrant was a new firm, but it is really new *products*, and not firms, with which the analysis is concerned. The new products might just as well be produced by firms already producing other products within the group as by new firms.[8] Indeed, it is obviously more profitable for an existing firm to produce a new product which fills some "hole" in the spectrum than to continue to expand output of its existing product past a certain point. Thus it could be expected that the older firms in the group might be multiproduct firms. In the absence of other influences, in particular, any kind of economies that gave a competitive edge to existing firms over new entrants, the resulting structure would be a mixed one, with some multiproduct firms (typically, but not necessarily, the older ones) and some single-product firms.

The equilibrium configuration of such a structure with respect to the number and prices of products would be identical with that of monopolistic competition, provided the following conditions are satisfied:

1. There are *no interproduct economies* such that a firm which is already producing within the group can produce another group product at lower cost than a firm newly entering the group.

2. *No quasi-monopoly power* is derived simply by virtue of producing several products within the group.

3. There is *no collusion* among the multiproduct firms.

The last point is made here because the existence of multiproduct firms obviously makes it easy to form coalitions that have few members but control many products, whereas the formation of effective coalitions over a large number of single-product firms is much more difficult. It will be assumed, however, that there is no collusion, even with multiproduct firms, and the analysis will be confined to the remaining two conditions.

Consider first the possibility of a firm acquiring some quasi-monopoly power, in the sense of being able to discourage entry in some portion of the spectrum, by virtue of its control over the production of several goods. The crucial factor here is the distribution

8. Schmalensee has argued that "hole filling" by existing firms is a form of predatory behavior, designed to block entry by new firms. The analysis here does not suggest that this gives any special advantage to existing firms unless the hole is filled in order to preserve the integrity of a bloc of products which are contiguous on the spectrum (see Schmalensee, 1977).

of the firm's products over the spectrum. If the products are scattered so that the products adjacent in the spectrum to one of the firm's products are the products of other firms, whether multi- or single-product firms, then it is clear that the firm possesses no particular advantage over a single-product firm with respect to combatting entry near one of its products. Reactions to such entry are restricted to price or specification adjustments for a single product and thus are the same as those for a single firm. A large multiproduct firm may, of course, possess the financial resources to engage in loss selling or other techniques of product warfare, but so may the firm which is entering—which could be one of the other firms already in the industry or a well-financed new firm. The existing firm has no advantage which arises *solely* because it already produces other goods in the group.

The situation is different if the products of the existing firm form a contiguous *bloc* of products in the spectrum, so that each of the firm's products, except those at the ends of the bloc, is flanked by other products of the same firm. In this case, the existing firm has many more options available for combatting entry within its bloc, because it can vary prices or specifications of all the goods which are adjacent to any potential entry. The firm, although not possessing true monopoly power in the sense of being able to prevent entry under any circumstances, possesses quasi-monopoly power because it can obviously deter entry to some degree. Since this power is derived from control over a bloc of contiguous products, the firm will go to considerable lengths to ensure that its bloc is not fragmented, and knowledge of this will further deter entry into the bloc and increase the quasi-monopoly power. Protected by its potential deterrant power, the firm can operate like an island monopolist to some degree, although it can be expected to offer more products and charge lower prices than if it possessed a true monopoly over its bloc of the spectrum. In particular, it could be expected to produce fewer goods per unit of spectrum distance than would be produced under monopolistic competition.

In the absence of interproduct economies or collusion, therefore, the effect of multiproduct firms on the equilibrium of the market may range from zero, if the products of the firms are scattered across the spectrum (so that the equilibrium is the same as under monopolistic competition), to quasi-monopoly behavior, if one or more firms have assembled blocs of contiguous products. In general, the formation of such blocs is easier the fewer the number of effective characteristics in the group, because the number of different products which can be adjacent to a given product rises rapidly with the number of dimensions of the spectral space.

Interproduct economies occur when the costs of producing a product in the group are lowered, if the same firm also produces other group products. These are economies of the firm rather than of the product, unlike the scale economies assumed to this point—which depend only on the output of a particular product. It will be assumed that there are still economies of scale in the production of each product, even when there are also interproduct economies, but that the whole cost structure of one product is lowered by the production of others. The simplest case, and perhaps the most realistic, is when a part of the fixed cost associated with the production of a product within the group consists of information costs which need not be replicated when another group product is produced. In this case, the economies of scale parameter $\theta$ for a given level of output of any good decreases as the number of goods produced by the firm increases, but the marginal costs of each product are unaffected. It is also possible to consider models in which marginal cost is affected by the number of products; however, the analysis will concentrate on the case in which multiproduct firms can spread part of their fixed cost over several products but there are no true production externalities that affect variable costs.

Under these circumstances, a firm already in the industry will earn a higher profit from producing a new good than will an outside firm which enters with only this good. The existing firm will, however, have the same equilibrium price and output as a new firm since variable costs are the same for both. Up to the point at which the total number of goods in the group is the number that would be the equilibrium for single-product firms, the only difference between the performance of multiproduct firms and single-product firms will be the higher profits of the former, which are able to capture the interproduct economies.

But the multiproduct firms can continue to increase their profits beyond this point, since they can make profits when single-product firms would just break even. They will increase product differentiation beyond the single-firm level, and new product entries from firms within the industry will continue until the multiproduct firms themselves just break even. If the interfirm economies are exhausted at $K$ products, where $K$ is small compared with $N$ (the number of goods that would be produced under single-firm monopolistic competition), the equilibrium structure can be expected to consist of firms which each produce at least $K$ products. The number of products and pricing will correspond to an industry equilibrium given by the condition

$$R = \theta_K, \tag{9.46}$$

where $\theta_K$ is the degree of economies of scale appropriate to the firm producing $K$ goods. Since $\theta_K < \theta_1$ (the single-firm value), the degree of product differentiation will be greater than would be achieved with single-product firms. In this ideal scenario, the interproduct economies are all passed on to the consumers.

If $K$ is relatively large, however, the picture is different. If $K$ is large enough, there may be room for only one firm which can obtain the full economies, and this firm will possess the quasi-monopoly power outlined earlier. With a smaller value of $K$, the equilibrium number of firms may be small enough for bloc assembly and thus for some weak quasi-monopoly.

It should be noted that a large value for $K$ does not necessarily lead to elimination of all but one firm. This is because the full interproduct economies apply only to new goods. The firm producing the largest number of products has only a marginal competitive advantage over other firms also producing many products, and buying out the right to produce some of these products would involve paying for the economies being lost by the other firms. Thus an industry that historically contained several firms may continue with these firms (or some of them), with the full potential for interproduct economies remaining unattained by any firm.

The possibilities for quasi-monopoly with interproduct economies are, as already suggested, of the same kind as occur when there are no such economies. They are, if anything, heightened by the difficulty of entry from outside the existing group of firms. Although collusion has been ruled out in this analysis, it is obvious that the nonexistence of any real threat of entry from outside is likely to lead to implicit "accommodations" by firms already in the industry. If blocs can be assembled, these will be largely immune from outside entry since a new entrant can only compete successfully by either a massive invasion of the bloc with several products or by a simultaneous invasion of several blocs—both very difficult to accomplish. The firms already in the industry have little incentive to disturb the blocs of others, and much to lose from retaliation, so the structure will be a relatively stable collection of island quasi-monopolies.

If the products of each firm are scattered, however, the existence of interproduct economies does little to generate quasi-monopoly power. At best, the relative difficulty of outside entry (easier than with blocs, but still requiring entry with several products) may enable the existing firms to capture some of the interproduct economies for themselves.

 **Chapter 10**

# Further Explorations

## 10.1 Introduction

THIS FINAL CHAPTER is devoted to taking up several topics that suggest extensions of the analysis already given or represent larger problems to which the previous analysis can make an important contribution. Each section of the chapter is concerned with one such topic and is little more than a brief sketch designed to suggest the possibilities for further investigation. Any conclusions or propositions given are tentative, and there is no complete or rigorous analysis for any of the topics.

## 10.2 Welfare, Variety, and GNP

For the kind economy with which this work has been concerned, namely, one in which there are diverse preferences distributed uniformly over some part of the potential goods spectrum and some economies of scale at sufficiently low levels of output, it has been shown (in Chapters 3 and 4) that it is not optimal to produce any good at its minimum average cost level of output. This result has a simple but important corollary:

If preferences are diverse and there are economies of scale, the configuration which gives maximum real GNP per capita is not optimal on either the full or second-best criteria.

Under conditions of uniformity there are no index number problems within the group since all goods will have the same real or shadow price, and thus real GNP can be found by simple addition of the quantities of all goods produced within the group, for the paradigm case. The group's contribution to real GNP can be found the same way when there are outside goods.

For given total resources in the paradigm case, or a given resource allocation to the group in the more general case, it follows that measured, real GNP can always be increased by moving from the optimal configuration to one in which either there is a single good (if $\theta$ is constant or minimum average cost occurs at a very high level) or there are exactly as many goods as enable each to be produced at minimum average cost. This always results in a reduction of the degree of product variety, on either the full-optimum or second-best criteria and is thus always a move away from the optimum, except in the case in which the optimum solution is already a single good.

The divergence between the maximum-GNP solution and the optimum solution is, of course, due entirely to the existence of preference diversity within the economy. The divergence vanishes if all individuals have identical preferences.

As would be intuitively expected from this last statement, the measured real GNP of an economy will fall with an increase in the diversity of preferences among its population (expressed as the overall range of diversity) if other properties of the economy are held constant. Consider a simple paradigm economy in which the range of preference diversity increases while the total population remains constant and in which there is a homogeneous (constant $\theta$) production technology. As shown in Chapter 3, the optimum size of segments will be unchanged since neither of the elasticities in the optimum condition described by Eq. (3.9) is affected by the change. Thus the number of goods will increase in proportion to the increase in the range, but the quantity of each good will vary inversely with the range because the total population is constant, and thus the density of consumers on the spectrum will be inverse to the range. Total GNP, which is the number of goods times the quantity of each good, would remain constant if the welfare levels of those consumers receiving their most-preferred goods remained constant. But each good is being produced in a smaller quantity when the range is greater, so its average resource cost is higher. Thus, if the resources of the economy are unchanged, the original GNP level cannot be sustained and must fall. The welfare level of the individuals (which is uniform across the population for the optimum solution in this model) will, of course, also fall.

This argument, which can be shown to hold if there are outside goods and if economies of scale decline with output, shows that there will be greater divergence between the maximum GNP attainable with given resources and the measured GNP associated with the most efficient use of those resources to attain a *uniform* level of welfare over the population, if the diversity of tastes in the population is greater.

If economic performance is measured by the level of GNP, then there is a conflict between this and equity as a performance goal when there are diverse preferences. It is always possible to increase GNP by abandoning equity, and the more diverse the tastes, the greater the increase. From an obverse point of view, equity is a goal which cannot be achieved costlessly, since one of the costs is lower real goods output from given resources and the greater the diversity, the greater the cost.

It was argued in the very first chapter of this book that diversity might be an increasing function of real income or welfare levels, that is, that preferences might show little dispersion when individuals must achieve basic consumption goals, like preventing hunger, but become more diverse when these goals are no longer dominant. If this hypothesis is sustained, it would predict a slowing of the rate of increase in ordinary measures of performance (such as real GNP) as economies develop and preferences become more diverse.

## 10.3 Intra-industry Trade between Identical Economies

Virtually any kind of difference between economies can result in potential gains from trade. The differences need not be on the pro- duction side, although differences in production possibility sets are the main tools of pure trade theory; gains can be generated from differences in preferences *between* economies having idential resource and production conditions. The analysis here will show that gains from trade can be generated from internal diversity of preferences within each economy, although preferences are identical between the economies in the sense that the aggregate demand curves or community indifference curves of the economies are identical. The gains are generated from the internal preference variations (the distributions themselves being identical between the economies) since they vanish if all individuals in each economy have identical tastes. Thus there are gains from trade between identical economies having identical populations.[1]

Consider two uniform economies, identical in all respects including size. There is a single product-differentiated industry, and resources not used in this industry are used to produce a single-characteristic nontradable good which it is convenient to refer to as leisure. Each economy has the properties of the paradigm case of Chapter 2.

Inititally, the two countries operate in isolation, with an optimum number of configuration of goods (product differentiates) in each. Since the economies are identical, the number and configuration will be the same in both countries. Economies of scale are assumed, so that the optimum number of goods in both countries is some finite number $n$. Now suppose that costless exchange is possible between the two countries, subject to the restriction that trade is to be balanced. The world is then a uniform economy, identical in structure to each of the component economies, but with twice the number of consumers.

If the technology is homogeneous of degree $k$ ($> 1$), the degree of economies of scale ($\theta = k$) is independent of size, so that the optimum number and configuration of goods is the same for the world as it was for each of the isolated economies, but the quantity required of each good is increased. Using the trade-balance requirement and

---

1. It has been apparent for some time that international trade theory is at its weakest in explaining the very high trade between basically similar economies, much of which appears as the exchange of the same products when given at the usual level of aggregation. Thus much trade occurs between similar economies, exchanging goods within each group. See Grubel (1967).

the property that the prices of all goods must be the same in each economy, it is obvious that the world optimum is achieved when each country produces the world requirement of half the total number of goods and exports half its output in exchange for those goods it does not produce. Since the same goods are produced (in the world as a whole) before and after trade, each country will cease production of half its goods and increase production of the other half. If there is absolute identity between the economies, it does not matter which goods are produced in which country, and, in practice, small random factors would determine the split.

In the homogeneous case, it if is assumed that consumption of goods does not change and all gains from trade are taken out in increased leisure resulting from reduced resources in the industrial sector, these gains can be measured. Before trade, the resources used in the industrial sector would be $V = nF(Q)$ for each country. After trade, industrial resource use would be $V' = \frac{1}{2}nF(2Q)$. For homogeneity of degree $k$, $F(Q) = Q^{1/k}$, so that the proportionate gain from trade is $(V - V')/V$, which is equal to $1 - 2^{(1/k)-1}$.

Multilateral trade will increase the gains from trade. If there are $m$ identical, uniform economies, each will produce $n/m$ goods for a gain, under the above conditions, of $1 - m^{(1/k)-1}$.

The above gains are calculated for a zero income elasticity for goods, in which case world production of every good after trade will be double the production in each country before trade, assuming there are two countries. It is more likely that the increased real income due to trade will be partly spent on more goods, so that output levels of every good could be expected to more than double after trade, as compared with outputs in either country beforehand.

If the technology is homethetic but not homogeneous, so that the economies-of-scale parameter $\theta$ varies with scale, the optimal number and specification of goods for the world after trade is opened need not be the same as in each country before trade—the number might be greater or smaller. It will remain true that each country will produce half the total number of goods required for the world (again, for a two-country world), and both countries will experience the same gain from trade. In general, however, the goods will have different specifications from those produced before trade, which requires restructuring of industry as a whole and not merely shutting down half the production lines and expanding others.

No matter whether the technology shows constant or variable *degree* of economies of scale, the gains from trade will exist as long as there are initial economies of scale ($\theta_o > 1$) and there is scope for specialization after trade. The last proviso requires that the optimal number of goods is at least two, which in turn requires some minimal degree of range in consumer preferences relative to the returns-to-scale properties. In particular, there can be no gain from trade if consumers have identical preferences.

Now consider two economies which are identical in all respects except size, the populations of the two countries being proportional to parameters $S_1$ and $S_2$.

Initially, attention will be confined to the case in which the technology is homogeneous of degree $k$ (giving $\theta = k$), where $k$ is greater than unity so that there are increasing returns. With uniform economies and a constant degree of economies of scale, the number and specification of goods at the optimum will be independent of size. Thus the two economies will produce the same $n$ goods in isolation, and, after trade, the world will also produce those same $n$ goods. For simplicity, it will be further assumed that the income elasticity of demand for goods is zero, so that the per capita consumption of all goods is the same in both countries, when the countries are isolated. Without loss of generality, $S_1$ and $S_2$ can then be taken to be the quantities produced in the two countries before trade, with $S_1 + S_2$ the world outputs after trade.

As in the case of identical countries, production after trade will be split among the two countries such that any particular good is produced entirely in one country. Let $n_1$ and $n_2$ be the number of goods produced in the two countries, with $n_1 + n_2 = n$. With identical per capita consumption in both countries, the exports of country 1 will be given by $n_1 S_2/(S_1 + S_2)$ (prices are the same for all goods, owing to uniformity), and its imports will be given by $n_2 S_1/(S_1 + S_2)$. The trade-balance relationship then gives $n_1/n_2 = S_1 S_2$, with the number of goods produced in each country after trade being proportional to the respective sizes. Thus the smaller country will show the greatest drop, as a result of trade, in the number of goods produced.

Now consider the gains from trade. To simplify the arithmetic, write $b = 1/k$, and $S = S_1 + S_2$, obtaining the expressions for the resource use in each country before trade (unprimed) and after trade (primed),

$$V_1 = nS_1{}^b \qquad V_1' = nS_1 S^{b-1}$$
$$V_2 = nS_2{}^b \qquad V_2' = nS_2 S^{b-1}.$$

The proportionate gains from trade $(V' - V)/V$ are given by $1 - (S_1/S)^{1-b}$ and $1 - (S_2/S)^{1-b}$ for the two countries. Since $b < 1$, the proportionate gains from trade are higher for the smaller country, as are the absolute per capita gains which are equal to $nS_1{}^{b-1}$ or $nS_2{}^{b-1}$ times the respective proportional gains. The reason for the higher gain per capita for the smaller country is, of course, that before trade the per capita real income is lower in the smaller country than in the larger country (owing to the effect of economies of scale) but after trade the two income levels are equal.

If the income elasticity of demand for goods is not zero, as assumed above, the analysis is somewhat more complex, since the different pretrade levels of per capita income may imply that the relative goods output levels are no longer in the same ratio as the populations and that the world outputs are no longer the same pre- and posttrade. So long as goods are not inferior, however, the general pattern will be as before, with the greatest posttradereduction in the number of goods, and the greatest per capita gain, occurring in the smaller country. The pattern should also hold for a nonhomogeneous (but homothetic) technology, unless the relationship between the degree of increasing returns and the level of output follows a particularly ill-behaved path. As in the identical country case, a minimum degree of diversity in preferences is necessary for gains from trade to exist.

For a given degree of economies of scale, the optimum number of goods will vary directly with the range of diversity, as shown above. It has already been noted that gains from trade through economies of scale can occur only if the optimum number of goods is at least two, which requires some minimum range of diversity. It is appropriate now to make a brief investigation of other effects of the range of diversity.

If the technology is homogeneous, the degree of economies of which affects the scale of output by affecting the optimum number of goods for a given size of the economy. In this case, the proportionate gains from trade between economies identical in all respects but size are not affected by the range of diversity, provided the minimum range requirement is satisfied. This is apparent from the preceding analysis, in which the proportionate gains were shown to be independent of the number of goods and the scale of output for a homogeneous technology. For a technology with variable $\theta$, on the other hand, the degree of economies of scale is not independent of the scale of output, and thus the effect of trade (including its gains) will depend on the range of diversity.

What about trade between economies with different ranges? The problem in analyzing this is to find an acceptable sense in which the economies are similar in all respects except range. Analysis begins by considering two economies with different ranges such that, in isolation, there is a set of $n$ goods which are produced in both countries in the same quantities and $m_1 + m_2$ other goods which are produced in one of the countries but not the other. This implies that the two ranges overlap over the $n$ common goods and that the populations in both countries are such that they give the same number of consumers over the common part of the range. The two populations must then be proportional to $m_1 + n$ and $m_2 + n$, respectively.

Now consider each economy to be partitioned into two parts, that part which produces the common goods and that part which produces the goods consumed only in that country. If trade is opened up between the parts of the two economies with the common goods, the results will be the same as for trade between two identical economies. Each country will produce $\frac{1}{2}n$ of the goods, and there will be the usual gains for the common sectors, taken in isolatio from the rest of their economies.

If the partitions separating off the remaining parts of the economies are removed, there will be further effects. Consumers who, before trade, consumed a good close in specification to the one of the common goods will find the common goods greatly reduced in price and will shift to consumption of one of these. This will cause repercussions down the spectrum of the noncommon goods, and there will be a reorganization of both the numbers and specifications of these goods. This reorganization will *distribute* the gains from trade over the whole population (not uniformly, however) but will not affect the size of those gains, except to a minor degree.

Thus the gains from trade will accrue primarily from the common sector, but will be distributed over the whole economy. The absolute gains will be essentially the same for both economies, but the per capita gains will depend on the total populations. Hence it can be expected that the per capita gains will be greatest in the economy which has the greatest overlap (smallest ratio $m_i/n$) and thus the smallest range.

For two countries with the same consumer *density* (the same number of consumers per common good), the per capita gains from trade would be greater in the country with the smaller range of diversity. For countries with the same *total population*, the situation is not clear-cut. In this case, the country with the smallest range will have the largest number of consumers in the common-good sector, and thus the least gain per consumer in the common sector, but will have this gain less diluted by consumers outside the sector. Thus the per capita gain as a function of range in this case is subject to two influences in opposite directions. It does not seem worthwhile, in a pioneer investigation, to set up a formal model to try and assess the strengths of these opposing influences.

## 10.4 Variety in Capital Goods

Although the emphasis in this book has been on the optimal variety of consumer goods, there is also a problem of the optimal variety of capital goods. For capital goods which produce services directly to consumers, such as housing, this is obvious enough, and the analysis of such cases is basically similar to that of indivisible consumption goods, except that the degree of variety depends on the properties of the whole stock and not on the variety of current production. If the good is highly durable and there are important economies of scale in its production (which do not seem to exist in housing), it would obviously be efficient to build up variety over a period by concentrating on one type at a time and using scale economies extensively.

It would obviously be inefficient to have current output at any time reflect the full degree of variety in the total stock.

There is certainly a problem of variety in industrial capital goods as well. All machines, from textile looms to locomotives to lathes to computers, can be produced in a variety of designs, and each variant is more suited to some production processes than to others. Most such machines are subject to some kind of scale economies in production. Indeed, one of the features of technological development has been the movement from custom-built machines to a range of standard models, which is clear evidence of the existence of such economies. Steam locomotives, for example, were essentially custom designed and built for each user and each use, whereas modern diesel locomotives roll off an assembly line. The same development has taken place in computers, from individual designs to standard models.

The analysis of optimal variety in capital goods is, however, more complex than that of variety in consumer goods. Such simplifying analytical devices as the uniformity assumption, which is a reasonable assumption for a spectrum of consumer preferences, are much less appropriate for expressing the relationship between the performance of available capital goods and the performance of each firm's most-preferred design. There is one simplifying feature in the capital-goods case, however, in that the effect of being restricted to an available standard model is measured in cost terms and can be directly compared across firms. If it can be assumed that there is a preferred machine specification for each productive activity and that costs increase with the difference between this specification and that of an available model, the overall pattern of the optimizing problem will have basic similarities to that of the second-best problem in the consumer-goods case.

If capital goods have low durability, so that they can be treated essentially as intermediate goods, the optimum problem is to produce a given basket of final products with the least use of resources, taking into account both the scale economies in production of intermediate goods and the additional resources required in final production from the use of inputs which are not specifically designed for the activity concerned. If the capital is highly durable, the same considerations arise as in the housing case with respect to variety in current production in relation to variety of the stock as a whole.

There is a special feature of variety in capital goods that does not exist in the consumer-goods case. This is the possibility of designing the machines themselves to be more flexible or more specialized—large mainframe computers with a range of software, for example, versus small computers designed to perform specialized tasks. Another choice is thus introduced into the situation—the choice between the flexible machine and the specialized one.

There is no equity involved in the capital goods case since the choice is confined to variety and efficiency. For the same reason, there is nothing in the structure of the capital-goods model comparable to uniform welfare density or uniform income, and the demand for a highly specialized machine will depend on the size of the industry which would use it. The demand may be sufficient in some uses to justify production of a machine to the ideal specification for that use, whereas other activities may have to use machines designed to several things well, but none perfectly.

Thus it is reasonable to conclude that there is a problem of optimal variety in the capital stock (and in nondurable producer's goods generally) and that the optimal variety will depend on the degree of economies of scale in the capital-goods industry, as well as the structure of the consumer-goods industries. The problem is inherently more complex than in consumer goods, but some of the principles of solution can be carried over from the analysis of the latter.

## 10.5 The Optimal Division of Labor

Work dominates the lives of many and, if the term is taken to include work within the household as well that sold on the market, is a major component in the life of almost everyone who is not either a child or retired. This is an obvious-enough statement, yet work as such plays almost no part in traditional welfare economics. It makes its appearance only as disembodied "labor," an input required to produce goods and the supplying of which diverts the individual's time away from nonwork or "leisure." The individual values both leisure and the goods that can be produced by direct labor or can be purchased with money acquired from the sale of labor, but no value (positive or negative) is associated with the work activity itself. A broader approach has appeared in the more recent work on human-resource economics, but with emphasis on the consequences for labor supply rather than for welfare economics.

It seems quite likely that a significant part of an individual's total welfare is derived (positively and negatively) from work itself, not merely from the *consequences* of work as represented by income or lost leisure. That is, the job itself carries positive and negative aspects which are independent of the time consumed or the pay received, and these enter in an important way into the individual's total well-being. Economists have not doubted this, and have even tried to make some allowance for it in certain contexts,[2] but have never integrated it fully into a welfare setting. This has been primarily because of the lack of a suitable analytical framework within which to make such an integration.

The welfare associated with work itself depends on the relationship between the job and the individual, just as the welfare associated with consumption depends on the relationship between the individual and the specific bundle of goods available. To analyze this relationship in the case of work requires bringing some order to the definition of a job and some way of associating this with personal preferences.

First it is important to separate the idea of a "job" from that of "working conditions," such as attractive or ugly workplaces, good or bad cafeteria services, and the like. Some jobs may be traditionally associated with good or bad working conditions, but the two are independent in principle. Even the interior of a coal mine could be brightly lit and have white paint over the rock faces—it is a question of cost. Working conditions can always be treated as positive or negative fringe benefits and taken into account in relating wages in one workplace to those in another.

The "job" is taken to mean the employment of particular types of

2. As in the traditional idea of "nonmonetary advantage" used to explain why an individual works in one occupation when he or she could earn more in another.

skill and effort in a particular combination, so that jobs can be differentiated by varying the proportions in which these various skills and efforts are required.[3] The traditional unskilled-laborer's job called for a considerable degree of pure muscular effort and the following of simple instructions with no use of problem solving, reading, or arithmetic skills. A skilled mechanic's job, on the other hand, called for the following of complex instructions, usually written and typically involving calculations, and varying degrees of problem solving. The toolmaker's job involved extensive problem solving, along with the other skills of the master mechanic. The traditional analysis of the differences among these jobs, designed primarily to explain wage differences, was to use a single parameter called "skill," the quantity of which was lowest in the job of laborer and highest in the job of toolmaker.

A welfare analysis of work requires that the job be regarded as multidimensioned, as requiring plural "skills" rather than a singular abstract "skill," with different jobs requiring these skills in different proportions. These skills required in a job are then exactly analogous to the characteristics associated with a good. Indeed, the term "characteristics" could be used also for the attributes of a job, but there is some advantage in keeping to the term "skills."

Just as jobs vary in the combination of skills they require, individuals vary in the skills they possess and the combinations in which they prefer to have them employed. This last point is crucial. It is not just which skills are possessed by the individual, but in what proportions they are used, that determines that individual's welfare from work. A physically strong person who is also a very good problem solver may prefer a job which uses both skills (a football quarterback, perhaps) to one that uses only one, even if all other considerations, including pay, were the same.

This leads to the first propostion in the welfare economics of work, that of the *optimal match*:[4]

Among all the allocations of persons to jobs which satisfy the

---

3. See Welch (1969) for an analysis along somewhat similar lines.

4. Rosen (1978b) discusses the optimum-match problem from the point of view of output maximization.

requirement that every person holding a job has all the skills needed
to perform it, there is an optimal allocation.

Since the set is confined to that of appropriate allocations in the
sense that everyone can do his or her job, the output of the economy
is unaffected by any reallocations. Among these reallocations, there
is, on any one criterion, an allocation or set of allocations which best
matches the preferences of the individuals to the characteristics of
their jobs.

The above proposition is based on the assumption that the number and specification of jobs in the economy is given. But just as it
is possible to consider an economy in which the number of specifications of goods are variable—the main point of this book—it is
possible to consider variations in the number and types of different
jobs. It is reasonable to assume that considerable flexibility is possible in the way in which production is structured, so that different
structures associated with different distributions of jobs of various
specifications are possible. In general, variations in the structure can
be expected to give variations in production for a given distribution
of skills in the population. The structure which gives maximum output
does not necessarily maximize welfare from work, and the change in
output (which affects welfare from consumption) must be balanced
against the change in welfare from work.

Thus there would seem to be a second proposition in the welfare
economics of work, that of the *optimal division of labor*:

If the number and specification of jobs can be varied, there is an
output-maximizing division of labor which gives the greatest output
from the skills available in the population and an optimal division of
labor which gives the greates overall welfare from work and consumption. The output-maximizing and optimal divisions of labor need
not be the same.

The two propositions on the welfare economics of work have
been put forward as plausible assertions, although the existence of
the optima has not been established here, let alone their properties.
But it does seem that the problem could be investigated along the
general lines of the anlaysis of optimal product variety given earlier.
A spectrum of job specifications analogous to the spectrum of goods

specifications seems to provide a basic structure into which can be fitted the preferences of individuals over jobs of different kinds. If it can be assumed that costs of management (and perhaps costs of capital) are lower when many workers are performing standardized jobs than when different workers are doing their tasks in different ways, there is an effect analogous to economies of scale in the goods case. Greater variation in jobs enables more workers to be performing the kind of job they prefer but increases organization costs, so that there is a solution to the optimal degree of job variety which is analogous to the optimal degree of product variety.

It should be noted that the optimal division of labor in the welfare sense may involve *fewer* job varieties than the output-maximizing division of labor. Workers may be more productive if they always screw in the same bolt on the assembly line, but they may prefer to vary their role, so that welfare maximization may call for a single job of "general assembler" rather than "front-bolt assembler" and "rear-bolt assembler," although the latter division would be output maximizing.[5]

It is not clear to what extent markets of any kind can contribute to solution of many of the problems of the optimal division of labor so long as the only effects are on the welfare of the individuals concerned. If, as is often assumed to be the case, jobs are actually performed more efficiently by workers whose preferences fit the jobs than by workers with the same skills but different preferences, the welfare effects become externalized, and it is in the interests of managers to ensure the best match between jobs and workers.

## 10.6 Variety and Economic Development

Although economies of scale are not exclusively related to industrialization, as is apparent from the preindustrial enclosure movement in England, they are one of its main features. Thus the analysis of the

5. There has been growing interest in recent years on the part of firms in the possibilities of arranging jobs to increase worker satisfaction from the job (welfare from work). Automobile manufacturers, including Ford and Volvo, have experimented with assembly-line changes designed for these purposes.

earlier chapters of this book would seem to predict a simple scenario for the effect of industrialization on product variety—that it would decline from the infinite variety of a constant-returns-to-scale custom-production preindustrial economy to the limited variety appropriate to the existence of economies of scale. Although the industrialization process does not seem to have been studied from this specific point of view, casual information on English society in the mid-nineteenth century as compared with the mid-eighteenth does not appear to support such a scenario. If anything, variety was greater in Victorian England.

It is not difficult to see that the product-variety scenario was heavily overlaid by other influences. Two of these are of particular importance: the change in the level and distribution of real income and the development of entirely new product classes which were not possible with a preindustrial technology. In addition, as pointed out in Chapter 1, most craftsmen in a preindustrial society have a limited range of things which they know how to make. It is not unlikely that the very rich, who could draw on the services of the small number of truly creative craftsmen, faced less variety after industrialization, but the middle class could now afford, for example, to select from a limited range of cast-iron decorative architectural details where before they could not afford custom-made wrought iron or carved stone details. Potential variety may have been reduced in many product classes, but affordable variety was increased.

Contemporary developing economies do, however, face the problem of relating product variety to development strategy. Is it better to produce to a single specification and gain the maximum possible economies of scale or to develop some variety from the beginning? This may not be regarded as entirely an economic decision, since a developing country emerging from a structure of great income inequality may place much symbolic significance on naïve uniformity and deliberately avoid variety, even when there are no economies of scale. As suggested in the introductory chapter, there is a strong incentive for the government of a poor country to *want* uniformity of preference since this will simplify almost every economic decision.

If an industry is subject to strong economies of scale, there seems little doubt that the appropriate development strategy, given that the product class is to be produced domestically, is to produce little variety and gain the greatest economies, at least during the initial development stage. Maximizing the growth of GNP outweighs equity considerations because of the positive feedback into faster future growth, just as an equitable distribution of money income may be subordinated as a goal for the same reasons. Equity problems are probably minimal at this stage in any case, if the argument given earlier—that dispersion of tastes increases with income—is accepted. Any kind of "people's car" that actually runs may suit almost everyone in a relatively poor society, since anything more than basic transportation is still a luxury beyond the horizons of most consumers. There is an information problem as well; most consumers do not know what specification would suit them best until they have some experience with the product class and some sense of feasible characteristics, so that the potential variety in preferences would be difficult to estimate at the initial stage.

There is still an optimum problem, however, even if it is decided to produce to a single specification, and that is the choice of the actual design. Given that a single good is to be produced in a product class, there is an optimal specification for that good. For a uniform preference spectrum with uniform density, this is the product in the middle of the spectrum, but a different specification would be optimal if density were not uniform. Consideration should be given to the longer run, however; it could be better to produce a specification which is not strictly optimal for a single-product solution but which is one of the specifications that will fit into an optimal multiproduct pattern at a later stage.[6] A plant designed to build a product which rapidly becomes obsolete may be poor strategy, even if the short-run gains seem considerable.

The possibilities for trade are critical in the solution of the variety and optimal-specification problems. If two developing countries can

6. It might be a serious mistake, in particular, to estimate the potential demand for some product group and then plan a giant factory with capacity to supply all the potential with a product of a single specification.

trade with each other, the joint optimum solution is clearly for each country to produce a good of a different specification, the choice of specifications ideally being determined by considering the optimum specifications for a product class of two goods and a variety of preferences given by taking both populations together. If the countries are small and the output at which scale economies are exhausted is large, the optimum may even call for only one country to produce the product class, the other country producing the single good in another group.

If the production of a particular group of goods is left to the private sector, the analysis of Chapter 7 becomes relevant. Monopolistic competition will generally tend to produce too great a variety, and the argument that the simplicity of leaving market organization to the market may outweigh any efficiency loss because it is coupled with greater equity due to greater variety has less weight when equity is subordinate to efficiency. This would suggest that entry should be controlled, perhaps by the licensing system discussed in the earlier chapter, if the conditions of perfect monopolistic competition are satisfied. Realistically, it is highly improbable that a new industry in a developing country will have the characteristics of perfect monopolistic competition, even with free entry and vigorous entrepreneurship. Imperfect information is almost certain to be predominant, leading to less variety than in the "perfect" case—by coincidence, this could even be the optimal variety or close to it. Even under perfect conditions, the excessive degree of product variety occurs only at the long-run equilibrium and not in the initial stages. The problem most likely to arise in the initial stages of market development is the wrong assortment of products, rather than too many products, so that there is overexpansion in some varieties (with consequent redundant capital investment) whereas other varieties are not produced at all.

Consideration of the appropriate degree of job variety may be even more important in the early stages of development than the degree of product variety. Industrialization creates new jobs as well as new products, and the design of these jobs is likely to be based on experience in advanced industrial sectors in other countries. There may be as much to be gained in welfare from appropriate job design as from appropriate product design, in addition to productivity gains which might ensue from jobs better suited to existing skills and preferences.

## 10.7 The Politics of Variety

Since the property of optimal solutions to the variety problem is that no good is to be produced to the point at which all economies of scale have been used up, it follows that each individual stands to gain if there is increased output of the particular good with which he or she is supplied, assuming that the decreased cost is passed on to consumers. Thus a coalition of all the consumers receiving the same good has an interest in reducing the degree of variety in the economy, *provided that the good they receive is not eliminated.*

In a political context, therefore, it is possible to form a majority coalition by assembling individual coalitions of the above kind, provided the consumers of each good are guaranteed that their good will not be eliminated. Such a coalition could, under majority rule, ensure that the degree of variety was restricted as much as possible without eliminating any of the goods of interest to members of the coalition. The easiest coalition of this kind to form would be a center coalition, consisting of consumers receiving goods which are adjacent on the spectrum and away from the edges of the spectrum. A law which prohibited the production or sale of goods having specifications beyond those of the coalition in any direction would then force all consumers to accept the coalition goods and would decrease average costs, and the coalition members could gain. Those who would otherwise receive goods at the fringes of the spectrum (who would be perceived as eccentrics by the members of the center coalition) would lose, of course. They would be required to accept a good which, even at the lower cost due to greater scale, was less desirable than one closer to their most-preferred good but more expensive, since this is the implication of the original optimum.

The gain would not generally be spread evenly over members of the coalition, however. In fact, some may not gain at all, and some may lose. In the case of the center coalition, the next-best good for those outside the coalition, after their optimal good is removed, will be a good at the *edge* of the subspectrum of goods still available. The output of these goods will increase, and their costs will fall, bringing gains to those coalition members who consumed these goods initially. Consumers further inside the coalition could still gain by switching to the cheaper edge good, and there would be consumers for whom such a switch would be optimal. Switching would, however, reduce the output and increase the cost of the goods next to the boundary goods, so that some members of the coalition would lose unless all coalition goods were boundary goods.

Thus, although it might be relatively easy to form a center coalition on the promise of gains for all, the gains will not be received by all unless there is a redistribution from coalition members at the edges to those at the center. In the absence of such compensation payments (which can always be made because the gains at the edges outweigh the losses at the center), a center coalition will not persist unless the part of the spectrum it represents contains no interior goods. Whether such a coalition is possible depends on the dimensionality of the spectrum (number of relevant characteristics of the goods), which determines how many neighbors a good may have, and on the optimum number of goods initially, which determines how many goods will be involved in the coalition. It seems a reasonable conjecture that it is not possible to form such a coalition among consumers distributed with uform density over a uniform spectrum, but is certainly possible with nonuniform density and a sufficiently small number of initial goods. In particular, if there are two goods initially and nonuniform density, so that the consumers of one good form a majority, those consumers in the majority can gain by prohibiting the production of the other good.

In the uniform-density case it is always possible to form a majority coalition so that all members gain without redistribution among themselves, but this would be an extraordinarily difficult form of coalition to put together. The desired coalition should consist of consumers whose most-preferred goods are *not* adjacent on the spectrum or are, at most, adjacent to one other coalition good. In the two-characteristics case, giving a line spectrum, a coalition consisting of those consumers whose preferred goods consist of one pair of adjacent goods and then every second good along the spectrum would, in the uniform-density case, produce the desired results. It would contain more than half the goods (and thus have a majority of the population) and would be such that every coalition good received some non-coalition consumers when the latter's goods were eliminated, and thus all coalition members would gain.

The structural resemblance of this last case to the firehouse example with which this book commenced is immediately apparent. In fact, it is only in a locational context in which groups of consumers could be placed on a spectrum with sufficient accuracy to enable such a coalition to be formed. In the firehouse case, a coalition of those residents who live closer to the firehouses that will remain than to those that will be closed, plus one additional resident, could form a majority that would vote for the faster-equipment, fewer-firehouses alternative.[7] The additional resident could be someone who is slightly closer to one of the firehouses destined to close but who will still gain by the faster service.

In principle, it is always possible to form a majority coalition that, under the guise of standardization or rationalization, could reduce variety in such a way that the coalition members gain at the expense of the outsiders. Unless there is some redistribution scheme *within* the coalition, however, the gains may not accrue to all members, and thus the coalition may not be stable. The most likely cases for success of such coalitions are either localized public services (like the fire-houses) or goods (public or private) subject to large-scale econo-mies, so that there are potentially few consumers, and with uneven distributions over the spectrum.

For any good in which the variety and specification is determined by political decision—primarily, but not exclusively, public programs and public goods—there is a majority interest in reducing variety at the expense of equity in order to increase the efficiency with which the goods preferred by the majority coalition are produced.

7.  Note the firehouse example as given in Chapter 1 is such that the average response time is the same in the two policies being compared, and two-thirds of the population gain while one-third lose with the fewer-firehouses policy. A majority could still be found for the fewer-firehouses policy even if the equipment speed was less than doubled, so that the average response time was lowered. This would not be "efficient" by the criterion used in Chapter 1, but the majority could still gain at the expense of the rest by eliminating some firehouses.

 **Appendix A**

# The Compensating Function

## The Goods Spectrum

THE ANALYSIS IN this work assumed infinite potential product differentiation within a group, so that the number of goods is not finite and thus the group cannot be identified by decomposing a finite technology matrix. It is, however, assumed that there is a *finite subset of characteristics* such that goods possessing these characteristics (some, perhaps, in zero amounts) possess no other characteristics and no goods possessing other characteristics possess characteristics from the subset. Under these circumstances, this subset of *group characteristics* is sufficient to define the group, since any good, whether previously identified or not, which possesses group characteristics can be placed within the group.

From now on, attention is devoted only to a single group. Let $z$ denote a vector of the $m$ group characteristics and $x$ a *normalized z-vector*, such that $x_i = z_i/(\Sigma^m z_i)$. The vector $x$ has only $m - 1$ independent components since $\Sigma x_i = 1$. The vector $x$ will be referred to as the *intrinsic specification* for a potential good within the group. A good is considered to be uniquely defined by its intrinsic specification: Two goods with characteristics in the same proportions are considered to be the same good, whereas goods with characteristics in different proportions are different goods.

Characteristics vectors $\lambda z$ and $z$ represent the same intrinsic

**335**

specification and thus are associated with different quantities of the same good.

The set of all intrinsic specification vectors $x$ over the unit simplex represents the set of all potential goods within the group and will be referred to as the *goods spectrum* for that group. It is assumed that all potential goods over the whole spectrum or over the same compact subset of the spectrum can be made available if this is appropriate, so that there is infinite potential variation in goods specification or infinite potential *product differentiation* within the group. It will be assumed that the set of production possibilities forms a convex set with a finite number of extreme points, so that it is possible to identify a finite number of potential goods which mark the "end" of the spectrum in that neighborhood.

## The Product-Differentiation Function

Let $z$ be the vector of the group characteristics made available *after* being embodied in the appropriate quantity of a single good of intrinsic specification $x(= x(z))$. Then the minimum total resource requirement for producing those characteristics so embodied is given by some function

$$V = \Phi(z),$$

where $V$ can be regarded as a single resource or a bundle of resources in fixed proportions. The function $\Phi(z)$ is the *product-differentiation function*.

The product-differentiation function is assumed to be homothetic, so that

$$\Phi(\lambda z) = F(\lambda)\,\Phi(z)$$

for all $z > 0$ and $\lambda > 0$. It is also assumed that $\Phi$ is a positive increasing function of $z$ and that it is quasi-convex, that is, that the contours $\Phi = c$ are either hyperplanes with semipositive normals or are curved surfaces which are concave toward the origin (like transformation surfaces in standard analysis).

## Definition of Quantity

Let a good of intrinsic specification $x^o$ be arbitrarily chosen as a kind of "numeraire," and let some arbitrarily chosen amount of that good which provides total characteristics $z^o$ be chosen as the *unit quantity* of that good. The *linear homogeneous function* $\phi(z)$ is defined in the following way:

$$\phi(z) \equiv a_o \, \Phi(z)$$

for all $z$ such that $\Phi(z) = \Phi(z^o)$, where $a_o$ is a constant scalar chosen so that

$$a_o \, \Phi(z^o) = 1.$$

Then $\phi(\lambda z) = \lambda \phi(z)$ (linear homogeneity), so that

$$\phi(\lambda z) = \frac{\lambda a_o}{F(\lambda)} \, \Phi(z),$$

and thus the functions $\phi$ and $\Phi$ have contours of identical shape and differ only in the labels attached to the contours.

The function $\phi(z)$ is the *quantity function*, the quantity $q$ of a good of intrinsic specification $x(z)$ being defined by

$$q = \phi(z).$$

For the numeraire good, the quantity measure associated with an amount of the good providing $\lambda$ times as much of every characteristic as the unit quantity is given by

$$q = \phi(\lambda z^o)$$

$$= \lambda \phi(z^o)$$

$$= \lambda$$

which conforms to the appropriate notion of a quantity measure for this case. Let $z^1$ be the characteristics associated with some amount of a good of intrinsic specification $x^1$ which is such that $\phi(z^1) = \phi(z^o) = 1$. This defines the unit quantity of good of that intrinsic specification, and it is easily seen that a characteristics vector $\lambda z^1$ derived from this same good will correspond to quantity measure $q = \lambda$.

Note the two basic properties of the quantity measure:

1. Unit quantities of all goods are such that they use the same resources as the unit quantity of the numeraire good. Both the intrinsic specification of the numeraire good and the level of characteristics chosen as the unit quantity are arbitrary.

2. The quantity of any particular good is given by the ratio of the total content of any characteristic to the content of that characteristic in the unit quantity since the characteristics proportions remain constant by definition of a good.

It follows from the two basic properties above, and the homotheticity of the product differentiation function, that the quantity definition has the important property that *equal quantities of different goods require the same resources*. Note, however, that the quantities of a single good are proportional to the characteristics, *not* to the resources required. Resource contents are used to bring the unit quantities of *different* goods to a common measure but not to measure relative quantities of the same good.

## The Fully Separable Group

The utility or preference functions of individuals are assumed to be given in terms of characteristics and not in terms of goods as such. Preferences among collections of goods are derived from preferences over the collections of characteristics to which the goods give rise. Thus there is no problem in dealing with consumer preferences over an infinite spectrum of potential goods, since the number of group characteristics is assumed to be finite.

The group has been referred to as intrinsically separable if it possesses no relevant characteristics in common with goods outside the group. For the group to be fully separable, it is necessary that consumers make choices among group goods separately from their choices between group goods and other goods, and this involves properties of the preference function, as well as the intrinsic properties of the goods themselves. It is sufficient for full separability that the utility function be separable in the usual sense into subutility functions on sets of characteristics and that one of these sets of characteristics coincide with the intrinsic characteristics of the group.

The group can be treated as separable under rather less stringent conditions, as, for example, when the group shares some characteristics with other goods, but their contribution to the total consumption of those characteristics by the individual is very small.

## The Most-Preferred Good

The *most-preferred good* of a particular individual is defined as a good having the intrinsic specification which that individual would choose if allocated a specific quantity of resources and permitted to use those resources to produce a single group good entirely for his own use. It is obviously the solution to the problem:

$$\max_{z} \; w(z), \qquad \text{subject to} \;\; \Phi(z) = \bar{V},$$

which has a solution of the form

$$w_i = \mu \, \Phi_i, \qquad i = 1, \ldots, m,$$

where $w_i$, and $\Phi_i$ are the partial derivatives of the functions $w$ and $\Phi$ with respect to $z_i$ and $\mu$ is a Lagrange multiplier. The intrinsic specification of the most-preferred good is given by the point at which an indifference surface is tangent to the appropriate contour of the product-differentiation function.

## Compensation

Since $w$ is strictly quasi-concave and $\Phi$ is quasi-convex, the most-preferred good determination will possess a strong maximum at the preferred-good specification. If a consumer is not provided with his most-preferred good, but with some other *available* good (from the group), attainment of the same level of preference will require characteristics combinations on a higher contour of $\Phi$ and thus a higher contour of $\phi$, which represents a higher quantity of the available good than the quantity of the most-preferred good that would have been sufficient. This is the concept of *compensation*—that the quantity of an available good required to enable an individual to attain a given preference level will be greater than the quantity of the most-preferred good. The ratio of the quantity of the available good to the quantity of most-preferred good that gives the same utility level is the *compensating ratio*. It is obvious that the compensating ratio depends, among other things, on the extent to which the intrinsic specification of the available good differs from the intrinsic specification of the most-preferred good.

## Distance

It is convenient to discuss the properties of compensation in terms of some measure of the "distance" between the specification of the most-preferred good and that of a particular available good. If $x^*$ is the intrinsic specification of the most-preferred good and $x$ is the intrinsic specification of some other good, then the distance measure $u$ is some function

$$u = \delta(x, x^*),$$

where $\delta$ is any acceptable distance function, such as, but not confined to, the Euclidean distance between $x$ and $x^*$. The essential properties of $\delta$ are that $\delta(x^*, x^*) = 0$ and $\delta(x, x^*) > 0$ if $x \neq x^*$ and that the function satisfies the triangle inequality. In the main text, the distance function is chosen to be the arc length along the contour of the quantity function, but there are other choices. Ultimately, the appropriate choice is that which satisfies the *uniformity property* discussed later, if such a measure exists.

## The Compensating Function

Let $q^*$ be the quantity of an individual's most-preferred good, of intrinsic specification $x^*$, that enables him to attain preference or utility level $\bar{w}$, with the total characteristics provided by that quantity of the most-preferred good being $z^*$. Let the consumer be provided with a quantity of some other good, with specification $x$, such that he still attains preference level $\bar{w}$. Then the characteristics obtained from that quantity of the available good, $z$, must satisfy the relationship

$$w(z) = \bar{w}.$$

The quantity of the available good required is given by the quantity function

$$q = \phi(z),$$

and the distance of the available good from the most-preferred good is given by the distance function

$$u = \delta(x, x^*).$$

Now the specification vector $x$ depends only on the properties of $z$, and the specification of the most-preferred good, $x^*$, is given, so that the distance function can be written as

$$u = \delta(z)$$

within the specific context. Also, $h = q/q^*$ is the compensating ratio for the individual in question with respect to the most-preferred and specified available good, so that there is a system of three relationships

$$w(z) = \bar{w}, \quad q^*h = \phi(z), \quad \text{and} \quad u = \delta(z)$$

between the $m + 2$ variables $z_1, \ldots, z_m$, $h$, and $u$. In general, given the number of relationships, it is insufficient to give a variable as a function of just one other variable. If $m = 2$, however, the three relationships are sufficient to determine $h$ in terms of $u$. Cases in which $m > 2$ will be discussed later, when the notion of uniformity has been introduced. At this stage, the analysis will be confined to the two-characteristic case with $m = 2$, for which it is possible to solve the system for $h$ in terms of $u$. The function $h(u)$ will be referred to as the *compensating function*. Note that the function is fully determined in the sense that for every specification $x$, there is a unique value of both $h$ and $u$. On the other hand, the function $h(u)$ is not necessarily single valued, even when $m = 2$, since there will be two different goods with specifications at any given distance $u$ from the most-preferred good, one on each side, and the compensating ratios will not necessarily be the same.

From this point on, the arbitrary normalization of the characteristics vector, introduced to provide a preliminary identification of different goods ("intrinsic specification"), will be dropped, and *specification* will now be taken to mean position on the spectrum, measured in terms of the distance function.

## Properties of the Compensating Function

By solving the system for small deviations away from the most-preferred good point (henceforth referred to as the origin), the following equation is obtained:

$$h'(u) = \frac{dh}{du} = \frac{1}{q^*} \frac{w_1 \phi_2 - w_2 \phi_1}{w_1 \phi_2 - w_2 \phi_1}.$$

At the most-preferred good specification (the origin), $w_1/w_2 = \Phi_1/\Phi_2 = \phi_1/\phi_2$ (since the contours of $\Phi$ and $\phi$ are identical), so that $w_1 \phi_2 = w_2 \phi_1$ and thus $h'(0) = 0$. Also, from the definition of compensation, $h(0) = 1$. These properties are relatively trivial, and the real purpose in determining $h'(u)$ is as a step toward the second-order derivative $h''(u)$.

## Convexity Properties

By taking the derivative of $h'(u)$ with respect to $u$ through the system and using the relationship $w_1/w_2 = \phi_1/\phi_2$ appropriately, it can be shown that, at the origin,

$$h''(0) = \frac{w_1}{q^*(w_1 \delta_2 - w_2 \delta_1)^2} (w_1 K_1 - \phi_1 K_2),$$

where

$$\phi_1{}^2 K_1 = \phi_2{}^2 \phi_{11} - 2\phi_1 \phi_2 \phi_{12} + \phi_1{}^2 \phi_{22}$$

and

$$w_1{}^2 K_2 = w_2{}^2 w_{11} - 2w_1 w_2 w_{12} + w_1{}^2 w_{22}.$$

Now $K_1$ and $K_2$ are immediately recognizable as expressions giving the degree of quasi-convexity/concavity of the functions $\phi$ and $w$, respectively. In particular, $K_1 \geq 0$ since $\phi$ is quasi-convex, and $K_2 < 0$ since $w$ is strictly quasi-concave. The stronger the convexity or concavity of the contours of the functions, the smaller the $K$ values, $K$ being zero if the contours are linear.

Thus an extremely important property of $h(u)$ has been established, namely, that $h''(0) > 0$, so that $h(u)$ is strictly convex at the origin. *It will be assumed that* h(u) *is strictly convex over the whole range of* u *being used in the analysis.*

Note that the degree of convexity of $h(u)$ [as measured by $h''(0)$] is, in effect, a weighted sum of the numerical values of the degrees of convexity or concavity of the two functions $\phi$ and $w$. The more strictly quasi-convex $\phi$ or the more strictly quasi concave $w$, the larger the degree of convexity of $h(u)$.

## Summary of Basic Properties

Since $h''(0) > 0$ and $h'(0) = 0$, it follows that $h'(u) > 0$ for all $u > 0$, within some finite range of the origin. Also, since $h(0) = 1$, it therefore follows that $h(u) > 1$ for $u > 0$, within some distance of the origin. Since it is assumed that $h''(u) > 0$ everywhere, the properties near the origin can be considered to hold over the whole range used in the analysis. The basic properties of $h(u)$ can thus be summarized:

1. $h(0) = 1$.
2. $h(u) > 1$ for all $u > 0$.
3. $h'(0) = 0$.
4. $h'(u) > 0$ for all $u > 0$.
5. $h''(u) > 0$ for all $u$.

Note that $h(u)$ is not necessarily single valued, but there is a single-valued function if deviations from the origin in only one direction are considered.

## The Elasticity of Compensation

The elasticity of compensation $e_h(u)$ is defined as the elasticity of the compensating function with respect to specification distance:

$$e_h(u) = \frac{d[\ln h(u)]}{d(\ln u)} = uh'(u)/h(u).$$

Certain properties of $e_h$ are immediate from the definition and the properties of $h(u)$:

1.  $e_h(0) = 0$.
2.  $e_h(u) > 0$ for all $u > 0$.

To derive further properties, it is useful to introduce the function $\underline{h}(u)$ = ln $h(u)$, which has the following properties:

$$\underline{h}(0) = 0$$

$$\underline{h}(u) > 0 \text{ for all } u > 0$$

$$\underline{h}'(u) = h'(u)/h(u) = 0 \text{ for } u = 0$$
$$> 0 \text{ for all } u > 0$$

$$\underline{h}''(u) = (hh'' - h'^2)/h^2,$$

where the primes denote derivatives with respect to $u$, not ln $u$. It is obvious that $h'' > 0$ (convexity of $h$) is necessary but not sufficient for $\underline{h}'' > 0$ (what might be termed *logarithmic convexity* of $h$). However, $\underline{h}''(0) = h''(0)/h(0) > 0$, and it will be assumed that $\underline{h}''(u) > 0$ for all $u$ over the range of variation required in the analysis.

The compensation elasticity can be written in terms of the logarithm of the compensating function as

$$e_h(u) = u\underline{h}'(u),$$

so that two additional properties of $e_h$ are:

3.  $e_h'(u) = \underline{h}' + u\underline{h}'' = 0 \text{ for } u = 0$
$$> 0 \text{ for } u > 0.$$

4.  $e_h''(u) = 2\underline{h}'' + u\underline{h}'''$.

The values taken by the first derivative result from the assumed logarithmic convexity of $h(u)$; weaker condition would be implied by the assumption that $e_h'(u) > 0$ for all $u > 0$, made directly, since $\underline{h}'' > 0$ is sufficient but not necessary for $e_h'(u) > 0$. The sign of the second derivative remains undetermined since it depends on third-derivative properties of the compensating function.

## The Cumulative Compensating Function

Considerable use will be made of the cumulative compensating function, the relevance of which will be apparent when the uniformity assumption is introduced. This is defined as

$$H(u) = \int_0^u h(v)\,dv \quad \text{with } H(0) = 0.$$

The following properties of $H(u)$ are immediately determinable:

1.  $H'(u) = h(u) \geqq 1$, $H'(0) = 1$.
2.  $H''(u) = h'(u) \geqq 0$, $H''(0) = 0$.
3.  $H(u)$ is a convex function and is strictly convex except at $u = 0$.

By using the standard properties of convex functions, the following useful pair of inequalities can be given:

4.  $u \leqq H(u) \leqq uh(u)$ and $u < H(u) < uh(u)$ if $u > 0$.

## The Elasticity of Cumulative Compensation

Great simplifications in the analysis can be made by the appropriate use of the elasticity of the cumulative compensating function, defined as

$$e_H(u) = \frac{uH'(u)}{H(u)} = \frac{uh(u)}{H(u)}.$$

From preceding inequalities, it follows immediately that

1.  $h(u) \geqq e_H(u) \geqq 1$ and $e_H(0) = 1$.

For the remaining properties, the results of Appendix B can be used. The function $H(u)$ satisfies the requirements of Lemma 1a in Appendix B, and thus

2.  $e_H'(0) = 0$ and $h'(u) > e_H'(u) > 0$ for $u > 0$.
3.  $e_H''(0) = \frac{2}{3}h''(0) > 0$ since $h(0) = 1$.

These results certainly hold within some finite range of the origin and will be assumed to hold over the relevant range. Note relationship 3, which implies that the degree of convexity of $e_H(u)$ at the origin is directly proportional to the degree of convexity of $h(u)$.

## A One-Parameter Compensating Function

Since the compensating function is strictly convex, a linear function is not acceptable as a compensating function, and the simplest acceptable function is a quadratic. It is easily seen that a quadratic representation $h(u) = a_o + a_1u + a_2u^2$ must satisfy the conditions $a_o = 1$ [since $h(0) = 1$] and $a_1 = 0$ [since $h'(0) = 0$], so that the quadratic must be in the form $h(u) = 1 + a_2u^2$. It is convenient to write the quadratic form as

$$h(u) = 1 + 3au^2.$$

Owing to the various restrictions on the form of $h(u)$, the equation reduces to a quadratic with only one variable parameter. This parameter is unrestricted except that it must be positive, and the resulting form is useful in examining the effects of changes in the compensating function properties on various system properties. Since the only variable parameter is the convexity, which can be related to economically meaningful properties of substitution between group goods, this is a convenient simplification.

   The derivatives and integral of this compensating function are as follows:

$$h''(u) = 6a$$

$$h'(u) = 6au$$

$$H(u) = u + au^3.$$

These relationships, and $h(u)$ itself, obviously satisfy all the properties required of the compensating function.

   Less obvious are the logarithmic properties of $h(u)$. Denoting, as usual, $\ln h(u)$ by $\underline{h}(u)$,

$$h''(u) = \frac{6a(1 - 3au^2)}{(1 + 3au^2)^2}.$$

Now $\underline{h}''(0) = 6a$, and $h(u)$ is logarithmically convex at and near the origin, as was shown to be necessarily true for a compensating function in general.

Note that the limiting value of $u$ for logarithmic convexity is when $3au^2 = 1$. Now the size of $u$ itself has no direct economic interpretation, but it can be noted that $h(u) = 1 + 3au^2$, so that $3au^2 = 1$ would imply $h(u) = 2$. Thus the condition that $h(u)$ be logarithmically convex requires $h(u) \leq 2$. The latter has a direct economic interpretation, since $h(u) = 2$ means that the available good is so different from the most-preferred good that two units of the available good are regarded by the individual concerned as equivalent to only one unit of the most-preferred good. This can surely be interpreted as a "large" difference between the two goods.

The values for the compensation elasticity and its derivatives are

$$e_h(u) = \frac{6au^2}{1 + 3au^2},$$

$$e_h{}'(u) = \frac{12au}{(1 + 3au^2)^2},$$

$$e_h{}''(u) = \frac{12a(1 - 9au^2)}{(1 + 3au^2)^3}.$$

Note that in this case $e_h{}' > 0$ for *all* values of $u$, even though $h(u)$ is not logarithmically convex for large values of $u$, because logarithmic convexity is a stronger condition than increasing elasticity of compensation. The second derivative is positive only for

$$au^2 < \tfrac{1}{9}[h(u) < \tfrac{4}{3}],$$

which shows that even in this case its sign cannot be taken as fixed.

The cumulative compensation elasticity is given by

$$e_H(u) = \frac{1 + 3au^2}{1 + au^2},$$

$$e_H{}'(u) = \frac{4au}{(1 + au^2)^2},$$

$$e_H{}''(u) = \frac{4a(1 - 3au^2)}{(1 + au^2)^3}.$$

It is easily found that $e_H$ and $e_H{}'$ satisfy all the properties expected and that $e_H''$ is positive over the same (large) range as that over which $h(u)$ is logarithmically convex.

Finally, since the parameter $a$ in this function represents the degree of convexity, the effect of its variations can be found. It can be shown that variations in $a$ affect none of the functions. Except at $u = 0$, at which all functions are invariant with respect to the parameter, the functions $h$, $h'$, $H$, $e_h$, and $e_H$ all increase with the degree of convexity.

## The Uniformity Property

The spectrum possesses the *uniformity property* if there exists a distance measure such that the compensating ratio *for every individual* with respect to a good at specification distance $u$ from the individual's most-preferred good is the same as that for every other individual with respect to any other good at the same distance from that individual's most-preferred good. If the uniformity property exists, there is a *universal* compensating function which gives the compensating ratio for any individual with respect to any good, once the specification distance between that good and the most-preferred good for the individual are given.

It is obvious that an individual compensating function $h(u)$ depends on (1) the choice of distance measure, (2) the shape of the indifference contour of the individual, and (3) the shape of the product-differentiation contour. To have $h^i(u) = h^j(u)$ for all individuals $i$ and $j$ not only requires proper choice of the distance measure but is possible only if the changes in shapes of the indifference contours moving from one individual to another along the spectrum are related in a suitable way to the shape of the product-differentiation contour.

A simple example in which an appropriate relationship exists is that of a product-differentiation contour which is a portion of the surface of a hypersphere of radius $R$ with center at the origin (in characteristics space), and for which the indifference contours for different individuals are portions of hyperspheres having the same radius $r$ but tangent at different points on the product-differentiation contour in accord with the most-preferred specifications for each individual. It is obvious that if the distance measure is chosen as the shortest arc distance along the surface of the product-differentiation contour between the points representing the specifications (or equivalently, the angle at the origin between rays passing through the two points on the surface), the relationship between any indifference contour and the product-differentiation contour beneath it is the same everywhere. In this case, there is certainly a universal compensating function, the form of which is

$$h(u) = (1 + \beta) \cos u - [\beta^2 - (1 + \beta)^2 \sin^2 u]^{1/2},$$

where $\beta = r/R$. This can be shown to have all the assumed properties over the range of $u$ for which $h(u)$ is defined—the range being limited by the spherical nature of the indifference surfaces and being smaller the smaller is $r$ relative to $R$.

This example shows that, if the uniformity property holds, the number of characteristics presents no problems. The compensating function in the example is the same whether the contours are circles in two dimensions or hyperspheres in $m$ dimensions.

It is not proposed to go into further details on the exact relationships which must hold between indifference contours and the product-differentiation contour in order for the spectrum to possess uniformity property or to discuss the determination of appropriate distance measures. It is shown in the main text that, if the uniformity property holds, the distance measure can be derived, in principle, from observations. The purpose of the brief discussion and example given here is to emphasize that the assumption of uniformity rests on the relationships between the indifference and product-differentiation contours and that it is possible to give an example of relationships between contours having properties that guarantee uniformity. The uniformity assumption is very strong but provides the basis for a workable analysis, and it is both simpler and better to make the assumption directly rather than to try and devise general relationships between preferences and production conditions sufficient to guarantee it.

 **Appendix B**

# Some Special Properties of Elasticities

THIS APPENDIX IS devoted to the development of several lemmas in which the properties of the elasticity of a function with respect to its argument are related to the properties of the function itself and its first-, second-, and third-order derivatives. Although the relationships are purely mathematical, the properties which are derived are of key importance in the proof of several important economic propositions in the main text, in which use of one or another of these lemmas occurs with some frequency in relation to properties depending on the elasticity of the cumulative compensating function $g$ and the elasticity of market quantity with respect to market width $e_Q$.

The lemmas make use of a basic property of convex/concave functions of a single variable, namely, that

$$f(x_1) - f(x_0) \geq (x_1 - x_0) f'(x_0)$$

for a convex function, with the inequality reversed for a concave function and with a strict inequality for a strictly convex or strictly concave function.

## Lemma 1a

If $x(u)$ is a continuous function of $u$ with properties

$$x(0) > 0, \quad x'(0) = 0, \quad x'(u) > 0 \qquad \text{for all } u > 0$$

350

and if $X(u)$ is defined by

$$X(u) = \int_0^u x(v)\, dv, \qquad X(0) = 0,$$

then the elasticity of $X(u)$, defined as

$$e_X(u) = \frac{uX'(u)}{X(u)} = \frac{uX(u)}{X(u)},$$

has the following properties:

1.  $e_X(0) = 1$ and $(x(u)/x(0)) > e_X(u) > 1$ for all $u > 0$.
2.  $e_X'(0) = 0$ and $(x'(u)/x(0)) > e_X'(u) > 0$ for $u > 0$, at least to some finite value $u_0$.
3.  $e_X''(0) = [(x(0) + 1)/3x(0)]x''(0)$.

*Proof*: Since $X'' = x' \geqq 0$, $X$ is convex, with $X(0) = 0$, so that basic property of convex functions implies

$$ux(0) \leqq X(u) \leqq ux(u),$$

with strict inequalities if $u > 0$, since $X(u)$ is strictly convex for $u > 0$. From this, the inequalities in property 1 follow directly, as does the limiting value $e_X(u) \to 1$ as $u \to 0$.

Now suppose that $e_X'$ is not greater than 0 for $0 < u \leqq u_0$, where $u_0$ is some finite value. Then it would be true that $e_X' \leqq 0$ for $0 \leqq u \leqq u_0$. But $e_X(0) = 1$, and implies that $e_X \leqq 1$ for $0 \leqq u \leqq u_0$, which contradicts the previous result that $e_X > 1$ for all $u > 0$. Thus if $e_X' < 0$ for some $u$, this can only occur after $e_X'$ has been positive over some finite range of $u$ commencing at the origin.

Differentiating the expression for $e_X$ gives

$$e_X'(u) = \frac{ux'}{X} - \frac{x}{X}(e_X - 1)$$

$$\leqq \frac{ux'}{X} \qquad \text{since } e_X \geqq 1$$

$$\leqq \frac{x'}{x(0)} \qquad \text{since } X(u) \geqq ux(0),$$

with a strict inequality if $u > 0$. This, together with the previous result, gives

$$0 \leqq e_X'(u) \leqq x'(u)/x(0) \qquad \text{for all } u \geqq 0.$$

Since $x'(0) = X''(0) = 0$, it follows that $e_x'(0) = 0$.
The second derivative of $e_x(u)$ can be put in the form

$$e_x'' = \frac{ux''}{X} + (2 - e_x)\frac{x'}{X} - \frac{2xe_x'}{X},$$

where the arguments of the functions have been omitted for simplicity.
Consider the limits of this expression, term by term, as $u \to 0$.
Since $\lim_{u \to 0} u/X(u) = 1$, the first term becomes $x''(0)$. For the second term, the limit of $x'(u)/X(u)$ cannot be determined directly, but the use of l'Hôpital's rule shows it to be $x''(0)/x(0)$, while $2 - e_x(0) = 1$.
Again, by using l'Hôpital's rule in the third term,

$$\lim_{u \to 0} xe_x'/X = \lim_{u \to 0} \left(e_x'' + \frac{x'e_x'}{x}\right)$$
$$= e_x''(0).$$

Thus

$$\lim_{u \to 0} e_x''(u) = x''(0) + \frac{x''(0)}{x(0)} - 2e_x''(0).$$

From this follows relationship 3 above.


**Lemma 1b**

If $x(u)$ is a function with properties identical with those of the function of Lemma 1a, except that $x'(u) < 0$ for all $u > 0$, then the properties of $e_x(0)$, $e_x'(0)$, and $e_x''(0)$ are identical with those of Lemma 1a, whereas the properties of $e_x(u)$ and $e_x'(u)$ have the same form as those of Lemma 1a, except that the directions of the inequalities are reversed.
The proof follows exactly the same lines as the proof of Lemma 1a, except that the directions of all inequalities are reversed because $X(u)$ is now concave instead of convex.

## Lemma 1c

If $x(u)$ is a continuous function of $u$ such that $x(0) > 0$, $x'(0) = 0$ and $X(u)$ is the cumulated value of $x(u)$ as in Lemma 1a, then

   i.   $e_X(u) < 1 + e_x(u)$ if $x'(u) > 0$ for $u > 0$.

  ii.   $e_X(u) > 1 + e_x(u)$ if $x'(u) < 0$ for $u > 0$,

where $e_x(u)$ is the elasticity of the uncumulated function $x(u)$, defined by

$$e_x(u) = \frac{ux'(u)}{x(u)},$$

and $e_X(u)$ is as defined in Lemma 1a.

   *Proof*: From the definition of $e_X$,

$$\ln e_X = \ln u + \ln x(u) - \ln X(u),$$

so that

$$\frac{d(\ln e_X)}{d(\ln u)} = 1 + e_x - e_X.$$

Thus

$$e_X = 1 + e_x - \frac{d(\ln e_X)}{d(\ln u)}$$

$$= 1 + e_x - \frac{u e_X'}{e_X}.$$

But $e_X' > 0$ if $x' > 0$ (Lemma 1a) and $e_X' < 0$ if $x' < 0$ (Lemma 1b), and results i and ii then follow directly.

## Lemma 2a

If $x_1(u)$ and $x_2(u)$ are continuous functions of $u$ with properties

$$x_1(0), x_2(0) > 0, \qquad x_1'(0) = x_2'(0) = 0,$$

and either $x_1'(u)$ and $x_2'(u) > 0$ or $x_1'(u)$ and $x_2'(u) < 0$ for all $u > 0$, and if $X_1(u)$ and $X_2(u)$ are the respective cumulative values of $x_1(u)$

and $x_2(u)$, then

$$e_{x_1} > e_{x_2} \quad \text{for all } u > 0.$$

implies

$$e_{X_1} > e_{X_2} \quad \text{for all } u > 0.$$

*Proof*:

$$\frac{d}{du}\left(\frac{x_1}{x_2}\right) = \frac{x_2}{ux_1}(e_{x_2} - e_{x_1})$$

$$< 0 \quad \text{for all } u > 0$$

$$= 0 \quad \text{for all } u = 0, \text{ since } e_{x_i}/u$$

$$= x_i'/x_i \to 0 \text{ as } u \to 0.$$

Now

$$X_2 = \int_0^u x_2 \, dv$$

$$= \int_0^u \frac{x_2}{x_1} x_1 \, dv$$

$$= \left(\frac{x_2}{x_1} X_1\right)_0^u - \int_0^u X_1 \frac{d}{dv}\left(\frac{x_2}{x_1}\right) dv$$

$$> \frac{x_2 X_1}{x_1}$$

after integrating by parts and using the inequality derived above. Thus $x_1/X_1 > x_2/X_2$, and the result follows immediately from multiplication of both sides of the inequality by $u$.

## Lemma 2b

If $x(\alpha, u)$ has properties with respect to $u$ identical with those of $x_i(u)$ in Lemma 2a, and $\alpha$ is some parameter, then

$$\frac{\partial}{\partial \alpha} e_x(u) > 0 \quad \text{for all } u > 0$$

implies

$$\frac{\partial}{\partial \alpha} e_X(u) > 0 \quad \text{for all } u > 0,$$

provided that

$$\frac{\partial}{\partial \alpha} e_x(0) = 0.$$

Under otherwise identical circumstances,

$$\frac{\partial}{\partial \alpha} e_x(u) < 0$$

implies

$$\frac{\partial}{\partial \alpha} e_X(u) < 0.$$

*Proof*: First note that

$$\frac{\partial}{\partial \alpha} e_x(u) = \frac{\partial}{\partial \alpha} \left( \frac{u x'}{x} \right) = u \frac{\partial}{\partial \alpha} \left( \frac{x'}{x} \right),$$

so that

$$\frac{\partial}{\partial \alpha} e_x > 0 \quad \text{for all } u > 0$$

implies

$$\frac{\partial}{\partial \alpha} \left( \frac{x'}{x} \right) > 0 \quad \text{for all } u > 0.$$

Then

$$\frac{\partial X}{\partial \alpha} = \int_0^u \frac{\partial x}{\partial \alpha} \, dv$$

$$= \int_0^u \left( \frac{1}{x} \frac{\partial x}{\partial \alpha} \right) x \, dv.$$

Then, integrating by parts and commuting $\partial/\partial\alpha$ and $d/dv$ gives

$$\frac{\partial X}{\partial \alpha} = \frac{X}{x}\frac{\partial x}{\partial \alpha} - \int_0^u X\frac{d}{dv}\left(\frac{1}{x}\frac{\partial x}{\partial \alpha}\right)dv$$

$$= \frac{X}{x}\frac{\partial X}{\partial \alpha} - \int_0^u X\frac{\partial}{\partial \alpha}\left(\frac{x'}{x}\right)dv.$$

Now

$$\frac{1}{e_X}\frac{\partial e_X}{\partial \alpha} = \frac{1}{x}\frac{\partial x}{\partial \alpha} - \frac{1}{X}\frac{\partial X}{\partial \alpha}$$

$$= \frac{1}{X}\int_0^u \cdot X\frac{\partial}{\partial \alpha}\left(\frac{x'}{x}\right)dv$$

$$> 0,$$

since $(\partial/\partial\alpha)(x'/x) > 0$ for all $u > 0$. The result of reversing the sign of $(\partial/\partial\alpha)(x'/x)$ is that $\partial e_X/\partial\alpha < 0$.

## Lemma 3a

If $x(u)$ is a continuous function of $u$ such that $x(0) > 0$, $x'(0) = 0$, and $x'(u) > 0$ for all $u > 0$ and if $z(u)$ is defined by

$$e_z(u) = \gamma e_x(u) \qquad \gamma \neq 0, 1,$$

then the elasticities of the cumulated values $Z(u)$ and $X(u)$, denoted by $e_z(u)$ and $e_x(u)$, respectively, are related, to a close approximation, by the equation

$$e_z(u) - 1 = \gamma[e_x(u) - 1] + \gamma(\gamma - 1)\phi(u, \gamma),$$

where $\phi(u, \gamma) > 0$ for all $\gamma$ and all $u > 0$ and $\phi(u, \gamma) \to 0$ as $u \to 0$, the elasticities being defined as in previous lemmas.

For sufficiently small values of $u$, $\phi(u, \gamma)$ is given by

$$\phi(u, \gamma) = \frac{(e_X - 1)^2}{2e_X + \gamma(e_X - 1)^2}.$$

In particular, the following inequalities hold:

$$e_z(u) - 1 > \gamma[e_x(u) - 1] \quad \text{for } \gamma < 0 \text{ or } \gamma > 1,$$

$$e_z(u) - 1 < \gamma[e_x(u) - 1] \quad \text{for } 0 < \gamma < 1.$$

At $\gamma = 0$, $e_z(u) = 1$ for all $u$ and $e_x(u)$, and at $\gamma = 1$, $e_z(u) = e_x(u)$.

*Proof*: Since $x(u)$ is a function of $u$ only, $z(u)$ is a function of $u$ and $\gamma$ only, so that $Z(u)$ is a function of $u$ and $\gamma$ only. The elasticities $e_x(u)$, $e_z(u)$, $e_x(u)$, and $e_z(u)$ are all single-valued functions of $u$, for given $\gamma$, so that it is certainly possible to write $e_z(u)$ in the form

$$e_z(u) - 1 = \gamma[e_x(u) - 1] + \gamma(\gamma - 1)\phi(u, \gamma), \tag{B3.1}$$

where $\phi$ is an unknown function.

Then

$$e_z{}' = \gamma e_x{}' + \gamma(\gamma - 1)\phi', \tag{B3.2}$$

where $\gamma$ is treated as a constant parameter and primes denote derivatives with respect to $u$. From this it then follows that

$$\frac{e_z{}'}{e_z} = \frac{\gamma e_x{}' + \gamma(\gamma - 1)\phi'}{1 + \gamma(e_x - 1) + \gamma(\gamma - 1)\phi}. \tag{B3.3}$$

By using the definition of $e_x$, taking logarithms, and then differentiating with respect to $u$, as in Lemma 1c, it follows that

$$e_x - 1 = e_x - \frac{ue_x{}'}{e_x},$$

with an equivalent result for $e_z$.

Then, since $e_z - \gamma e_x = 0$,

$$e_z - 1 - \gamma(e_x - 1) = \gamma \frac{ue_x{}'}{e_x} - \frac{ue_z{}'}{e_z}. \tag{B3.4}$$

From the definition of $\phi$ it follows that

$$\gamma(\gamma - 1)\phi = \gamma \frac{ue_x{}'}{e_x} - \frac{ue_z{}'}{e_z}$$

$$= \gamma \frac{ue_x{}'}{e_x} - \frac{\gamma e_x{}' + \gamma(\gamma - 1)\phi'}{1 + \gamma(e_x - 1) + \gamma(\gamma - 1)\phi} \tag{B3.5}$$

$$= \gamma(\gamma - 1) \frac{(e_x - 1)ue_x{}' + \gamma\phi ue_x{}' - e_x u\phi'}{[1 + \gamma(e_x - 1) + \gamma(\gamma - 1)\phi]e_x}.$$

Thus, canceling the factor $\gamma(\gamma - 1)$, which is nonzero since it is assumed that $\gamma \neq 0, 1$, gives

$$e_X \phi + \gamma(e_X - 1)e_X \phi + \gamma(\gamma - 1)e_X \phi^2$$
$$= (e_X - 1)ue_X' + \gamma \phi ue_X' - e_X u\phi'. \qquad \text{(B3.6)}$$

If $u$ is sufficiently small, the first-order expansions $e_X(0) = e_X(u) - ue_X'(u)$ and $\phi(0) = \phi(u) - u\phi'(u)$ can be used, so that the right-hand side of Eq. (B3.6) can be written

$$(e_X - 1)^2 + \gamma(e_x - 1)\phi + e_X(\phi_o - \phi) \qquad \text{(B3.7)}$$

since $e_X(0) = 1$ (Lemma 1a).

As $u \to 0$, $e_X \to 1$ and $\phi \to \phi_o$, so that the right hand side of Eq. (B3.6) vanishes at $u = 0$ and thus $\phi(u) \to 0$ as $u \to 0$. For small $u$, therefore, second-order terms in $\phi$ can be neglected and Eq. (B3.6) can be written as

$$e_X \phi + \gamma(e_X - 1)e_X \phi$$
$$= (e_X - 1)^2 + \gamma(e_X - 1)\phi - e_X \phi \qquad \text{(B3.8)}$$

after using Eq. (B3.7) and noting that $\phi_o = 0$.

Solving for $\phi$ in Eq. (B3.8) then gives

$$\phi = \frac{(e_X - 1)^2}{2e_X + \gamma(e_X - 1)^2}. \qquad \text{(B3.9)}$$

Noting that $e_X - 1$ is of the order of $u$, it follows that $\phi$ is a second-order function. Thus $\phi$ can be treated as "small" even when $e_X - 1$ is not so treated. The result can be strengthened, therefore, by noting that, since $e_X$ is convex (Lemma 1a), the general inequality

$$ue_X' \geqq e_X - 1$$

can be used instead of the first-order approximation, which gives the result that the right-hand side of Eq. (B3.6) is no less than Eq. (B3.7), rather than approximately equal to it. The first-order approximation for $\phi$ is still used, since this is equivalent to a second-order approximation for $e_X$.

Instead of Eq. (B3.9), this leads to the inequality

$$\phi \geqq \frac{(e_X - 1)^2}{2e_X + \gamma(e_X - 1)^2}, \qquad \text{(B3.10)}$$

with $\phi$ converging to the right-hand expression as $u$ becomes smaller.

The expression on the right-hand side of Eq. (B3.10) is clearly positive for all $u > 0$ when $\gamma > 0$. If $\gamma < 0$, the expression is positive for sufficiently small values of $u$, whatever the magnitude of $\gamma$, since $(e_x - 1)^2 \to 0$ and $2e_x \to 2$ as $u \to 0$.

The inequalities

$$e_z - 1 > \gamma(e_x - 1) \quad \text{for } \gamma < 0 \text{ or } \gamma > 1$$

$$e_z - 1 > \gamma(e_x - 1) \quad \text{for } 0 < \gamma < 1$$

follow directly from Eq. (B3.1) and the property $\gamma > 0$.

*Note*: Although $\phi$ is a function of $\gamma$ as well as of $u$, through $e_x$, its properties are dominated by the properties of $e_x$, and the parameter $\gamma$ has a minor influence. If the elasticities of $\phi$ with respect to changes in $e_x$ and $\gamma$ are calculated, the ratio of the former to the latter is given by $2(1 + e_x)/(e_x - 1)^3$. This is a large number when $u$ is relatively small, as assumed in the context of the lemma. Thus, if there are two functions $z_1$ and $z_2$ such that $e_{z_1} = \gamma_1 e_x$ and $e_{z_2} = \gamma_2 e_x$, the two functions $\phi_1$ and $\phi_2$ determined by applying the lemma to $e_{x_1}$ and $e_{x_2}$ will be approximately equal to all small values of $u$. (See Lemma 3c for a formal analysis.)

## Lemma 3b

If $x(u)$ and $z(u)$ are as defined in Lemma 3a, then

$$e_z' > \gamma e_x' \quad \text{for } \gamma < 0 \text{ or } \gamma > 1$$

$$e_z' < \gamma e_x' \quad \text{for } 0 < \gamma < 1$$

for sufficiently small values of $u$.

*Proof*: From Eq. (B3.9) in Lemma 3a,

$$\phi = \frac{(e_x - 1)^2}{2e_x + \gamma(e_x - 1)^2}$$

for sufficiently small $u$. Differentiation with respect to $u$ then gives

$$\phi' = 2 \frac{1 + e_x}{(e_x - 1)^3} \phi^2 e_x'. \tag{B3.11}$$

Since $x'(u) > 0$ for $u > 0$, $e_x > 1$ and $e_x' > 0$ (Lemma 1a), so that

$$\phi' > 0 \quad \text{for } u > 0.$$

The results then follow by using this property in Eq. (B3.2) of Lemma 3a.

Note that the value of $\phi$ in Eq. (B3.11) cannot be treated as negligible by virtue of the factor $\phi^2$ in the numerator, because of the factor $(e_x - 1)^3$ in the denominator. In fact, since $\phi^2$ is of the fourth order, the whole expression is of the first order.

## Lemma 3c

If $x(u)$ is as defined in Lemma 3a, if $z_1(u)$ and $z_2(u)$ are defined by

$$e_{z_1}(u) = \gamma_1 e_x(u)$$

$$e_{z_2}(u) = \gamma_2 e_x(u),$$

and if the functions $\phi_1$ and $\phi_2$ are defined by Eq. (B3.9) of Lemma 1a for $z_1$ and $z_2$, respectively, then the differences between $\phi_1$ and $\phi_2$ and between $\phi_1'$ and $\phi_2'$ are of the fourth order and can be neglected for small values of $u$.

*Proof*: From Eq. (B3.9),

$$\frac{1}{\phi_1} = \frac{2e_x}{(e_x - 1)^2} + \gamma_1,$$

and

$$\frac{1}{\phi_2} = \frac{2e_x}{(e_x - 1)^2} + \gamma_2,$$

so that

$$\frac{1}{\phi_1} - \frac{1}{\phi_2} = \frac{\phi_2 - \phi_1}{\phi_1 \phi_2} = \gamma_1 - \gamma_2$$

and

$$\phi_1 - \phi_2 = (\gamma_1 - \gamma_2)\phi_1\phi_2 \tag{B3.12}$$

But it has already been shown (in Lemma 1a) that $\phi$ is a second-order function in $u$, and so the right-hand side of Eq. (B3.12) above is of the fourth order.

Also, from Eq. (B3.11),

$$\phi_i' = 2 \frac{1 + e_X}{(e_X - 1)^3} \phi_i^2 e_X' \qquad i = 1, 2,$$

so that

$$\phi_1' - \phi_2' = 2(\phi_1^2 - \phi_2^2) \frac{1 + e_X}{(e_X - 1)^3} e_X'. \qquad (B3.13)$$

But, from Eq. (B3.12),

$$\phi_1^2 - \phi_2^2 = (\phi_1 + \phi_2)(\phi_1 - \phi_2)$$
$$= (\gamma_1 - \gamma_2)(\phi_1^2 \phi_2 + \phi_1 \phi_2^2).$$

Thus $\phi_1^2 - \phi_2^2$ is sixth order.

Since $e_x'$ and $e_x - 1$ are of the first order, the right-hand side of Eq. (B3.13) is of the fourth order, as asserted.

 # References

Alcaly, R. E. and A. K. Klevorick. 1970. "Judging Quality by Price, Snob Appeal, and the New Consumer Theory." *Zeitsch. Nationalekonomie* 30:53-64.

Archibald, G. C. 1967. "Monopolistic Competition and Returns to Scale." *Econ. J.* 77:405-12.

Archibald, G. C. and G. Rosenbluth. 1975. "The 'New' Theory of Consumer Demand and Monopolistic Competition." *Quart. J. Econ.* 89:569-90.

Arrow, K. J., H. B. Chenery, and R. M. Solow. 1961. "Capital-Labor Substitution and Economic Efficiency." *Rev. Econ. Stat.* 43:228-32.

Arrow, K. J. and F. H. Hahn. 1971. *General Competitive Analysis*. Holden-Day, San Francisco, Calif.

Auld, D. A. L. 1972. "Imperfect Knowledge and the New Theory of Demand." *J. Polit. Econ.* 80:1287-94.

—— 1974. "Advertising and the Theory of Consumer Choice." *Quart. J. Econ.* 88:480-89.

Barker, T. S. 1974. "The Variety Hypothesis as an Explanation of International Trade." IIES Seminar Paper No. 41, University of Stockholm.

Barten, A. P. 1977. "The Systems of Consumer Demand Functions Approach: A Review." *Econometrica* 45:23-52.

Barzel, Y. 1970. "Excess Capacity in Monopolistic Competition." *J. Polit. Econ.* 78:1142-49.

Beckmann, M. 1968. *Location Theory*. Random House, New York.

Bernardo, J. J. and J. M. Blin. 1977. "A Programming Model of Consumer Choice among Multi-Attributed Brands." *J. Consumer Res.* 4:111-18.

Blackorby, C. G., G. Lady, D. Nissen, and R. Russell. 1970. "Homothetic Separability and Consumer Budgeting." *Econometrica* 38:468-72.

Brems, H. 1951. *Product Equilibrium under Monopolistic Competition.* Harvard University Press, Cambridge, Mass.

Brumat, C. and L. Tomasini. 1977. "A Probabilistic Extension of Lancaster's Approach to Consumer Theory." Western Management Science Institute (University of California at Los Angeles), Working Paper No. 266, May 1977.

Chamberlin, E. H. 1933. *The Theory of Monopolistic Competition.* Harvard University Press, Cambridge, Mass.

—— 1953. "The Product as an Economic Variable." *Quart. J. Econ.* 67; reprinted in E. H. Chamberlin, *Towards a More General Theory of Value,* Oxford University Press, New York, 1957.

—— 1957. *Towards a More General Theory of Value.* Oxford University Press, New York.

Colantoni, C. S., O. Davis, and M. Swaminuthan. 1976. "Imperfect Consumers and Welfare Comparisons of Policies concerning Information and Regulation." *Bell J. Econ.* 7:602–15.

Demsetz, H. 1959. "The Nature of Equilibrium in Monopolistic Competition." *J. Polit. Econ.* 67:21–30.

—— 1964. "The Welfare and Empirical Implications of Monopolistic Competition." *Econ. J.* 74:623–41.

—— 1972. "The Inconsistencies in Monopolistic Competition: A Reply." *J. Polit. Econ.* 80:592–97.

Dixit, A. K. and J. E. Stiglitz. 1977. "Monopolistic Competition and Optimum Product Diversity." *Amer. Econ. Rev.* 67:297–308.

Eaton, B. C. and R. G. Lipsey. 1976. "The Non-Uniqueness of Equilibrium in a Löschian Location Model." *Amer. Econ. Rev.* 66:77–93.

Galbraith, J. K. 1967. *The New Industrial State.* Houghton Mifflin, Boston.

Geistfeld, L. V. 1977. "Consumer Decision Making: The Technical Efficiency Approach." *J. Consumer Res.* 4:48–56.

Goldman, S. and H. Uzawa. 1964. "A Note on Separability in Demand Analysis." *Econometrica* 32:387–98.

Gorman, W. M. 1959. "The Empirical Implications of a Utility Tree: A Further Comment." *Econometrica* 27:489.

Graft, D. A., S. E. G. Lea, and T. L. Whitworth. 1977. "The Matching Law in and within Groups of Rats." *J. Exp. Anal. Behav.* 27:183–94.

Grieson, R. E., ed. 1976. *Public and Urban Economics: Essays in Honor of William S. Vickrey.* Lexington Books, Lexington, Mass.

Griliches, Z., ed. 1971. *Price Indexes and Quality Change: Studies in New Methods of Measurement.* Harvard University Press, Cambridge, Mass.

Grubel, H. G. 1967. "Intra-Industry Specialization and the Pattern of Trade." *Canad. J. Econ. Polit. Sci.* 33:374–88.

Hanoch, G. 1975. "The Elasticity of Scale and the Shape of Average Costs." *Amer. Econ. Rev.* 65:492–97.

Henderson, J. M. and R. E. Quandt. 1971. *Microeconomic Theory: A Mathematical Approach,* second ed. McGraw-Hill, New York.

Hendler, R. 1975. "Lancaster's New Approach to Consumer Demand and its Limitations." *Amer. Econ. Rev.* 65:194-99.

Hogarty, T. F. and R. J. Mackay. 1975. "Some Implications of the 'New Theory of Consumer Behavior' for Interpreting Estimated Demand Elasticities." *Amer. J. Agr. Econ.* 57:340-43.

Hori, H. 1975. "Revealed Preference for Public Goods." *Amer. Econ. Rev.* 65:978-91.

Hotelling, H. 1929. "Stability in Competition," *Econ. J.* 34:41-57; reprinted in G. J. Stigler and K. Boulding (eds.), *Readings in Price Theory,* pp. 467-84. Richard D. Irwin, Homewood, Ill., 1952.

Ironmonger, D. S. 1972. *New Commodities and Consumer Behavior.* Cambridge University Press, Cambridge.

Kaldor, N. 1935. "Market Imperfection and Excess Capacity." *Economica* 2:33-50; reprinted in G. J. Stigler and K. Boulding, (eds.), *Readings in Price Theory,* Richard D. Irwin, Homewood, Ill., 1952.

Klevmarken, N. A. 1977. "A Note on New Goods and Quality Changes in the True Cost of Living Index in view of Lancaster's Model of Consumer Behavior." *Econometrica* 45:163-74.

Kuenne, R. E., ed. 1967. *Monopolistic Competition Theory: Studies in Impact. Essays in Honor of Edward H. Chamberlin.* Wiley, New York.

Ladd, G. W. and M. Zober. 1977. "Variations on a Theme by Lancaster." *J. Consumer Res.* 4:89-101.

Lancaster, K. J. 1966. "A New Approach to Consumer Theory." *J. Polit. Econ.* 74:132-57.

—— 1971. *Consumer Demand: A New Approach.* Columbia University Press, New York.

—— 1974. *Introduction to Modern Microeconomics,* second ed. Rand McNally, Chicago.

—— 1975. "Socially Optimal Product Differentiation." *Amer. Econ. Rev.* 65:567-85.

—— 1976a. "Information and the Consumer." Paper delivered at the Conference on the Economics of Information, held at the City College of New York, May 1976.

—— 1976b. "The Pure Theory of Impure Public Goods." In R. E. Grieson (ed.), *Public and Urban Economics: Essays in Honor of William S. Vickrey.* Lexington Books, Lexington, Mass., 1976.

—— 1977. "The Measurement of Changes in Quality." *Rev. Income Wealth,* Ser. 23, 157-72.

Leland, H. E. 1977. "Quality Choice and Competition." *Amer. Econ. Rev.* 67:127-35.

Leontief, W. W. 1933. "The Use of Indifference Curves in the Analysis of Foreign Trade." *Quant. J. Econ.* 47:493-503.

Lerner, A. P. and H. W. Singer. 1937. "Some Notes on Duopoly and Spatial Competition." *J. Polit. Econ.* 45:145-86.

—— 1977. "The Measurement of Changes in Quality." *Rev. Income Wealth,* Ser. 23, 157-72.

Lipsey, R. G. and K. Lancaster. 1956. "The General Theory of Second Best." *Rev. Econ. Stud.* 24:11-32.

Lipsey, R. G. and G. Rosenbluth. 1971. "A Contribution to the New Theory of Demand: A Rehabilitation of the Giffen Good." *Canad. J. Econ.* 4:131-63.

Lösch, A. 1954. *The Economics of Location.* Yale University Press, New Haven, Conn.

Lovell, M. 1970. "Product Differentiation and Market Structure." *Western Econ. J.* 8:120-43.

Marx, K. 1891. *Critique to the Gotha Programme.* English translation, Moscow.

Meade, J. E. 1974. "The Optimal Balance between Economies of Scale and Variety of Products: An Illustrative Model." *Economica* 41:359-67.

Menger, C. 1950. *Principles of Economics* (translation of 1934 German test). Free Press, Glencoe, Ill.

Michael, R. T. and G. S. Becker. 1973. "On the New Theory of Consumer Behavior." *Swedish J. Econ.* December 1973, pp. 378-96.

Mills, E. S. and M. Lav. 1964. "A Model of Market Areas with Free Entry." *J. Polit. Econ.* 72:278-88.

Muellbauer, J. "Household Production Theory, Quality, and the 'Hedonic Technique.'" *Amer. Econ. Rev.* 64:977-94.

Nash, J. R. 1950. "Equilibrium in *N*-Person Games." *Proc. Nat. Acad. Sci.* 36:48-49.

Negishi, T. 1960. "Monopolistic Competition and General Equilibrium." *Rev. Econ. Stud.* 28:196-201.

Nelson, P. 1970. "Information and Consumer Behavior." *J. Polit. Econ.* 78:311-29.

—— 1974. "Advertising as Information." *J. Polit. Econ.* 81:729-54.

Nicosia, F. 1974. "Towards an Empirical Theory of Consumer Behavior based on the Economics of Goods-Characteristics." *J. Marketing Res.* 11:115-20.

Nikaido, H. 1975. *Monopolistic Competition and Effective Demand.* Princeton University Press, Princeton, N.J.

Nove, A. and D. M. Nuti. 1972. *Socialist Economics: Selected Readings.* Penguin Books, Harmondsworth, England.

Pollack, R. 1972. "Generalized Separability." *Econometrica* 40:431-53.

Ratchford, B. T. 1975. "The New Economic Theory of Consumer Behavior: An Interpretive Essay." *J. Consumer Res.* 2:65-75.

Rawls, J. 1971. *A Theory of Justice.* Harvard University Press, Cambridge, Mass.

Roberts, G. S. 1975. "Lancaster's New Demand Theory: Its Application in Portfolio Analysis." *J. Econ. Lit.* 13:45.

Roberts, J. and H. Sonnenschein. 1977. "On the Foundations of the Theory of Monopolistic Competition." *Econometrica* 45:163-74.

Rosen, S. 1974. "Hedonic Prices and Implicit Markets: Product Differentiation in Pure Competition." *J. Polit. Econ.* 82:34-55.

—— 1978a. "Advertising, Information, and Product Differentiation." In D. G. Tuerck (ed.), *Issues in Advertising*. Washington, D.C., American Enterprise Institute.

—— 1978b. "Substitution and Division of Labor." Unpublished working paper. 1978.

Rothenburg, J. 1976.."'Inadvertent' Distributional Impacts in the Provision of Public Services to Individuals." In R. E. Grieson (ed.), *Public and Urban Economics: Essays in Honor of William S. Vickrey*. Lexington Books, Lexington, Mass., 1976.

Rothschild, M. 1973. "Models of Market Organization with Imperfect Information: A Survey." *J. Polit. Econ.* 81:1283-1308.

Salop, S. 1976. "Monopolistic Competition Reconstituted or—Circular Fashions in Economic Thought." Paper presented at the North American Meeting of the Econometric Society, Atlantic City, 1976.

Sandmo, A. 1973. "Public Goods and the Technology of Consumption." *Rev. Econ. Stud.* 40:517-28.

Schmalensee, R. 1972. *The Economics of Advertising*. North-Holland Publishing Co., Amsterdam.

—— 1977. "Brand Proliferation and Entry Deterrence: The Ready-to-Eat Cereals Case." Paper presented at Bell Conference on Industrial Organization, 1977.

Schultz, T. W. 1961. "Investment in Human Capital." *Amer. Econ. Rev.* 51:1-17.

Sherer, F. M. 1970. *Industrial Market Structure and Economic Performance*. Rand McNally, Chicago.

Smithies, A. 1941. "Optimal Location in Spatial Competition." *J. Polit. Econ.* 49:423-39; reprinted in G. J. Stigler and K. E. Boulding (eds.), *Readings in Price Theory*. Richard D. Irwin, Homewood, Ill., 1952.

Spence, A. M. 1975. "Monopoly, Quality and Regulation." *Bell J. Econ.* 6:417-29.

—— 1976a. "Product Differentiation and Welfare." *Amer. Econ. Rev.* 66:407-14.

—— 1976b. "Product Selection, Fixed Costs, and Monopolistic Competition." *Rev. Econ. Stud.* 43:217-35.

Stern, N. 1972. "The Optimal Size of Market Areas." *J. Econ. Theory* 4:154-73.

Stewart, F. 1977. *Technology and Underdevelopment*. Macmillan, New York.

Stigler, G. J. 1949. "Monopolistic Competition in Retrospect." In *Five Lectures on Economic Problems,* Chapter 2, Macmillan, New York.

—— 1961. "The Economics of Information." *J. Polit. Econ.* 69:213-25.

Strotz, R. H. 1957. "The Empirical Implications of a Utility Tree." *Econometrica* 25:269-80.

Sweezy, P. M. 1939. "Demand under Conditions of Oligopoly." *J. Polit. Econ.* 47:568-73.

Triffin, R. 1940. *Monopolistic Competition and General Equilibrium Theory.* Harvard University Press, Cambridge, Mass.

Welch, F. 1969. "A Linear Synthesis of Skill Distributions." *J. Human Resources* 4:311-327.

White, L. J. 1977. "Market Structure and Product Varieties." *Amer. Econ. Rev.* 67:179-82.

Willig, R. 1973. "Welfare Analysis of Policies Affecting Price and Products." Discussion Paper, Stanford University Center for Mathematical Methods in the Social Sciences, 1973.

 **Index**